WALLACE STEVENS AND THE ACTUAL WORLD

WALLACE STEVENS
AND THE ACTUAL
WORLD

Alan Filreis

PRINCETON UNIVERSITY PRESS   PRINCETON, NEW JERSEY

Copyright © 1991 by Princeton University Press
Published by Princeton University Press, 41 William Street,
Princeton, New Jersey 08540
In the United Kingdom: Princeton University Press, Oxford
All Rights Reserved

Library of Congress Cataloging-in-Publication Data
Filreis, Alan, 1956–
Wallace Stevens and the actual world / Alan Filreis.
p.   cm.
Includes bibliographical references and index.
ISBN 0-691-06864-X (alk. paper)
1. Stevens, Wallace, 1879–1955—Political and social views.
2. Political poetry, American—History and criticism.
3. Stevens, Wallace, 1879–1955—Knowledge—History.
4. World War, 1939–1945—Literature and the war.
5. War poetry, American—History and criticism.
6. History, Modern, in literature.   I. Title.
PS3537.T4753Z636   1991
811'.52—dc20   90-2364

This book has been composed in Adobe Janson

Princeton University Press books are printed
on acid-free paper, and meet the guidelines
for permanence and durability of the Committee
on Production Guidelines for Book Longevity
of the Council on Library Resources

Printed in the United States of America by
Princeton University Press, Princeton, New Jersey

1   3   5   7   9   10   8   6   4   2

for Susan

There is going to be a *Selected Poems*. . . . The book seemed rather slight and small to me—and unbelievably irrelevant to our actual world. It may be that all poetry has seemed like that at all times and always will. The close approach to reality has always been the supreme difficulty of any art: the communication of actuality, as poetry, has been not only impossible, but has never appeared to be worth while because it loses identity as the event passes. Nothing in the world is deader than yesterday's political (or realistic) poetry. Nevertheless the desire to combine the two things, poetry and reality,
is a constant desire.
—*Stevens at the height of the 1952 presidential campaign*

I take it that the bearing of the phrase "actual world" is toward something outside us, something objective, whose actuality is somehow an empirical one which tends to look after its own affairs without consulting us, and even at times resisting whatever it is in us which we like to call by names like subjective, private, human as opposed to nonhuman, although even the human and the subjective lie ready for objective scrutiny if we change our vantage-point and let them stand opposite us rather than let them oppose a thing, a world, beyond them. . . . Are we prepared to take this stand? Perhaps we are if we are philosophers of a certain logical stubbornness.
—*Allen Tate*

Final for him, the acceptance of such prose,
Time's given perfections made to seem like less
Than the need of each generation to be itself,
The need to be actual and as it is.
—*Wallace Stevens, "St. Armorer's Church from the Outside"*

Contents

List of Illustrations

PUBLISHED WORKS

CP: Wallace Stevens, *Collected Poems of Wallace Stevens* (New York: Alfred A. Knopf, 1954).

L: *Letters of Wallace Stevens*, ed. Holly Stevens (New York: Alfred A. Knopf, 1966).

NA: Wallace Stevens, *The Necessary Angel: Essays on Reality and the Imagination* (New York: Alfred A. Knopf, 1951).

OP: Wallace Stevens, *Opus Posthumous*, ed. Milton J. Bates (New York: Alfred A. Knopf, 1989).

SM: *Secretaries of the Moon: The Letters of Wallace Stevens & José Rodríguez Feo*, ed. Beverly Coyle and Alan Filreis (Durham: Duke University Press, 1986).

WSR: Peter Brazeau, *Parts of a World: Wallace Stevens Remembered* (New York: Random House, 1983).

ARCHIVES

Preceded by cue titles as they appear in the notes.

Arkansas: Manuscripts Department, University of Arkansas Libraries, University of Arkansas (Fayetteville).

Beinecke: The Yale Collection of American Literature, Beinecke Rare Book and Manuscript Library, Yale University.

Brown: Manuscripts Department, John Hay Library, Brown University.

Chicago: Rare Book and Manuscript Department, Joseph R. Regenstein Library, University of Chicago.

Columbia: Rare Book and Manuscript Library, Butler Library, Columbia University.

Dartmouth: Dartmouth College Library.

Getty: Getty Center for the History of Art and the Humanities, Santa Monica, California.

Harvard: Harvard University Archives, Pusey Library.

Houghton: Houghton Library, Harvard University.

Huntington: Henry E. Huntington Library, San Marino, California.

Illinois: University Archives of the University of Illinois, Champaign-Urbana.

Massachusetts: University Archives, University of Massachusetts at Amherst.

Princeton: Rare Books and Manuscript Department, Firestone Library, Princeton University.

Rosenbach: The Rosenbach Museum and Library, Philadelphia.

Société Paulhan: Société de Lecteurs de Jean Paulhan, Paris.

Stanford: Special Collections Department, Stanford University Libraries.

Syracuse: George Arents Research Library for Special Collections at Syracuse University.

Texas: Harry Ransom Humanities Research Center, University of Texas, Austin.

INTERVIEWS

Fernand Auberjonois: December 22, 1987, Los Angeles, California.

Stanley Burnshaw: May 18, 1989, New York, New York (with Harvey Teres).

Philip May, Jr.: June 3, 1987, West Chester, Pennsylvania.

Samuel French Morse: January 7, 1983, Milton, Massachusetts.

José Rodríguez Feo: October 17, 18, 19, 1983, New York, New York (with Beverly Coyle).

Willard Thorp: May 7, 1986, Princeton, New Jersey.

WALLACE STEVENS always felt a strong desire to make his poetic career a "general moving forward" fully in spite of the fact that the motion of his career as attorney at The Hartford Accident and Indemnity Company, in his own metaphor, traced a circle. A competing desire was to experience and write about "longed-for lands" (*CP* 486) while remaining at home in the United States. To read Stevens's career from 1939 is to understand these two desires as characteristic American attempts at discerning the motion of an individualized poetic self within wartime and postwar place and time. If the poems could be marked by a program, a career in themselves, as has occasionally been argued—a "Whole of Harmonium," with a troublesome middle and a distinct end[1]—then they might also be described as traveling a way outward toward wartime and postwar peripheries from a central, unmoving prewar identity. They might be said finally to have succeeded in three of their boldest claims: (1) that poetic effects replicate foreign realities as "experiences in themselves"; (2) that one can make "poetry out of . . . the day's news"; and thus, (3) that such poems do mark an approach to "the actual world."

Experiencing the foreign.   The precise psychological reasons why Stevens never visited Europe are less important to this book[2] than how this astonishing fact endorses the poet's shifting conception of imaginative power in relation to a world of events and trends he often admitted was well beyond him. Holly Stevens has offered a sensible explanation for her father's unwillingness to tour the world in his later years, when he might have made the time and certainly could have set aside the funds to do so. She argues that the Second World War had destroyed the cultural center the poet had so long imagined, especially the France he considered, to use Walter Laqueur's relevant phrase, "the museum of Europe."[3] Stevens had already learned to take his pleasure from postcards and letters received from these longed-for lands. To Leonard C. van Geyzel, his correspondent in Ceylon, he wrote: "These letters from persons living such different lives in far-off places are experiences in themselves" (*L* 486). To Thomas McGreevy, the Irish Catholic poet, in responding to one letter typically full of Irish matters, Stevens wrote: "I feel quite at home in Dublin, thanks to you" (*L* 795). In dozens of his most playful letters the language is transported by the feeling of being comfortable overseas while remaining in his office chair or staring out his bedroom window at home. "I have often seen Seville before," he exulted at news that his young Cuban friend, José Rodríguez Feo, was to visit Spain, "but never smelled the heavy fragrance of its orange blossoms. And I have seen Granada but never felt the noise of its mountain water. Also, I have been in Madrid but this time it was a change to get away from the Prado and to go to restaurants and sit by the door and look out at the 18th century" (*L* 837). At times he was grateful to his traveling friends and acknowledged that his "true" sense of Europe, Asia, and the Caribbean, to the extent that this sense went beyond the tourist's, was contingent upon their varying talents for conveying those places in words. "One of the real pleasures of my life is to have such an agreeable correspondent in Paris," he wrote Paule Vidal, his postwar art and books agent (*L* 702). Yet at other times he made it clear that his friends merely traveled "for" him, that the touring Other was actually himself. His encouragement of their postcards and letters from abroad was so often repeated, and their replies were so consistently the occasion (in subsequent letters) for language most closely resembling that of the poetry, that we may characterize this special exchange as a plan of "generous self-interest," borrowing a phrase—appropriately, as I will argue—used by historians of the cold war to generalize about Americans' postwar disposition toward Western Europe.[4] Stevens's European correspondents in particular collected views and wrote him versions of himself seeing them. In his words, "I suppose that if I ever go to Paris the first person I meet will be myself since I have been there in one way or another for so long" (*L* 665).

In the twenties, when making the tour of longed-for lands seemed almost required of the American modernist, William Carlos Williams urged friends to find a sense of direction by taking time from work to visit Europe, as Williams did for an entire year. Stevens responded to Williams's project by describing the responsibilities that prevented *him* from moving outward, in rhyming images of routine and circularity: "But oh la-la," he wrote Williams in 1925, "my job is not now with poets from Paris. It is to keep the fire-place burning and the music-box churning and the wheels of the baby's chariot turning" (*L* 246). The trope was hardly an improvisation, even then, in the twenties—for in order to keep the machine of his family and home perpetually turning, Stevens had already quite consciously adjusted himself to the idea of going nowhere. He wrote about himself at his office desk as existing at the focus of others' movements. So the proscribing circle was powerfully self-descriptive, the decision to live off the postcards of others entirely consistent with the figure made by American work. Such a decision gave new force and clarity to what might otherwise have been an entirely unremarkable view of place. Stevens would live and work *in* Hartford, and *in* would be one of his tiny engines driving the huge, American linguistic business of distinguishing *here* from everywhere else. On the one hand, he wrote one traveling friend, "*You* appear to have had a good summer with your trip or trips *to* the Continent," while on the other hand, "*We* stayed at home *here in* Hartford" (*L* 763; emphasis added). "Here in Hartford," he wrote another friend, "we have the advantage of receiving postcards" (*L* 645). From *in here* one's sense of direction was derivative, taken up lightly, as one takes up or "picks up" a souvenir from a visited place. "I have received a letter from a friend in Europe," he wrote. "This has refreshed me. . . . One picks up a kind of freedom of the universe, or at least of the world, from the movements of other people." After receiving a series of postcards from this moving friend, Barbara Church, Stevens gratefully replied: "I feel as if I had been knocking about in Europe. . . . How cheerful they look on one's desk."[5]

Making poetry of the day's news. "[T]o make poetry out of commonplaces: the day's news," as Stevens once plainly put it (*L* 311n), really did involve for him the act of exploring the newspapers for *materia poetica*. The Stevens who could not apparently be held accountable for any "specific scene or time or action" in his writing, as Delmore Schwartz put it in 1940,[6] was conscientiously affirmed in the fifties, by admirers who had their own cultural motives—motives I have attempted to describe in my final chapter—for lauding Stevens as having "dared to speak for the virtues of the imagination . . . [in] a world that has had its chief pride in objectivity, documentary realism, statistics, and unadorned facts."[7] Daring, however, had little or nothing to do with Stevens's acute perceptions of his time, place, and limitations in a world that changed rapidly and radically in his day; nor do facts adorned lose unconditionally their identity as fact, nor realities severed from documents their basis in the rhetoric of the real. This was a poet who not only read about and understood the American idea of containment; his keen judgment of its significance actually preceded the popularization of this key diplomatic metaphor and shaped subsequent poems' sense of Americans' distant obligations. Earlier, he felt and recorded the great shift from isolationism to internationalism; his "war poems," as I demonstrate, mark such a rhetorical course. Still earlier, three weeks after the invasion of Poland in 1939, he followed "news of the development of the war" vigilantly enough to report American public opinion with accuracy to Leonard van Geyzel. The news did not make Stevens feel simply "horror of the fact that such a thing [the German invasion] could occur" (*L* 342) but also the "extraordinary pressure of news" itself, "news . . . of a new world so uncertain" (*NA* 20) that to know the reality reported one first had to develop a sense of the mediation that we have come to call, in short, "the media." His own brief experience as a journalist in the first years of the century—a time of great journalistic pace and expedience, to be sure— helped him develop a feeling for the sometimes distorted relation between the "news" and the new. He paid close, day-to-day attention to big and small events, pointing his correspondents toward both front- and back-page stories, mailing them clippings, and several times locating old friends through telling details found buried deep in minor items.[8] In reading the *New York Times*, he might find and describe for Rodríguez Feo a story about a wanted war profiteer discovered hidden among the resorts of Cuba (*L* 533, *SM* 85n), or examine the trial of Judith Coplon, who was charged in 1949 with passing secret documents to a Russian at the UN (*SM* 160), or follow the story of a friend who had been denounced by Joseph McCarthy and Roy Cohn as a red working at the Voice of America.[9] He was an inveterate reader of the *Hartford Times*; he came to feel it was an essential part of his day (*L* 829) and knew its style and arrangement of features (*L* 646). Evidently he read his local paper story by story, front to back—it takes "an ungodly time," he once said (*L* 856). His routine in the late forties, if not throughout his years in Hartford, was to read this paper immediately upon returning home from work; after that there might be time for poetry, but only after that (*L* 594). He deemed himself very much a man of the world in part *because* he was firmly set in the routines of home.

Approaching the "actual" world. The American Stevens presented in this book emerges as a person who variously comprehends and ignores the world of his time and who writes a poetry that, at its most characteristic, reproduces this comprehension and ignorance. To put it in terms we have learned from received criticism, the poems make both assumptions and claims about reality, assumptions and claims that are then elaborately qualified in the practice of a poem. This is the Stevens we seem to have admired most, Stevens as his own "harassing master" (in the oft-quoted phrase of "An Ordinary Evening in New Haven"). But to put the point in terms more specifically congenial to the reading of a twentieth-century American Stevens: the poet every so often proposes a new agreement or pact between himself and "our actual world" just as he continues to make naturalizing claims *against* that world. By the phrase "the actual world" he really did mean historical conditions, at times in order to denigrate his interest in such externalities as the last resort of a man whose already famous interiority made him feel desperately irrelevant. In this account of two major periods of Stevens's life and work, the war years and the postwar years, I have described in new detail two such occasions—two moments, a national moment and what is accurately if clumsily called a postideological moment—in which desperate feelings of irrelevance gave way to engagement, when Stevens felt determined to make a "close approach to reality" in an effort to reconcile previous discrepancies between his poetic language and the cultural language around him. In describing these apparently different moments, I want to demonstrate that the very terms in which such renewed offers were made responded with great specificity to historical and political forces pressing on Stevens from outside the career; that this American career should not only be defined as having its own motion and time out of time; and that the forces impelling the motion between two or more texts marking courses in the career, marking developments of greater significance to our idea of Stevens than any one poetic effort observed discretely, may thus be read as originating from beyond even this otherwise persuasive individualist in such a way as to call up critical biography—and other critical subgenres strange to Stevens scholarship, such as diplomatic history—in the service of American literary historiography.

San Marino, California
December 26, 1989

Acknowledgments

My work began and was sustained in the research libraries, where curatorial staffs, directors, and archivists—many now friends—have been extraordinarily responsive to my long and short visits and ceaseless requests for help. I owe special debts to Jonathan Walters of the Joseph R. Regenstein Library, University of Chicago; Eileen Cahill, formerly of the Rosenbach Museum and Library; Jean F. Preston of the Department of Rare Books and Special Collections, Princeton University Library; Jacqueline Paulhan of the Société des Lecteurs de Jean Paulhan; Patricia Willis and Patricia Middleton of the Beinecke Rare Book and Manuscript Library, Yale University; Bryant Duffy, Sara Hodson, Aldo Perdomo, Fred Perez, Virginia Renner, Daniel Woodward, and Mary Wright of the Henry E. Huntington Library; Eugene Gaddis of the Wadsworth Atheneum; Michele Palmer of the Center for Oral History, University of Connecticut; Kyle Reis of the Ford Foundation Archives; Sarah Polirer of the Harvard University Archives in Pusey Library; Cathy Henderson and Ken Craven of the Harry Ransom Humanities Research Center, The University of Texas at Austin; Linda Seidman of the University of Massachusetts Archives; Kenneth Cramer and Philip Cronenwett of the Dartmouth College Library; Blanche T. Ebeling-Koning of the McKeldin Library, University of Maryland; Kathleen Manwaring of the George Arents Research Library for Special Collections, Syracuse University; Daniel Traister of Special Collections, Van Pelt Library, University of Pennsylvania; Bonnie Jean Woodworth of The Hartford Insurance Group, Corporate Library; Margaret Sax of the Watkinson Library, Trinity College; Barbara Filipac of the John Hay Library, Brown University; Linda Gutierrez of the Center for Visual History; Norma Ortiz and Charlene Kaufmann of Special Collections, University of Arkansas Libraries; Beverly Laughlin of the Hartford Public Library; Bernard R. Crystal of the Butler Library, Columbia University; Noriko Gamblin and Marcia Reed of the Getty Center for the History of Art and the Humanities; Michael Ryan of Special Collections, Stanford University Libraries; Robert T. Chapel of the University Archives, University of Illinois Library at Urbana-Champaign; Eva Wallgren of the University of Göteborg Library, Göteborg, Sweden; and Vicki Denby of Harvard's Houghton Library.

My research was supported by a yearlong National Endowment for the Humanities Research Fellowship, a Huntington Library–Exxon grant in 1986 and a Huntington-Mellon grant in 1989, a research stipend provided in association with the Esther K. and N. Mark Watkins Chair at the University of Pennsylvania, and grants for travel and equipment from the American Council of Learned Societies, the University of Pennsylvania Research Foundation, and the IBM Advanced Education Project. David DeLaura, Stephen N. Nichols, Alice van Buren Kelley, Martin Ridge, and A. Walton Litz helped make this financial assistance possible.

For their extraordinarily energetic work as research assistants, I very gratefully acknowledge Wendy Bach, Sarah Fremerman, Millicent Gaskell, Carlton Jackson, Jr., Elizabeth Neighbor, Suzanne Maynard, and Judith Pascoe at the University of Pennsylvania; Robin Barsky and Caroline Carville at the Universities of Virginia and Arkansas, respectively; Thomas and Eva Franzkowiak in Germany; and Laura Lynch in Dublin. For their help with translations I wish to thank Susan Albertine, Rebaia Corley, Emmanuel Rimbert, and Sandra Webb (French); Maria Theresa Meyer, Marci Sternheim, and Sienah Wold (Spanish); and Lloyd Hustveldt (Swedish). David Gansler and Lauren Solatar, David and Ellen McWhirter, Bruce Rosenberg and Ann Harleman, Barbara Albertine, Cindy Wallace, Stuart Kaufer, Manny and Lucille Filreis, and my loving, tolerant parents, Samuel and Lois Filreis, dished up not only ample hospitality but good measures of sanity at day's end during my research trips.

For reading portions of this book and offering substantive suggestions, I want to thank Nancy Prothro Arbuthnot, Milton Bates, Robert Buttel, Arthur D. Casciato, Beverly Coyle, Joanne Ferguson, John Lewis Gaddis, John Gimbel, Theodora Graham, George Lensing, J. C. Levenson, Ruth Lindeborg, Luther Luedtke, the late Samuel French Morse, Raymond Nelson, John Noakes, Roy Harvey Pearce, José Rodríguez Feo, Harvey Teres, and Thomas Underwood. David Wyatt, aside from seeing Chapter 5 through its several lives and providing the most insightful criticisms I have received, first brought me to the Huntington materials in 1982.

I am also grateful to a number of generous people for taking time to teach and advise me about certain issues: Paul Fussell, Philip Nord, Eugen Weber, and Gerhard L. Weinberg offered help with the Vidal material in Chapter 1; Jane Morse with the Morse material in part 1 of Chapter 2; Fernand Auberjonois, Dominique Aury, Frederic Grover, Bernard Leuilliot, and Jacqueline Paulhan with the Paulhan material in part 5 of Chapter 2; Harry Levin, Walter Kaiser, Kevin Van Anglen, and the late Theodore Morrison with the PBK material in Chapter 3; Percy Colin-Thomé, H.A.I. Goonetileke, H. L. Seneviratne, Jacqueline Lee Mok (of the USIS), Anne van Geyzel, and particularly Jonathan Walters with the Sri Lankan material in Chapter 3; Beth Dalin with the Ebba Dalin material in Chapter 5; David R. Clark, Richard Haven, Jean Tucker, and H. L. Varley with the Massachusetts material in Chapter 6; and Myron Baskin of the Freedom of Information section in the State Department with the USIA material, also in Chapter 6.

Samuel A. Abady, Charles Adams, the late Peter Brazeau, Cleanth Brooks, Stuart Curran, Richard Eberhart, Wendy Flory, Robert Gallimard, S. K. Heninger, Daniel Hoffman, Faith Jackson, William Koshland, James Longenbach, James K. Lyon, Glen MacLeod, Margaret Maurer, Harry C. Payne, Jane Pinchin, Donald G. Sheehy, Sylvia Simons Sights, Wendy Steiner, John B. Stevens, Jr., the late Willard Thorp, James Thorpe, and Jane MacFarland Wilson each supplied needed information, gave counsel at sticking points, sent me following new leads, or contributed timely encouragement. Exceptionally encouraging were A. Walton Litz, Marjorie Perloff, and the late Terrence Des Pres. One could not have had stronger editorial and institutional support than I have had; I wish to thank in particular Robert E. Brown and Robin Ginsberg at Princeton University Press, and Kathleen Roos. Holly Stevens has been patient with me and unfailingly supportive; I am grateful to her also for having so carefully fashioned several essential tools of the trade—especially the magnificently edited *Letters of Wallace Stevens*.

I want to praise and thank most of all two whose help has been unceasing, Peter Tarr and Susan Albertine. From the moment I began to undertake the project, Pete and I have exchanged ideas daily in long long-distance telephone calls; that he has left a deep impression on this book is but the merest sign of his intelligence, generosity, and capacity as a friend. Susan, truly "friend and dear friend," read every word a number of times, applied her enviable editorial skills, caught me when I was near a fall, and always offered her astonishing good sense; her own work in American literature has informed this study in ways neither of us could have predicted. She has made everything seem possible.

Grateful acknowledgment is also made to the following:

Alfred A. Knopf, Inc., for permission to reprint previously published material from *Letters of Wallace Stevens*, Copyright © 1966 by Holly Stevens; *Opus Posthumous: Poems, Plays, Prose* by Wallace Stevens, Copyright © 1957 by Holly Stevens and Elsie Stevens, renewed 1989 by Holly Stevens; *The Necessary Angel*, Copyright © 1951 by Wallace Stevens; *The Collected Poems of Wallace Stevens*, Copyright © 1954 by Wallace Stevens;

Oxford University Press and Richard Eberhart for permission to quote portions of "Formative Mastership" from *Collected Poems, 1930–1986*, Copyright © 1960, 1976, 1987 by Richard Eberhart; and Richard Eberhart for permission to quote portions of "Closing Off the View";

New Directions Publishing Corporation for permission to quote portions of "A Place (Any Place) to Transcend All Places" from *William Carlos Williams: Collected Poems, 1939–1962*, volume 2, Copyright © 1944, 1948 by William Carlos Williams;

Farrar, Straus & Giroux, Inc., for permission to quote portions of "Seasons of the Soul," "Ode to Our Young Pro-Consuls of the Air," and "Ode to the Confederate Dead" from *Collected Poems: 1919–1976* by Allen Tate, Copyright © 1952, 1953, 1970, 1977 by Allen Tate;

and Jane Morse for permission to quote lines from the dedication in Samuel French Morse, *Time of Year*, Copyright © 1943 by Samuel French Morse.

Portions of Chapter 4 appeared, in somewhat different form, in the introduction to *Secretaries of the Moon: The Letters of Wallace Stevens and José Rodríguez Feo* (Durham: Duke University Press, 1986); I wish to thank Beverly Coyle, my co-editor, and Duke University Press for permission to use this material. Part 1 of Chapter 2 has appeared, in slightly different form, as "Stevens's Home Front" in the *Wallace Stevens Journal* 13, 2 (Fall 1990).

The following individuals and institutions kindly granted me permission to quote from previously unpublished materials: Fernand Auberjonois for his letters to me and portions of our 1987 interview; Jonathan Bishop for John Peale Bishop's letter to Stevens; Cleanth Brooks for his letters to Stevens, Tate, and me; Ashley Brown for his letter to Tate; Kenneth Burke for his letter to Tate; Helen Church Minton for Henry Church's letters to Paulhan, Tate, and Stevens, and for Barbara Church's poem and her letters to Moore and Stevens; Beth Dalin for Ebba Dalin's letters to Stevens; Richard Eberhart for his letters to Stevens; Margaret Farrington for Thomas McGreevy's letter to Stevens; Joseph Frank for Richard P. Blackmur's letter to Tate; Helen Ransom Forman for John Crowe Ransom's letters to Brooks, Warren, and Tate; Jill Janows, producer of *Wallace Stevens: Man Made Out of Words*, Center for Visual History, for a portion of Richard Rogers's interview with John Lukens; Henry A. Kissinger for his letter to Stevens; R. M. Ludwig, representing the estate of Willard Thorp, for portions of my 1986 interview with Professor Thorp; Marianne C. Moore, Literary Executor for the Estate of Marianne Moore, for Moore's letters to Barbara Church; Jane Morse for Samuel French Morse's letters to Katherine Frazier and Gordon Cairnie; Mary O'Connor for William Van O'Connor's letter to Brooks; Jacqueline Paulhan for Jean Paulhan's letter to Jean Lebrau; Donald Stanford for his letter to Tate; Holly Stevens for many of her father's letters; John B. Stevens, Jr., for his and Anna May Stevens's letters to their uncle; Helen Tate for Allen Tate's letters to Ashley Brown, Marianne Moore, Donald Stanford, Oscar Williams, Morton D. Zabel, and Stevens; Anne van Geyzel for Leonard C. van Geyzel's letters to Stevens; Béatrice Wahl-Hamet for Jean Wahl's unpublished Drancy poems and his inscription to Stevens; William Eric Williams and Paul H. Williams for unpublished material by William Carlos Williams, Copyright © 1990, used by permission of New Directions Publishing Corporation, acting as agents for the Williamses; Adam Yarmolinsky, Executor of the Babette Deutsch estate, for Deutsch's letter to Stevens; and Special Collections, University of Arkansas Libraries; Collection of American Literature, Beinecke Rare Book and Manuscript Library, Yale University; Joseph R. Regenstein Library, University of Chicago; Dartmouth College Library; Houghton Library, Harvard University; Henry E. Huntington Library; Société des Lecteurs de Jean Paulhan; Princeton University Library; Rosenbach Museum and Library; Department of Special Collections, The Stanford University Libraries; George Arents Research Library for Special Collections, Syracuse University; Harry Ransom Humanities Research Center, The University of Texas at Austin; and Special Collections, Washington University Library.

Part One

STEVENS'S NATIONAL MOMENT

CHAPTER 1

Playing Checkers under the Maginot Line

It is difficult
to get the news from poems
yet men die miserably every day
for lack
of what is found there.
—*William Carlos Williams*

[T]he demnition news, added to the demnition
grind at the office, makes me feel pretty much as a
man must feel in a shelter waiting for bombing to
start. We live quietly and *doucement*, but, for all
that, the climate is changing. . . . It might be that it
would be better to wait a little while, until there is
a change of weather.
—*Stevens, writing to Henry Church about
Church's idea to republish* Mesures (L *365*)

War is the periodical failure of politics.
—*Stevens* (OP *191*)

THE FOREIGN correspondents who would form one of Wallace Stevens's
links to the world at war, and later to the world at cold war, were of little
help, actually, in sorting out the confusions of the war's very first phase. In
spite of that—indeed because of it—they are the unlisted *dramatis personae*
of a number of poems Stevens wrote between the Anschluss and Pearl
Harbor, work that can be characterized as presenting a form of American
isolationism. To be sure, these people themselves assumed no single political position; their ideas in fact ranged from a colonial socialism (Leonard
van Geyzel) to a mild form of French defeatism (Anatole Vidal). If Stevens
derived from the information these contacts provided him—or, more to
the point, from what they did not provide him—an affirmation of his own
disengagement, it was not because this affirmation was among the motives
behind these correspondences in the first place. It is characteristic, then, of
a book hinging on Stevens's developing notion of politically unconscious
impulses that we begin with what he was not told and could not have

known about the actual world in danger—not primarily in order to establish benign or malevolent purpose for omission but rather to lay a groundwork for Stevens's construction of political fact.

Leonard C. van Geyzel. Stevens's politically astute correspondent in Ceylon, a place symbolizing dislocation, would become quite disturbed about the war. He would eventually offer Stevens a glimpse of a postwar position shaped by an intellectualized if not active leftism, entailing an evenhanded assessment of the Soviets' contribution to the Allied war effort.[1] But such insights came later; until well into 1941, van Geyzel merely joked about his island's peripheral relation to the European crisis, a geopolitical trope Stevens took to heart, as it would confirm his own sense of Ceylon's exquisite severance from history.

Henri Amiot. This Frenchman had long since returned to Paris after a stint in the United States working with The Hartford, and at signs of war's imminence was absorbed into the French army. But only one note came to Stevens from the front, and it did not describe the agonies of *attentisme*, as much a diplomatic as a military stance of waiting and seeing assumed by the French nervously assembled behind and below the psychologically inviolable Maginot Line. When "phoney" war ended with the offensive war of May and June 1940 and the rapid disintegration of Reynaud's uncongenial coalition in late June, Sergeant Amiot, assigned to one of the doomed detachments, was undoubtedly among the multitudes taken prisoner; before the German invasion his unit had been stationed in Le Mans, which by June 17 was behind the lines. An eyewitness to war, to the rapid, bewildering collapse of Stevens's cherished France, was lost to him[2]—until, that is, a postcard arrived after the liberation of Paris. "[Y]our postcard told me that you were still alive," Stevens then replied (*L* 480). But that was four and a half years after the Germans moved on France.

Anatole Vidal. Right up to the time Vidal, like van Geyzel and Amiot, disappeared from Stevens's foreign landscape during the worst years of the conflict, letters from this kindly French art and book dealer concerned items such as a lively Jean Marchand, an Edmund Ceria harbor vista, even a small Corot—works Stevens might purchase from Paris sight unseen. Perhaps this very procedure, Vidal's special agency, made depictions of the European scene seem visually unreal and abstract, inappropriate or unavailable to the correspondence. The extent to which the intrusions of war affected Vidal's business—we can now be certain he and it were both greatly affected—Stevens could not then have known, for his agent's verbal descriptions dwelt on how "it all went on in an orderly way," to borrow pertinently from "Connoisseur of Chaos" (1938), and were evidently designed to describe an art world advantageously for a customer who would want to read in words (and not see in pictures) how that world carried on, even as Panzer divisions gathered opposite the Maginot in unimaginable numbers and with undreamt-of force.

Walter Pach. Much closer to Stevens than was van Geyzel or Vidal— those two long-term correspondents whom Stevens would never meet in person—was the art collector and critic Pach, "an old friend of mine" (*L* 490). They had known each other at least since the time Pach was one of the co-organizers of the Armory Show.[3] Having spent part of the year in Europe, periodically reporting back to Stevens about fresh young painters and writers there, Pach was now compelled to remain in New York; in fact, despite his general authority on all things French, in 1939 and 1940 he would have known only as much of the immediate troubles as Stevens knew.

Ferdinand Reyher. A correspondent dating back to the mid-teens, who also spent a good deal of time in Europe, Reyher had been refused by the U.S. Army in 1917 because of his German background;[4] now he was engaged in helping a famous German antifascist. Regaining contact with Stevens at least briefly in February 1939—it was their first exchange in well over a decade—Reyher wrote to solicit Stevens's aid in bringing Bertolt Brecht to the United States after his escape from Nazi Germany. The man whom Brecht called his "American Cicerone" urgently informed Stevens that Brecht was "in exile, about to be tossed out of the green and white haven of Denmark, but writing with the humorous bitter fever of a papal legate." Reyher hoped Stevens would read "the English translation of his Beggar's Opera novel, *A Penny for the Poor*, . . . a sardonic exercise in plot." But Stevens did not apparently respond to Brecht's crisis or look into his antifascist writings; instead, he induced Reyher into the pattern of their old relationship, which was characterized by Stevens's requests for hard-to-find books and Reyher's energetic efforts to locate them. His reply must have seemed to Reyher a clear sign that the old self-involvement had not yet given way, for Stevens now asked the man busily assisting Brecht to locate a copy of his own *Owl's Clover*; and Stevens, so far as we know, never so much as mentioned Brecht again.[5]

Henry Church. Here was a man friendly with many French and German intellectuals endangered by the rise of Nazism. He began regularly corresponding with Stevens in 1939, after the poet had given permission to have some of his works translated and published in Church's and Jean Paulhan's little magazine, *Mesures*. That as war became imminent, and then broke out, Church chose wisely to remain in the United States (he and his wife had come for a visit in July)[6] only made it more difficult for him to describe the situation from the inside.[7] To the extent, then, that Stevens can be said to have been insufficiently compelled by the magnitude of the crisis in its early phase, it may have been due to Church's propensity for sentimentalizing the political events affecting his precious adopted French home. Thus, in the war's first months, Church's second- and thirdhand news from his many literary and academic friends in Europe, passed along incidentally to Stevens in Church's scrawled or poorly typewritten letters, may have been misperceived as the lamentations of one hypersensitive, wealthy exile, weakened by a weak heart, worrying over hard-to-confirm reports of his many imperiled possessions and his fancy estate in—after June 1940— an occupied zone. Indeed, as Willard Thorp remembered the Churches at Princeton in the months before and after the decision not to return to their Ville d'Avray home, Henry seemed to take the invasion of France "as if it were a personal attack on him"[8]—just the sort of maudlin view of international affairs Stevens would have the most difficulty accepting.

It seems certain that Stevens's first general response to these correspondents was a readiness to withdraw into the basic fact of American distance. Indeed, by the time he prepared a statement for the 1939 *Partisan Review* symposium, his isolationist position was clear and apparently simple. "I don't think that the United States should enter into the next world war," he wrote. This statement was composed, submitted, and printed before the late-August Nazi-Soviet agreement that allowed the Germans to carry out their plans for the invasion of Poland on the first day of September. The qualifying phrase he added to this comment ("*if* there is to be another" war) obviously does not indicate his otherwise fine sense of rhetorical timing. Still, his eleventh-hour statement appeared in the Summer 1939 issue[9]—that is, before such an "if" became an anachronism of delayed publication; others who participated in the symposium, such as the fellow-traveling Horace Gregory, were given a less fortunate context, as their statements, saved for the autumn issue, might be misunderstood as straddling the meaningful date. Stevens's isolationist impulse, of course, raises problems much greater than those created by the ambiguity of a literary magazine's untimely appearance—though, to be sure, any tardiness in an era of rapid-fire events, of ever-shifting intellectual alliances both at home and abroad, is not a matter to be lightly discounted; nor is sorting out accidental from substantial bad timing wholly beyond the reconstructive effort of the literary historian. Much of this book depends on just such a reconstruction, however qualified by ideological reflection; it reveals first that Stevens was hardly alone among writers in giving expression to what we might hastily conclude was an unremarkably conservative view of the prospects for American intervention overseas. There were other American intellectuals who would only a few years later espouse a fervent "new nationalism," as it would be called, who would energetically support the American artist's involvement in the "total war" (meaning, for all but a few intellectuals of Stevens's generation, not the battle itself but the creative war "effort" on the home front). Yet these others sent the *Partisan* views substantially similar to Stevens's. Of the nine writers whose comments were printed in the symposium, only two, veterans of literary wars John Dos Passos and Lionel Trilling, could be said to have been prepared to support the war effort in any way. Neither actually worked from an interventionist premise; Dos Passos only said he would, if necessary, be ready to get back his "old job" driving an ambulance, and Trilling merely said more straightforwardly than other respondents that a new world war was "the great objective and subjective fact which confronts every writer."[10] Mild as Trilling's endorsement of the war seems now, however, it was then a distinct and arguable position.

Stevens, clearly on the other side of the argument, was yet in safe *liberal* company in opposing American involvement. But what side was that exactly? The coalition was broad and not easily defined even then, let alone now. Sherwood Anderson ("I do not believe in any war") and Katherine Anne Porter ("[D]on't be betrayed into all the old outdated mistakes") were isolationists primarily because they were pacifists;[11] Porter had seen the Nazis—in the person of Göring—close up.[12] Louise Bogan and Richard Blackmur were ready to oppose American involvement actively; so they said. James T. Farrell and Horace Gregory, like Porter, still felt the sting of the Great War; Gregory wondered satirically if the symposium question meant that the last war had now "actually ceased,"[13] and Farrell mocked the idea that he, as an American, would ever have any "economic interests" in places like Danzig, Teschen, or Tunisia—standard isolationist logic from an ex-communist, soon-to-be ex-radical, who was moving so surely rightward that he might be said even here to be meeting the communist line coming round the other way.[14] Allen Tate's remarks were certainly the strongest of the ten offered. Tate and Stevens appeared to share much the same ideological ground, in fact, each assuming, as Tate put it, "The writer, *as* writer, has no responsibility when war comes."[15] In a later phase of the war, the evident alliance between Tate and Stevens would cause the latter great discomfort. Still, the 1939 *Partisan* symposium helped set out the controversial literary-political terms in which the Tate-Stevens relationship, the most important poetic interaction of Stevens's war years, must be told.

That ten American writers in the summer of 1939 were unready or unwilling to support U.S. involvement in another world war cannot be at all surprising, even given the fact that American communists, who still held sway over many noncommunist writers, strongly supported all forms of war against fascism—this preceding, crucially, the Nazi-Soviet Pact, after which, and until June 22, 1941, intervention was opposed as supporting another "imperialist war."[16] While the basic agreement between Stevens and his fellow writers does accurately suggest a consensus among American intellectuals, it hardly presented the sort of association, or camp, one might have expected a major political issue to have produced only a few years earlier. To restore Stevens's symposium statement to the context provided by nine other American writers, then—to show his fitting in so neatly—only partly satisfies a justifiable curiosity about the literary-political meaning of his isolationism as (to most of us today) an inevitably unattractive position. There is a far more revealing qualification to it, which will emerge as the main theme not only of this chapter but of this study: insofar as Stevens's statement that the United States should not enter another world war *is* unique among the others'—especially unlike the pacifists'—it is so in speculating, prematurely it might seem, on the particular burdens to befall the *postwar* American imagination. The United States should not enter the war, Stevens was suggesting before it had begun, "unless it does so with the idea of dominating the world that comes out of it."[17] If his wartime poems give any expression whatever to such an acutely critical prediction of the world to come in the late forties and early fifties, they are for that reason alone worth studying as unique anticipations of cultural cold war—odd as Stevens's association with the cold war may initially seem to readers of the later chapters here. Thus Stevens's early opposition to World War II—it was brief, an attitude that would diminish and then disappear in 1941—was not intended, as Bogan's was, to stimulate an "active opposition" to it,[18] nor, as Blackmur's was, to demonstrate how a new worldwide war, just like the last one, would be a "very complete debauching devil," the ugly issuance of a greedy munitions-making class,[19] but was something wholly different—a source of great fear that American writers, if they are eventually coerced to support a total war uncritically, will not at the same time be sufficiently prepared for the responsibilities that will come with unqualified victory and the ascendency of American culture.

It may also seem odd that such an astute prediction could have derived from so outmoded a politics as isolationism. Yet isolationism was hardly then outmoded; quite the contrary. Stevens's apparently straightforward prewar statement contains in fact a complex version of the already complex logic of isolationism—logic that, even in its most reductive forms, plentifully available in Republican party rhetoric, was neither monolithic at the time nor ideologically predictable;[20] one removes the name and affiliation from any of Robert Taft's speeches of 1939–1940, for instance, only at the risk of being no longer able to place the speaker politically.[21] Crucially, the same could be said of many liberals, whom an exiled Klaus Mann saw as indulging the "illusion . . . that the United States, for some shadowy reason, was absolutely immune to the germ of Fascism." "Many of my liberal friends," Mann recalled in 1942, "seemed to believe that the New Deal could succeed even if Europe went Fascist."[22] Inscribed in a poetry such as Stevens's, far more rhetorically flexible than Senator Taft's podium talk and the conversation of Mann's liberal friends, American isolationism was at this strange and important moment a moving ideological target. Thus, if for American noncombatants there were at the very least three distinct phases of political—and, I will argue, poetic—American rhetoric about the war, we must certainly not write about Stevens's wartime poetry as if in it he could hold a single line from 1939 to 1945 or as if the story of his own response was a single episode or chapter in his career.

Once indeed it can be assumed that Stevens, in reacting quite distinctly to each of three phases, was not essentially different from other Americans at least in this one respect, then the conventional effort of treating the poet as in all ways unique among, for instance, his colleagues at The Hartford—and in general his American peers—can be usefully doubted. When Stevens saw his poetry as responding to the wartime world, he would not allow himself to consider the substance of such responses exceptional. It is surely too easy to say that these admissions are one with the poet's humble fibs about his own unimportance. Why not modify this view in a revision based on Stevens's own shrewd view, to allow at least provisionally for the conclusion drawn generally here—that when his poetic efforts made him feel small in relation to worldwide conflicts, both hot and cold wars, it was because great political positions had impressed themselves upon him? The effects of these impressions are not predictable from period to period, not even perhaps from year to year; nor, thus, are they assimilable into a discrete, maintained, or defended ideology—something to be called, simply, *Stevens's politics*. But they are nevertheless ideologically expressive, for they arise as particular counterarguments to particularly compelling arguments, and thus must be investigated instance by instance, argument by argument. What Stevens had learned from his interaction with the literary left in the thirties, a subject for a book all its own, was that his poetry could find something important to say about Americans' social and political life. So, too, during the early forties, while he moved away from many elements of the liberal-left position he had absorbed for the sake of tempering his argument against what he had called "the pressure of the contemporaneous" (*OP* 230), he clearly retained a basic commitment to "the actual world" that he had initially thought was unfairly forced upon him. Making the rapid transition with Stevens from the thirties to the forties, one must attempt to follow his use and misuse of successive counterarguments, especially at the moments when these pose as original arguments taking the side of "reality"; it is exactly when Stevens evidently offers such arguments as original that one can learn precisely how and why they have their sources elsewhere. By the bitter end of the thirties, during which poetry was regularly measured by its engagement with political crises, Stevens thought of his verse as helping him maintain an interest in the preoccupying events around him. What he had told a Harvard audience in late 1936, in announcing a workable definition of the political unconscious, was still by 1940 true to his feelings: "We are preoccupied by events," he had said, *"even when we do not observe them closely"* (*OP* 229; emphasis added). That striking idea was perhaps even less relevant then than two and a half years later: the effects of the Depression could have been observed indeed *very* "closely" when Stevens offered his definition, right there in his Hartford, in the local parks through which he walked daily and even in the offices of The Hartford where, he would have us believe, he put his head down and ground away at his work until it was done. (That he was more attentive to his workplace surroundings than he and some of his critics like to let on is a story submerged, though still available, in interviews, some excerpted in print and many unpublished, conducted by Peter Brazeau in the seventies with Stevens's co-workers.)[23] Yet a few years later, as war approached, the absorbing events were not local at all but distant and unseen, taking place in "longed-for lands"—long imagined, that is, but never visited. The Europe of Stevens's imagination would be severely tested by the Europe pressed by imaginable crisis turning rapidly unimaginable—as depression, *here* as *there*, became institutionalized fascism, *there* as not *here*. Faced with an increasingly ardent wish to enlarge his sense of place so as to supersede the tropes he had long before invented to explain the foreign to his well-developed domestic self, an effort that would serve perhaps to rationalize his decision not to travel in Europe, Stevens did respond to the war in a characteristically American way and kept rather close to an American chronology: 1939 to December 7, 1941; December 7, 1941, to June 6, 1944; mid-1944 and beyond.

The central critical narrative of this book follows Stevens as the first and second phases of world war, more or less discrete eras of his disengagement and commitment respectively, gave way to an even more important phase in my view (the last wartime period, during which the acclaimed Stevens of the late forties and early fifties came into being). In 1945 the nagging contradictions between American disengagement and commitment, reformulations of thirties oppositions filtered through wartime isolation first and nationalism second, found resolution in a postwar poetry characterized by what many cold-war historians describe as a new and brilliantly disarming twist in the interventionist's claim: an innocence yet worldly, a sentimentalism yet imperial, a benevolent assimilation to match an abstract sense of place yet mightily referential—a special American power, rhetorically but not actually postdating colonialism, that would at once reconstruct and contain the world.[24] Stevens's poetry, in this view, reached fullest maturity just as American politics assumed that ideology itself had been exhausted; the conjunction will suggest that the period of 1942 through 1955 is every bit the "major phase" Harold Bloom argued for so energetically in his effort to reveal Stevens as "the most advanced rhetorician in modern poetry and in his major phase the most disjunctive."[25] But to say even this much about a complex issue—to tie the cultural cold war to notions of an "advanced" rhetorical sense in the late Stevens, and to maneuver Bloom's sense of Stevens's rhetorical mastery onto a historical ground Bloom himself would not want to share—is to leap ahead.

First there is the difficulty of judging how and in what poems Stevens reacted to the war; deciding whether he did so responsibly or irresponsibly, systematically or trivially—questions raised forthrightly by Marjorie Perloff's 1985 essay on "Notes toward a Supreme Fiction"[26]—cannot involve generalizations about the war itself. Such an assessment will entail, rather, an exposition of particular aspects of the various military and cultural efforts in Europe, Africa, and Asia that were evident to the worldly man of Hartford who had already made it his literal business to insure a home front while at the same time maintaining an interest in events well beyond home. Certainly in the first phase of war, prior to U.S. involvement, when the isolationist position was always strengthened by the fact that American culture had not yet been habituated to importing news from abroad that would reshape American daily life itself, Stevens was *already* an experienced gatherer of foreign things. Central to his imaginative power at this moment was his conception of himself as someone capable of measuring the proximity to reality of reports presented by his own foreign correspondents against the distinct irreality of the radio, the American news dailies, the opinion weeklies, and the literary quarterlies. The result of this strikingly postmodern comparison was an extraordinary confusion of reality and mediated irreality that would somehow be reproducible in poetry.

Stevens and his family were sightseeing in Virginia when war broke. If his letter to Leonard van Geyzel, written a few weeks later, on September 20, amply expressed his "horror of the fact that such a thing could occur" (and not incidentally that he was following "the news of the development of the war"), it also accurately identified the special form of indecision now embodied in American attitudes. One felt general sympathies for the British and French, Stevens observed for van Geyzel's benefit (Stevens always assumed that his Ceylonese friend knew little about world events); yet there was also fervid sentiment for continued isolation: "The country is more or less divided between those who think that we should hold aloof and those who think that, at the very least, we ought to help the British and the French. Our sympathies are strongly with the British and the French, but this time there is an immensely strong feeling about *staying out*. I hope that this war will not involve you in your far-off home" (*L* 342; emphasis added).

The poem "Martial Cadenza" (*CP* 237–38) works out a response to the invasion of Poland that gives expression to the "more or less divided" American mind. It is difficult, of course, to be as sure about the poem as about the newslike letter to van Geyzel, and yet one can be certain that at the time of his September 20 letter Stevens had a precise sense of the news coming in; an article running that morning described how the "horror" conveyed and/or aroused by all the news reports was itself a potent "weapon in war."[27] As important, surely, was his accurate judgment of the continued strength of the isolationists. Note that on the day Stevens generalized for "far-off" van Geyzel that "there is an immensely strong feeling about *staying out*," there appeared stories of isolationist stamina under these headlines: "Industry Demands Nation Keep Peace," "Fifty Mayors Pledge Aid in Neutrality," "Survey Shows War Cuts Party Lines; Republicans and Democrats Agree on U.S. Staying Out."[28] Stevens was describing not only his own but a characteristically American partisan nonpartisanship, the precise, though seemingly imprecise, rhetorical manifestation of a cultural impulse to "hold aloof." He recognized not only that the world had suddenly changed—but, too, that such a change could be best apprehended through an American's abstract sense of European time and place set in contrast to his own ultimately stable, quotidian sense of each. The rhetorical redundancies of "Martial Cadenza" replicate the uneasiness in the American reaction he reliably cited for van Geyzel. The effort to locate a ground for the poem's anxieties about *now* through a conversely firm sense of *here* is a passionate one, yet confused: "more or less divided" while "an immensely strong feeling." "It was like sudden time in a world without time, / This world, this place, the street in which I was." The speaker has seen a star again and identifies his own power as derived from the freedom to view the star again and again. This freedom to act and see the same way repetitively works with his "immensely strong feeling" of *confusion* about the war—not schizophrenia, as has been sloppily argued,[29] but an American paradox: intensely focused indecision[30]—to make evident in the poem that its stammer, a rhetorical fumbling for solid ground, is its only appropriate idiom: "Again . . . as if it came back, as if life came back"; "But as if evening found us young, still young"; "that which is not has no time, / Is not, or is of what there was"; "this evening I saw it again / At the beginning of winter, and I walked and talked / Again, and lived and was again, and breathed again / And moved again and flashed again, time flashed again." The poem presents so insistent a sense of being, breathing, and living that one cannot but wonder about the extent to which the poet has realized these are in doubt.

"Martial Cadenza" was the result of a promise made to an associate editor of *Compass*, Parker Tyler, on October 4. This was about the time Stevens received Anatole Vidal's first letters about the European crisis. Vidal wrote on October 17 to report that his associate, a certain Rott, had been serving with the army since the first day of invasion in the East. Vidal reported that Rott, somewhat bored by phoney war, was occupying himself by admiring paintings and other art objects he saw *while on duty*, and that he was even able to find the time to sketch a still life here, a landscape there. This reassuring story seemed calculated to offer the American client a sampling of conditions continuously favorable to business, and strongly suggested that the flow of paintings from Paris to Hartford need not stop.[31] Though perhaps for reasons that have little finally to do with his politics, pro- or anti- German, Vidal's letter of November 18 nevertheless pushed hard for proceeding with normal business relations with Stevens—so hard that it might also have conveyed the idea that the expected German invasion might not in the end represent a threat to French cultural activity. Vidal, after all, took pains to note that shipments of paintings to Canada and the Antilles "have arrived perfectly without incident."[32] More important to the safe passage of paintings Stevens might purchase, Vidal also revealed to Stevens that he had had "friendly and prolonged arrangements with the Germans, around 1900, and then commercial agreements in South America with businessmen of the same nationality and also as correspondent of a German bank in São Paulo and in Rio do Sul—thus here is how I judge the present conflict, as objectively as it is possible to do."[33] Before concluding that in order to counteract the Germans' "religion" of "*la Force*" "we, the French, the most exposed to the perils of slavery," must fight on as individualists inevitably do,[34] Vidal explained to Stevens that "[t]he Germans are a great people by virtue of their work, their organization, their tenacity, and would have become masters of Europe in an atmosphere of peace and freedom."[35] What caused this outpouring? Stevens had evidently suggested to his Parisian agent that the war would not last long. In flatly rejecting this naive prediction, Vidal reiterated his faith in business as usual and the acclimation of the aesthetic mind to war: "Contrary to what you think, I fear that this war will be very long. I'm inclined to believe that it is necessary to set ourselves up morally and materially in this state, unstable as it might be."[36]

Stevens's later comments about Vidal to Henri Amiot—that Vidal "respected many of the things that I respect"; that with Vidal Stevens felt he could "make myself understood"; and that it was therefore "a real pleasure to exchange letters with him"[37]—hardly, of course, constitute evidence that among the things Stevens and Vidal commonly "respected" was the Germans' potential to be "masters" of a peaceful Europe. And since the letters to Vidal do not survive, we are only left to guess at Stevens's response to the guarantees of continued unhampered trade and specifically to the scenario of business as usual with the Germans. It would not have been uncharacteristic of Stevens's attitude toward wartime writing in this first phase for him to have replied to Vidal as he did to van Geyzel, by saying, "I *make no reference* in this letter to the war. It *goes without saying* that our minds are full of it" (*L* 356; emphasis added). Such a comment, aside from being rhetorically typical of Stevens at any point, would in this very special instance send a clear signal that his correspondence with the French agent must keep strictly to the matter of art. Yet the question about art's inevitable relation to German power had now been posed; it could hardly be ignored even as the correspondence continued otherwise undisturbed. Were inherent opposites—for Vidal, embodied in French as directly opposed to German ways—reconcilable, in spite of everything, for the purposes of conducting art's business? Stevens's previous notion of art and antagonism in "Connoisseur of Chaos" had been that aesthetic relation mediated warring concepts and that the resulting fiction of "essential unity" in a painting satisfied in this unique way. Such a theoretical position suggests that he might indeed have understood Vidal's letter about the Germans as describing the impact of the European conflict on the man who arranged for the sale of these paintings as "the present realized" in a "vivid thing in the air that never changes" (*CP* 238). It might be that, as "Martial Cadenza" contends, the more rapidly things moved the more inexorably they remained the same, geographically and temporally. Vidal's curious version of *c'est la guerre* for Stevens was this: "If from a biological point of view man has hardly changed (massacres, tortures, war in Spain, Poland) the only true good that he must strive to reach is freedom . . . which allows him . . . to act according to . . . the atavisms of the race."[38]

The ideological basis of Vidal's assessment of the Germans for Stevens is difficult to discern, but the attempt is surely justified. Eugen Weber, author of *Varieties of Fascism*, observes that "Vidal's letter echoes familiar right-wing themes aired during and after the First World War," though this is less a sign of *Lavalisme*, of any specific readiness to collaborate with the Germans, who would indeed pillage the Parisian art world Vidal loved so well, than yet another indication of the thoroughness with which the rhetoric of the *Action française* had by this time penetrated the otherwise apolitical French psyche. His remarks do reproduce the kind of French stereotypes of the German character that derived from the campaigns of 1870 and were being "dusted off" (Professor Weber's phrase) in late 1939. Vidal seems reconciled to the sinking liberal republic, and his apparent respect for the revived German sense of communal tenacity, which was already challenging French individualism from within, suggests that the old bookseller was making a serious if unsystematic effort to accommodate himself to the climate of ideological instability.[39]

Whatever the precise motive for Vidal's long letter about art under the Nazi threat, the fact is that his three final letters to Stevens, written in 1940 prior to the invasion that began on May 10, dropped the subject of the Germans entirely. These last letters occupied themselves, as they always had in peacetime, with describing the work of new artists whose paintings Stevens might like to buy—in particular, Edmund Ceria, whose *Harbor Scene* was Stevens's final purchase until after the war.[40] From this we can only conclude that Stevens responded to the November 18 letter by tacitly consenting to continue with business as usual, with both men assuming the fact that such a policy might suddenly become impossible.

For all its attention to a world to which we cannot go back, then, Stevens's "Connoisseur of Chaos" had already made explicit its interest in the less and less tenable disposition of "business as usual" and the great debt to Vidal's agency. The painting by Jean Marchand that Vidal had recently selected for Stevens is mentioned in line 12 of the poem. In making the settlement of inherent conflict analogous to the "pleasant" inevitability of "the brush-strokes of a bough, / An upper, particular bough in, say, Marchand," "Connoisseur of Chaos" spoke of a world resolving oppositions satisfactorily. Even the choice of one painting in favor of another, akin to the never-quite-certain choice of one word over another, need not ever have been made ("in, *say*, Marchand"), according to the elaborate rules guiding the translation of the visual to the verbal in the Vidal-Stevens agent-buyer relationship. That is, as particular as this interartistic pointing might seem—an *upper, particular bough* in a particular painting the poet now owned and could study as he wrote his lines[41]—these resolutions were *generally* achievable in art produced in a world hardly altered after canonized books no longer sufficiently resolved its conflicts (ll. 13–16). The perception of violence, converted into order through an illogic made logical by the poem's propositional discourse ("A" proposed with "B"), depended on how "great" the violence of the disorder was, for the greater the violence, the sharper the perception of the need for order. Only a great disorder leads to so willful a conception:

> A. A violent order is disorder; and
> B. A great disorder is an order. These
> Two things are one. . . .
>
> . . . .
>
> And if it all went on in an orderly way,
> And it does; a law of inherent opposites,
> Of essential unity, is as pleasant as port,
> As pleasant as the brush-strokes of a bough,
> An upper, particular bough in, say, Marchand.

(*CP* 215)

We know that by early 1939 Stevens had read Charles Henri Ford's book of poems *The Garden of Disorder* and had decided that "[n]ext to order, disorder is the great temptation," even though "[t]here are no end of intermediates." And: "There is nothing to dis-order except the making of it."[42] This marked a change that was obviously in turn marked by the times, from "Connoisseur of Chaos" of 1938 to "Man and Bottle" of late 1939. In the earlier poem Stevens had pointed to an increasing disorder that had not yet degenerated into outright conflict, when a conflict between the German mastery of order (Vidal's sense of *la Force* victorious) and the French addiction to disorder (Vidal's sense of cultural individualism doomed to defeat) could be appeased, rendered "intermediates," only at certain obvious risks and would finally be "resolved" for the vanquished French as Vichy's politically fictive "New Order." But by the time of "Man and Bottle" both the disorder and the tone that indicated a craving for mediation had deepened; that poem engaged Stevens's new effort to be "the master of disorder."[43]

Composed around the time Vidal's November letter arrived in Hartford, "Man and Bottle" defines the mind in opposition to "the man"; it is the mind, and not "the man" himself, that abides the naturalizing logic about a war that had by then begun.

Man and Bottle

The mind is the great poem of winter, the man,
Who, to find what will suffice,
Destroys romantic tenements
Of rose and ice

In the land of war. . . .

. . . .

It has to content the reason concerning war,
It has to persuade that war is part of itself,
A manner of thinking, a mode
Of destroying, as the mind destroys,

An aversion, as the world is averted
From an old delusion, an old affair with the sun,
An impossible aberration with the moon,
A grossness of peace.

It is not the snow that is the quill, the page.
The poem lashes more fiercely than the wind,
As the mind, to find what will suffice, destroys
Romantic tenements of rose and ice.

(*CP* 238–39)

If for someone like Vidal, who wanted to continue buying and selling art, it had to be able to live with war, so too for Stevens in "Man and Bottle" art "has to content the reason concerning war." "It has to persuade that war is part of itself," and this self-rationalization constitutes not only "A manner of thinking" but "a mode / Of destroying," which is precisely how the mind can be said to hold the power to destroy an attitude of "aversion" in which "the world is averted." Vidal's efforts to rationalize the continuing world of art in wartime obtain here, having taught Stevens an important lesson about National Socialist hegemony—how in justifying imagination in wartime the defeatist mind may unwittingly take on qualities of the mode that will destroy it. (How better to explain Vidal's absorption of the rhetorical basis of German peacetime mastery?) The destructive mode also destroys the attitude that enables poems and paintings to go on as if they still responded to peacetime conditions—the sort of art, for instance, that never had in the first place made mimetic claims and thus might attract the often unreasonable reproach, "Don't you know there's a war on?"[44] Such a poem (not necessarily "Man and Bottle," but the poem described in the poem— "it") presents itself as inserting into a contingency ("in the land of war") an aesthetic attitude beyond the reach of events to which one may choose not to refer.

Vidal was not the only model for Stevens's wartime connoisseur of chaos; Walter Pach was also. Stevens's old friend Pach advised him about dealing productively through a foreign agent to purchase paintings sight unseen. And it was Pach who recommended, in January 1938, that Stevens carry out the search for a painting by Marchand.[45] But if Stevens seriously "wants to own pictures," Pach had counseled in 1937, and did not himself wish to go to Paris, he would have to find, and then place unwavering trust in, a dealer whose European disposition the American consumer of art would have to study as diligently as he studied the paintings themselves.[46] Since we lack Stevens's letters to Vidal, we must judge in part from Stevens's postwar letters to Vidal's daughter Paule, who after her father's death assumed the role of Stevens's Parisian agent-correspondent; from these we may fairly conclude that Stevens took quite seriously Pach's stipulations. Stevens was indeed always careful to imply that Paule Vidal should buy him only paintings that she herself liked—or, to be more precise, only those works that, *because* she liked them, she could convey successfully to him in words, in her letters, an agent's letters thus taking on the demanding task of describing modern visual art in language;[47] we know that Anatole explained this "difficulty" to Stevens.[48] True intermediacy between the poet and the world of art he chose not to know firsthand, a wished-for limitation the European crisis only made easier to justify, would depend as much on the special relations between agent and buyer as on the actual features of the paintings.

The insight of "Man and Bottle" provided a contribution, then, to Stevens's evolving idea about how the American imagination "has to persuade that war is part of itself" in order to maintain a response to the climate of art even as it was being changed by war. In this view "Man and Bottle" has two competing senses as a title phrase. The phrase first implies a unity (man *and* bottle) characteristic of a work of modern art, in which the human figure and the nonhuman form may be joined to share basic qualities. There is a second, idiomatic sense of *bottle* here, I think—a connotation of the relation between a man and his bottle that competes with the poem's obvious modernism. In this, man seeks refuge in a readily available form or, as it were, *takes to the bottle* in an opposition to war.

This second sense of *bottle* may have been written into the poem as something of a private and seemingly trivial joke between Stevens and the Pachs, Walter and his wife Magda, as I will suggest shortly. More important, it does *not* resolve the crisis of wartime art; "and" suggests not unity but strain. To be sure, the poem's title does suggest that the words to follow will encourage the mediation of subject and object; and when the poem addresses the issue of the romantic mind locating itself as subject in that which suffices "in the land of war," it does seem to propose a form of wartime representation consonant with the modern: the poetic subject, in knowing war, knows war to be somehow "part of itself," so "man" (a human shape) and "bottle" (a basic form, say Gris's or Picasso's bottle-shaped figures) are one. The poetic mind viewing war in this visually analytic way begins to work in the ways of war; the poem works violently, claiming not just to be *like* the mind but to *be* the mind itself—"the mind *is* the great poem of winter." Yet bottle has another sense, in which the irreconcilable differences between man and bottle posit a resistance to the very fact of war. The mind's poem is thus an independent agent in the pitched periodic battle against the natural cycle of the weather—wintry cold no less than seasonal (or "periodical") war; its very formalities warm in a time of cold. It teaches a response to a boreal vehemence and denies war's harshness. Modernism, in such a context, would seek to unify the two by at once subjectivizing and formalizing the man and having him share qualities of *bottle*; in my reading, the poem offers a temporary humanist repudiation of this, for it is marked, paradoxically, by an *awareness* of a resulting insensitivity—"aversion"—to real crises. Thus, as the title phrase cuts across the aesthetic to the idiomatic, it also tentatively moves to a more realistic realm, somewhat restoring bottle's status as object, to the province of the "man" surveying objective conditions and finding that this bottle may also suffice in the effort to ward off the violent winter months of 1939–1940.

The idiomatic reading of man's wartime relation to bottle is indeed supported by Stevens's dealings with Walter and Magda Pach that season. The Pachs' visit to Hartford, where they saw Stevens and an exhibit of paintings at the Wadsworth Atheneum, was returned by Stevens in late November. At the Pachs' Manhattan studio, a central conversational topic was surely the precarious status of modern painters and painting in Paris, where Pach had always spent much of his time; he had known Matisse, Derain, Picasso, and Braque there and once told Stevens it was "the most exciting spot on the globe."[49] The prospect of losing touch with Paris would have been all the more poignant for the socializing threesome, as on the walls around them were many of Pach's spectacular French acquisitions, among these a Cézanne lithograph, *Baigneurs*,[50] Raoul Dufy's *Under the Trees*,[51] Antoine Gros's *Portrait of a Woman*,[52] a Delacroix study for *Cicero Accusing Verres*,[53] Constantin Guy's *Portrait of a Lady*, Matisse's *Reclining Nude*, and Raymond Duchamp-Villon's abstract bronze *Horse*.[54] Pach had just then concluded his ample book on Ingres—its publication may have been the ostensible reason for their little party—with a plea that Europeans strive to remain "equal to the task of continuing their tradition" and with confidence that Paris "rocks but does not go under."[55] The only surviving record of the evening the three spent together indicates that Magda Pach fixed them a seasonal drink, her *Glühwein*, which Stevens apparently enjoyed in quantity. After Stevens returned to Hartford, it was Magda who wrote him to suggest the pun of *the bottle* that might help one resist the season's lashing cold: shortly after his visit she mailed Stevens her recipe, noting that "[i]t was one of the drinks one likes once [in] a while *when the wind blows and snow is in the air*" (emphasis added).[56] To the Pachs in particular—for whom the poem may have been, in one sense, an elaborate note of thanks for an uproarious evening of forgetting the Germans' warmongering with *Glühwein*—Stevens's "bottle" was to be understood as an object tenably of service to a modern art of war.[57] But if man and bottle can be said to split "man" even momentarily from "mind" in the poem, they also complete the ratio by keeping poet momentarily from form, reality from imagination, sentiment from abstraction, and a modified (or "neo-") Romantic from the modern. When, under the Pachs' influence, the "mind" as subject is dissipated in the realization that an art of war advances from self-persuasions and rationalizations, and when "bottle" is literalized to warm just as the lash of the poem about war's reality chills, the title can play off a thoroughly nonpoetic sense of the object. The implication was also, though cryptically, a friendly admonition to Pach: the war had brought those who traded on Europe's cultural achievement, American promoters of European modernism, to the point of admitting modernism's final powerlessness against actual political degeneration; the poem elaborately offers itself as evidence.

Two days before the end of 1939, when the boreal wind was indeed blowing and the temperature was, Stevens observed, "zero out of doors," he dictated an important letter to Hi Simons (*L* 345–46). He restated in sum the related points he had made in "Man and Bottle" and "Of Modern Poetry" (1938): a poem itself entails the act of finding what suffices (*CP* 239–40). He was seeking, he told Simons, "the discovery of a value that really suffices." The letter was designed in part to provide Simons an explanation of a poem Stevens was then writing or had just finished. As an example of the sort of thinking that went into this latest poem, Stevens quoted and explained an expression in a French journal he had read the night before. The phrase, as he remembered, was

> something like this: "the primordial importance of spiritual values in time of war." The ordinary, everyday search of the romantic mind is rewarded perhaps rather too lightly by the satisfaction that it finds in *what it calls* reality. But if one happened to be playing checkers somewhere under the Maginot Line, subject to a call at any moment to do some job that might be one's last job, one would spend a good deal of time thinking *in order to make the situation seem reasonable, inevitable and free from question.* (*L* 346; emphasis added)

That in late 1939 Frenchmen were rationalizing realities of the European situation by discussing spiritual values was evidence to Stevens that the wartime mind sought to resolve normal oppositions between spiritual values and individual war effort in order to supplant a political contingency, the historical preconditions of war, with a universal value—to replace what is reasonable with something "in order to make the situation seem" reasonable, reality with "what it calls" reality. The soldier playing checkers under the Maginot Line, waiting to be called upon to serve and die, had to remain unaware that he himself participated in the effort to keep the reasons for dying unquestioned. Stevens continued:

> I suppose that, in the last analysis, *my own main objective is to do that kind of thinking. On the other hand,* the sort of poem that I have in the winter number of THE KENYON REVIEW, from which every bit of anything of that sort has been excluded, *also has its justifications.* In a world permanently enigmatical, to hear and see agreeable things involves something more than mere imagism. *One might do it deliberately* and in that particular poem *I did it deliberately.* (*L* 346; emphasis added)

How did Stevens intend for his Maginot Line–to–poetry analogy to serve as an explanation for Simons that the goal of his own recent writing had been indeed "to do that kind of thinking"? What kind was *that*, precisely? The problem with the casually constructed scene of an entrenched, expectant soldier is that it is not clear whether Stevens wanted Simons to read the recent poems as accommodating themselves to political "justifications" that force upon participants the acceptance of war as an absolute or, alternatively, if he thought they helped repudiate the latest form of such justifications as making war palatable and thus possible. It is hard to say, in other words, from his seemingly definitive remarks, if indeed at the end of

1939 Stevens now deemed "Variations on a Summer Day" (*CP* 232–36), the poem "that I have in the winter number of KENYON REVIEW," a success or a failure in the effort to raise verse *not* about war to a level above "mere imagism." In avoiding explicit reference to war, did the summery poem "deliberately" expose, reproduce, or avert "this kind of thinking"? The gloss for Simons was further complicated by the fact that the poem's twenty "variations" commemorate an experience that had taken place just before the September 1 outbreak of war, a dating that would help to explain the December 29 statement as a form of looking back at the point of significantly belated magazine publication—at a poem, that is, that seemed only a few months after it had been written to be at turns enchantingly and alarmingly innocent of subsequent world events. Such might honestly be claimed at a moment that called out for retrospection, the final days of a tragic year. The eleventh-hour avowal would not be convincing if the belatedness associated with this poem *predicted* eerie bad timing by thematizing "portent" and setting the boat-of-human-will on a drifting course: "you drift, / You, too, are drifting, in spite of your course; / . . . if there is a will, / Or the portent of a will that was, / One of the portents of the will that was" (variation iv).

Straddling the start of war in Stevens's mind, somehow looking back *on* and yet *with* prewar innocence, these "Variations" have written into them signs that they memorialize not only the pleasing aimlessness of a vacation but also the loss of innocence, always to be associated with the summer of 1939. (This became a trope of other poets' early war poems, for instance, W. R. Rodgers's "Summer Holidays" and Oscar Williams's "A 1940 Vacation.")[58] In resisting reference to war, the poem replicated a crucial phase of omission, what Stevens naturalized as the seasonal or "*periodical* failure of politics." Note that in April 1941, in "The Noble Rider and the Sound of Words," the prewar metaphor of news-as-weather has not changed: even the "pressure of reality," a strain or force, is explained as "the *drift* of incidents, to which we accustom ourselves *as to the weather*" (*NA* 19). Such a special form of "aversion"—"as the world is averted," in "Man and Bottle"—is manifest even in the one stanza of "Variations" that comes close to the issue of war poetry. This risked least the criticism that Stevens's poetry was produced merely as the result of a few pleasant brushstrokes—stood furthest, in other words, from offering itself independently as a nice "agreeable thing," yet unable finally to resist aestheticizing a historical event (an officer and his troops were killed):

> Everywhere the spruce trees bury soldiers:
> Hugh March, a sergeant, a redcoat, killed,
> With his men, beyond the barbican.
> Everywhere spruce trees bury spruce trees.

> (var. xii)

The "agreeable thing" here is the spruce tree grown up over the graves, arising out of the bodies of Revolutionary War–era soldiers; they and their sergeant were *English* soldiers, one-time enemies, now (apparently) allies. James Baird, in explaining how "Variations on a Summer Day" records Stevens's last prewar vacation in the summer of 1939 at Christmas Cove, Maine, has noted that the history of Pemaquid Point involved the destruction of Fort Frederick during the American Revolution by local residents acting to prevent British occupation of the area. He has briefly described the significance of Stevens's "Hugh March" as a British soldier who fell during this skirmish (Baird even conducted an unsuccessful search for a gravestone of an English soldier of that or similar name).[59] Stevens obviously meant the soldier of "Variations" to be an Englishman; the poem can thus be said to have reproduced a special rhetorical confusion that was at this time an integral part of isolationist logic: Would the United States come to Britain's side if war broke out? Holly Stevens recalled of this vacation that her father "spent a lot of time" with a fellow guest who was an RAF officer, in conversations that "undoubtedly included discussion of the situation in Europe."[60] Memorializing the dead of an enemy, now a pending ally, implied the historical fluidity of the transatlantic alliance. Baird's idea of the relation between "Variations" and the Stevenses' Maine trip was based on a reference Holly Stevens provided (*L* 341n.7). An unpublished letter written by Elsie Stevens from Maine, dated July 1939, to which Baird could not have had access,[61] describes the Pemaquid Point–Christmas Cove area in the kind of detail registered in "Variations on a Summer Day," and helps confirm the close relations between that poem and a last, blissful prewar moment. Elsie reported (to her mother) the lovely "water between the islands and the 'rock-bound' coast of Maine . . . islands . . . mostly rocks seem to grow very white in the sunlight, and the brilliantly green spruce trees . . . [and] many birds . . . gulls . . . + we saw some herons on an island the other day when we passed in a boat."[62] Stevens wrote:

> Say of the gulls that they are flying
> In light blue air over dark blue sea.
>
> (var. i)
>
> A repetition of unconscious things,
> Letters of rock and water . . .
>
> (ii)
>
> The rocks of the cliffs . . .
>
> (iii)
>
> One sparrow is worth a thousand gulls,
> When it sings. . . .
>
> (vii)

Now, the timothy of Pemaquid

(xi)

Everywhere spruce trees bury spruce trees

(xii)

Even the star over the Atlantic (addressed in the fourth variation), common point of reference for people on *both sides* of the issue that otherwise divides, may not be the guide it once was. The referential point may itself now be the "will, if there is a will, / Or the portent of a will that was." Will has been qualified almost to nothing, and the associative "Atlantic star," universally stable, a rare sign of fixity in a time of rapid movement, a point beyond all political argument for or against war, now drifts, unfixed. It becomes another sign of the general failure of will. Stevens's own brief reading of "Variations" suggests an ardent desire to resecure the unmoored star, for the star, like the poem itself according to the disclosure for Simons, resists the effort to establish a stable, practical relation between two points—the drifting boat of the poem itself, now without guidance, improvising its way. Rather, the star only obscures the navigational relation: it shifts points of reference so that the effect is to deny the validity of reference generally. So the overall effect of the poem, to borrow the language of the ninth variation, is to produce a profusion of confusing relations ("cloudy world . . . produces / More nights, more days, more clouds, more worlds") and to resist the division of the world into two sides: "Star of Monhegan, *Atlantic* star, / Lantern without a bearer, you drift, / You, too, are drifting, in spite of your course" (iv).

"Variations on a Summer Day" does stand, then, as an attempt to disconnect obvious connections—to make "no reference to . . . the war," or, in other words, to suggest that "[i]t *goes without saying* that our minds are full of it" (*L* 356; emphasis added), as Stevens had remarked to van Geyzel. Yet in being "deliberate" in this effort it can be said to have made just such a reference—to what is in effect an isolationist's ideal position. It supposes that in avoiding contact with the warring world—in *not* "destroying . . . / An aversion, as the world is averted"—it nevertheless bears signs that Stevens acknowledged the problem of making poetry out of war's reality. Such an enigmatic strategy was not perhaps quite enough to hold all the variations together under the general rubric defined for Simons. But by "Martial Cadenza," probably the next poem Stevens wrote, the same strategy had somewhat matured.

Of course "Martial Cadenza" is explicitly a song of war, whereas "Variations" consciously charted the dangerous course of innocence by improvisationally evading direct connections between *here* and *there, now* and *later*. "Martial Cadenza" more pointedly bears the marks of the indecision characteristic of American thinking about the place and time of war; it is a perfect example of the paradox of the "kind of thinking" the Maginot Complex brings. The poem mildly proposes that the star the poet sees fixes him in historical time, though the repetitive, qualified assertions of the first and especially the second sections tend to undermine this, as I have already observed. Thus Stevens may sympathize with those on the other, more troubled side of the Atlantic who share a view of the same fixed point beyond them. Section iii of the poem expresses skepticism about this equation, asking a bold, pertinent question:

> What had this star to do with the world it lit,
> With the blank skies over England, over France
> And above the German camps?

The speaker who can seriously pose such a doubtful question about so central an issue ("What had this star to do with" the situations in England, France, and Germany?) remains largely unaware of the ways in which he fixes himself to the ground on which a war is being fought. This obvious lack of awareness undermines the poem's claim to an understanding of England and France "and"—*equally*, the conjunction here implies—the German camps. Similarly it compromises any renewal of the speaker's human will in the act of transatlantic sympathy. Even the question "Which side are you on?"—itself central to the cultural politics of U.S. intervention, as it derived from leftist antifascism earlier[63]—goes unanswered in this war song. The trope of the commonly viewed star leaves indistinct the essential differences between the English, the French, and the Germans on the one side, and the neutral-seeming star-gazing American on the other. The speaker tries to consider the "sides" to be equated by nature and not distinguished by other great differences (such as German fascism and French republicanism; England, France, and Germany on the same "side" of an ocean from the point of view of isolationist America). Yet finally the taking of sides here *was* partisan by default of the implied American subject-position, with Stevens's United States standing alone on its "side" of the conflict, the others somewhere else altogether.

The main insight about war in this so-named war song is precisely what undermines its general assumptions about understanding: there existed a "*silence* before the armies," and these armies were "*without* / Either trumpets or drums, the commanders *mute*, the arms / On the ground, fixed fast in a profound defeat." If the modern armies themselves were silent, would not songs of war become obsolete? Thus "Martial Cadenza," promised to Parker Tyler as near to the shock of the Polish invasion as October 4, at a time when reports reaching the United States began to describe in detail the new, frighteningly efficient and mechanized force of invasion (*Schreckkrieg*), did at first seem to cast doubt on the possibility of a successful new poetry of war. Since the old battle formalities, trumpets and drums (and horses), were now entirely outmoded on one side and rapidly "dismembered and disembowelled" on the other,[64] what *modern* form should a war poem take so as not to side with the forces of modern belligerence? Yet such an insight into the new style of war, and the suggestion of a poet incapable of adapting his sounds to the trumpetless advance, worked to defeat the other informing trope of the poem: with the return of the winter star came a renewed sense of connection to the troubled world. This star "came back," was seen "again," *was* time and yet was out of human time, existing "*apart from any past.*" The more historical things change, in other words, the more satisfying the return of "The vivid thing in the air *that never changes.*" War was not a failure of political will, unique and specific each time; it was "the *periodical* failure of politics," coming on like the seasons, like weather. War "came back" then, in 1939, as the winter star always does and will—reasonably, inevitably, free from question.

In January 1940 Stevens shored up his sense of American distance by stipulating the close association of news and weather; that association provided him with another powerful strategy for naturalizing the fact of war in its first phase. At the request of Hi Simons, he looked back at his early poems and decided that the "ever jubilant weather" of "Waving Adieu, Adieu, Adieu" (1935; *CP* 127–28) was not a symbol for an event but an event in itself. Weather had become a form of reality just as surely as other " 'immediate' things in the world" (*L* 349). In this climate of heightened reality, when the supreme fiction "Must Change" to account for a rapidly shifting sense of the extrinsic, weather-as-event became the matter of the poem. When Simons again suggested an elaborate symbolic explication of the Blue Woman section of "Notes toward a Supreme Fiction" (*CP* 399–400), Stevens responded by reading the canto as making the human figure not *like* the weather but composed of it: the event of writing the poem has as both its source and subject "the weather of a Sunday morning early last April when I wrote this." This taught him that the invention of a fiction originated in an acute sense of reality as event. "One of the approaches to fiction is by way of its opposite: reality, the truth, the thing observed. . . . Eventually there is a state at which any approach becomes the actual observation of the thing approached" (*L* 444). So, too, news reformulated as weather could give special pleasure; what the poet found significant was not the reality of the day itself but the threat of immediacy that came, say, from seeing on a clear night a star that could be observed by people in parts of the world where events pressed strongly on the mind. "There are many 'immediate' things in the world that we enjoy," he wrote Simons. "We are physical beings in a physical world; the weather is one of the things that we enjoy" (*L* 348–49).

It was surely as a measure of defense that Stevens now took to referring to war news euphemistically as a kind of weather, for instance in the following letter to Henry Church of August 1940, where he explained why, for the time being, Church ought to postpone his plans for a literary endowment and put off efforts to continue publishing his and Jean Paulhan's *Mesures*.

> The last month or two have been so very realistic for me that at the moment I question whether you ought to go on with your idea at once. It might be that it would be better to wait a little while, until there is a change of weather. The crisis in Europe may come out of a blue sky, but I don't expect it to do so. I am afraid that what is going on now may be nothing to what will be going on three or four months from now, and that the situation that will then exist may even involve us all, at least in the sense of occupying our thoughts and feelings to the exclusion of anything except the actual and the necessary. I don't mean that I think that we are going to become involved in war, but there may be a complete blockade of England and by England. That at least is what I expect. This will isolate us and leave us to be played on by a huge variety of excitements. How could MESURES exist under such conditions? If, by reason of exhaustion of one or all of the nations now at war, late next spring a peace should be evolved, then the appearance of a magazine devoted to the values to which MESURES is devoted would be a joy.... [T]he fact that the PARTISAN REVIEW, so much closer to politics, so much more in the movement, should seem to be growing more and more attenuated speaks for itself. (L 365)

Stevens's argument here—a new literary project might give the impression of supporting values inappropriate to a time of war and should wait for peace to arrive—is undermined by a reductive metonymy of the weather, which has the effect of refiguring the occupation by then of sizable parts of Europe as the passing of a storm or the reemergence of the sun in a sky once again blue. As occupation was reduced to a necessary *preoccupation* with the news of reality, so isolation was to be euphemized as the state of being socked in by a stalled front. In the grammar of news-as-weather, a possible peace settlement was passively constructed, a condition that might just "be evolved," naturally. As such, an end to the war seemed not less remote but more; indeed, the letter was successful in convincing Church not to go forward with *Mesures* then, even though, as we will see, Church's eventual plan—Stevens knew this, but only after Pea Harbor—involved engaging his journal in the effort to give hope to occupied France.

The new dependence on radio and newspapers, then, did not destroy Stevens's sense of American distance as natural in 1940 and 1941; rather, it reinforced it, enabling him to pair the political "news" (news of *elsewhere*, abroad) with the unavoidable "weather" (weather of *here*, at home). For Stevens, the inveterate newspaper reader and radio listener,[65] the convergence had already become a daily fact: the news was increasingly taken up with the weather. "The weather," in the mediated form of what we call a "weather report," was often the most essential form of the news for Americans isolated from the war; indeed, official national weather forecasts, now expanded and given prominence, served to aid the politically contentious and costly goal of national defense or "preparedness" by implying the possibility of sudden attack, under appropriate weather conditions, and further naturalized war preparation, otherwise a political strategy of interventionists.[66]

That the phrase "the sound of words" should be understood as pertaining to the radio full of news is the helpful suggestion of Terrence Des Pres's analysis of the April 1941 lecture, "The Noble Rider and the Sound of Words." There Stevens spoke of the difference "between the sound of words in one age and the sound of words in another age" and argued that in this difference might be discovered the source of a new "pressure of reality" (*NA* 13). Des Pres takes this to mean that "the sound of words depends [only] in part upon their sense." More important, he implies, is "the degree of their referential commitment."[67] Des Pres is surely right to suggest that Stevens's lecture marked a new awareness that the poet's claims to a "highly complex and unified content of consciousness" could not hold up against a new, intensely referential language that "every newspaper reader experiences today." There was, Stevens argued in his lecture, "an extraordinary pressure of news"—"news incomparably more pretentious than any description of it, news, at first, of the collapse of our system, or, call it, of life; then of news of a new world, but of a new world so uncertain that one did not know anything of its nature, and does not know now" (*NA* 20). Des Pres argues that Stevens

> is correct, even prophetic, to dwell on the impact of "news." Through the media the world comes at us every day nonstop, and in ways that undermine the distance imagination needs to make sense of what we behold. . . . [T]he cause of reality's change is time's acceleration and the collapse of space, the increasing reach and beat of political clamor—events "that [in Stevens's words] stir the emotions to violence" . . . events beyond the capacity of mind to tranquilize, reduce or transform them.[68]

And it is exactly here that Stevens, as Des Pres observes, turned to the impact of history on poetry. "[T]he pressure of reality is, I think, the determining factor in the artistic character of an era" (*NA* 22).

But recognizing history's impressions on poetry did not necessarily mean a new sense of "obligation" in Stevens's case (*NA* 27); at least in April 1941, it seems only to have emphasized mediation between the reported thing and the thing itself. A special problem presented by "Noble Rider," then, lies in the common assumption that the new consciousness of the news inevitably contributed to the demise of the isolationist line—that the more Americans heard about the European crisis on the radio and read about it in newspapers, the closer to the events of war they felt and thus the greater the chance of their accepting U.S. intervention. Yet as Selig Adler pointed out in *The Isolationist Impulse*, even "those news-packed days" of the first war years did not necessarily mean the end of isolationist thinking.[69] Indeed, Bruce Bliven, a liberal editor of the *New Republic*, implied that watching the newsreels gave the European reality a distinct sense of *un*reality: "[A]s I watch the motion picture of events unreeling on the screen of time . . . I feel . . . that I have seen it all before"—a reference to the Great War clearly implying that it would be a mistake to get involved again.[70] So, too, American dependence on news for a proximity to reality, though overwhelming to others as to Stevens, could itself become part of the isolationist argument warning of an incomplete sense of the emergency. Americans were asked if they had "confidence in the news from Germany": only 1 percent answered that they had "complete" confidence, and 66 percent felt no confidence at all.[71] When Stevens discussed the advent of radio-created closeness as an aspect of the pressure of reality, he was not suggesting that this necessarily led to engagement with the actual world: "We lie in bed and listen to a broadcast from Cairo, and so on. There is no distance. We are intimate with people we have never seen and, unhappily, they are intimate with us" (*NA* 18).

The "pressures of reality" thesis, elaborated in early 1941, expressed just such a dislike of mediated closeness to the warring world. When in "Noble Rider" Stevens announced that "the poet must be capable of resisting *or evading* the pressures of reality," he did not seem to mean resistance and evasion as opposites. "Resistance" at this point looked a good deal more like evasion than resistance, especially the "resistance" we have come to know from, for instance, the experience of some of the French or a few of Warsaw's Jews; here the concept followed from Stevens's assertion that "[t]he poetic process is psychologically an escapist process" (*NA* 30). Stevens himself would reject this pre–Pearl Harbor position a few years later, and I will suggest that this rejection had much to do with the fact that he had contact by then with French writers who were indeed perilously involved with *Résistance* in the strict sense.

In finding engagement in "Noble Rider," then, Des Pres has significantly predated[72] a distinct form of political shrewdness that would translate into a sense of national responsibility in the second, or Americanized, phase of the war. Only with Stevens's later formulation of the poet's relation to the actual world at war—only in "The Figure of Youth" lecture of midsummer 1943—would he speak of "an agreement with reality," no longer of a resistance to it. Yet Des Pres is right to note that "the martial element in Stevens has seldom been recognized," and to foster with his urgent tones a revision of the critical consensus "on the urbane Stevens, the ornate and carnivalesque Stevens"—and, most helpfully, to locate a "Stevens embattled."[73]

CHAPTER 2

Formalists under Fire

THE SOLDIER'S WAR AND THE HOME FRONT

> After all, we keep warm at home. . . . However, it
> may be worse because no one knows whether or
> not there will be oil enough even to take care of
> the ration tickets.
> —*Stevens to Arthur Powell, mid-December 1942*

> He is just as practical in the realm of pragmatism as
> he is idealistic in the realms of the imagination.
> —*Powell, after quoting Stevens's statement above,
> in a letter to Hi Simons*

> [W]e can not and will not deny our soldiers the
> finest equipment in order to cater to the whims of
> those who don't seem to realize that their country
> is at war.
> —*Robert P. Patterson, undersecretary of war,
> deploring citizens' complaints about new nationwide
> gas and oil rationing, December 1, 1942*

> [T]he supplying of oil to our armed forces and
> those of our Allies is no less than a prerequisite to
> survival. . . . [T]he successful carrying out of this
> task is one . . . which calls for . . . continuing sacri-
> fice, affecting directly or indirectly in some way
> every man, woman and child.
> —*Harold Ickes, upon being named head of the new
> Petroleum Administration for War, December 3, 1942*

> It is here, in this bad, that we reach
> The last purity of the knowledge of good.
> —*Stevens, in "No Possum, No Sop, No Taters" (1943)*

IN MARCH of 1944, Wallace Stevens spoke at length with a young captain
on furlough. This same man, Fernand Auberjonois, recalled for me that it
was an "occasion when we spoke at some length about the war."[1] The

· Swiss-born Auberjonois, friend of Henry Church and contributor to *Mesures*, had immigrated to the United States in 1933. He volunteered for service in the American army almost immediately after Pearl Harbor, having already established the NBC Radio French-language program that he proudly transmitted to listeners in occupied France. His specialty became propaganda and intelligence (later he worked at the Voice of America).

Stevens knew Captain Auberjonois well by the time they dined together in 1944; Auberjonois was often a dinner guest at the Churches' Cleveland Lane home in Princeton, and the young man had joined the Churches and Stevens there and in New York on several occasions.[2] He had attended the Churches' party for Stevens after the presentation of "The Noble Rider" at Princeton in 1941. Stevens was initially intrigued because Fernand was the son of the Swiss painter René Auberjonois. Stevens never failed, upon meeting people who knew intimately the lives of painters, to ask specific questions about work habits and personal oddities; later he came to recognize René Auberjonois as "a theorist grown abstract with age," a "figure" that "absorbs me" (*L* 607). As for Fernand, he soon became absorbing, too: "He seems to be fresh and clean and right," one of the few acquaintances of whom Stevens would say, with no apparent equivocality, "I look forward to seeing more of [him]" (*L* 582). When Stevens met up with the Churches, he invariably asked about the young man.

He particularly followed Auberjonois's overseas service, curious also about the adjustments of the family the captain had left behind in Princeton. He knew, for instance, that when the water heater broke down at the Auberjonois residence, the Churches took what was for them an extraordinary measure: Fernand's wife, Laura, and their two children moved into the Cleveland Lane house.[3] Throughout the war, Fernand's APO letters home were being shown to the Churches, who in this way were trying desperately to keep up with the progress of the Free French,[4] "and I know," Auberjonois has written, "they were being shown to Stevens who, apparently, always asked about us when he came to see Barbara and Harry."[5] The Churches also closely followed the work of the young French section chief of NBC's international branch—"very interested in this contact with the French, and they were hoping I could be heard by friends of theirs in Ville d'Avray."[6] Auberjonois's outfit produced a pamphlet, *France Speaks to America: Letters from a Frenchwoman to the International Division of the National Broadcasting Company* (the letters were in fact addressed to Auberjonois personally). These fervent notes, postcards from a volcano, described the "collective self-examination" undertaken by a conquered people that "reawakened in each Frenchman a feeling of being French" and an equally strong hope that Auberjonois would convey to Americans "how UNITED you and we are." They expressed sentiments that should be understood, Auberjonois urged NBC's American listeners, "with your heart as well as your mind." The power of such appeals is hard to measure, but those who have made the attempt are certain it was great indeed.[7] Of these forceful pleas from France, Auberjonois has recalled for me: "I know the Churches were deeply moved and showed them to W.S."[8]

In early 1944, then, when Stevens and the captain met again, the poet naturally wanted to talk about the war. The captain had been engaged by the Office of Strategic Services as an intelligence officer attached to the unit that was more or less secretly planning the invasion of the European mainland. Of course the very fact of an invasion, long an imminence, was hardly a secret to any discerning American like Stevens who heard the usual rumors of war. To be sure, as the young captain remembers, he "could not have said much about what was going to happen in June 1944. Not in detail."[9] Yet it is certainly significant that in Stevens's "Repetitions of a Young Captain," a poem published that spring before the Normandy landings of early June,[10] the soldier-speaker should alter Stevens's concept of the "major man" expressly in relation to a maneuver involving "millions" of men in a time of war. To Stevens, before the actual landings became a major American fact, the thought of these millions was, indeed, "An image that leaves nothing much behind." A man in such a situation, one of millions of men "In a calculated chaos," stands tall only insofar as he is part of the immense human whole:

> Millions of major men against their like
> Make more than thunder's rural rumbling. They make
> The giants that each one of them becomes
>
> In a calculated chaos: he that takes form
> From the others, being larger than he was,
> Accoutred in a little of the strength
>
> That sweats the sun up on its morning way
> To giant red, sweats up a giant sense
> To the make-matter, matter-nothing mind,
>
> Until this matter-makes in years of war.
> This being in a reality beyond
> The finikin spectres in the memory,
>
> This elevation, in which he seems to be tall. . . .

That an American poet would anticipate by several months a major episode of a major war—especially in generalized images like those the "Young Captain" presents—is hardly a meaningful event in itself. But that Stevens would is meaningful, if only because it shows his sensitivity to the not unreasonable contemporary claim that even after Pearl Harbor, for example in "Notes toward a Supreme Fiction" (written in the spring of

1942), his poems bore no signs of passion about the war. Typical is Harvey Breit's view, in a *favorable* notice of "Notes": "This last volume of Stevens's poems is nearly an anachronism. Its wholeness, its lucidity, its exactingness, its sanity, make you marvel that it managed its construction inside the wartime temper and that it somehow found living space between the abortive and the truncated."[11] Yet the mostly unexamined facts of Stevens's realization of the American sense of the war's second phase, December 7, 1941, through 1944—his understanding of the vicissitudes of the home front, but also his knowledge of various military campaigns and even his perception of the danger of life under Nazi occupation—belie this assessment of Stevens's writing in this particular period, even when, as with Breit's view, such an assessment is intended to praise the poems. What is especially important about the timely meeting with the furloughed Young Captain is that it allowed an experienced soldier-poet, a captain who had already survived landings in North Africa and Sicily, to demonstrate that he recognized Stevens's attentiveness to the war.

Fernand Auberjonois, who has written a memoir of his ordeal as a soldier-writer, was well aware that the language used to describe the reality of war is but a version of the reality described; he knew that such description can make no absolute claim to bear witness to life *in extremis* without building in the qualification that words and war are not ever wholly one. Stevens's poem anticipates the belated, perhaps faltering recitation of a soldier whose part in a major experience was itself minor but whose noncombatant listeners depended on the accuracy of the retelling. The poem deftly reproduces the difficulties of the secondary account; these images, these "Millions of major men," are, indeed, only and exactly "Repetitions" of the real; but, as such, as Emil Fackenheim has suggested, they are no less—and sometimes more—essential to understanding.[12] No poem of war replicates the war itself; yet qualified as it will inevitably be by the intricacies of memory and the screen of language, the war poem might beneficially attend to the difficulties of testimony, thus sustaining an essential indirectness that was already, as it happens, characteristic of Stevens's rhetoric. The captain-speaker is aware of these psycholinguistic obstructions: a ruined building he recalls "*had been* real. It was *something* overseas / That I remembered, *something* that I remembered overseas" (emphasis added). It was *something*, significantly, that while existing then in the unreal—the "new reality" of poetic disclosure—had once "stood" unambiguously "in an external world." The third section of the poem recites the story of the millions of men; just before this, the captain falls into appropriate awe of the difficulty of retaining an event so primary. In this recession or secondariness, the remembered event is *figuratively* a thing: "*Like* something I remembered overseas." Again, then, the trauma of recollection affixes itself to the trauma of event. Not *overseas*—the clear, pointing syntax of

"Over There"—but *It was something overseas that I remembered.* The war poem absorbs eventfulness into the paradox of accounting for what happened in relation to the reality of an occasion now forever lost. If the language describing events and reactions wielded by "The War Poets," as they were ubiquitously called, created a new telling absolutely, making the real original or fresh or "poetic" and thus a bit unreal-seeming in the very effort to retain the real—and, in the strict sense, *inarticulate* or (in Stevens's words) "desperate with a know-and-know"—then the meaning of the event may elude the nonwitness, and the experimental witness-poet may be accused of anachronism or irresponsible obscurity. If the language used to describe events is, on the other hand, utterly imitable and straightforward in its effort to bear witness with precision, then the teller may not have made realization difficult enough to allow for the pathos of memory and intensified subjectivity as the event fades—in the case of the June 1944 landings, appropriately so, as the image of individuality would fade especially into the total image of the millions involved. Confronted with the materiality of life *in extremis*, testimony and literature made a hard but necessary alliance. Expectations raised by the fidelity to life's experience in testimony were transferred to literature, as expectations raised by the fidelity to poetic language in literature were transferred to testimony. Stevens knew how the subgeneric sharing might work. The Young Captain's Repetitions, his relation of the millions of men in section iii, is followed, shrewdly, by a qualification that marks the boundaries of this paradox. The speaker-poet joins the eyewitness to history (the Young Captain), and in one voice they powerfully anticipate the objection that will be raised up against their version of the witness to war—namely that "these were only words," not the real thing.[13] As the detractors' anticipated doubt is strong, so the protest by the soldier and the war poet together is urgent:

> If these were only words that I am speaking,
> Indifferent sounds and not the heraldic-ho
> Of the clear sovereign that is reality,
>
> Of the clearest reality that is sovereign,
> *How should I repeat them, keep repeating them,*
> As if they were desperate with a know-and-know,
>
> Central responses to a central fear . . . ?

> (*CP* 307–8; emphasis added)

Redesignating the nationalist war-poem subgenre by defying normal expectations created by it, Stevens's poem about war firmly stands as a "central response" to war's eventfulness. In this view, a war poem assimilating the difficulty of writing war poems is certainly itself a war poem, for a "central fear," a home-front fear, "sweats up a giant sense" of war *especially* in the otherwise isolationist "matter-nothing mind." What matters, ironically, is the "matter-nothing mind." The fear reasonably feared by the mind that "matters" is that no poem allowing an event of war to be related sufficiently conveys the horror of the "external world" as witnessed, especially as the captain himself only retains it as a vague but vast feeling, a distant visitation—"something overseas." But Stevens and the Young Captain, combining forces, can together forestall the fate of retelling: their words are "only words" because they carry the realization of the subject-position and never do claim to be or become the reality reported. Yet how else may such a reality be conveyed to those whose sense of "overseas" is much vaguer still than "something"? So the soldier's emotional departure is reported. His inevitable return to the front after furlough is exactly enough of a war-poetry cliché to remind with its sentimentality that there is an "external world" to which the poet (this noncombatant poet, Stevens) does not go, a place not imaginable except in words of description without place and reiteration without stop. "*Constantly*, / At the railway station, a soldier steps away, / . . . And goes to an external world, *having / Nothing of place*" (emphasis added). Yet a very strong image, such as the millions of men in section iii, remains. Even the captain, when coming finally home, must prepare to "nourish" himself "On a few words of what is real in the world."

One of the facts of war Stevens learned from the young captain on that day in March of 1944 was simply that the soldier's life was not unremittingly dangerous. There were periods of boredom. Auberjonois described for Stevens military life in North Africa in 1943. "Outside of the operational upheavals," he later wrote, "the life of an occupying army is monotonous."[14] "Repetitions of a Young Captain," accordingly, signals a final revision of the earlier heroic conception of the "major man," a version that characterized the pre–Pearl Harbor war poems (and several poems written during or very soon after December 1941, such as "Examination of the Hero in a Time of War," published in April 1942). In its earlier forms the "major man" stressed the mythic, the unreal, and the fabulous, as in the frequently quoted "Asides on the Oboe" of 1940, where the hero is "The impossible possible philosophers' man, / . . . The central man, the human globe, / . . . the man of glass, / Who in a million diamonds sums us up" (*CP* 250). The figure of the major man tends toward the irrational and the antihistorical, serving as it did a Nietzschean model urged, and somewhat screened, by Church;[15] in Milton Bates's accurate characterization of "Examination of the Hero," the champion "arises spontaneously and unaccountably."[16] But by 1944, Stevens's representative man has been refigured; accountability is all. He is more overtly American and much more democratic. He is only, from war experience, "larger than he was" (he only "*seems* to be tall") because he "takes form / From the others." A democratic version of the major man, in other words, suggests that by 1944 (and even earlier, as I will show) Stevens saw that the pure poet's valorous figure, the harlequinized "MacCullough" of "Notes," for instance—of whose role as wartime hero we are right to be skeptical, as Marjorie Perloff is[17]—must finally be modified by the repetitions of the young captain who was actually there. Later, when José Rodríguez Feo asked Stevens to define the "major man" for him, Stevens wrote "Paisant Chronicle" as his answer on one day, and then a few days later wrote again to say: "I came across the words *major men* in REPETITIONS OF A YOUNG CAPTAIN. In that poem the words major men merely mean the pick of young men"—recalling, correctly, that the use of the concept in the spring of 1944 had meant to identify American fighting men sent in powerful but powerfully dehumanizing waves, the oxymoronic *special* force of *regulars*, the real heroes of D-Day (*L* 489).

Stevens was keen also to know about the Young Captain's "monotonous" life in North Africa. "Stevens was interested," Auberjonois has recalled, "in my having met French writers and poets in Algiers and in the fact that I had written, while there, for the literary magazine *Fontaine* which had taken over as a vehicle for free expression from the collaborationist *NRF* [*Nouvelle Revue Française*] in Paris."[18] What was perhaps astonishing and delightful to Stevens—that "[s]urely one had a great need to write, and to read" while serving in war,[19] and that one could manage to do both—was a commonplace to his young captain. Furloughed from the front in Tunisia, Auberjonois would hasten back to Algiers "to check *Fontaine* in order to find out who in France or in exile had written what and under what pseudonym."[20] Even the scene near the desert front was a "tolerable purgatory"[21] of anisette, jazzmen, and fried food. But Algiers was a very special literary haven, where *Fontaine*, cofounded by Henry Church's old friend Jean Wahl, acted as "a rallying point" for French, English, and American writers "both mobilized and civilian, who tried to write while on leave."[22] The most strikingly clear image of the Young Captain's story about Algiers was the regular meeting-place itself. This was the balcony of number 43 Rue Lys du Pac, which served as a kind of "loge of a theatre" (a figure Auberjonois liked to repeat), where the *Fontaine* writers "gathered in the evenings *not* to speak of circumstances or events" of war, and, raising glasses of red wine, "disengaged themselves from the *gangue*."[23] Yet this psychologically protected cultural space also offered a direct view of actuality: perched above the Algiers harbor, the *Fontaine* group had found, as Auberjonois remembers it, a "perfect place to watch the German (or Italian) bombers zooming over the hill and dropping bombs on or near the ships down below. *It was, to us, a spectacle*" (emphasis added).[24] This striking image enabled Stevens to imagine for the Young Captain of his poem a special, excusable obliviousness to the war associated not with the non-combatant poet but with the soldier-speaker himself. Part of the *something* this intrepid "pick" of a man remembers overseas is indeed that "The people sat in the theatre, in the ruin, / *As if nothing had happened*." The theatre of combat, a "ruin" of war literally and of culture figuratively, in the otherwise inexplicable opening image of the poem (*CP* 306), exists to help the enlisted imagination withstand the violence of war from without—Stevens's "tempest cracked on the theatre" underscores Auberjonois's descriptions of the "paroxysm" of the air attacks seen from the balcony in Algiers[25]—while a desperately literate culture is sustained. This sustenance symbolizes, in Stevens's words, a *something* that "stood still in an external world," the resilience if not inviolability of poetic thought and culture—an otherwise surprisingly confident notion of the survival of European, specifically French, culture in the trying months of 1943 and early 1944. It must have fascinated Stevens to hear from Auberjonois that when disembarking in Morocco the first thing the soldiers in his group did was to search "in vain for a cultural elite" there.[26] The preservation of poetry in a time of the terrible North African campaign did not contradict the purposes of *Fontaine*, which were, reconcilably, to disengage the French writer from the loss of normal freedoms and the smashing defeat of his country and yet at the same time encourage him to view wartime writing as liberating it.

It is even possible that for one rare moment Stevens conceived of his own writing as a liberating force in a small yet practical way. Auberjonois confirmed what Stevens, from Henry Church through Jean Wahl and Jean Paulhan, already knew about *Fontaine*: in Algiers, Auberjonois and others prepared a special number of the review in miniature format and delivered it to the Free French in London, where it was printed on rice paper and then dropped by parachute into France. "I never met anyone who saw it fall . . . but an RAF pilot risked his skin to let go several thousands," Auberjonois has explained; yet he has also warned, I think appropriately, "Do not disdain these symbolic gestures."[27] Such small literary victories may have been symbolic to Stevens with a special intensity, for he was informed, at about that time, that Jean Wahl was at work translating portions of "Notes toward a Supreme Fiction," which the exiled French writers wanted to use in *Fontaine*.[28] Such evidence requires us to imagine Stevens imagining an RAF pilot risking his skin to drop his notes on the supreme fiction into occupied France; nor, surely, can we help but imagine Stevens imagining his verse undergoing selection by the literary *Résistance* as a "contribution about freedom," translated into French, printed in tiny type on lightweight paper, and launched into Nazi territory.[29] Not qualitatively different, I would urge, is the idea generally of the fighting man at rest, reclining on a balcony with a glass of wine, shoring up his aestheticism against a time of universal pain, but continuing to feel that pain, as one that gave Stevens the boldness he would need to begin his ambitious aesthetics of pain, his "Esthétique du Mal," another poem of 1944, with this provocative wartime image: a man leisurely reads "paragraphs on the sublime," contemplating "pain on the very point of pain" while lying, apparently out of harm's way, on a balcony at night. It was only from this unusual station in the general environs of pain, in relative comfort but still general discomfort, suffering an expectation of volcanic disruption that is at the same time ethereal, that the troubled writer-figure on the balcony is able to use this elaborately constructed poem to "communicate / The intelligence of his despair" (*CP* 314). From this disturbing point, in the second canto of a fifteen-canto poem, the figure of the poet is emboldened to restrain, within the same poem, the opposing tendencies of, on one hand, a canto describing this special hell in studied, traditional stanzas—modified terza rima in homage, certainly, to Dante ("His firm stanzas hang like hives in hell")—and, on the other hand, the famous seventh canto, "How Red the Rose That Is the Soldier's Wound," a war-poem set piece. What both Stevens and Auberjonois meant by the image of the balcony (Auberjonois in being there but later making productive use of its symbolism; Stevens in borrowing it for the troubled but contemplative speaker) was to indicate that in wartime the soldier-writer had the unusual opportunity "to *look over the whole thing* and to think about it as part of it." These words Stevens wrote, incidentally, to a young poet, Samuel French Morse—then an army sergeant (*L* 450; emphasis added).

Of course if Fernand Auberjonois had been the only soldier Stevens knew personally during World War II, we might as easily ascribe the Young Captain's anxieties about the rhetoric of retelling to Stevens's obliviousness as to a new nationalist acuteness. But, as with most nonmobilized Americans during a war in which an astonishing 17 percent of their fellow citizens were in uniform at once,[30] Stevens was hearing other stories as well. The war experience of Sergeant Sam Morse was of special curiosity, as the Cummington Press, Stevens's publisher for two of his three wartime books (*Notes toward a Supreme Fiction* and *Esthétique du Mal*),[31] was the source of this information. Morse, Katherine Frazier wrote Stevens from Cummington, was serving in the army, adjusting to the soldier's life; he even seemed, she wrote, to be writing poems about the war.[32] Stevens agreed to write the introduction to Morse's first book; and given Frazier's hint that Morse was becoming a war poet, Stevens may have been surprised to find not a single reference to the war in the typescript Cummington sent on. It was reasonable, of course, to read into the dedication—to the soldier's mother—and see a young man, at the dedicatory last moment, promising a return from service: "spare, inadequate / And sometimes grim, the poems stand. / Take them for what they are, *and wait*" (emphasis added).[33] Wartime dedication or no, Stevens wrote the introduction gladly, doing his bit for a young poet cut off from his poetic milieu, New England. The New England matrix was incessantly there: "[H]e tries to get at New England experience," Stevens wrote, "at New England past and present, at New England foxes and snow and thunderheads" (*OP* 244). But so was the thrill, though largely suppressed, that *Sergeant* Morse of the U.S. Army Air Corps would provide Stevens, at New England's home front, a new perception of life-and-death matters, of old things told definitively anew. "[A]s people live and die, each one perceiving life and death for himself, and mostly by and in himself, there develops a curiosity about the perceptions of others. This is what makes it possible to go on saying new things about old things." This was exaggerated praise of the poems themselves, as Morse much later admitted to me.[34] What purpose did it serve, then? It was Stevens's subtle way of saying to the young poet-soldier that he would be pleased to have the view: "The fact is that the saying of new things in new ways is grateful to us" (*OP* 243). Frazier sent Stevens's introduction to Morse where he was temporarily stationed—in Florida—and soon she quoted back to Stevens Morse's elated response. Not only does Stevens do "beautifully what an introduction ought to do"; it was also truly a foreword, Morse felt, in that it gave the poet now working under difficult conditions "a clue for future work" and helped "a possible audience discover what is there." Stevens aided Morse's readers, Morse realized, by giving them the "wise and profound implication that poetry is more important than the work of a single poet," by helping in the general effort to view "poetry" at this moment—not poems but the whole project of American poetry—as just the sort of imaginative collectivity the nation was urging for all endeavors.[35] Stevens's unremarkable comments show the extent to which he too would engage wartime clichés when he felt they would serve to comfort. "The lot of a soldier," he told Morse, "is one of the great experiences, and I hope you are happy to be having it" (*L* 450).[36] How far Stevens had come from the skepticism of his 1939 statement describing soldiers waiting under the Maginot Line, in which he sought to demystify the justifications of nationalism, deeming wartime politics to be little more than a means of enabling individual soldiers to die willingly *pro patria* (*L* 345–46). There is no trace of that doubt here.

Other soldiers gave him pictures of their particular wars. From his sister's daughter, Jane, who married a certain recently drafted Hayward Stone, he received long letters about the soldier's imminent departure for service overseas; his niece wrote him straightforwardly about the intensity of the couple's last days together.[37] His views of the experiences of Private Stone, and that of his own nephew, John Bergen Stevens, Jr., were significantly a woman's views—views from the home front. To be sure, his direct correspondence with John was itself gratifying, especially when they discussed their common genealogy; John was pleased to be descended from the Dutch and not from the Germans, for obvious reasons. Actually, however, John's letters were notable for what they did *not* say about a soldier's attitude toward wartime politics. "As to the state of the world at present—the less said about it the better. I think we all understand what we want," John wrote in a letter mostly taken up with family genealogy—the past rather than the present.[38] The aversion to discussing war matters is at least partly explained by restrictions placed on what a serviceman could write about battles and troop movements; and indeed most of John's letters to his uncle bear the signs and seals—and intrusions—of military censors. In another letter John brought himself to the brink of saying exactly why he was delighted to know for certain that the Stevenses and Barcalows had come from Holland rather than England; that is, while he might have said explicitly why he disliked the idea of being English, and Alliance-sensitive censors be damned, for his father's brother Wallace he need not say more than that he was "pleased to know that [the family line] is definitely Dutch, although *I trust you will not ask me just why*."[39] From zones of war—this letter was mailed from the Pacific—certain national biases were better left undefined. Not surprisingly, but crucially—and typically—Stevens knew a good deal more about the impact of war on his nephew from the young man's wife back at home, Anna May, whose second child, Laurie, was born on May 8, 1942, after John had gone off to war. It was not only a long while before John saw his child—in June 1944 he still had not seen her[40]—but at least a month before he even knew that he and Anna May had had a daughter.[41] Alone and raising two children, Anna May confessed freely to her husband's uncle Wallace that she had no one to talk to. She was grateful to him for sending her phonograph records, which, she told him, she played over and over.[42] Her words for him were home-front words: "I've been alone so long and have had so much thrust upon me that I firmly believe in taking things as they come"; she described how to her judgment in John's two years of war "he has grown up."[43] Anna May's continued support of the war must have impressed Stevens with a sense of the indomitability of the American home front, for despite having had "so much thrust upon" her, she held the national line: "We all wish for the termination of this wastefulness, but we are all determined to stick it out."[44] John Bergen Stevens, Jr., served as an infantry officer for four years; three of those years were spent in combat duty in the Pacific.

At some point before midsummer 1943 Wallace Stevens chose to make a pact with national reality. What will account for the difference between the Stevens of April 1941 who spoke of poetry as "resisting or evading the pressure of reality" and the Stevens of August 1943 who announced that poetry must make "an agreement with reality"? The cause of such a major change of position is the Americanization of the world war, even if December 7, 1941, does not precisely date the shift. But no doubt in any case the change came soon after, for the fact of the nation's involvement in the world war, though so long imagined, was an overwhelming one for most Americans. Pearl Harbor may have attained a retroactive symbolism for Stevens particularly, as a little while later his daughter, Holly, used the transformations wrought by the Japanese attack as the basis for explaining to her distressed father her reasons for quitting Vassar College and going to work in the Hartford insurance world, a move that disappointed him perhaps more than any other single personal event in his adult life. But college, as Holly Stevens has later described it, gave her "no purpose after Pearl Harbor and the entrance of the United States into World War II" (*L* 397), whereas a low-level position in an insurance company offered her a chance to lead a willfully "democratic" existence (during this period "Holly made friends in every spectrum of the social scale," one of these friends has recalled).[45] To borrow for Holly her father's now suddenly outmoded concept for the imagination: college was an evasion of the pressure of reality. Whatever the specific cause for Stevens's new accord with the actual world, and whatever its precise date, certainly the state of that world, in a crisis that now involved many of the people around him, was the general cause. No surprise, then, to hear him saying things he had not said since the last of such agreements, made just after the advent of the Popular Front in 1935—statements urging that "one has to live and think in the actual world, and no other will do" (*L* 292) and that one must be concerned with "how to write of the normal in a normal way" (*L* 287). By July 19, 1942, that is, he could return to such a rhetoric of engagement: "The contemporary poet," he wrote Hi Simons, "is simply a contemporary man who writes poetry. He looks like anyone else, acts like anyone else, wears the same kind of clothes, and certainly is not an incompetent" (*L* 414).

Like other competent, contemporary Americans, then, Stevens was forced to face the problems of the home front—oil rationing, drastic changes in the workplace, the enormous dislocations of soldiers coming and going, and shiftings in the American language as it adapted itself hastily and clumsily to the war. Not uncharacteristically, he met this last change with a measure of irony. In late February 1942 he described for Barbara Church how the frost had covered bits of debris strewn on the lawns of his neighborhood "in the early mornings." But here he stopped short to correct himself, bemused by the pervasiveness of war usage: "perhaps I ought to say in the early war mornings" (*L* 404). This cynicism notwithstanding, he too formed for himself metonymically evasive, shorthand references to the war that became a part of daily life—in one, for instance, the war was "all the hubbub."[46] And while it may have been typical of Stevens to doubt the need for such an all-out propaganda campaign to sell U.S. involvement overseas to the American people as was being mounted by the Office of War Information—with help from big literary names like Archibald MacLeish and Malcolm Cowley in its Writers' Division and in less important offices young poets such as John Pauker and Frederic Prokosch (both of whom would later write about Stevens)[47]—at the same time he may not have been aware of the extent to which he himself accepted the position being enterprisingly promoted. After all, the qualities he liked in Fernand Auberjonois—cleanness and rightness—were the very ones that led this literate, naturalized American to the OWI himself, a fact Stevens learned from Church.[48] But more, the soldier canto supplementing "Notes toward a Supreme Fiction" in May 1942 is marked by the distinct impressions of the new, positive American rhetoric—perhaps, as some argue, to the detriment of the whole poem. The measurable "change in the atmosphere" Stevens felt (when the Cummington Press *Notes* was receiving little attention)[49] also explains, as I will argue, Stevens's special use of the now-ubiquitous word "victory" in 1943, in his announcement of the agreement with reality; his audience on that occasion, not incidentally, was dominated by refugees.

Stevens did, after all, continue to work every day in a workplace that was rapidly and radically changing. Talk of the war was ubiquitous, especially, one easily imagines, among the younger, draft-age employees at The Hartford who were preparing themselves for enlistment. The company's magazine, the *Hartford Agent*, made much of employees' contributions to the war effort, regularly printing lists of men and women from The Hartford who had entered the service; it ran large photographs of enlistees as they left the home office, smiling and waving, and cited the military feats of those who dropped in at Asylum Avenue to say hello while on furlough.[50] The Hartford also spoke proudly of stateside employees' "moral and patriotic duty" to preserve the trade of field agents who had left for the service.[51] Perhaps the greatest sign of change brought on by the war at The Hartford, and certainly the most visible, was what the *Agent* referred to as "women in the agencies." Holly Stevens's reason for moving from Vassar to war work is affirmed by general studies such as Francis Walton's *Miracle of World War II*: after December 7, 1941, "Women instantaneously asked, 'What can we do?' "[52] The oft-noted influx of women into the American wartime workplace was of special importance to the insurance industry, where so many of the jobs vacated by men were clerical, jobs in service as opposed to manufacturing—a path already well worn by twentieth-century working women. The *Agent* chose to highlight this phenomenon as part of the company's nationalism, to praise, in harmony with Susan B. Anthony II and others, "Women's Winning Role in the Nation's Drama."[53]

"They"—The Hartford's confident women—were displayed in group photos spread over two pages. The *Agent* carried a new regular feature entitled, perhaps unnervingly to some traditionalists among the company officers,[54] "They're Running the Agencies Now."[55] To be sure, most of the men at Stevens's rank were too old to be serving in the armed forces, and the company's particular choice of slogan suggesting that women were *running* the insurance business was not an accurate description at the home office even as it might have been out in the field, into which Stevens himself ventured much less frequently than earlier; so, too, there is no telling what side of the question Stevens was taking when he jotted the phrase "Women & Nationalism" in one of his notebooks of adages, save that the issue was on his mind.[56]

Holly Stevens's experience as a young woman wanting war work, starting at the bottom, as a clerk with nearby Aetna, would have made a plain fact of the war at home even plainer to her father, even in these months when she and he were not regularly interacting: if the war would alter the insurance world permanently, such change was containable at the lower ranks, where most of the women entered and remained.[57] This and other[58] dramatic changes in personnel may not have substantially altered Stevens's manner of thinking about the war's effect on his work, but the modifications in insurance policies and the way the industry radically changed its relation to the national government would certainly have made their mark. To be sure, he worked for a while on a committee overseeing Harry Williams's management of all war operations, which included "some whopping big shell contracts" with both the army and navy,[59] and secret arrangements with the Manhattan Project. Williams told Peter Brazeau that Stevens "handled the responsibility perfunctorily." But Williams also recalls that Stevens asked "intelligent questions when he did get interested in a particular project," and if his memory of hurried weekend meetings at 118 Westerly Terrace—Williams would have spent Monday through Friday in Washington working with defense and regulatory officials—is generally that Stevens was "kind of useless" (*WSR* 61), this impression may be due less to the poet's inattentiveness than to the discomfort he felt discussing insurance business on a day always reserved for "spasms" of gardening, catching up on art journals, eating two-inch-thick slices of liverwurst delivered from Milwaukee,[60] "dozing outdoors,"[61] and, occasionally, poetry. It is perhaps more helpful to remember that the company's home-front projects extended well beyond insuring the development and manufacture of weapons, and that as colleague John Lukens recalled for Richard Rogers, director of the PBS *Voices and Visions* documentary, Stevens "saw every contract bond claim, which was the most important type of claim and case that came into the company. Almost—he insisted that almost everything go across his desk."[62] We can be sure that Stevens knew well that his industry must rapidly shed its traditional resistance to government involvement, for the transformation far outdid any reform enacted by the New Deal: in 1938 direct federal expenditures formed 9.1 percent of the Gross National Product; in 1940 the figure rose to 9.2 percent; by 1942, however, it had become 22.0 percent.[63] If American conservatism did not give up certain aspects of its antigovernment rhetoric, it might have to relinquish its entire sense of what was good for business—for now nationalism was good for business. In Hartford there were a large number of defense-related industries, for example Billings & Spencer, Colt, Pratt & Whitney Tool, and especially United Aircraft. The Army and Navy Munitions Board placed Stevens's city on the list of fourteen "most vital strategic industrial areas in the country." Stevens's Hartford changed forever, with no fewer than eighteen thousand new residents, mostly working and "pink-collar" class, moving to Hartford in just one war year.[64] Plants manufacturing war materials rapidly increased in insurable values; some factories now assessed at $100 million had been not a fraction as valuable only months earlier, even though little may have changed in the visible, physical plant. So the war yielded huge new areas of business for the insurance companies. The Hartford considered its main contribution to the national effort to be protecting such companies as the Diamond Hill Machine Shop of Cos Cob, Connecticut, which converted to war production after being assured by The Hartford of its ability to cover the astonishing rise in value; and when Undersecretary of the Navy James Forrestal awarded the small company the Army-Navy E award, The Hartford shared the credit, and rightly.[65] Stevens's own day-to-day dealings with surety bonds were altered by these increased values, at least quantitatively; qualitative changes came as new federal procedures governed war-damage insurance.[66] The same respected surety department that had managed the famous "construction miracles"—the contract bonds written for the construction of the Hoover Dam and the San Francisco–Oakland Bay Bridge had been undertakings of The Hartford—now turned its attention to the so-called Texas Towers that would be anchored in the Atlantic to serve as outposts for detecting incoming enemy attacks. Indeed, The Hartford's greatest if least obvious contribution to the war effort may have been in the work of the departments handling surety and fidelity bonds. Surety bonds helped engineers and government planners organize and protect otherwise hurried bidding and contracting procedures. War work was also to be done, though with less patriotic fanfare, in the fidelity department, where "blanket bonds" sheltered government-sponsored projects against loss through employee dishonesty. Stevens—who held uniquely creative views on, for instance, the "morbid[ity] of an embezzler . . . [who] keeps a memorandum" on his corporate theft[67]—was involved in these "certificate[s] of good character" just at the moment when home-front propagandists seized the idea (to the delight of employers) that employee theft was treasonous (see illustration).[68]

"Stop," artist unknown, 1944.

Shifts in the rhetoric with which the company viewed itself and the insurance industry were hardly restricted to the surety and fidelity business, of course. Whereas in the lean years of the thirties the emphasis had always been placed on success that follows individual, competitive work,[69] now cooperation, teamwork, and "unity" were the ideals. Corporate rhetoric was inverted: "it was their *collective* and not their *individual* effort," a company historian later wrote, "that contributed most importantly to the nation's war effort and to victory."[70] And having opposed in the thirties most government involvement in the insurance business, executives in Stevens's company now freely entered into agreements administered by wartime oversight boards; this may have amused Stevens, who had stood virtually alone in his field when endorsing the Social Security Act as conducive, not detrimental, to the continued good fortune of private insurance as an idea and a business.[71] Now here were many of the same men who had despised the New Deal's principle of government intercession, still otherwise stalwart business conservatives, sitting down at the conference table with Roosevelt's emissaries, collaborating on the creation of a War Damage Corporation, a government shield that would have caused many of these men to see red a few years earlier. Yet lucrative new terms and regulations were established under which "war damage" to insured defense industries, doing work previously not covered under standard policies, would now be amply secured—to the benefit of the American insurance establishment. This is not, then, to suggest that the industry suffered in wartime while individuals' belts were being tightened—rather, that propaganda directed at employees from within the company, designed to encourage the salespeople to sell more and larger policies (ever The Hartford's goal, war or not), could defer to rhetoric of the new nationalism—unity and individual sacrifice. There was a double game at home, and The Hartford played it. "War Furnishes Dozens of Arguments for Products Liability Insurance" is one unusually honest profit-minded headline in the *Hartford Agent*.[72] More typical is the article in the same *Agent* describing how Hartford employees would have to be watchful of "wartime sales methods." This approach and others served to bind the traditional goal of increased sales to the rhetoric of national propaganda aimed at all American home-front employees, such as that motivating the ubiquitous Rockwell poster displaying a frontline soldier, machine gun earnestly aimed, and bearing the caption "Let's Give Him Enough and On Time" (see illustration). "Wartime conditions have challenged the agency's ability to maintain [the prewar] standard, for it is determined not to fall into that dangerous frame of mind which uses war as an excuse for slip-shod methods."[73] The requirement for insurance coverage under the new compacts with the government was hardly inessential or unreal. So, too, the company's campaign to cope with shortages of the most basic supplies, such as paper, may have seemed to short-term, war-minded employees only incidentally a means to save money, even as that obviously undisturbed corporate goal was clothed in patriotic rhetoric; old-timers and other skeptics would remember that requests from the top to cut back on the use of office supplies were issued as energetically in peacetime. Yet what the *Agent* dramatically called the "Paper Situation" forced the company to request that even its officers, though business was great and getting greater, use 25 percent less paper than the year before, to

"Let's Give Him Enough and On Time," Norman Rockwell, 1942.

write and type on half-sheets whenever possible.[74] We know that Stevens, who wrote several thousand personal letters at the office (most dictated and then typewritten by Hartford employees on company time), adapted to the "Situation"; it is a small irony, indeed, that one of the surviving letters he sent to Allen Tate, explaining his skeptical attitude toward poetry doing its bit, was typewritten and carbon-copied on half-sheets provided by The Hartford for the emergency.[75]

Of course, paper presented the mildest of home-front problems. If that shortage affected Stevens to any degree—and even while it was characterized sardonically by one poetry critic, surveying the great quantity of facile war verse, as "a publisher's best friend"[76]—it did not bring the war home nearly as forcefully as the rationing of heating oil and restrictions on travel. But the very real prospects in the winter of 1942–1943 of a sizable home without heating oil, and a life without travel, forced Stevens to accommodate to the realities of the home front his old conception of imaginative "impoverishment" (or "poverty," in the word he more often used). The result of this new thinking, a poem called "No Possum, No Sop, No Taters," gives direct expression to a war-induced ordeal that seems to have frightened Stevens into a special awareness: the heating oil that had been delivered to 118 Westerly Terrace on January 21, 1943 (a hundred gallons), and which would have to last for another month, would not in fact last, he calculated, even another week.[77] There are other expressions of discomfort in Stevens's letters; such statements perhaps do support arguments that he was insulated from the greater suffering around him. But this truly was an exceptional moment for him, his fear both real and powerfully representative; in the frightful winter of 1942–1943 Wallace Stevens would be no less cold than many. The federal deputy oil administrator went so far as to predict that "some New Englanders might freeze to death this winter," and others agreed, putting the supply of heating oil ahead of gasoline on the rationing priority list.[78] The cold was so unrelenting that some curbs on use of fuel oil were eased.[79] Stevens wrote Philip May in Florida, wondering how he would "go through the very coldest period of the year" with no heat.[80] But home-front rhetoric about heating oil, leading to thoughts of escaping on Florida vacations, combined with still more uncompromising rhetoric against inessential travel. Posters around Hartford, as in other American cities, asked, "Is Your Trip Necessary?"— a question Stevens would pose and answer affirmatively in his new poem, indicating the extent, as I will suggest shortly, to which he could modify his old thesis about the imagination, the poverty or "Snow Man" thesis, for the home front. That he did so at just this moment, when home-front propaganda implied that "nonessential" travel could lead to American deaths, suggests a nationalist response.[81] This little episode did not begin with such feelings, however, as he planned, with May, a return to sunny Florida, where he had not traveled since 1940, partly because the navy had requisitioned his favorite resort, the Casa Marina in Key West. As Stevens considered renting in Winter Park, Sarasota, and Phil May's own Neptune Beach, he was not able to bring his rather strong powers of persuasion to bear on the West Hartford oil man, who was operating strictly under the new rules of rationing. Eventually, Stevens was able to prevail upon the oil man, but, significantly, he never made the return to Florida; nor, of course, was he in any real danger of freezing, though the language of his letters to May, when the southern escape still had a strong hold on his mind, is dramatic. Yet the weather's special *new* relation to the news—the record cold and the extraordinarily drawn-out war—suggested to him the bleak verse of "No Possum, No Sop, No Taters," a poem in which the old trees, standing under the cold sun in a frozen field, are subtly and ominously likened to horribly wounded, captive men, trying to cry out the story of their own version of wintriness:

> Bad is final in this light.
>
> In this bleak air the broken stalks
> Have arms without hands. They have trunks
>
> Without legs or, for that, without heads.
> They have heads in which a captive cry
>
> Is merely the moving of a tongue.

The poem is a brilliant wartime rewriting of "Farewell to Florida," that important transitional poem, as critics have suggested,[82] drawing the line between the period of fecund *Harmonium*-like poems and the bleak poems of the early thirties. But this "Farewell" is without even a last look at the warmth of the South—so far is it from the harsh realities of the moment. The title, borrowed from a phrase he used in a 1940 letter to the same Phil May,[83] gives us the only hint that there is a place where human life survives, though even there the attributes of the fecund life are a peasant's regional fare; even a recovery of the fertile, Floridean imagination would mean a tightening of the belt, a reduction in the standard of life—a new tolerance of the barrenness, bleakness, and (relative) poverty: possum, taters, and sop (a meal itself a sop against even less). Even that much is negated by the situation recorded in the poem: *no* possum, *no* sop, *no* taters. Borrowing from the negative rhetoric of "The Snow Man" (1921), this crisis poem restores reality to that abstraction—for the first time a "poverty" poem can make the abstract claim of nothingness and yet respond in doing so to a physical and social reality, to things as they are. For things as they are, at this moment, were never more real as they were *not*. This was the reality of the home front—doing without. The poem about doing without, about rationing and restrictions, begins by telling us what is not, what is no longer (the imagination, like the horrible limblessness it depicts, has reached an end). Yet suddenly—and this, I argue, is typical of Stevens's agreement with reality in the war's second phase—out of the "savagest hollow of winter-sound" comes a poetry of national redemption, a moral sustenance that is discovered only by standing at a distance from what was once considered fertile. The speaker here decides resolutely to join a watchful crow "for company," gaining perspective on the cold situation and on his initial negative response to it. In *not* "escaping or evading the pressures of reality" ("Noble Rider"), now more than ever a "cold" and "hard" reality, in *not* going to Florida, symbolically and biographically the source of the escape inscribed into the early career as poet, Stevens has chosen to remain with the horrible legless, handless figures standing out in the cold. By this point, the approach to reality—saying *no* to *there* is an acceptance of *here*, the hardness of the home front and the cold realities of national restrictions—becomes an aesthetic decision for the poetry spoken in contemporary moral terms:

> It is here, in this bad, that we reach
> The last purity of the knowledge of good.

THE NEW NATIONALISM

I like to hold on to anything that seems to have a
definite American past.
—*Stevens on Thomas Cole* (L 626)

I have found . . . no natural scenery yet which has
affected me so powerfully as that which I have seen
in the wilderness places of America.
—*Thomas Cole, quoted by James Thrall Soby
for a 1943 exhibit, "Romantic Painting in America"*

To assist American artists and to contribute to the
victory of life (artistic creation) over death (Nazi
barbarism) was seen as a national duty.
—*Serge Guilbaut in* How New York Stole
the Idea of Modern Art

The moments of enlargement overlook
The enlarging of the simplest soldier's cry
In what I am, as he falls. Of what I am,

The cry is part.
—*Stevens, "Chocorua to Its Neighbor" (1943)*

The ill fated Chocorua refused to destroy himself
by that terrific leap. And suffered death beneath
their hands.
—*Thomas Cole, explaining his use of the
Chocorua legend*

If the loss of Florida to wartime was at once a setback for the rhetoric of the
imagination and an advance into wartime reality, the loss of Paris, while
presenting a very different constraint, had the same effect. The two losses
were closely related in one important way: forced to face the realities of
remaining in Hartford, the cold facts of the home front, Stevens realized
that there were to be restrictions on a home-front art as well. Being de-
prived of Vidal's agency meant limiting forays into the international world
of modern art to New York, where he got a strict schooling in the new
wartime Americanism. Once thriving on regular letters from the well-
connected Vidal, messages from a world of painting that he would never
see with his own eyes but one that had been painstakingly described for
him, he came to know well the transformation taking place in the nearest

center. Indeed these were the years when, to use Serge Guilbaut's phrase, New York "stole the idea of modern art" from Paris. Stevens himself saw at firsthand how the war made its impact on art collectors and critics, such as his friend Walter Pach, who could no longer spend part of his year searching out new French talents and modes. The years 1942 through 1945 generally saw the making of a New York art scene without ties to Paris. The clearest fact of European war for people with Pach's and Henry Church's transatlantic connections—that French art was no longer being exported as European sources of art were being destroyed—surely made itself clear to Stevens as well: with Vidal's help, Stevens had just begun to reach his stride in purchasing French paintings. What would be his reply to the forfeiture of Paris as art center? Would he, like many another, turn to American painting? Or to the Americanization of European modernism?

In New York the reply of art critics and museum directors rapidly emerged. They were beginning to learn how to take advantage of the terrible situation, adapting a new cultural nationalism to the long-cherished idea of an independently modern American art. Samuel Kootz's position was just one of the most obvious forms of this adaptation: "We can expect no help from abroad today to guide our painters into new paths, fresh ideas." The aesthetic advantage was plainly derived from military disadvantage: painters were now "hermetically sealed by war against Parisian sponsorship. . . . [W]e are on our own."[1] If Stevens reacted positively to this strategy—and he did, as we will see—it would take a less obviously self-serving argument than Kootz's to elicit such an affirmative response. But both vehement and subtle forms of aesthetic nationalism were readily available. And the fact is that Stevens was very much absorbed by a general resurgence of American interest in museum exhibits, many of them designed to reproduce a new patriotic rhetoric and to elicit a nationalist response. Evidently, the rhetoric worked well. Attendance at exhibits of modern art increased astonishingly, as did memberships in the Museum of Modern Art particularly.[2] Stevens was one of the crowd. His museum-going peaked in the two most anxious American war years, 1942 and 1943. Judging only from explicit references in published and unpublished letters dating from those two years, I find Stevens at no fewer than ten major exhibits; the actual total, including shows he attended but did not mention in surviving written records, is likely of course to be greater.[3] This is not to count, moreover, the many exhibit catalogues he collected and closely examined. Some of these came from museum visits; others were sent him by special arrangement when he could not make the trip to New York to see the paintings for himself. In 1942, to Wilson Taylor, a Hartford Insurance colleague who worked in the New York office, and who shared—or at least kept up with—the poet's interest in art exhibits, Stevens wrote: "Catalogues are to me what honeycombs are to a bear."[4] And when he did venture to see the exhibits for himself, he might take in two or three or more in a day. "To him," Taylor later recalled (*WSR* 84), going to galleries "was just part of life." He remembered that Stevens would carefully scrutinize listings of the current exhibits on the train from Hartford: "I don't think he ever came down that he didn't read *The New Yorker* on the way" (*WSR* 84).

Discriminating as he was, always wary of exuberant crowds at popular exhibits,[5] Stevens could hardly have avoided the new nationalist rhetoric backing them. The Metropolitan's huge "Artists for Victory" show was typical of the period. "Art is a method of unifying people," announced Clifton Fadiman over the radio, urging his fellow citizens to attend.[6] Even moderates like the *New York Times* art critic, Edward Alden Jewell, wanted to see "an art that engaged with its historical period, an art that stood for the values being defended by the allied armies."[7] The museum catalogues were full of expressions of such engagement. The interaction between the Alliance, historicism, and "values" was everywhere assumed, left unexamined as a new political relation—even (or perhaps especially) by critics like Jewell at the *Times* who had been known until then for their interest in modern abstraction and who were largely unaware that a moral conversion from formalism was going to be required. Manifestations of this assumed relation were to be found in every corner of the museums. Even the captions that accompanied exhibited paintings, tracing provenances that took one perhaps through occupation and into exile, were liberally if only somewhat intentionally inscribed with the American Century thesis: America was the inevitable safe harbor for great art under duress elsewhere; once in America, art had no Elsewhere. Proudly displayed were paintings such as Max Ernst's *Europe after the Rain*, bought and shown by Hartford's Atheneum in 1943 after it had been literally rescued and smuggled out of Europe;[8] a certified wartime provenance might be deemed part of the value of the painting. This point was especially pronounced when the paintings on show were indeed European, for here the useful idea was that happy cultural relations between the United States and its allies "are literally weapons for wartime use," as Alfred Frankfurter put it,[9] and that the Americanization of otherwise displaced modern art—even if in fact the United States was only serving as an exhibition setting—strongly implied the formation of a cultural defense, reduced French art to the status of dislocation, and raised the status of American art to centrality.

The defense of culture was the presiding metaphor at exhibits Stevens saw for himself. One show of French paintings pleasingly denied the fact of Nazi occupation in its very title: it was an exhibit, as Stevens described it to Wilson Taylor, "of pictures of France *from Paris to the sea*" (emphasis added).[10] The wished-for "France" that swept so freely did not then exist of course—not from Paris to any sea. The title was, along with much else, usefully hopeful. Later in 1943 the same gallery, Wildenstein's on East 64th Street, where the gallery staff knew Stevens and he them by name[11]— "Wildenstein's in the morning (after 10) is my idea of a good place to be," Stevens had written[12]—displayed van Gogh by explicitly connecting the Dutch painter to Americans' responsibility to aid the occupied Nether-lands. The very fact that fourteen of the van Goghs shown were loaned out of Holland constituted a strenuous "war effort" in itself; the exhibit organ-izers did not fail to proclaim this. The catalogue proudly noted that the show was mounted in support of American and Dutch war relief. Attend-ing Wildenstein's van Gogh exhibit on Saturday, November 6, 1943, Ste-vens could not help but come away with a feeling reinforced by Frank-furter's notion, presented in his introduction to the exhibit catalogue, that van Gogh's art shows him to have been "the very epitome of the dilem[m]a of the modern world," someone who "courageously tr[ied] to solve the problems" against which great artists fight—an obvious attempt to make van Gogh's private struggle seem appropriate to the many national strug-gles of 1943.[13] Van Gogh's "mastery of reality" encouraged Stevens, in his own work, "to seize the whole mass of everything and squeeze it," as he wrote to Church (L 459). Frankfurter, editor of *Art News*, was still more explicit in his introduction to the catalogue accompanying the 1942 Cézanne show mounted at the Rosenberg Gallery—"for the benefit of Fighting France."[14] Wilson Taylor procured for Stevens the catalogue for this exhibit,[15] and possibly the special issue of *Art News* assembled for it,[16] and what with his general recognition that "Cézanne has been the source of all painting of any interest during the last 20 years,"[17] it is likely that at some point he stopped in at Rosenberg's to see the paintings for himself. Whether from the catalogue alone or in the gallery itself, Stevens saw a Cézanne fully remade for wartime. The newspapers certainly did their part; one of Jewell's two articles about the exhibit was headlined "CEZANNE SERVES RESURGENT FRANCE." It was accompanied by a halftone of *Mont Ste. Victoire*, the title now implicitly taking on wartime meaning.[18] Stevens gave a sign of having assimilated Frankfurter's and the *Times*'s revision of Cézanne to such good purpose when a little later, in the introduction to the army's Sergeant Morse, Stevens quoted Lionello Venturi (from an essay in the same Rosenberg catalogue) on Cézanne's "*moral* beauty" (*OP* 244; emphasis added). Frankfurter's wartime Cézanne overcame the usual rule against "interpret[ing] the life-work of an artist merely as a metaphor illustrating a topical truth," for "in the ordinary course of events"—mean-ing, if it were not wartime—such a historicist reduction "would be as wrong in taste as in proportion." But there *was* a war going on; so, indeed, rules against engaging even the greats as illustrations of a "topical truth" (such as all-out victory for the Allies) having been broken, the Cézanne

Stevens saw in 1942 was rendered "completely . . . a symbol of the Fighting French." The painter now expressed no less than the "will to *freedom*." Closer still to the political point: "Those Frenchmen who, distant from their homes, are fighting under General de Gaulle for the restitution to their native land of its ancient tradition of liberty, equality, and fraternity, are fighting for the same principles to which, in art, their great countryman Cézanne devoted his life." Cézanne could even be superimposed on a particularly American sort of freedom, as the catalogue, quoting Lincoln, imagines that great American liberator addressing the French painter (and through Cézanne the French people), acknowledging " 'the solemn pride that must be yours to have laid so costly a sacrifice upon the altar of freedom.' "[19]

From his experiences with Vidal's deft management of Franco-American intermediacy, Stevens might fluently read the subtext of a catalogue celebrating Americanized French art and glean a sense of the cultural work that went into mounting such an exhibition, let alone rationalizing the convergence of Abraham Lincoln and Paul Cézanne in a catalogue. Perhaps the exhibits' subtexts were even more intelligible to him after some years of familiarity with the inner workings of Hartford's ambitious Atheneum. In the thirties he had assiduously followed the energetic collaboration of James Thrall Soby and A. Everett ("Chick") Austin, who raised the status of the Atheneum from Victorian respectability to what the French collector Paul Rosenberg would call the world's only "genuinely modern museum."[20] The most difficult part of Soby's and Austin's effort to awaken Hartford's citizens and its potentially great museum from a cautious, premodern mode of financing acquisitions was to make publicly palatable new exhibitions of the postcubist Picasso, the surrealists, and the "neo-Romantics" (Eugene and Leonid Berman, Tanguy, Tchelitchew). Stevens knew Austin's and Soby's work exhibit by exhibit,[21] and the latter's rapid rise in the museum world must have brought into sharp focus for Stevens a certain style of museum politics that would become perfectly suitable to wartime, when official funding was available once a measure of public acceptance had been won. And Stevens, having witnessed such curatorial cunning, would be able to observe in wartime the way in which, for example, in mounting the Cézanne show, Rosenberg's people managed to secure and bring to the United States several Cézannes from Jakob Goldschmidt.[22] Stevens's up-to-date factual knowledge of Goldschmidt's precarious situation—a prominent Jewish Berliner and a favorite target of Goebbels, he succeeded in retaining his paintings and bringing them out of Germany, as Reich authorities were calling for his arrest, because he was in favor with Mussolini, who interceded for him[23]—suggests that the poet from Hartford knew enough about dealings in New York to view these paintings with a sense of appropriate relief merely that they had survived

Nazi acquisitiveness, and not without a certain awareness of the present threat to all European art.

Between 1942 and 1944, then, it was becoming evident to Stevens that looking at paintings in wartime could produce one of two general effects. It could calm one, inducing one to remember the prewar peace in which artists had flourished and experimented, thus quietly strengthening one's resolve to resist intellectual defeatism by conjuring a culture whose art was worth fighting a war to save. Alternatively, however, it could serve as a diversion from the world at war. Stevens seems at least once to have understood the risks involved in the second approach. After a weekend in Boston, during which he visited the Grenville Winthrop collection then on exhibit at the Fogg Museum, he wrote Church with genuine regret about such an apparent act of retreat: "Cambridge is so full of war that walking round a museum seems somehow to be a sad mistake."[24] But as for the calm that stiffened resolve to see the war through, to save Vidal's France, he was, I am equally certain, well aware of what Guilbaut has identified in museum and exhibit politics—the conscious design of "new nationalists" in the modern art world. When Stevens visited the Corot exhibit at Wildenstein's in late 1942, called "The Serene World of Corot: An Exhibition in Aid of the Salvation Army War Fund," and saw, for instance, Corot's blissful *L'Etang de Ville d'Avray*, he thought immediately of the exiled Churches, whose sadness at being separated from their own Ville d'Avray home had always interested him. The wartime Corot of this exhibit was a person who "stood resolute and calm in the midst of the surging spirits" around him. It was assumed that Corot would appear to the viewer of 1942 "as . . . a distinctly peaceful and luminous figure in a century filled with agitation"[25]—a thesis that could not help but legitimize the already strong American image of the typical Frenchman so badly needing relief from abroad after his nerve had failed in the spring of 1940. Now that the United States was France's active ally, however, the same American's representative Frenchman was intellectually "peaceful" and aesthetically "luminous," radiating soft cultural light amidst the hardened and barbarous German occupiers, remaining "calm" yet "resolute" (that is, inviolable, *resistant*)—all in the tradition of Corot, whose composition recalled the great French love of the land. New York's wartime Corot indeed presented a "serene world" Stevens knew the Churches needed to see again: "This is so full of Ville d'Avray," Stevens wrote Henry Church of the Wildenstein show, "that you and Mrs. Church would be sure to find it very much more than worth while."[26]

Despite the inducements of the wartime catalogues, Stevens might not have responded at all to the new nationalism in painting had it not been for James Soby, the Hartford-centered collector and a great admirer of Stevens's poetry.[27] Soby's direct involvement in the cultural politics of the war effort surely lent new and needed modernist credentials to the project, especially as he was known, from his Hartford years, as an uncompromising internationalist. He had had little to do with American art; his coming aboard in wartime would seem all the more impressive for that. He had indefatigably promoted (and bought) the neo-Romantics, whose art was as far from nationalism, even French nationalism, as one could get. Soby began to spend more time in New York than in Hartford:[28] immediately following the attack on Pearl Harbor, on behalf of the Museum of Modern Art, he began consulting with army and navy morale officers as to how the American museum "could put its facilities most helpfully at the service of the men in the armed services." Then in January 1942 he was named director of MOMA's Armed Services Program, proclaiming that the desire among enlisted men for art books and color reproductions of great works could be satisfied by MOMA's contributions and that these would create new "lasting interest" in art as "a greater stimulant to [soldiers'] conversation than fiction or picture magazines."[29]

Having followed Soby's purchases, knowing Soby's own collection of neo-Romantic works painting by painting, Stevens now familiarized himself with the facts of Soby's wartime arrangement.[30] "The glimpses that I have had of your collection have been precious to me," Stevens had written Soby in 1940;[31] by 1943, when he wrote Church that he was "intensely interested" in Soby's private acquisitions,[32] Soby was already too busy serving his country (and MOMA) to display his collection at Farmington or in Hartford as he once had with inspiring regularity. Stevens did see Soby at MOMA,[33] of course, but this must have made it only clearer to the poet from Hartford how the scene had shifted. The eyes of Hartford's museum-goers turned toward New York, where under Soby's direction, MOMA signed thirty-eight contracts with the OWI, receiving a total of $1.5 million in war grants, and became, in Russell Lynes's phrase, "a minor war industry."[34] Soby sponsored, for instance, a Support America Contest, awarding the prize to a poster that elaborated the "Buy a Share in America" theme.[35] "By showing how greatly the war effort depends upon the human element," another of Soby's patriotic catalogues announced, "the exhibition will enable every citizen to recognize his position in the nation's effort."[36]

Soby's position at MOMA did allow him to continue one particular part of the work he and Chick Austin had done in the late thirties at Hartford's Atheneum: he brought the neo-Romantics along with him, as it were, into new-nationalist aesthetics. He could now Americanize them, could make them tolerable to American wartime tastes—no simple task, as they had been known as dreamy, nostalgic, even reactionary.[37] He would have to find a way to strip neo-Romanticism somewhat of its exclusively European context. That even Eugene Berman would now be strategically refigured for Americanism must have struck Stevens particularly, for only a few years earlier, in 1937, it had been one of Berman's dreamlike, misty seascapes, a painting Soby himself owned and exhibited in Hartford, that Stevens had boldly reproduced in one of the "Blue Guitar" cantos.[38] As Stevens may have guessed that Americanizing Berman would be pushing both the neo-Romantic and new-nationalist points too far at once, he would also have been right about Soby's sense of strategic limits: although some critics hailed the presence of Tanguy in the United States as bound "to lighten the darkness" of the war years,[39] Soby was still anxious about nativist antagonism to the continued promotion of European over American art. Despite the risks, he remained steadfastly devoted to European painters, and he evidently came to view his task as enlarging the nationalist enthusiasm to include internationalism itself, inimical to nationalism as that might have seemed. It only shows the elasticity of the idea—its special hegemonic power, Guilbaut would argue—that the new nationalism could accommodate internationalism, and offers a clue as to how it would lead to American cultural politics of the postwar years. To be sure, the integration was not easy to manage; its promotional phrases had to be turned just so if not to seem utterly contradictory. Soby's friend and ally Alfred Barr was dismissed as MOMA director in 1943 after he, with Soby, sponsored the exhibits of Morris Hirshfield and Joe Milone, in an effort to "establish an American tradition modeled on that of the Paris school by presenting the world of 'naive' American artists"—an effort that flopped.[40] This was a major piece of art-world news Stevens would have heard recited, almost surely, by Barbara or Henry Church, who would have heard it in turn from their friend James Johnson Sweeney, Barr's immediate successor at MOMA.[41] If Soby wanted to continue promoting Berman and the other European neo-Romantics, it could not hurt to be associated so closely with the OWI, especially as this brought MOMA and himself into favorable visible contact with Archibald MacLeish, author of "The Irresponsibles," that impassioned, unspecific essay that had quickly become the new-nationalist manifesto. Of course, as Stevens was well aware, MacLeish and Soby knew each other before the battle began between nationalists and "irresponsibles"; both men lived in Farmington, outside Hartford.[42] Perhaps because he knew he was effectively shielded, as an ally of the well-placed propagandist MacLeish and as director of MOMA's impeccably loyal Armed Services Program, Soby continued to advocate the neo-Romantics in a manner not immune to new-nationalist criticism. While its supporters had already extended MacLeish's thesis to include irresponsibles in the modern art world—it had been directed at writers, and by the word "writers," Paul Fussell observes, MacLeish apparently meant only "novelists"[43]—at least one of these zealots, in shifting aim from "writers" to painters, began to criticize the manner of fantastic, unworldly, and sentimental painting the neo-Romantics practiced and Soby had long fostered. In "American Art a

Year after Pearl Harbor," published in *Art News*, Milton Brown complained that "the catastrophe of war has exposed so pitilessly the inherent weaknesses within our art," its "inability . . . to participate in this moment of crisis": the target was painting belonging to any "school of elegant effeminacy," art that provided "figures in so *sentimental* a golden haze that one expects the momentary appearance of a rainbow."[44] Brown's dislike of "sentimental" figures—an attribute winning commendation only a few years earlier in Soby's *After Picasso*—took sharpest aim.

Soby's counterresponse was brilliant. He found that he could formulate what the neo-Romantics were doing in wartime terms: all the major neo-Romantics were now living in the United States as exiles and were turning their attentions to their new American surroundings.[45] How better to earn the approval of Brown and his nationalist allies? To remind American critics that the neo-Romantics ought to be objects of their concern, Soby helped mount an "Artists in Exile" exhibit at Pierre Matisse's gallery and wrote "Europe," one of the two catalogue essays, where he succeeded in modifying the new nationalism so that it resembled in fact a resurgent modernism. He saw "the beginning of a period during which the American traditions of freedom and generosity may implement a *new internationalism in art, centered in this country*." The American national spirit was to reach out to Europe and offer sanctuary to European artists while at the same time centering Europe in America. Soby did also warn against too much submission to the demands of the most zealous new nationalists: "[I]t would be disastrous to apply rigid standards of nationalism to the arts," Soby wrote, "however necessary these standards may be in other applications during time of war." But even the most inflamed cultural patriot, he was confident, would find that "a sympathetic relationship with refugee painters and sculptors can have a broadening effect on native tradition."[46] This crucial strategy—internationalize the new-nationalist impetus and yet take great care not to contradict it, and claim to avoid "the dread bait of imperialism" that might inevitably follow increasing American cultural power[47]—enabled Soby to manage perhaps his most unusual wartime museum project. This was the 1943 exhibit entitled "Romantic Painting in America," which prominently featured the landscapes of Thomas Cole. The show suitably appealed to nationalist popularizers like Kootz, who in staking out "New Frontiers in American Painting" had himself implied a kind of aesthetic American manifest destiny, even as he obviously also meant frontiers of formal experiment.[48]

The new context for Cole also appealed to Stevens, whose later feelings for Cole's work centered on the painter's sense of Americanness (*L* 626). Soby himself wrote the introduction to the catalogue for the American Romantics show, which aimed at making Cole fashionable enough to museum-goers accustomed to Tanguy and Tchelitchew—to people precisely like Stevens who had remained largely uninterested in American art—by suggesting as strongly as possible a connection between the ahistorical neo-Romantic manner—their landscapes expressing childhood memory and personal emotion—and the style of these premodern American Romantics; and also by putting Cole in direct relation to the French traditions, for instance Claude and Poussin,[49] two painters whose landscapes interested Stevens.[50] Thus MOMA stressed a peaceful nineteenth-century Cole for the warring twentieth, and an American perceived as respecting European inspirations; but so also did Soby's MOMA remake Cole as an artist who could help painting fight the present war. Soby arranged to show a number of Cole's landscapes, including the *Scene from Cooper's The Last of the Mohicans* (1827), which Stevens had undoubtedly seen at the Wadsworth Atheneum.[51] Also displayed in this 1943 exhibit was the painting entitled *Mount Chocorua, New Hampshire* (1827).

When Oscar Williams asked Stevens for contributions to *New Poems 1943*, advertised as "an anthology of war poetry"—it would compile "the current work of poets who have intensely felt the fact of war"[52]—one of the poems Stevens sent was a new one, "Chocorua to Its Neighbor," a work that asks to be read in the new-nationalist context Soby's MOMA had now given Cole's painting. The poem is a story told by the mountain, Mount Chocorua, about the human figure whose experience in climbing Chocorua becomes a fable for the rejuvenation of the romantic spirit in a time of crisis. At first, the mountain-speaker depends on a sublime perspective. This lofty view allows him to see men collectively, indifferently, "To perceive men without reference to their form / . . . not [in the case of the climber] / One foot approaching, one uplifted arm" (*CP* 296). But slowly, as the mountain itself realizes what the man who climbs him is coming to know about himself and his world, the perspective of the telling shifts toward that of the climber. At first the climber is defined in the usual terms of Stevens's major man (in sections v and vii, for instance). In the eleventh section of the twenty-six-section poem, the climber, now quoted by the mountain-speaker, claims that mountain and climber are speaking in the same voice. Thus, when the mountain turns again to the view of humanity in the villages and cities far below, he speaks more sympathetically of the people whom the climber protects and defends, by taking the trouble to climb, by risking the fall of a falling soldier. Finally, then, the mountain confesses his sympathy directly: "I, Chocorua, speak of this shadow [the climber figure] as / A human thing" (*CP* 300). He has realized that the man risked everything in search of "what / Was *native* to him in that height" (301).

The story of Chocorua, for Cole as for Stevens, involves an Indian warrior named Chocorua, who, after the French and Indian Wars, is hunted by vengeful white men and flees to a high and nearly inaccessible peak in the White Mountains. Chocorua and his pursuers reach the summit, whereupon Chocorua refuses to jump, forcing the white men to kill him with their own hands. The legend goes that the area near the mountain remains pure, Native American terrain; Chocorua is said to have cursed the area so that settlers' cattle could not be raised there. Finally the mountain itself took the name of the heroic Indian who climbed it and who, refusing to destroy himself, forced his enemy to commit an explicit act of war.[53] In the context provided by MOMA's strategic wartime use of American romanticism, the most important moment in Stevens's "Chocorua" occurs when the speaker of the poem resolves to learn from a "native" spirit to relinquish the lofty perspective that too easily distinguished the speaker's view of events from what seemed initially to have been the limited view of the humans living and warring below. Indeed, this point is made in terms of the war. In the lofty view:

> The armies are forms in number, as cities are.
> The armies are cities in movement. But a war
> Between cities is a gesticulation of forms,
> A swarming of number over number, not
> One foot approaching, one uplifted arm.
>
> (CP 296)

This opening perspective, a grand but deceiving one, reveals only the *forms* below, tiny in relation to the mountain, warring in such a way as not to be the least bit troubling—a swarming of numbers, not individual tragedies. By the twenty-fourth section, the "uplifted arm" *not* distinguished earlier is now "the great arms / Of the armies, the solid men" who "make big the fable" of the hard-to-tell (301); note the great distance Stevens has come from the muted armies of "Martial Cadenza" in his isolationist period. Along the way—up the mountain, as it were, of engagement— Stevens may discover that an individual hero—the climber-Chocorua, like the Young Captain—enables "others like him" to remain "safely under roof," and Stevens takes time to list those whose home-front safety is protected and defended by the soldier-climber, in a cataloging rhetoric that is hardly less expressive of democracy than Whitman's:

> The captain squalid on his pillow, the great
> Cardinal, saying the prayers of earliest day;
> The stone, the categorical effigy;
> And the mother, the music, the name; the scholar,
> Whose green mind bulges with complicated hues.
>
> (CP 300)

All on the list are safe; they are equal only (yet crucially) in that they are equally defended. "Chocorua to Its Neighbor" deliberately creates an

American art out of what was at the very moment of its composition a distinctly international theme. It calls, as shrewdly as Soby did, for a universal good to have "a broadening effect on native tradition." Yet its nationalism is indeed subtle enough to include the sufficient warning, in its revision of the mountain view—Cole's dominant mode revised for a time of democratic leveling—that, again in Soby's words, "it would be disastrous to apply rigid standards of nationalism to the arts, however necessary these standards may be in other applications during time of war." On one hand, then, Soby's wartime Cole must suggest that Americans' dependence on European tradition could be affirmed, and so imply that the war must be fiercely fought in Europe to save the culture on which our own is derived: "Cole's art was based upon the 17th century European tradition to a degree from which no love of New World scenery could completely free him." At the very same time, Soby's Cole must be overtly patriotic, an artist who decided that he had seen "no natural scenery [in Europe] yet which has affected me so powerfully as . . . the wilderness places of America." These are precisely the tensions driving Stevens's own "Chocorua'' as an American landscape for a war fought elsewhere, and presumably it is the reason he deemed the poem appropriate to send to Oscar Williams's war-poem anthology.[54]

The Americanization of modes previously centered in Europe and now welcomed in the New World was strong evidence of the American commitment to preserving modernist culture, as to aiding individual exiled painters, even if the commitment seemed insufficient to painter-soldiers like Ralston Crawford, who urged (in an article Stevens almost certainly saw) "pictures pertaining to: 1. Guys dead, (including odor). 2. Guys with their noses missing. 3. Guys with one arm on another part of the deck,"[55] and George Biddle, who had been dispatched "to active theaters to paint war scenes" and to do "action drawings."[56] Most nationalists, however, felt that the very fact of MOMA's making the effort to mount a show with Thomas Cole was a great victory, for in this way American painting might finally meet its general responsibility of "unifying people," in Fadiman's phrase. For a variety of reasons, those who now called for American *writing* to involve itself in the war effort had high standards of service—expectations much closer indeed to Crawford's in the Pacific and Biddle's in North Africa than to Soby's at MOMA. When these standards were applied to Stevens, a battle for his allegiance began.

The new nationalism in writing began as a negative campaign—namely, in MacLeish's attack on "the irresponsibles," first in an essay and then in a small book going under that title. But the chief characteristic of MacLeish's jeremiad was to advocate what Van Wyck Brooks characterized as a positive and constructive American literature—and what Brooks's and

MacLeish's detractors mocked as a "Chamber-of-Commerce spirit."[57] MacLeish, who had contributed several paragraphs to Roosevelt's 1940 acceptance speech, then defined "soft" or "white" propaganda in his so-called Strategy of Truth at the Office of Facts and Figures and OWI, now took his case to the American people. He repeatedly promoted optimism and attacked "divisionism" and defeatism among writers.[58] He reminded writers that the destruction of "the integrity of words" was a greater crime against the state than the destruction of a machine or manufacturing plant.[59] He attacked writers who insisted on presenting "the point of view of the defeated man."[60] After Pearl Harbor, he insisted that as "the American mentality" was changing "from defensive to offensive," so should that of American writers and critics. "What is true of the people as a whole in the war fought for the domination of the world should be true as well of the intellectuals—the writers and the scholars and the librarians and the rest—in the war fought for the countries of the mind."[61] MacLeish's pronouncements, especially in "The Irresponsibles," which sparked a great deal of immediate comment (much of it favorable),[62] had an enormous impact on subsequent responses to the war by American writers, including Stevens—like "no document of our time," Brooks felt.[63] American writers and intellectuals had failed to see how "the imagination," as "weapons of ideas and words," could be "devot[ed] to th[e] warfare."[64]

Faced with such arguments, what writer could disagree with the new nationalism without seeming to oppose the war to save culture or, worse, to be soft on fascism? To a certain extent, as critics such as Dwight MacDonald pointed out, Brooks's and especially MacLeish's attacks on the irresponsibles were themselves irresponsible.[65] The fact remains, however—few writers who, like Stevens, read the weeklies and quarterlies would fail to notice it[66]—former leftists were now in the position of celebrating democracy, working for its total victory over the fascist right. Dos Passos, resister in the First World War, now flew to England to help win this one; Max Eastman and Malcolm Cowley busily wrote war propaganda for the government. These and many others were more or less on MacLeish's side, whether they admitted it or not, in suggesting that writers who sat back "as spectators of a war against ourselves" and who saw art as "an ornament, a jewel,"[67] did so only at the risk of losing the things they loved because of the purity of their detachment and the pretense of their objectivity. It was hard to disagree about the danger, even while one may have disagreed about the causes new nationalists had identified to meet it. If only at first out of respect for Church's predicament, Stevens may not have felt he was in a position to oppose the new-nationalist claim that American writers whose imaginations had in all other ways extended to Europe had also been unaroused "witnesses . . . to the destruction of writing . . . in great areas of Europe and to the exile and the imprisonment and murder of men whose crime was scholarship and writing."[68] Willard Thorp, Church's and Allen Tate's friend, whom Stevens met during his visit to deliver his 1941 Princeton lecture,[69] came to MacLeish's side. Thorp was probably the only person with direct access to the growing Church-Stevens relationship to do so. Thorp agreed that scholars' justifications for irresponsibility included "scholarly aloofness," "dispassionateness," and "devotion to permanent values," and he called for a keener sense of contingency in academic values, a new self-reflective historicism. The scholar, he argued, must not "neglect . . . that portion of his author's career which was turned toward the world of his time"; in shifting focus, such a scholar would be similarly turning toward that world.[70]

No evidence survives to suggest that Thorp argued his support of MacLeish for Stevens, though Professor Thorp did remember discussing the new-nationalist controversy with Church and noted for me his surprise at the extent of Church's interaction with Stevens at the time.[71] We will see, in any event, that Stevens did respond positively to the nationalist thesis by first reacting *negatively* to Allen Tate's abhorrence of it. MacLeish's allies had immediately turned some of their ire against Tate's and Ransom's particular brand of wartime formalism. To the extent that MacLeish himself meant to include the agrarians and New Critics in his initial attack, it was generalized to include the purest poets and the most formalistic critics.[72] But Van Wyck Brooks, in "What Is Primary Literature?" and "Coterie-Literature" a year later, specified this indictment. Among the "secondary" or "coterie" critics and writers who, "[l]acking all that makes for content, . . . said that . . . the only essential matter is form," and developed "a learned game for students to play . . . round and round in a little circle of references," he named Eliot, Richards, Cleanth Brooks, and Ransom.[73] It is not surprising that Ransom and Tate joined those attacking Brooks in the *Partisan Review*—with Trilling, Williams, and Henry Miller from one side and Louise Bogan from the other. It was clear to anyone with an acumen for such things that a new consensus was forming, the edges now rallying back against a growing middle.[74] As formalists under fire, Ransom and Tate were especially delighted to have certain company from the left. Brooks reserved his strongest words for the New Critics: Ransom's literary criticism suggested to Brooks "the joy of Bruno [*sic*] Mussolini hunting out the Ethiopians."[75] Such shots scattered widely enough to hit Stevens. It was Weldon Kees who made the connection between Eliot, Richards, Brooks, Tate, Ransom—and Stevens: all stood to be criticized by the new nationalists. Kees's review of *Parts of a World* began: "Wallace Stevens has been, and still is, very much what Van Wyck Brooks has blithely called a coterie writer.' His audience is probably more restricted than that of any other poet of his importance."[76] To be sure, Kees's review is positive, even from Brooks's point of view. "In the face of today's

disintegration and chaos," Kees wrote of Stevens, "a good deal of his earlier serenity and self-possession has gone. There are new tones of anguish,
grief and disgust, and an awareness that our society is moving . . . to 'a
falling and an end' [*CP* 214]." But it was also clear—and this is central to
the response Stevens would make—that Stevens's reviewers, and presumably his readers, were getting into the habit of looking at poems he had
written before the war, in the late thirties (the earliest poem in *Parts* was
written in 1937), and reading into them anachronistically "anguish, grief
and disgust" about the war's American phase. Kees quoted "Girl in a
Nightgown" to demonstrate that "Stevens was never blind to threatenings
of disaster," even though the "disaster" of that poem signifies the booming
of a *prewar* spring, an individual's physical reawakening to the swelling
green world outside her window. "It is shaken now. It will burst into
flames, / Either now or tomorrow or the day after that"—*it* referring, for
Kees, to the inflamed world at war.[77] Even in spite of the praise of Stevens's
political topicality, if his response to such reviews as Kees's was even
slightly what it had been in 1935, when he by most accounts overreacted to
Stanley Burnshaw's, this one may well have sent him to Brooks's claims of
American intellectual failure, looking to discover on which side of what
controversy he had been placed. Stevens's wartime interaction with Tate,
especially because Henry Church was the chief reason for it, would force
his position to move chromatically toward clarity.

ALLEN TATE'S WESTERN FRONT

> The enemies of liberty, here as in other countries,
> practice the destruction of the integrity of words.
> . . . And nowhere have they used these *Kulturwaffen*
> to destroy a word more skillfully than with the word
> "democracy"—the word essential to our cause—
> the word which *is* our cause—the word we must
> defend whatever else we lose, or fail to fight for, or
> do not defend.
> —*Archibald MacLeish*,
> "*The American Cause*"

> There is already going to be a strong movement in
> favor of bigness, Americanism, and "democracy,"
> and a hatred of the subtle and the intelligent—
> which is the way our totalitarianism will develop
> on the literary front.
> —*Allen Tate*

> I wonder whether there is enough of the peasant in
> Tate: *Il faut être paysan d'être poète.* The KENYON
> group ["Seasons of the Soul"] is acute and intricate
> and Tate has every right to be proud of it, but his
> pride is a little like Pierre duPont's pride in his
> espaliers.... I like sap and lots of it and, some-
> how, this Kenyon group seems to me like poetry
> written under glass.
> —*Stevens on Tate,*
> *in a letter to Henry Church* (L 461)

> He never *faces* experiences: his poems are *about* ex-
> periences or the impossibility of knowing anything.
> —*Tate on Stevens in 1971*

The new nationalism was not initially responsible for bringing together
Stevens and Tate, but it did accelerate their relations. Years before Tate's
name began to appear with some frequency in Church's wartime letters
from Princeton, Stevens had already been familiar with the younger man's
poems. They had met once, in Hartford, and while it may not have been an
altogether pleasant meeting for Tate,[1] there was obviously an affinity to be
explored. By the time Church brought the two poets together again in the
early forties, Stevens certainly knew Tate's collection *The Mediterranean &
Other Poems*, including "Aeneas at Washington," "Shadow and Shade,"
"To the Lacedemonians," "The Ivory Tower," "The Anabasis," and "The
Mediterranean" itself; that book had been one of Ronald Lane Latimer's
Alcestis Press editions, and Stevens owned a numbered copy. Tate, for his
part, had followed Stevens's career assiduously. In a confession he would
finally regret having made, Tate admitted to Stevens how much he had
"admired" "Sunday Morning" in his poetic youth—"more than any contemporary poem of our time," he wrote, "for what it taught me, and for its
own magnificence."[2] The facts of Tate's interest were impressive: when
Stevens later sent a gift copy of *Transport to Summer*, Tate stated that he
already knew all but three or four of the fifty-six poems in the collection
from their earlier publications—no small sign of esteem, even at a time
when Stevens was otherwise confident that his readership was slowly but
surely growing, as it would suggest that Tate had taken the trouble to
follow new, yet-uncollected work to such far-off corners as *Arizona Quarterly* in Tucson, *Pacific* at Mills College, and *Orígenes* in Havana.[3] Characteristically, Stevens did not reveal the extent of his increasing engagement
with Tate's work, but the evidence indicates that he was always a good deal
more than curious about it, even if *incurious* characterizes his disposition

toward much contemporary poetry.[4] I would argue indeed that the inter-action between Tate and Stevens, during the war years in particular, was as acute as any Stevens had with another poet of recognized stature.[5] Stevens exchanged a copy of his *Notes toward a Supreme Fiction* for Tate's *Reason in Madness* (1941), a collection of essays he then read with care (*L* 393, 420). He saw, in manuscript, Tate's translation of *The Vigil of Venus* (*L* 460n). He read *The Winter Sea* (1944) closely after having followed the maga-zine publications of at least two poems that would go into the collection, "Jubilo" and "Seasons of the Soul" (*L* 461, 487, 488). The bibliographic facts of the exchange account for its fullness but not its intensity, for it was a relationship driven by disjunction between a personal mistrust on one hand and perceived but never quite articulated aesthetic and ideological affinity on the other; this disjunction itself seemed increasingly improper to Stevens at a time when common purpose was so strongly urged upon American intellectuals. At moments when the aesthetic and ideological af-finity was tested, the personal mistrust reared up most visibly. The severest of such tests came just as the new nationalists turned their attention and their ire toward the New Critics. The resulting battle for Stevens must be heard shot by shot: at points the nationalists pinned Stevens to Tate and the New Critics; for Stevens, at such times, Tate let on that he assumed that Stevens was indeed with them, while to others privately and at least once in print Tate suggested that Stevens was incapable of being with them; and all the while, Stevens was suggesting to Church that they were not to be trusted.

In 1939 Tate had come to Princeton as resident poet in the university's first Creative Arts Program. (He, in turn, brought Richard Blackmur there a year later; Stevens followed these developments and by 1943 could write Tate and know the letter would be shown to Blackmur as a matter of course.)[6] After leaving Princeton and returning to Monteagle, Tennessee, Tate carefully maintained his association with Church and continued to exchange books and letters with Stevens, soon in his capacity as the editor of the *Sewanee Review*. Stevens would publish six poems and one essay there, often as the result of a personal appeal.

Church's role as intermediary between the two poets, though it tended at points to distort their senses of each other, always at least saved the relationship from degenerating into hostile silence. Stevens was certain to tell Church of Tate that "there is a great deal to him" (*L* 401), but this was partly because Stevens knew that Church's assistance to Tate at Princeton was vital to both; and Tate was integral to the Church scene there. Fernand Auberjonois remembers Tate and Caroline Gordon as frequent dinner and swimming guests at Cleveland Lane.[7] When Tate returned to Princeton in 1943 to deliver one of the *Mesures* lectures, he stayed at the Churches' house for four days.[8] At the end of the war, looking back on his having become acquainted with Stevens through the Churches, Tate told Marianne Moore: "they've all been very kind to me."[9]

If Church, then, patron of a circle of intellectuals now dispersed and living (and writing) at risk, could summon something of a new circle at Princeton, it would certainly include Tate as a central figure whose skills in navigating the choppy waters of institutional politics were often evident, and whose prominent position in a critical group now enduring its own dispersal (though, of course, at no risk) to Baton Rouge, Monteagle, and Gambier was already legend. Stevens was at least excited for Church, whom he knew craved cultural centrality; Stevens himself had not belonged to anything that could even remotely be called a salon since the New York days with the Walter Arensberg crowd, and even then the company had been more casual than insightful, and not even at times congenial.[10] A less generous side of Stevens resisted Tate for his famous belonging, and occasionally this feeling extended to Church himself for being obsessed with the idea of a circle in exile. A big house and swimming pool in a college town do not a coterie make. Poets who were joiners were not poets in the purest possible sense, he felt; mistaking the edges for the center, they could not ultimately be themselves. Tate was not used to *this* sort of reaction to the work of his own well-defined group, most other peers having indicated to him that they rather envied his subscribing to so coherent a project (no matter what the project). Tate's and Stevens's mutual friend Blackmur had made one such declaration of envy, and this had come, not incidentally, in connection with Blackmur's effort to understand Stevens's poems.[11] Stevens's idea that on the contrary he should hold to a program entirely his own, that he would operate best in a circle of one, was his convenient way of explaining to himself no less than to others how and why he had come to Hartford and remained. If he wanted Princeton to be central for Church, he also toyed with his own sense of periphery, once inventing his relative distance and conceiving of Princeton as absorbed, suburblike, into the infinitely greater center of New York (*SM* 150). During his 1941 visit to Princeton to deliver his *Mesures* lecture, Stevens saw firsthand the skill with which Tate positioned himself in and at the university, and he must have seen that what Ransom described for Tate as "the Princeton version of the war between creative literature and scholarship" was already being waged.[12] Such facility with institutional wrangling, in combination with reviews he might have seen of Tate's anthology, *Princeton Verse Between Two Wars* (1942), emphasizing Princeton as the shifting scene of the "war" Ransom somewhat feared—even Tate's strong ally Robert Penn Warren decided that that book was a sign "of a tendency to bring the arts, as practiced, and not merely as a subject for scholarship, into closer contact with the academic world"[13]—caused Stevens to harbor like a grudge the belief that Tate was actually in his element in the Ivy League. By March 1942, indeed, Mary Colum, unhappy that "[t]his country at the present time has quite a few literary coteries"—there is no doubt that she was referring to Van Wyck Brooks's "Primary and Coterie Literature," as at least Cleanth Brooks realized—concluded that there was already enough of a "Princeton Group" to be so named. The problem, for Stevens, was that if he was pleased that Church could help establish a coterie recognized as such by the likes of Mary Colum, he was not so sanguine about being subsumed under such a heading himself—as he was, in fact, in Colum's summary. She was reviewing the Princeton book Tate edited, sponsored by Princeton's Creative Arts Program, funded by Church in Princeton, published by the Princeton University Press, and containing Stevens's Princeton lecture, "The Noble Rider."[14] Her piece only expedited the division of the camps into discrete halves, throwing Stevens headlong into one, just as Cleanth Brooks, writing to Tate, threw *her* in with "MacLeish-V.W. Brooks and Co."—along with all those who fired at the formalists merely in "defend[ing] their special interests."[15] It galled Stevens, I think, to have to learn from the *New York Times* that he played even a minor role in endorsing the ideas he would soon criticize in Tate. Colum put Stevens with Tate under the general heading of "the Princeton Group" that ought to "get out of the studies and away from the campuses and sit up nights discussing their ideas."[16] If Stevens knew how poorly this characterized him, he also sensed that the desire for acceptance and security ran deep in Tate. Later, when Tate left for the University of Minnesota, a distant region of academia Stevens could hardly imagine for a southerner so apparently attached to the South, he wrote Church: "Minnesota ... is neither north nor south. It is just Minnesota. And Allen may realize there that the worlds in which his amours and phobias have nourished themselves up to now no longer surround him" (*L* 730).

To read Tate's critical essays and poems in the context of the various critical disputes then publicly raging is to be aware of the manner in which he nourished his phobias as a shrewd strategy for "encouraging others ... to do their best," as Donald Stauffer once kindly put it. Stevens perhaps had special insight into Tate's "giving full rein to his prejudices and enthusiasms,"[17] since nourishing phobias—at least feeling that he had insulted someone when he probably had not—was an aspect of Stevens's own anxious public bearing. After the April 1941 visit to Princeton, letters between Church and Stevens ceased for some nine months, with Stevens fearing that he "must have done something in Princeton ... and that you had x-ed me out." He confessed: "I cannot tell you how humiliated I was by the thought." One possible source of "the trouble" at Princeton, Stevens speculated, was his having asked Caroline Gordon ("Mrs. Tate") to change places with him at the Churches' dinner table in order that he might converse more conveniently with someone else (*L* 400); not only did Tate notice Stevens being "abysmally rude" to Gordon, but he remembered the offense always.[18] Tate evidently felt that Stevens's social awkwardness arose from intellectual timidity. How could he possibly be a poet of ideas that mattered when, as Tate later recalled, "he never wrote at length about his ideas to any of his peers," choosing instead people like the "shallow young Cuban, [Rodríguez] Feo"?[19] The way in which the literary world had come to Stevens while Stevens barely moved outward to that world perfectly demonstrated what was wrong with the poetic mode Americans respected: Stevens never, it seemed, took sides, nor a single step toward sides others passionately took. It was not merely, as Tate once confessed to Stevens, that "I envy your gift of putting into verse the immediate, 'speculative' moment."[20] Nor that in Stevens's best poems Tate saw what he himself could not achieve; of "Sunday Morning" he wrote, "I knew then that what you were doing was not for me: I could never reach it."[21] Nor even that when Stevens hit the mark, as he did in two of the ten sections of "Things of August," it could cause Tate to admit that he was "moved" by Stevens's verse and that it forced him to look "into my own special limitations." For the entire project of modern American poetry seemed at risk, symbolically, if even the affinities between Allen Tate and Wallace Stevens could never be realized or acted upon: Tate identified the second and third sections of Stevens's "Things of August" as direct causes for "the occasion of stating certain differences from the work of an older contemporary which I admire and have learned from."[22] Tate's admiration for the second section may have been, in part, a cunning way of pointing out that he felt similarly about his own best lines: Tate evidently sensed that Stevens was borrowing from, and then contradicting, his own "Seasons of the Soul" (1944). In part ii of that wartime poem, entitled "Autumn," Tate wrote:

> It had an autumn smell
> And that was how I knew
> That I was down a well:
> I was no longer young.[23]

In his own poem about autumnal premonitions, Stevens was writing what seemed to be a direct reply:

> Break through.
> Have liberty *not* as the air within a grave
>
> Or down a well. Breathe freedom. . . .
>
> (*CP* 490)

In 1975 Donald Stanford pointed out to Tate that the very poem he told Stevens he admired was one in which "Stevens echoed your famous phrase concerning the well from 'Seasons of the Soul' " and agreed that that was what had caught Tate's attention and inspired the letter about the differences between them.[24] If "Things of August" contained a reply to "Seasons of the Soul," the difference was plain. Tate had been caught in a moment of intense confession—later: "I will leave this house, I said"; then: "I saw my downcast mother / Clad in her street-clothes, / . . . Who had no look or voice"[25]—and Stevens countered by suggesting that *Tate*, of all poets, ought to "Break through" from the past that seemed to bind him, that he should seek and "Have liberty" and disdain images such as the deep well of autumn: fall, at least in this Stevens poem (not in others), was a means by which the poet looks forward, not back. Tate responded to Stanford's suggestion of Stevens's borrowing by insisting that his concept of angelism was not in any way dependent on Stevens, citing Jacques Maritain to prove it; Tate added, "Stevens's Angelism I found very boring."[26]

Tate also discovered himself in the third section of Stevens's "Things of August": *he*, it seemed, was the poet who

> in this intelligence
> Mistakes [desire] for a world of objects,
> Which, being green and blue, appease him,
>
> . . . .
>
> According to his thought, in the Mediterranean
> Of the quiet of the middle of the night,
> With the broken statues standing on the shore.
>
> (*CP* 491)

Could this have been Stevens's belated observation on the Allen Tate of the Alcestis book, *The Mediterranean & Other Poems*, the poet obsessed with putting together the broken bits of intellectual classicism found lying about the modern romantic scape, the poet of "To the Lacedemonians" or "To the Romantic Traditionalists"? If so, the difference between them—the issue Tate's confessional letter raised—was raised in the poem. The "certain differences" between Stevens and Tate, then, were characterized by the difference between "High poetry and low: /Experience in perihelion / Or in the penumbra of summer night." One of these positions produced, in an unnamed poet (Stevens's speakers' often self-referential "he"), "The solemn sentences, / Like interior intonations, / The speech of truth in its true solitude" (*CP* 490). So Tate, reading himself into Stevens's displaced third person, I think, replied in kind—in the low poetry, as it were, of a confessional letter, with his own "interior intonations" that Stevens would happen to overhear. Tate knew he was not in any meaningful sense a "low" poet, of course; he knew that Stevens knew the avowal to be unique. If Stevens truly felt that there was not "enough of the peasant in Tate" (*L* 461), he was only revealing his own anxieties about "closing off the view" of reality, as Richard Eberhart would put it much later. The main problem was not really, then, the "differences" between them, expressed here or earlier, for relative to the other wartime poets these two seemed always on the same side of *that* distinction, each bespeaking a "speech of truth," unaffected by fads of engagement—"High poetry" surely. Rather, Tate would feel in the first place compelled to make such a devastating admission to Stevens of his own limitations exactly as Stevens was incapable of responding in kind. Notwithstanding their disagreements of the war years, Tate's letter must have been a difficult one to write, a rare admission from a poet with a rival's keen sense, whose melancholy only infrequently pierced tremendous pride. He wrote Stevens that he was "much moved" by the new poems he had read, admitted his career-long admiration for "Sunday Morning" and confessed his own poetic weaknesses. He then apologized for expressing the "profound insight" Stevens had caused in him, and concluded by saying of this avowal that it "is my message to myself. The man who breathes the air of the well cannot breathe purer air unless it be the air of revelation." He had learned from Stevens nothing less than "a new way of putting a dilemma of our time—and it may be *the* dilemma."[27] Stevens's reply to this sentimental disclosure was immediate. But, to Tate, it was so extremely unresponsive as to seem intended as an insult. For one thing, Stevens remade the old sore point about Tate's academic ties and the presumption, mistakenly sustained by Stevens, that Tate had always been happiest as a Princeton man:

> When I got back from New York yesterday after spending several days there, I found your most welcome letter. As it happens, we had spoken of you and someone told me that you had apparently settled down in Princeton and had found a home there, which must mean a great deal to you. I know that when I come back from even a day or two in New York home regales me. To crawl into my own bed with all the windows open and to be able to lie there in the really sharp cold of this time of year is an experience that means far more than sleeping in one of the nickel-plated ovens that they give you in New York, even though it has ten lamps.

Stevens went on to say that he had attended a fancy dinner at his genealogy club, stopped in at F.A.O. Schwartz to order four or five items from the catalogue, describing the purchase of toys in the most impersonal diction possible ("one buys toys for a grandson nowadays"), and, "to top it all off, I had my hair cut at the Pierre" (*L* 658). Tate sometimes scribbled his reactions to letters he received; on the bottom of this one he wrote, "This is like a letter from an advertising man who doesn't want to lose good will but who can't bring himself to discuss the point at issue. If Stevens has ever done a generous thing, I never heard of it."[28] If confession, an obvious gesture of personal reconciliation and, what's more, a demonstration of poetic influence, was to be met by a trivial tale of elite clubs, fancy toys, and expensive barbers, then it was just as well that the confessor sniped back in private.

Other strategies fared a little better. Once, after "a very bright person used the Stevens stick to beat the Tate dog, by saying that my language is thin where yours is rich," Tate wrote Stevens with new high hopes that they would begin to discuss their poetic differences. This letter expresses something further of Tate's envy for Stevens's apparent obliviousness to such issues. "Your language sometimes conceals the 'subject,'" Tate wrote, "while my subject strangles the language." Finally, however, he told Stevens they should avoid comparisons "between poets who have a very few 'resemblances' in common," citing the key term of Stevens's "Three Academic Pieces," which he had just received.[29] While in this last remark Tate denied the value of the comparison, as he should never have taken the distinction of "High poetry and low" as implicating him, still he was smarting from being beaten (especially in reviews) with the Stevens stick and felt he deserved reply. Thirty years later he still remembered his gesture: he recalled for Ashley Brown "a letter I wrote Stevens about certain philosophical differences between us. He did not deign to answer it."[30]

This last dispute confirms the point that the disagreements between the two poets went far beyond the erratically personal into the systematically poetic, for there was something about Stevens's poetry that also made him seem personally incapable of responding to threats that challenged his ideas about poetry. Certainly this is indicated by Tate's astute remark about Stevens's language obscuring the subject and Tate's own subject "strangling" the language. A literary-political vocabulary that would be used to describe the basic differences between Tate and Stevens fully developed in the years of American involvement in the war, for this was the period in which the principles and a polemical reorganization of the New Critics were apparent to Stevens in direct relation to his own developing attitudes about the aspect of American culture that made it right for it to be asserted abroad. The fact that Stevens enjoyed teasing and even baiting the New Critics reveals an underlying skepticism about the practical implications of their positions. If he goaded Tate for subscribing contentedly to the Princeton world while Tate was at Princeton, he also joked about why anyone would want the isolation of the rural South when the world of modern poetry was obviously located elsewhere, such as indeed back at Princeton. Sending Tate his copy of *Notes toward a Supreme Fiction*, Stevens quipped: "this is not the sort of thing that you are likely to pick up at the railroad station in Monteagle" (L 427). He felt Tate's group to be "too sequestered," Cleanth Brooks remembers, "too much living in the past," that they "were not quite up to the present issues of the present day."[31] And he found himself, when the cocktails were either "too good or too many," confronting at a Yale party a fellow whom he soon misremembered as having been Brooks: "I got talking to Brooks," he wrote to Tate afterward, "about the fact that Louisiana was not a part of the United States at the time of the Revolution, etc."—more goading about the New Critics' alleged lack of patriotism (L 634). That Brooks had to set the record straight years later for Peter Brazeau—in fact, he said, "It was *Allen Tate*, among others, to whom he said something"—reveals the extent of Stevens's willingness to repress the genuine antagonism Tate embodied, once the alcoholic haze that had momentarily freed him cleared.[32] Composing a note in honor of Ransom's seventy-fifth birthday, a piece eventually published under the apparently definitive title "John Crowe Ransom: Tennessean,"[33] Stevens initially believed Ransom's home state was *Kentucky*; he had first sent the piece to Tate accordingly mistitled. Tate shot back: "It was I, not Ransom, who got his start in Kentucky."[34] But Stevens felt he knew enough about the former agrarians to be able to characterize them theoretically, distinctions more important than the borders separating Border States: as poets these men similarly abstracted the emotional value from even their most emotional subjects, and so his understanding of the relation between their regional origins, their hatred of modern American romanticism, and their political reaction in wartime was not as unknowing as might be suggested by the substitution of Kentucky for Tennessee or Brooks for Tate. His brief analysis of the primness of "The Bells of John Whiteside's Daughter"—"What is it that Mr. Ransom feels at the sight of [her], dead, except the same quizzicality that he felt at the sight of her alive?"—indicates significant insight into his distinction from them as a group.[35] And so I want to know as precisely as possible where Stevens got the charge of anti-emotion and abstraction, for it is at least clear that he heard it first in wartime. Indeed it was the basis of the general nationalist assault on the Ransom-Tate group, a countercharge made against formalist poetics in a time of war that Stevens was to deem increasingly valid, not so much again because he reacted favorably to the new nationalists who mounted the charge, but because he saw in Tate's hatred of democratic wartime politics the implications of his own poetic isolationism of 1939 to 1941. The claim Stevens would knowingly reproduce was, specifically, that the New Critics were principal among writers and scholars who were going to lose the things they loved because of the purity of their detachment, their lack of engagement with the culture of the United States as a unity—in short, the new nationalist claim.

Not many months after MacLeish's opening shot in the intellectual war about the actual war, some critics loosely allied with MacLeish turned the attack toward the Ransom-Tate group explicitly:[36] those poets, it was now decided, had never sufficiently qualified their contempt for the expectation that poetry will work in the service of a national program, even—especially—this overwhelmingly popular one. And if the new nationalists and their allies had known something of Tate's unpublished thoughts about the war, he would have been an even easier target. One can only imagine how MacLeish, with his loathing of defeatism, would have responded to Tate's private comment (in a letter to John Peale Bishop), "I am afraid now you are right: the Germans will win." Defeatism indeed! (Imagine, please, that MacLeish's response to the defeatism of Stevens's *published* "Extracts from Addresses to the Academy of Fine Ideas" of 1940 would have been hardly less severe: "Behold the men in helmets borne on steel, / Discolored, how they are going to defeat." Yet Stevens, with characteristic coyness, left the defeated ones unidentified; Tate, with characteristic daring, identified them exactly.) The Germans might not win, Tate had decided, but "the Allies will take so long to fight them off that we shall get into it, and I will go to gaol as an Isolationist, or worse." His isolationist logic, so much more explicit than Stevens's ever was, entailed his "strong sympathy for the Germans politically & economically, but not 'culturally'; the result is a perfect neutrality."[37] These statements, of course, were made before Pearl Harbor; Tate's dislike of American involvement would soften, and not merely to the extent that he staved off arrest.[38] What did not change, however, was his idea that American poetry itself must embody a discrete intellectual front, a resistance to the world at war *as a politically and aesthetically degenerated whole*, that it must defend its integrity against those nonmilitary intellectual warriors, these false poets who were really politicians, who would try to drag him to their side of the battle lines as they defined them. Nor would Tate's prediction change—a prediction based in part on what he saw in the patriotic responses of the American intellectuals like MacLeish—that what Stevens eventually told Tate was "the rising fury of the future" (*L* 483) would be led by mediocre "democratic" minds that will have used the crisis of the war to gain official status as democrats by attaching themselves to an unassailably popular cause. Judgments like that, overtly reactionary, reminded Tate of his and Stevens's ideological likeness, and only then fueled his desire for improved poetic relations with Stevens as well. The mediocre minds Tate feared did not foster democracy so much as they reinvented democratic tactics, what Dwight MacDonald maligned as *Kulturbolshewismus*, a totalitarianism effectively shielded by a democracy's ecstatic, self-protective rhetoric. Tate saw as MacDonald did—and earlier than MacDonald, it must be noted—that in order to fight totalitarians "we shall have to be like them; even if we won a war against them, they would still be the victors." He wrote: "If it comes to an issue between our sort of fascism *vs.* the German, I'm willing to fight; but for democracy, no."[39] This particular attitude was the one Tate allowed to emerge publicly, at some cost.[40] In his introduction to Robert Lowell's first collection, for instance, he hinted strongly of a nationalist conspiracy. After the war the "small public for poetry shall exclude all except the democratic poets."[41] The new nationalism, in his view, capitalized on cultural trends he had attacked consistently and articulately through the thirties—positivism, low mimeticism (or social realism), pragmatism, instrumentalism, collectivism (the extinction of "our moral natures in a group mind"), and, worst of all, "historicism." The last he sometimes saw as a form of liberal relativism, because it arose from an urge to contemporize the past to suit the purposes of the present.[42]

Stevens doubtless saw more than a little hypocrisy in Tate's rejoinder to the nationalists, for Tate was not himself without a few important official wartime connections and thus his own nationalist context—a point he was ready to admit even in the midst of his least generous description of the "vulgarity" and "confusion" caused by Van Wyck Brooks's "spy-picture conspiracy" theory of the coteries.[43] Serving the Library of Congress as consultant in poetry during 1943 and 1944—some wartime letters to Stevens came on government stationery—Tate issued a government publication, *Sixty American Poets, 1896–1944*, and wrote the introductory notes for each poet selected for the volume; Stevens was among them, accompanied by Tate's high praise.[44] With Bishop, in 1942, Tate edited an anthology called *American Harvest*, a book distributed by the Office of the Coordinator of Inter-American Affairs operating under the aegis of the Office for Emergency Management (OEM).

A notice in the *Catholic World* admiringly acknowledged the propaganda value of Tate's OEM work: Tate, it was observed, wrote "a special preface to aid Latin Americans in understanding this era of American writing."[45] Not surprisingly, however, many other reviewers criticized the Tate-Bishop anthology for not being overtly democratic enough. It was obvious to Tate where the now solidly interventionist literary left stood in relation to the new nationalism and why he, a known antinationalist, would have trouble with them. Louis Kronenberger's review of *American Harvest* in the *Nation* claimed that the selection was aesthetically exclusive and did not show sufficient interest in the kind of American writing "produced as a convulsive necessity of the *Zeitgeist*";[46] in other words, the book did not contain enough war poetry. The usual doubts about New Critical or agrarian exclusivity, then, became in this period even more ideologically focused than in the thirties, since the political orientation against formalism was now *official*, endorsed as patriotism and as "democracy" by an emerging cultural elite—Cowley and others who as radicals had been outsiders and now associated confidently with representatives of a public majority.[47] The anti-elitist view from this increasingly elite position saw Tate's selection, made at taxpayers' expense, to be "no more than a reflection of [Tate's and Bishop's] taste"[48]—a personal rather than a consensus (or "democratic") choice. (In these years, there were actually schemes for "democratic" anthology selections, involving a kind of popular election of the poets and poems to be included. Stevens was asked to serve on the editorial board of one such collection, along with MacLeish and others.)[49] The wide distribution of Tate's OEM book in Central and South America would only serve, the *Partisan* reviewer complained, as a false "missionary" for the "not . . . sufficiently rounded representation" of the "severely aesthetic" critics of Tate's and Bishop's camp "who see literature as art or nothing."[50] Reviewers who admired the book, like Joseph Warren Beach, were equally aware that it refused to admit any writing that did not pass the threshold "of technical performance at which art begins, . . . however interesting the subject-matter or ideology of the writer."[51] And it was precisely this nonideological test (which seemed to the book's detractors to be very much an ideological test) that caused the OWI writers to cry defeatism. Cowley's rejoinder was perhaps the bitterest of all: in work selected for the Tate-Bishop book, he said,

> Kay Boyle describes the fall of France; she makes it seem real and tragic, but very far away. Most of the other [included writers] are avoiding public issues; *have they been warned?* [Reading them,] one would never suspect that this country had . . . faced ten years of international crisis before being plunged into another war. One would think that Americans had no real problems except those of . . . poets trying to polish their verse and those of old men getting ready to die. (emphasis added)[52]

How far had Tate and Cowley come from the days, in the thirties, when *each* was deemed an extremist and Tate could disarmingly tell his opposite number, "all poets are automatically revolutionary."[53] Now just one of them was on the edge. Like Cowley's, Howard Mumford Jones's notice suggested that the real American subject was larger, more muscular, than the one Tate and Bishop offered as representative, and *Jones named Stevens* as indicative of the Tate-Bishop bias, lamenting that "the polished littlenesses of Mr. Wallace Stevens" would be "sent into the world with the blessing of the Office of Inter-American Affairs."[54] This statement was just mean enough to cause Tate to speculate privately that a real plot had been hatched, with the objective of forcing the U.S. government to withdraw its backing. It was in this context that Tate expressed his fear of the coming "strong movement in favor of bigness, Americanism, and 'democracy,' " of a new "hatred of the subtle and the intelligent," as he wrote angrily, "which is the way our totalitarianism will develop on the literary front. (See Alfred Kazin in the New Republic. Oct 19th.)"[55]

That issue of the *New Republic* must have been a painful one to read for Tate's allies, for it contained not just Kazin's "Criticism at the Poles," an excerpt from *On Native Grounds*,[56] but Cowley's scorching review. Much as Cowley and Kazin might disagree on other matters, they seemed made of whole nationalist cloth. Their criticisms were similarly motivated, Tate felt, having much less to do with the war than with the great challenge represented by the New Criticism. Certainly, to Tate as well as to Ransom, Kazin's attack on the New Criticism in the nativist *On Native Grounds* (1942), readable, authoritative, and well received, was part of the new liberal-totalitarian web—and here is where the web caught Stevens. If Stevens wanted to be extricated from the New Critical context, Kazin's excerpt in the *New Republic* did not help matters at all. For Kazin, Ransom's and Tate's "contempt for democratic society," the "cozy self-satisfaction of the[ir] esthetic cult," had given rise to a "post-ethical," supranational "technical art of extreme difficulty" like Stevens's, about whom Ransom made his "unforgettable remark" on a "calculated complexity" that made one "happy." Exactly as and because "[c]riticism had become expert at last," so was Wallace Stevens to be celebrated.[57] Kazin's work must itself be understood as a postideological attack on the "two groups of extremists" that had dominated thirties criticism (Marxists and agrarian formalists).[58] Its criticism of both movements marked the beginning of the end of ideology; as such, it induced some nonagrarians to come to the defense of their former detractors, such as MacDonald and Kenneth Burke, who now spoke out on the issues raised by what was by then ubiquitously called "the 'Brooks-MacLeish Thesis.' "[59] Delmore Schwartz, who could otherwise express doubts about Tate's acid style,[60] seemed willing to defend the American formalists specifically on the issues raised by Kazin. Schwartz wrote Ransom that the success of *On Native Grounds*, timed so conveniently with the war, "is a sign that it is part of the New Philistinism, which of course always grows up in times of crisis." Schwartz recognized that the nationalists' charge of political irresponsibility had everything to do with the fact that it was now "infamous" merely to write about the structure of a poem.[61]

Ransom chose the strategy of ignoring the new demands put on writers and editors to write and publish poetry as war effort, perhaps believing that this phase too would pass. The troubling aspect of Ransom's imperviousness would come to Stevens's attention in 1944 and get him started on the long work "Esthétique du Mal," his own poetics of wartime pain. Tate's tactic, less graceful than Ransom's, was to inscribe bold counterattacks into both poetry and criticism; in fact the difference between Ransom and Tate in wartime was the difference between a political view deeming itself to be withdrawn from politics and an overtly political hatred of politics; thus Ransom was less well suited than Tate to respond to criticisms like Kazin's, itself rationalizing a new nonpolitical center that thought itself to be left.[62] Tate had a way of drawing others on his side into the controversies; when, for instance, the Cummington Press published Tate's book *The Winter Sea* in 1944, Cleanth Brooks was on hand to point out explicitly in his review that "this is war verse that will hardly please Van Wyck Brooks." In these poems, Tate satirically "pays his respects to Van Wyck Brooks and the 'new nationalists' who 'give the yawp barbaric / Of piety and pelf.' " Tate was responding, insisted Cleanth Brooks, to "[t]he new attack on form" and "the fashionable glorification of formless bigness," and his reply in verse should be "required reading for some of our literary Pharisees who have been recently congratulating themselves on their failure to have a 'failure of nerve.' "[63]

If Ransom himself could not so easily be drawn into the fight, others would use him in the effort. Burke noticed how, in proposing "a kind of Separationist aesthetic," Ransom's The New Criticism adroitly disarmed the opposition's vocabulary: "democracy" and "unity," new-nationalist by-words, were especially vulnerable to formalist infiltration. Ransom, Burke saw, boldly likened the poem itself to a democratic organization that, in Burke's paraphrase, "gives a distinctive measure of local autonomy to the details, or 'texture' of the work." Prose, on the other hand, is "totalitarian" because it subordinates texture to the demands of the central plan. This could not have been politically shrewder, Burke noticed with an admiration he reserved for the ideologically astute.[64] In Tate's hands, the New Critical "unitary effect" was to be figured, tantalizingly, in the political trope of an embattled but attractively "neutral" center fending off rights and lefts: he explained how a "poetry of tension" established the unitary effect, demanding "not poetry of the extremes, but poetry of the center"— this explicitly in the context of his rejection of Edna Millay's leftist "mass language" used in the defense of Sacco and Vanzetti. "Unity" was vitally centrist, nonpartisan, even when the claim of unity helped Tate take his stand on the right.[65] It was as if the poetic isolationists—MacLeish's hated defeatists—were now claiming to have reached a nonaligned center, suggesting that the critical method for any decent democracy-loving American was in fact the one attending decisively to the poem. Burke plainly saw how "like most aestheticians in our present economy" Ransom "treats the aesthetic and the practical as opposites" and could only commend the implication of Ransom's figurative use of democracy, for here was the analysis of the poem itself, the New Critical keynote, functioning ideologically in the manner of purest democracy, while prose writers (read: "democratic" "social commentators" like MacLeish, urging the use of "mass language") engaged in a gussied-up absolutism.[66] A similarly brilliant New Critical ploy was to take back from the new nationalists a term they habitually used to criticize doom-saying, the now-politicized word "unity," which generated connotations of the home front—unity as opposed not to disunity so much as to disloyalty. Tate's essay "Liberalism and Tradition," collected into Reason in Madness (where Stevens read it), had reversed the charge in advance of MacLeish's famous articulation of it. Liberals, positivists, and historicists were the ones engendering disunity, while the Ransom-Tate group *had always been* the ones calling for unity. So "unity," the term now common to both camps though created out of very different elements, might serve as a basis for a compact between them. At the 1941 English Institute, held at Columbia, old historicists and New Critics assembled to argue over the significance of a single poem by Wordsworth; but the historicists on that occasion, Cleanth Brooks told Tate, "didn't care to fight,"[67] and the critic sent by Ransom[68] to summarize the results of the conference for the readers of the *Kenyon Review*, Donald Stauffer, reported the basis of agreement: each side readily agreed that "[a] great work of art possesses unity,"[69] even though Brooks, in his own view, was the only speaker who "actually tried to deal with the poem throughout as a poem."[70] And Stauffer, despite his claim that the two sides finally stood on common ground, could not resist paraphrasing points made at the conference from the point of view of the antinationalists, and provided a fine example of the sort of war metaphor that justifiably incensed the interventionists. For here the tendency of Tate and Ransom to invert nationalist terms, and so create an effective rejoinder, was taken to an unsightly extreme. "[I]nsofar as it is possible," Stauffer observed, "the standards for judgment should be found in the poem itself; *they should not be alien invaders, attempting to set up a New Order in an established land*" (emphasis added).[71] Spiriting away "unity" and "democracy" from the already tenuous historicist-nationalist alliance was harmless enough as a theoretical and polemical stratagem; calling *prose* itself "totalitarian," as Ransom did, was perhaps no more provocative; even labeling a "new attack on form" a "New Philistinism" was tolerable if imprecise. But the suggestion that literary critics who allowed historical conditions, such as a world war, to "invade" the judgment of a poem were setting up a "New Order"—the "New Order" could be nothing but a reference to Pétain's arrangement of the Nazi occupation of cultural as well as diplomatic France—only demonstrates how the fight between literary isolationists and nationalists could be bitter indeed. It was a bitterness Stevens would begin to taste.

Of course Tate, sharpest in his political satires, could himself be very rough on his nationalist opponents. His "Ode to Our Young Pro-Consuls of the Air," a poem Stevens saw, recounts the history of the controversy, first by mocking the new-nationalist complaint:

> In this bad time no part
> The poet took, nor chance:
>   He studied Swift and Donne,
>   Ignored the Hun,
> While with faint heart
> Proust caused the fall of France.

To the Brooks-MacLeish group, the failure of the modernists to respond to the rise of fascism "caused the fall of France." (Proust had been
among Brooks's examples.) Tate satirizes those who might have raised the
cry of premature anti-antifascism, a ridiculous, anachronistic charge. Then
when the Japanese attacked Pearl Harbor,

> It was defeat, or near it!
> Yet all that feeble time
>   Brave Brooks and lithe MacLeish
>   Had sworn to thresh
> Our flagging spirit
> With literature made Prime!
>
> Cow Creek and Bright Bear Wallow,
> Nursing the *blague* that dulls
>   Spirits grown Eliotic,
>   Now patriotic
> Are: we follow
> *The Irresponsibles!*

The bitter antiwar sentiment of the poem is not just isolationist but
simultaneously anti-imperialist; it is made clearest in relation to this invective against the new nationalists: "Young men, Americans! / You go to
win the world / With zeal pro-consular . . . / You partisans / Of liberty
unfurled!" Tate was actually asserting here that the accelerating, unchal-
lenged American commitment to "total war," aided and abetted by our
intellectual nationalists, would contribute to, not alleviate, the destruction
of civilization; worse, it would merely supplant a new imperialism for the
old—a forceful insight that the postwar Stevens, pointing to much the
same risk (as we will see in the second half of this book), might seem to
have derived only from the left. In Stevens's wartime response to Tate we
see the makings of a willful American displacement of domestic anxieties,
a description without place, as a defense against a criticism made from a
then-cogent right to an amassing, incoherent center that had already absorbed much of the left. In the last two stanzas of his antiwar ode Tate
imagines an American bombing mission in the following way, powerful in
its perception of an American imperial urge and resolutely braving accusations of treason: "Take off, O gentle youth" and, locating on "the Tibetan
plain / A limping caravan, / Dive, and exterminate / The Lama, late /
Survival of old pain. / Go kill the dying swan!"[72] What was so extraordinary
about this poem (and, likewise, the times that coerced it into being), with
its relentless elitist mockery of the terms under which the American involvement in the war was justified by intellectuals associating with a war-
minded political state, was that it appeared in the third of Oscar Williams's

wartime anthologies, *New Poems 1943*, a collection that Williams made a point of introducing as *designed to promote war poetry*. By this Williams obviously meant (and participating poets understood him to mean) poems generally or specifically *supporting* American entry; Williams's anthology selections, as Cowley later noted, were designed to reveal a "fundamental *agreement* about this war" (emphasis added).[73] Tate's "Ode" *was* war poetry, of course, but hardly the sort Williams expected and Cowley observed. Williams proudly wrote of his 1943 annual that "[i]t is the current work of poets who have intensely felt the fact of war."[74] Tate certainly felt his position "intensely," but the ode given Williams was not "doing its bit" in the least. Yet, Williams claimed, "Each poem included here is a 'war' poem, doing its bit . . . in the struggle towards the only victory worth having."[75] It can only have nourished Tate's phobias to find that critics were measuring Stevens's war-poem set piece, "How Red the Rose That Is the Soldier's Wound," against his own "Ode" by standards invented in Williams's anthologies: the leftist poet Harry Roskolenko deemed Stevens's war work so good that it "should make Mr. Tate's *Ode* pass away, as if into air."[76]

Long before Roskolenko paired them as befitting Williams's aims, Stevens is sure to have seen Tate's verse attack on the new nationalists in the context of the wartime anthology, for he himself figured prominently in *New Poems 1943*—with *five* poems. Not only did Oscar Williams choose to print "Chocorua to Its Neighbor," with its tactic of reconciling romanticism and modernism on one hand and wartime nationalism on the other, and "Dutch Graves in Bucks County," a poem that shows an even greater commitment to total war, but the anthologist also did not leave it to his readers to discern Stevens's development as a nationalist. To support his prefatory thesis that the poetry of 1943 must have done "its bit" to find its way into his book, Williams quoted Stevens's note on the poetry of war from *Parts of a World*. Thus the Stevens who appeared alongside Tate in Williams's book says: "In the presence of the violent reality of war, consciousness takes the place of the imagination." And: during this war there will be "a consciousness of fact . . . on such a scale that the mere consciousness of it affects the scale of one's thinking and constitutes a *participating* in the heroic" (emphasis added).[77]

POETRY AND THE ACTUAL WORLD

[T]he world of the 20th Century, if it is to come to
life in any nobility of health and vigor, must be to
a significant degree an American Century.
        —*Henry Luce, "The American Century,"*
                February 1941

There is no doubt some connection between
Grimm's law and the latest patriotic homily by Mr.
Henry Luce, but I do not know who could take the
responsibility for it.
        —*Allen Tate, in the* Partisan Review,
                Spring 1941

[H]e is . . . given to pursuing the enemy, thus tending not to let the enemy's thoughts develop.
        —*Kenneth Burke on Tate in 1942*

[P]oetry is always a matter of groups, cliques,
rival sets.
        —*Stevens (WSR 127)*

Whatever doubts about Tate's antinationalism were incited in Stevens by
such semi-accidental contexts as Oscar Williams supplied him, he also
began to hear from people whom he implicitly trusted on the issue—
Henry Church, for instance, who was much closer to Tate's situation than
he. After all, Church had written Tate several years before the publication
of the antinationalist ode, chiding Tate a little, trying to bring him around
to moderation: "Are you not a little hard on [Van Wyck] Brooks?"[1] It is
possible that Stevens might not have responded to the new nationalism at
all had Tate not hit upon Church as a potential donor to the New Critics'
wartime projects.

As Church was vaguely casting about for ways in which he could spend
his money to continue the work of *Mesures* and somehow contribute to the
effort to save the arts, Tate formed a small committee (Willard Thorp, a
MacLeish sympathizer but also a Princeton ally of Tate, was a member).
The committee took the idea for Church to their academic dean, Christian
Gauss. But once the Church money began to show itself, Tate began to
think in much larger terms. He did not know that Church had been writing
to Stevens about the idea of an endowment for many months already, and
that Stevens had constructed serious and lengthy replies. Stevens's letters

to Church of May 28, August 23, October 11, and October 15, 1940, especially the last with its elaborate "Memorandum" toward a Henry Church
Chair of Poetry, served as the broad basis for the project Church finally
undertook at Princeton. And it provided the impetus for the next major
poetic undertaking ("Notes toward a Supreme Fiction").[2]

Ever the shrewd businessman, skilled at putting off a sales pitch, Stevens
did not take long in realizing that Tate was drawing the bottom line for
Church. Among the casualties of Pearl Harbor was the college allocation
to Ransom's *Kenyon Review*. A month after the entry of the United States
into the war, Ransom wrote Tate, one of *Kenyon*'s advisory editors, suggesting that "[t]he crisis is not merely military, it's total, and it affects the
K.R. In other words, we will have to go on a reduced budget." Ransom's
scheme to keep the *Kenyon Review* from going under during the war crisis
was to approach "the boys" (Robert Penn Warren and Cleanth Brooks) at
the imminently collapsing *Southern Review* and ask them to "please come
in and 'merge' with the Kenyon Review"; at the same time Ransom knew
they would also need the support of "outside angels," but he could think
then of "no real prospects."[3] Tate wrote Ransom and suggested that this
might be just the sort of thing to enable the wealthy Church to keep his
hand in the world of letters and channel "the boys" some much-needed
money at the same time.[4] The idea, as it developed, was, in Ransom's
words, "a somewhat larger *Kenyon-Review–Southern-Review* partially subsi-
dized by Church." Ransom and Tate would offer Church "a literary stake,"
a "department of FOREIGN LETTERS or FOREIGN LITERATURE in each number." Church could thus continue the work of *Mesures* and contribute to an
important American journal at the same time.[5] Ransom was quite clear
about the extent to which Church's literary interests were of inherent significance; the *Mesures* writers would get "[m]ore space if he [Church] can
put in some money," Ransom added frankly in the margin of a letter to
Tate.[6]

American entry into the war only intensified Ransom's and Tate's desire
to convince Church to make a donation; the idea had actually come up a
year earlier, but now they decided to bear down. By March 1942 Ransom
was writing Brooks and Penn Warren in Baton Rouge that "[w]ith Church
as a best prospect I think the chances [of the merger] are very good."[7]
Meantime, at Princeton, as Fernand Auberjonois recalls, "Tate was court-
ing the Churches for possible contributions.... The whole southern
route was very much waiting for Church money. Stevens felt that they
were on the make."[8] Church had informed Stevens of Tate's approaches,
and Stevens's letter in reply betrays a real sense of anger at the New Critics
for trying to exploit Church's situation. Moreover, it was only by defending Church against Tate and Ransom that Stevens became aware of the
irony of the New Critics' position on how American poetry ought to re-

spond to the war. He was particularly upset by the thought that *Mesures*, of all the little magazines, would be absorbed into the *Kenyon*. He wrote:

> What you say about the estimate of the cost of printing an American MESURES surprises me. Yet you speak of having to make some concessions. . . . For one thing (since you ask me to comment) I cannot imagine you as content to share the pages of the KENYON REVIEW. This seems to me to be very much as if Ransom was giving you a chance to wear his old clothes in order to keep himself going. (*L* 365)

Church and Stevens had been working on the endowment of the poetry chair and the broad legal terms of Church's will (the details were left to Stevens's old friend Ned Bechtel). Church trusted Stevens's advice generally, and seems to have followed it here as well. He wrote a note to Tate: "The word sinecure is a stranger to my life and never was a part of my vocabulary. You misinterpreted my thoughts."[9] Church did make several sizable donations ($500 in the summer of 1942[10] and the same amount in the spring of 1943).[11] But he did not underwrite the *Kenyon* plan to the degree that Tate and Ransom had originally hoped (they wanted $2500 immediately[12] and more later). After making the 1943 donation, Church complained again to Stevens: Ransom "wants more," he reported. "It seems strange to me," he added, "the way a rich man is exploited over here."[13]

Church confessed to Stevens that he had given money to Ransom despite his opinion that *Kenyon* was "a dusty, musty tabernacle."[14] He would have been sadder still to know how Ransom felt about him personally: while telling Tate that Church was "our big shot contributor," he reported, "Church asked me to stay with him, and that might be a good policy, though not so much to my taste."[15] But Church knew something was amiss. "I am known through-out the U.S.A.," he lamented, "as the number one litterary [*sic*] poire. I am ashamed."[16] It is possible that Church had heard the news that *Kenyon* would not go ahead with plans to absorb the *Southern Review* despite Ransom's continued appeals to him *explicitly based on this plan*. There was no further mention of the *Mesures* section of each issue, as Ransom originally promised Church through Tate, even after Church's donations. Ransom and Tate would not have leaked Church the truth: "Mr. Church . . . is one I'll be careful not to tell about our not having an official merger."[17]

Stevens's sharp response to Church's cry of exploitation expressed the point of all his advice to Church about how to confront the causes of *Mesures*'s premature death: if France is the matrix of *Mesures*, then Church's money should be aimed as directly as possible at the situation in France, or should be used to create a world to reproduce the conditions that had made him happy before the war. Ransom's journal had nothing to do with such an effort. "Your experience with Ransom is the common experience," Stevens wrote.

> The trouble with all this is that people never let go. Moreover, they don't realize that a man who is interested at all is likely to be interested in things of his own choice. But the panhandlers make no allowance. In any case, I don't think THE KENYON REVIEW of great value, any more than anyone could possibly think Ransom a great spirit. There are other things that I should much rather help. (*L* 450–51)

Consider, in this context, Stevens's Princeton lecture: "The Noble Rider" resulted from a conscious decision to overcome the usual antipathy toward presenting a public self; Stevens made his appearance, in other words, for the sake of showing moral support for the besieged *Mesures* group, for the sake, generally, of the France Church was trying to re-create in Princeton—even if the lecture itself could not manage to move resistance beyond evasion. The evidence suggests that after giving his own Princeton talk Stevens followed the rest of the series as closely as he could from Hartford; as we have seen, he continued to offer Church advice as to new lecturers who might be invited. All the speakers seemed to understand that their task was to talk about poetry in the broadest possible sense. Stevens's memorandum and related letters supplied the basis for this definition. By "poetry" both Stevens and the *Mesures* lectures meant more than poems; in outlining his ideas for the poetry chair, Stevens had been writing as a legal advisor but also as someone keen to have Church's fortune support just the right project: "It would be possible for you to make no provision whatever with respect to a Poetry Chair in your will, but to establish such a Chair in your lifetime. Or you could work with the idea and then add a codicil to your will. For my own part, I think that the prudent thing to do would be to try to give form to the scope and function of such a Chair before spending any money on it" (*L* 376). Stevens went further, then, offering his guidance as to the function of the Henry Church chair, in the Memorandum attached to the letter just quoted:

> One does not intend a literary course, except as the theory of poetry is a part of the theory of literature. The intention is not to read poetry from archaic to contemporary; nor is the intention to teach the writing of poetry. And, by way of a final negation, the intention is not to foster a cult.
>
> What is intended is to study the theory of poetry in relation to what poetry has been and in relation to what it ought to be. Its literature is a part of it, and only a part of it. For this purpose, poetry means *not the language of poetry* but the thing itself, wherever it may be found. It does not mean verse any more than philosophy means prose. The subject-matter of poetry is the thing to be ascertained. . . .

[I]f it is objected that this is carrying humanism to a point beyond which it ought to be carried in time of so much socialistic agitation, the answer must be that humanism is one thing and socialism is another, and that the mere act of distinguishing between the two should be helpful to preserve humanism and possibly to benefit socialism.

The fundamental objection is that this would be a course in illusion. (*L* 377–78)

So the *Mesures* lectures should be theoretically sophisticated and yet speak at the same time to the problem not only of reality but of "extraordinary actuality," indeed to the point of benefiting socialism. Perhaps more important, the program was *not* to be about "the language of poetry," a "negation" that seems to have provided Stevens a way of saying that it ought not to give a platform for the kind of linguistic analysis Ransom or I. A. Richards would offer. The admonition against "the language of poetry" should have been explicit enough to steer Church clear of "foster[ing] a cult" of *this* kind—a group, clique, or rival set that institutionalized academic courses in illusion, mere surveys from "archaic to contemporary." But this warning was not in fact sufficient: if Stevens wanted Church to keep the likes of Richards and Ransom out, he perhaps ought to have named names.

When Church—or, more probably, his Princeton committee, acting largely without him[18]—put together the final program, the invited lecturers were told of a broad theme they should follow, a new one annually, and presented with an overall picture of the exiled *Mesures*.[19] This picture was based on Stevens's initial notes, and was plain enough to encourage some of the *Mesures* invitees to address issues raised by the war. One such lecture was Kenneth Burke's in the 1942 series. It generously satisfied Stevens's and Church's goals for *Mesures* in wartime America; it was truly an occasional talk, even while it obviously had been mined from Burke's then-current work on his "Grammars." It surely helped bring the 1942 lectures in line with the intellectual response to the contemporary crisis. So did another of the 1942 lecturers, Maxwell Anderson, "a playwright who has a play on Broadway, now, about the Nazis," as Church informed Stevens.[20] Stevens had gone to New York to see Anderson's *High Tor* at the Martin Beck Theatre a few years earlier, when Anderson's play generally followed the line of the literary liberal-left, as Stevens understood;[21] in 1941 the FBI opened its file on Anderson because of just this sort of thing, equating Anderson's dramas that functioned "as a counterattack against foreign propaganda in the United States" with " 'red' plays designed to encourage radicalism."[22] Even if he knew of Anderson's current political work, *Candle in the Wind*, only what reviews in the *New Yorker* and the *Nation* could have told him—that the action entailed an escape from a Nazi concentration

camp and that Anderson was "as successful as anyone else has been in trying to expose the chill horror of the Nazi philosophy"[23]—Stevens would
have had a new sense that Anderson's invitation to Princeton, like Burke's,
was at least a temporary reprieve from the formalist context of the 1941
lectures.[24]

Burke, for his part, made quite clear his own interest in the conjunction
of theory and the world: "Poetry," he told his audience, is "a kind of *action.*" The war, he said, has taught us a great deal already about the insuffi-
ciencies of the categorical separation of "poetry" and "rhetoric." Yet rhetoric in poetry induced American people to act when they needed to act; in
this Burke sounded much like MacLeish, and in fact in "The Tactics of
Motivation," a year later, he would sound *very much* like MacLeish—an
internationalist, an optimist about liberal education, a critic of the moral
dissipation that fostered isolationism.[25] Insofar as we will learn to reinte-
grate rhetoric and poetry in analyses of each, Burke confidently asserted at
Princeton, we can shed the prewar tendency to "distrust rhetoric *per se,*"
and we can outgrow that knee-jerk (he meant anti-Marxist) tendency. Only
then will we find our poetic expressions suited to the wartime world, where
the "diplomatic ways of admitting unpleasant truths" merely serve to hold
in check a total moral engagement with reality. Only when official rhetorical optimism has been demystified can poetry serve in any of three ways
that will help alleviate the crisis: when poetry cannot be (1) action itself, or
(2) preparation for action, it can be (3) an inducement to action.[26]

While Burke's *Mesures* lecture served the goals Stevens described for
Church, even "carrying humanism to a point beyond which it ought to be
carried in time of so much socialistic agitation," it would surely have struck
Tate, sitting in the Princeton audience—he was probably, indeed, Burke's
introducer[27]—as merely a sophisticated version of the same old new nationalism; this was despite the fact that Burke himself had already chosen
publicly to stand *between* the antipositivist formalists and the pragmatic
nationalists, admiring elements of both positions and moderately calling
for reconciliation.[28] That may not have been enough, for Tate and Ransom did not view the *Mesures* lectures as hinging on any effort Burke or
Stevens or Maxwell Anderson could make in articulating definitions of poetry broadened by wartime. Ransom especially thought Burke's role as
"appeaser and reconciler" indicated that he no longer knew what Ransom
"was talking about" and—a much greater sin—that "[h]e can't bear to think
of unresolvable oppositions."[29] This was the same Ransom who wrote to
Tate, referring to the *Mesures* program as "*your* institute at Princeton (the
Church-Tate one)." If that program could serve as a potential outreach for
undiluted forms of New Critical ideas—there is no doubt that Ransom felt
this way—then Burke's moderate suggestions to war propagandists about
"diplomatic ways of admitting unpleasant truths" would not suffice.

Throughout 1941 Ransom and Tate had been discussing the possibility of publishing under the auspices of the *Kenyon Review* a dictionary of critical terms; the Church money might literally underwrite "the language of poetry." The dictionary would be assembled at an institute they would set up, and Ransom presumed that the "Church-Tate" alliance at Princeton "could do it admirably."[30] Even Church may not have known it—certainly Stevens did not—but the invitation list for the first lecture series, the one that included Stevens, was scrutinized by Ransom with an eye to securing exclusive rights to publication for *Kenyon*.[31]

Insofar as in Stevens's own contribution to the series he had wished to address a few of the issues raised by Church's exile, and the "extraordinary actuality" that reinforced it, he was disappointed, I think, by the context in which his lecture appeared in print as an essay. Had he not, after all, concluded the talk by attempting to show that "self-preservation" required a poetics that "helps us to live our lives" (*NA* 36)? Isolationist or no, he had clearly analyzed the American sense of contemporary distress. Yet the context his lecture was given among the first series of *Mesures* lectures, and especially as it appeared in the book-length collection, which went under the title *The Language of Poetry*, undermined the preconditions of "self-preservation" to which Stevens referred. And Stevens's *Mesures* lecture was not the only thing undermined here; *Mesures* itself was. What had happened to the clear stipulation, in his painstaking memorandum, that in his usage the word "poetry means *not the language of poetry* but the thing itself"? Was Church himself implicated in the effort to contradict that essential piece of advice? Stevens probed a little further and found the answer, namely that Church was not primarily responsible. The most significant fact about *The Language of Poetry* was indeed that Allen Tate was its editor, and that the milieu was definitively New Critical.

The reception accorded the Tate collection made one aspect of the formalist-nationalist war abundantly clear to Stevens: one was to be judged by the wartime company one seemed to keep. His Princeton visit had only served to allow others to put him in the position of seeming to have joined one of the "rival sets" he wanted no part of. Church was not entirely innocent, of course; and the kindly misreadings Church inserted into his chaotic letters suggested that Stevens failed to get across even to Church his point about "the pressures of reality"—failed, that is, to distinguish himself sufficiently from the language-of-poetry critics. Then there was the problem of being placed with all those professional lecture-givers—Tate and Richards among them, experienced stumpers. "And what is there to say of Wallace Stevens' Report on the State of the Universe," William Troy wrote of the Tate collection in the *Partisan Review*, "except that it demonstrates conclusively that poetry [not prose, that is] has all along been his proper medium." The interaction between the imagination and, in Troy's disparaging phrase, "something that he calls 'reality' " is unclear not only because "[w]hat precisely he means by reality is never certain"[32] but also because Tate, Richards, and Cleanth Brooks were so persuasive in their denunciations of poetry claiming to reproduce the real. At the *Partisan Review*, then, notwithstanding Dwight MacDonald's defection to the antinationalists, Stevens saw his *Mesures* lecture fall victim to the general literary-political resistance thrown up against wartime formalism. (Troy did, at least, question the New Critics' obsession with paradox, as manifested in Cleanth Brooks's lecture, as follows: "Not all poets, despite Mr. Brooks' understandable admiration for Donne, do actually rely very much on paradox."[33] But in making clear that he knew a New Critical convention when he saw one, he only made still clearer that he knew what he was doing when he put Stevens with them.) Mary Colum, we recall, decided that "the Princeton Group" exemplified what Van Wyck Brooks described as the treason of the coteries; so when she turned to Stevens's contribution in Tate's volume, all she could say was that he was "like the others"—wordy and abstract. Cleanth Brooks, Allen Tate, I. A. Richards, Wallace Stevens—"all come out of the same type of mind, the same school of thought."[34] If Tate always had the power to make others' appearances in his collections and anthologies seem "perhaps too intimate," as even one of his admirers put it—was shrewd enough to make his contributors seem "depend[ent] largely on what Allen Tate has thought and written"[35]—then *The Language of Poetry* was the classic instance of the effective use of this power.

Until 1951, when it was published in a setting Stevens carefully controlled, his Princeton lecture existed in a context generated by the formalists' essays that were originally gathered around it, by Brooks's and Richards's no less than by Tate's introduction, which was an attempt to unify the four talks under one New Critical rubric. Thus their merits were judged by a single standard. In the influential *New York Herald Tribune* "Books" supplement, in a notice Stevens clipped and laid into his own copy of the volume,[36] Elizabeth Drew praised Brooks and Richards for giving us "concrete analysis" and reproached Wallace Stevens for being abstract. That would have been easy to take, if Drew's sense of Stevens's abstraction, which to her meant that he sees "life in the mode of contemplation, not of action"—note the contradiction of Burke's lecture—did not also carry with it the implication that the bona fide New Critics in the volume succeed because "concrete analysis" entails a kind of practical action in itself.[37]

Tate's effort to bring Stevens under the formalist banner is plain from his introduction to the volume. "Each of these men," he wrote of the four lecturers, "approaches poetry with a warning that it defies analysis."[38] Here Tate humbly acknowledged that "it is always proper" to invite Richards to such symposia,[39] even while Richards would not quite agree that poems make analysis untenable;[40] there is evidence to suggest that Brooks convinced Tate to consider the *Mesures* lectures a site for a great and timely reconciliation between Tate and Richards.[41] In any case, Richards could be counted on to restate the general psychoaesthetic idea that dominated the book, namely the structuralist tenet that "[w]e understand no word except in and through its interactions with other words";[42] this is not to mention the implied fortunate counteralliance of American and English formalisms. The advertising pamphlet issued by the Princeton University Press (and surely printed with Tate's approval)[43] specifically put Stevens in line with Richards's generalization: "Mr. Stevens also concurs in the general decision on the language of poetry which characterizes this symposium when he says: A poet's words are of things that do not exist without the words."[44] Tate's Stevens is thus made to ratify Brooks, Richards, and Tate himself. To the reader of the whole volume Stevens might seem to be a rather intimate member of the cross-citing critical family, even if, as Drew felt, he did not otherwise succeed. Both Brooks and Richards cite Donne and quote Eliot, following New Critical practice. Brooks's reading of "The Canonization" was to Drew "a brilliant example of all that such an analysis should be." And Brooks, not having the space in his talk to attack "superpositivism" himself, refers us to one of Tate's *Reason in Madness* essays at exactly the point where Tate in turn had referred us to Richards's *Coleridge on Imagination*, a work that had a direct influence on Stevens's own lecture.[45] Indeed, Stevens and Richards might have seemed to the unknowing reader of *The Language of Poetry* to have actively collaborated in presenting their papers, for each cited the *Phaedrus* to make much the same point. "[A]s Plato pointed out in the Phaedrus," Richards said, ". . . [h]e was concerned with 'the dialectic art' which I arbitrarily take here to have been the practice of *a supreme sort of poetry*." Stevens also was led from the *Phaedrus* to the idea of a supreme fiction: "unreal things have a reality of their own, in poetry as elsewhere. We do not hesitate, in poetry, to yield ourselves to the unreal" (*NA* 4). From his use of Plato, Richards goes on immediately to quote the *Phaedrus* on the nobility of language, Stevens's titular and introductory figure in "The Noble Rider and the Sound of Words": " 'Noble it may be,' " quotes Richards, " 'to tell stories about justice and virtue; but far nobler is a man's work, when finding a congenial soul he avails himself of the dialectic art to sow and plant therein scientific words, which are competent to defend themselves, and him who planted them.' "[46] Stevens's use of the charioteer permits him to "recognize what Coleridge called Plato's dear, gorgeous nonsense" (*NA* 3), just as Richards, in *Coleridge on Imagination*, quoted the letter to Thelwall in which Coleridge confesses his pure love of language, Plato's "dear *gorgeous* nonsense" (Coleridge's emphasis). To submit to the sound of words is truly to find in the "[a]wareness of words as *words*," as Richards insisted was Coleridge's idea, an immediate successor to a sudden rising light wind of the Imagination, in Coleridge's terms for Plato; a deference to a precise sense of musical delight, in Richards's terms for Coleridge; and a yielding to an unreality that becomes reality, in Stevens's terms for all, which were hardly thus his own making.[47]

While Tate's arrangement of the *Mesures* lectures in print made the most of Stevens's interaction with the Anglo-American formalist project, his seeming to be one of "the boys," this had already been Tate's notion some months before the book appeared. In the fall of 1941, as Tate was gathering the material together for the press at Princeton, he wrote Stevens to suggest not simply that he greatly admired "The Noble Rider" but strongly implying that it reminded him of his own critical position: "There is no other single, brief statement about poetry by a contemporary with which *I feel so much in agreement*. And I am taking the liberty to send you one of my books, in which I direct your attention to an essay called *Tension in Poetry*" (emphasis added).[48] Stevens's reply to this was that he "had read the paper on TENSION" before (*L* 393).

Ransom had been the first to use Stevens's poetry explicitly to justify the New Critical demeanor. His remarks on "Sea Surface Full of Clouds" in fact became both the received reading and a formalist standard.[49] "The poem has a calculated complexity," Ransom wrote, "and its technical competence is so high that to study it, if you do that sort of thing, is to be happy."[50] This oft-cited observation can only remind one of Ransom on *Macbeth*, itself a disarming, representative New Critical remark: "I do not know why [Shakespeare chose] *dusty death*; it is an odd but winning detail."[51] By the forties it had become something of a commonplace for both those attacking *and* those defending the Tate-Ransom group to bring in Stevens; this, and his experience with Tate's handling of the *Mesures* lectures, only heightened the anxiety Stevens felt about being enlisted by a faction under heavy fire—particularly, at this very point, by a faction whose attitude toward wartime poetry was judged morally irresponsible by the nationalists: for Stevens did not wish to seem disengaged on the issue of war in full view of Henry Church, whose desire to make up for the loss of *Mesures* Stevens respected. Yet, in the special Stevens number of the *Harvard Advocate* (1940), Tate wrote that Stevens's status as "one of the best poets alive" would be maintained if Stevens would stand by the *Harmonium* style, by which Tate was really saying Stevens would do well to return to the poetry he wrote before he had been diverted by social and political matters (in *Ideas of Order, Owl's Clover*, and *The Man with the Blue Guitar & Other Poems*). This line gained power belatedly; in the fifties, as we will see, it would serve to unite New Critics and cold-war liberals on the central case of Stevens. Tate wrote: "I could wish him—not to *remain* as he was fifteen years ago, because nobody can *remain* anything—but to find anew the genius for the floating images of *The Emperor of Ice-Cream*."[52] Privately, in a letter to Morton Zabel, Tate was even clearer on the point, pronouncing Marianne Moore's *What Are Years?* "somewhat above Stevens' two recent books"—*Parts* and *Notes*—"but not, of course, above his early and finer work."[53] A few critics began to follow Tate's (and Yvor Winters's)[54] lead in reclaiming the early poems as a way of diminishing the importance of the thirties detour. Elizabeth Drew and John L. Sweeney—Stevens would later come to know Sweeney personally—put out a book in 1942 with the contemporary-sounding title of *Directions in Modern Poetry*, pairing Ransom and Stevens as romantic ironists and emphasizing poems like "The Ordinary Women" (1922), "The Comedian as the Letter C" (1922), and "Sunday Morning" (1915); to be sure, they cited "Owl's Clover" (1936), but stripped of any reference to the "direction" of social poetry in the thirties.[55] A little later, when Delmore Schwartz defended Stevens against Geoffrey Grigson's 1936 attack on *Ideas of Order*,[56] it was to help Schwartz link Stevens to Ransom on the basis of their "mock-grand style" and "dandyism of surface."[57] Young critics were heeding the Tate-Winters-Schwartz thesis as well. William Van O'Connor, serving in the Pacific, was one who indeed followed Tate to the letter. In a few years' time O'Connor would become the first to comment at any length—and favorably—on Stevens's political conservatism,[58] but he was at this point able to suppress any form of that judgment by holding close to a rhetorical commitment—one might say slavishness—to New Critical practice. O'Connor's "Tension and Structure of Poetry" expressed total devotion to the "floating," inexplicable images as Tate and Ransom did; it was written in part to show a debt to Tate's definitive "Tension in Poetry," a desire O'Connor's unpublished letters to Tate document.[59] Unabashed about the obvious influence, O'Connor in his essay quoted Tate's "succinct pronouncement" that "the meaning of poetry is its tension" and Brooks's notion that poems are "resolved through struggle." The usual poets were assembled to be analyzed as examples of the New Critical thesis—Donne, Herbert, and Herrick for instance, but also, at relative length, Stevens's "Peter Quince at the Clavier" (1915). O'Connor's Stevens was the New Critic's model poet: one was delighted to find groups of lines extending to "explore" a single figure; "intensive" images abound (O'Connor borrowed Tate's distinction between "intension" and "extension"); intellectual resolution of tension would come at a poem's end; and the poet's words were "tools which shape the poetic structure and make the final statement just."[60] The New Criticism was obviously attractive to on-duty soldiers like O'Connor as agrarianism never could have been[61]—and Stevens was placed prominently on the soldier's checklist.

From the other side of the argument came Kazin, quoting Ransom's praise for Stevens in stating his general disapproval of the literary-political extremists under Ransom's influence. It is thus easy to see how Kazin's argument served the interests of the nationalists as a popular counterinfluence on earnest soldier-critics like O'Connor, already searching for critical projects to get peacetime careers underway; and the characterizations of the formalists in *On Native Grounds* were borrowed in presentations of zealous nationalists. After quoting Ransom lauding the "calculated complexity" and "technical competence" of Stevens's "Sea Surface"—to study Stevens is to be "happy," oblivious—Kazin shifted his aim from Stevens back to Ransom: "Criticism," he summarized, ". . . had finally turned its full attention upon the poem itself; it missed nothing; it was stainless in motive, happy only to study the calculated complexity of those few poems whose technical competence was 'high.' It had become 'a sort of thing,' a game of devotions by knightly grammarians, and it made one happy."[62] Burke, in order to defend Ransom from Kazin, quoted Kazin quoting Ransom on Stevens's delightful formalism, in a negative review of *On Native Grounds* that appeared in the *Chimera*, a magazine edited by some of Tate's students at Princeton. It is possible that Stevens and Church missed Stevens's enlistment in the skirmish caused by *On Native Grounds* in some of the journals, but they almost certainly learned from the Princeton group that in Burke's piece Stevens's poems had again been caught in the formalist-nationalist cross fire.[63]

Church began to contemplate the *Mesures* series for 1943. He wrote Stevens to ask for advice as to a theme and appropriate lecturers on that theme. Church apparently had a notion of calling the new series "Poetry and Actuality." Stevens's long reply reveals his special interest in this theme. Here is part of it:

> Your subject, when you come to think of it, is a terrifying subject: ACTUALITY. I shouldn't think of [Theodore] Spencer [whom Church had suggested as a speaker] as the right man to make a big thing of it.
>
> Given an actuality extraordinary enough, it has a vitality all its own which makes it independent of any conjunction with the imagination. The perception of the POETRY OF EXTRAORDINARY ACTUALITY is, for that very reason, a job for a man capable of going his own way. Your subject is not really POETRY AND ACTUALITY, but POETRY AND THE EXTRAORDINARY ACTUALITY OF OUR TIME. . . .
>
> What I am trying to lead up to is the idea that the anti-poet may be the right man to discuss EXTRAORDINARY ACTUALITY. . . . Such a man would bring us round to recognizing that the mere delineation of an EXTRAORDINARY ACTUALITY is the natural poetry of the subject. *It is not a subject that requires conjunction with the imagination.* (L 411; emphasis added)

The letter is important because it hastened Stevens's movement away from the isolationist rhetoric of his pre–Pearl Harbor work. When one is induced to speak of "the extraordinary actuality of our time," one is in a position to discover "poetry" in prose discourse on nonpoetic things; one learns to use words that are more securely attached to the world of extraordinary events, not as extraordinary in themselves but as a common language, as distendings of the ordinary. Stevens was beginning to insist on an agreement with reality that would cause a breakthrough in the summer of 1943; here he said, "It is *not* a subject that requires conjunction with the imagination." Rather, indeed, it was the sort of subject that an academic poet like Theodore Spencer[64] would *not* handle well, specifically because of his competence in analyzing literature (with his "more or less literary and correct . . . references to the Elizabethan dramatists, and so on"). Though Stevens was on all the Harvard mailing lists, he could not yet have known that Spencer had been chosen to deliver the 1943 Phi Beta Kappa Poem at Harvard, and that his poem, "The Alumni," the most patriotic of the wartime PBK offerings—including, as we will see, Stevens's own 1945 delivery—described both Harvard men and American poems doing their parts in war in precisely the unextraordinary language and antipoetic manner Stevens thought apt for Church's 1943 series.[65] Notwithstanding Spencer's own bid to be Harvard's nationalist poet, Stevens weighed in against him and in favor of Hemingway, that arch-antipoet and arch-anti-isolationist. Given the extraordinary actuality Stevens claimed to be seeking, is it really so surprising to hear him endorse the man who was operating his own counterintelligence network and chasing U-boats off the coast of Cuba with no less a compliment than that he is "the most significant of living poets"? Stevens had not so much come finally to admire Hemingway personally[66] or his novels aesthetically;[67] rather, he wanted to go on record as suggesting a nonacademic, nationalist literary *personage*—and who better than Hemingway? Who better, also, than Philip Rahv? By this time Stevens could say positively that the *Partisan* editor "looks at things from the social point of view (the social in a contemporary sense)." This was the very same Rahv who before Pearl Harbor had been a plausible candidate for presenting a *Mesures* talk but was, alas, "a Jew and a Communist."[68] Obviously, it was not Rahv who was moving but Stevens. Another sign of the change taking place was that Stevens overcame even his antipathy toward MacLeish. As a help to the *Mesures* program Stevens suggested that Church contact the new-nationalist favorite himself, the poet-turned-propagandist at the Office of Facts and Figures whose mere mention, in James Soby's recollection, had only a few years earlier turned Stevens "purple with rage" (*WSR* 119). Perhaps if MacLeish could be made interested in a series of lectures on the actual world, Stevens advised, *he* could get Hemingway interested. He did not merely mean that MacLeish would contact Hemingway as friend calling on friend; the implication was, obviously, that getting MacLeish involved could mean conferring upon the Church project official war-effort status; *that* might hook Hemingway.[69] Stevens was also willing to turn to Faulkner, who, "[f]or all his gross realism," could speak to the theme. He counseled Church to approach Tate, a fellow southerner who "very likely knows him personally," to be the emissary to Faulkner (*L* 412).

Church followed Stevens's advice on the theme for the 1943 series. It was indeed "Poetry and the Actual World." But the final list of speakers must have been a disappointment after all those spectacular suggestions: neither Hemingway nor Faulkner, nor even Rahv, but G. A. Borgese, whose "Outline of a Poetics" Stevens had admired (*L* 384), to be sure, and F. Cudworth Flint of Dartmouth—and, indeed, even after Stevens's warning against mere academic competence, Theodore Spencer. And the first of the year's lectures was to be delivered by Allen Tate.[70]

The point of Stevens's advice had been that if *Mesures* in 1943 was to address the issue of the extraordinary reality "of our time" with seriousness, as it had in 1942 with Anderson and Burke, it must reach beyond the universities and beyond poetry in the language-of-poetry sense. The speakers must face today's actuality, a "terrifying" subject. But Tate, in giving his *Mesures* lecture on Thursday, April 8, did not merely leave the terrifying subject unmentioned. He went further, satirizing those who would mention it. He did not merely deny the validity of war poetry; he criticized the theme of the lectures itself. He so severely scrutinized the given phrase, "Poetry and the Actual World," that by the end of his talk it was evident that he wanted to repudiate the concept of the actual world in a manner that indeed sent Stevens back to it: "The two terms for this occasion are, first, Poetry, and, second, the Actual World. Do we mean then by the actual world a world distinguished from one which is less actual or not actual at all? I suppose we mean both things; else we should say: Poetry and the World. We might again alter the phrase and get: Poetry and Actuality."[71]

Tate disliked the series theme because it implied by its "bearing" that there existed "something outside us, something objective, whose actuality is somehow an empirical one which tends to look after its own affairs without consulting us." The terms he used to disown the idea would have reminded anyone in the audience who had followed the *Mesures* lectures of Stevens's "Noble Rider," with its idea of resisting the pressures from without by a poetry from within: those who acknowledged an actual world pressing on the imagination from outside, Tate now said, a world "even at times *resisting* whatever it is in us which we would like to call by names like subjective, private, human as opposed to nonhuman," could only by sheer accident suggest validly the real truth, namely that an inner not an outer world of poetry "contains all that we can ever know of any other world or worlds that appear to lie beyond it" (emphasis added).[72] The social reality available to poets had been distorted to useless unrecognizability by the same poets' claims of variable points of view, and it was thus not a reality replicable in good verse. The claim to actuality suggested by the series theme, worse still, "smacks a little of our national reliance upon expert testimony." Any poet who declared, as the new-national experts did, that there was a world out there stable enough so that poets could help form policy "is not, as he talks about poetry, inside his verse, but outside it; and his report is as much under the obligation to make good as yours."[73]

Tate's bold criticism of the Stevens-Church theme reiterated the formalist claim that the true means of representing the real—even, or especially, the deadly real of 1943, where "a total violence"[74] compels us to respond—is to present the world in the "world's body" of the poem, in Ransom's conception. The "actual world" was to be found, if anywhere, in the utter world of the poem, "in its own final completeness." Tate did not hesitate to relate even this point to his distrust of the way the liberal intellectuals were handling the war. In a provocative extended figure, he equated certain literary-critical methods with military strategies. He turned the current phrase *total war*—a phrase used by supporters of war, specifically by those who wanted an invasion of the European mainland as soon as circumstances would permit—so that it became synonymous with *total criticism*, a concentration on the poem's art and nothing extraneous. Never mind that a conception of "total war" was plausible only on the assumption that a world of objective conditions not only existed but was in danger of being destroyed, and that "total criticism," in Tate's version, qualified the concept of conditions external to the mind to the point where the phrase "actual world" meant little.[75] Moreover, the rhetorical effect of Tate's analogy of criticism and war, and the impact of his title image (the fly in the closing scene of *The Idiot*), was to thwart the movement toward the real implied in the assigned topic. Even when first hinting that he felt at odds with Church's theme, he deployed his military figure: he and his audience were being sent "off into the *unknown regions* of 'actuality,' into which we have *received orders to advance*" (emphasis added).[76] Dostoevsky's hovering fly, embodying the actual world in a speck, allowed Tate to poke some further fun at allegiant American intellectuals, such as those who gave him his marching orders here, who were so bold as to believe they could encompass the wartime world in poetry. For Tate, perversely and polemically, "the world and the fly are the same thing."[77]

Tate had helped arrange university funding for the *Mesures*-in-America venture and had followed its course probably more closely than anyone: so it is not surprising that he embedded in his own 1943 talk responses to Burke's of 1942 and to Stevens's of 1941. Burke, it will be remembered, in his *Mesures* lecture, sided generally with MacLeish in criticizing irresponsibles like the American formalists who refused to acknowledge that political rhetoric had a central place in understanding poetry. If Tate was referring critically to Burke, he was brilliantly reversing this charge: the nationalists, calling for poetry to serve if it must as "operational technique,"[78] were actually the ones full of "*irresponsible* rhetoric." "The grammarians of the modern world," he argued, "have allowed their specialization, the operational technique, to drive the two other arts to cover, whence they break forth in their own furies, the one the fury of irresponsible abstraction, the other the fury of irresponsible rhetoric." Tate agreed that the philosopher is perhaps entitled to do his contemporary work in the service of the operational technique, "whether in the laboratory or *on the battlefield*" (emphasis added). But the poet's or literary critic's work was an entirely different matter.[79]

If Burke's *Mesures* lecture was indeed what Tate had in mind when he spoke of "irresponsible *rhetoric*," then Stevens's lecture was surely the one designated as "irresponsible *abstraction*." To see this, we must note first the cunning use of the new-nationalist buzzword "irresponsible"; Tate's *Mesures* lecture was one of his profoundly bitter wartime satires, certainly as caustic as the antiwar ode. He seems to have satirized Stevens at other points as well, for instance when he considered a term broader than "Poetry"—"the Imagination." Tate warned his audience at this point that if we are "trying to discover the relation between the Imagination and the Actual World," which is exactly what Stevens's "Noble Rider" had claimed to do (and in very similar terms), we must be prepared to sit and listen to "a host of comforting saws" about such an abstract relation. Among the old saws was the already famous (though largely misunderstood) Stevensean line that "[t]he Imagination is superior to Reality" (Tate's words).[80] This was a potshot at what to some had always seemed Stevens's loose talk about largely exclusive terms; here, for instance, is Stanley Burnshaw's recent casual reflection on the issue: Stevens is "constantly talking about reality and in a lot of the poems about the necessity of reality. Reality is all over the place. But what does he mean by reality? His reality is the imagination. . . . He uses a word like 'reality' but it means one thing to him one day and another thing to him another day."[81] Of course it was one matter for Burnshaw, who had wanted to push Stevens toward what he and the literary left (and in a very different era) had deemed representations of reality (by which they meant realism), to notice the epistemological confusion caused by Stevens's term "imagination." It was quite another matter for Tate, in the forties, to point out the same problem. For Tate, unlike Burnshaw, was trying to draw Stevens *away* from conditional wartime conceptions of reality, and to demonstrate for Stevens's benefit that the imagination could not be said to be a reality unless the poet's goal, like the propagandist's, is merely to provide his reader a "comforting" truism. Such a reason, to offer comfort, was itself contingent on the conditions—world war—that first required (and now defined) the comforting. Yet Stevens, Tate saw, was trying to make the equation in the manner of a generally applicable rule. Perhaps after having seen himself serving Tate as a satirical target, Burke mentioned Stevens in a letter that suggests that even he was weary of "imagination" used as a realist's misleading slogan. "Anent imagination as the slogan, . . . I wonder," Burke wrote Tate, obviously referring to Tate's lecture-essay; work on his "Grammars," Burke reported, was

> leading me slowly to the conclusion that lurking in "imagination" is the very essence of the heresy of *scientism*. Is it not a bit ironical, for instance, to see a supposedly fairly relatively new poet like Stevens trying to explain his supposedly fairly relatively new esthetic by discovering the Kantian line-up somewhat more than 150 years late? I think you'll have to let more philosophy into your criticism, if only to avoid its coming in thus unnoticed, and naively.[82]

With this letter (of 1944) one of the two targets of Tate's criticism had come forward to explain himself. Did Tate really expect to hear from the other also?

Stevens had not attended Tate's lecture. But he expressed interest in it and followed the 1943 series in letters from the Churches, beginning with the Spencer visit.[83] A little more than a week after Tate's talk Stevens and Church were corresponding about the image of the hovering fly. Prior to April 16, apparently the Churches and Stevens had met to dine in New York, as they often did in these years; Stevens referred to "The Hovering Fly" as "the title spoken of by Mrs. Church." Even if Stevens was likely to have known many details about Tate's lecture before its publication that summer, the subtitle alone, "A Causerie on the Imagination and the Actual World," would send a clear enough signal that Tate had deliberately contradicted Stevens's original warning to Church that the extraordinary reality of 1943 should *not* be spoken of merely in conjunction with the imagination. His final recorded comment on Tate's talk, referring to the title, was dismissive: "[T]he least one can do is to keep the flies off" (*L* 447). In other words, at least *he* was moving, while others, like Tate, stood stubbornly still.

Stevens was indeed moving, perhaps with more surety than at any other time in his poetic career. When that spring an invitation to present another paper came from Jean Wahl, the Sorbonne philosopher and friend of Henry Church whom Church had arranged to bring to the United States from occupied France, Stevens sat down in earnest to prepare a second lecture that would better describe his changing ideas. For this, then, he would modify his "pressures of reality" thesis so that his interest in the threatened actual world would be unmistakable. That he was willing, in wartime, to make a new pact with reality could no longer be mistaken, he hoped, for a desire to make his own key phrase "actual world" a world unto itself, or the new-national word "unity" a term for describing how a poem functions happily on its own.

CONVERSATIONS WITH REFUGEES

The exciting news about F.D.R.'s voyage to Africa
made us duly excited and full of admiration of the
President's energy and that french soil was chosen
makes it very sympathetique.
—*Barbara Church to Stevens, January 27, 1943*

Suppose the Henry Churches stayed in Ville
d'Avray, with Paris occupied by the Germans, and
his wife a German, a former German citizen. It
would have been simply impossible. . . . It simply
couldn't have been. And after '42 they would have
been sent to a concentration camp.
—*Fernand Auberjonois*

Jean Wahl, a Mesures contributor and professor a
la Sorbonne once, has just arrived. He was in a concentration camp in prison too, but does not bear
the Germans a grudge. They were told to mistreat
him and being obedient did so. He is now a professor of philosophy at Mount Holyoke.
—*Henry Church to Allen Tate, September 24, 1942*

Factory of death, Drancy at night,
Where the body, creaking, already feels the planks
The shoulders ache, I feel the hips groaning
But the mind remains supple and warm in the chilled air.

Usine à fabriquer la mort, nuit de Drancy,
Où le corps en grinçant tâte déjà les planches
Les épaules font mal, je sens gémir les hanches
Mais l'esprit reste souple et chaud dans l'air transi.
—*Jean Wahl, in a poem written at the camp in
Drancy, a way station for French Jews being deported
to Auschwitz*

[F]or the first time [we] have a sense that we live in
the center of a physical poetry.
—*Wallace Stevens at Mount Holyoke, in a lecture Jean
Wahl invited him to deliver* (NA 65)

The paper Stevens gave at Mount Holyoke College is energetically "the
cry of its occasion" (*CP* 473). Without even a partial reimagining of the

event, the essay seems of a piece with the others in being knottily allusive, rarefied, monotonous, aimless, unreal, and even uncommunicative, as some disappointed readers of *The Necessary Angel* have remarked.[1] Even admirers of Stevens's prose, like the poet Richard Eberhart, have viewed the Mount Holyoke paper as typifying Stevens's indirectness, his "indecision" and "lack of resolution"—at worst, so rhetorically conditional as to be self-contradictory; at best, so "*intelligently* conditional" as to go nowhere when it seems appropriate to stand still. Eberhart's imitation of the lecture's qualified assertions makes his point impressively: "It is often that if so and so should be true then such and such might follow, but if it were not quite so, or if there were thus and thus other possibilities then it might be that this or that could be the result." Yet in characterizing the rhetoric of "The Figure of the Youth" as going nowhere, Eberhart, who complained here[2] and later (*WSR* 149–50) of Stevens's confused sense of the poet's "sociological or political obligation,"[3] might have revised his sense of the indefiniteness of the 1943 talk had he known how firmly Stevens had tried to ground himself in the politics of wartime exile.

The remarkable context for Stevens's talk was Les Entretiens des Pontigny of 1943, the *décade*, or ten-day conference, cosponsored by Mount Holyoke College and the Franco-Belgian university-in-exile, Ecole Libre des Hautes Etudes (associated during the war with the New School for Social Research). For fifty or sixty refugee intellectuals attending the conference that midsummer, and probably for most of the American participants as well (James Rorty, Marianne Moore, Edmund Wilson, and others),[4] the mere fact that intellectuals exiled from Nazi-occupied Europe were attempting to continue their work, collectively facing the war situation, symbolized an enduring spirit that would seem to make victory inevitable. For the French and Belgian refugees, in particular, gathering together in numbers and in relative comfort at such a moment was a form of intellectual resistance. "[I]n a leaden time," one of the participants confidently said to the group, "and in a world that does not move the weight of its own heaviness," the intellectual, by recognizing himself as a poet in the broad sense, and by taking "measure of his obligation," can "feel . . . his own power to lift, or help to lift, that heaviness away."

But these were not the words of one of the refugees. They were spoken by one of the Americans—indeed, by Stevens, who arrived at Mount Holyoke on Tuesday, August 10, stayed overnight with the Churches at an inn in South Hadley,[5] and gave his talk the next morning, and then listened to at least part of the afternoon session on social and political issues before returning to Hartford. However generally or figuratively Stevens addressed the issue of the free poet's assistance to the unfree (only once does he mention the world crisis in specific terms), there is nothing uncommunicative about his manner, aimless about his point, or unreal about the world to which he refers with unusual intensity. The care he took with the talk involved a sharp sense of the politics framing the occasion and a desire to anticipate, point by point, the doubts of his listeners. Never more clearly does Stevens's preparation show his unwillingness to offend a particular audience, as deleted lines in the surviving manuscript indicate: at Mount Holyoke he referred to Jakob Burckhardt's historiography only after deleting the portion I have emphasized:

> Burckhardt thought . . . that poetry achieves more for the knowledge of human nature than history, *and he treats it in precisely the way you would expect from a professor at the University of Basel. He is so diffident about everything American that it is permissible to repeat in this reference to the University of Basle [sic] the diffidence that the French appear to feel toward any Swiss university.* Burckhardt considers the status of poetry at various epochs.[6]

If this was to be a conference repudiating disunity, national difference, defeatism, and traditionally divisive intellectual traditions, and, moreover, if Burckhardt's idea was to be taken seriously—that poets might teach history more compellingly than historians do—then one must suppress the desire to qualify such claims even with humor; one must not generalize unreliably, as an American, about a "French" view of others. Less qualified than usual, and yet unwilling to make generalizations for the French, Stevens's talk was nothing if not indeed an effort to communicate. Here he explained his idea that a poet must make "an agreement with reality" in terms that would have appealed to his refugee audience in very specific ways, in ways we can only assume he knew would be understood as attuned to the Franco-American rhetoric of total war, just then resurgent—a fine sense of the occasion that could not be conveyed in *The Necessary Angel.* When one makes an agreement with reality, Stevens told this special audience, and when one acknowledges that poetic truth embodies a "factual truth," then one's poetry "is a moment of *victory* over the incredible" and "what was incredible is *eliminated*"—and then, and only then, "something newly credible takes its place."

There is more than sufficient evidence to suggest that Stevens understood what the atmosphere at Mount Holyoke would be before he arrived at the conference. Jean Wahl's invitation had arrived in early April 1943, and happened to coincide with a renewal of Church's desire to endow a poetry chair. On March 30 Stevens wrote Church to elaborate still further on his ideas for the endowment (*L* 445–46), and on April 9 Stevens wrote directly to Wahl, describing his proposed paper in just such a way as to confirm, for us now (and possibly for Wahl, who was then conferring with Church), that it was going to be a delineation of the ideas for *Mesures*-in-exile; Stevens's tentative title was itself an echo from the Church memoranda,

"Project for Poetry" (*L* 446–47). Certainly one of the reasons Stevens urged the Churches to attend the conference that summer—at one point Church, suffering attacks of angina, decided not to risk the trip—was that he wished to honor Church, more elaborately than he had in the dedication to *Notes*; he would accomplish this by assimilating their private discussions into a public setting.[7] Stevens already knew about Wahl from Church, for Wahl had been a member of the Ville d'Avray "circle" before the war, a participant who had lent a good deal of importance to their gatherings, his philosophical writings being already then well known in France.[8] To accept such an invitation from Wahl, in short, would be doubly to show respect to Church, who had been understandably distraught when Wahl, a Jew, had been delivered to the concentration camp at Drancy. It is quite possible that Church's money—significant sums of it were still in France and Switzerland in then-dormant accounts relating to *Mesures* and accessible to Jean Paulhan[9]—had something to do with Wahl's being placed high on a list prepared for Vichy by one of the Jewish rescue organizations.[10] Wahl went almost immediately to the Churches after leaving the camp and fleeing France; "he didn't want to stay in Paris," Auberjonois learned in North Africa, "he'd had enough."[11] Church told Tate that Wahl had somehow managed to maintain a sense of serenity about the nightmarish experience; it might not have been naive of Church to say of Wahl that he "doesn't hold a grudge," for there are signs of admirable control: Wahl had managed to compose short, formal stanzas during his imprisonment, and having thus helped satisfy a strong will to bear witness, he seems indeed to have held up psychologically. Still, Church also knew, and told Tate, that Wahl's German captors "mistreated him" under orders.[12] A French report, made only eight weeks after Wahl's release, described the situation he had endured: "Those who have not with their own eyes seen some of those released from Drancy can only have a faint idea of the wretched state of internees in this camp. . . . It is said that the notorious camp of Dachau is nothing in comparison with Drancy."[13]

Through Church, then, and through Church's contacts—Auberjonois at war via his wife and the Churches, and now Wahl at South Hadley—Stevens could piece together the various fates of Europe's anti- and non-Nazi intellectuals. He knew that many of those who had been able to escape were now active in publishing French-language journals in places like Buenos Aires and—beginning in the months immediately preceding the *entretiens*—in Algiers as well. From its very first issue, Stevens had the privilege of observing the work of the journal *Lettres Françaises*, edited by Church's compatriot Roger Caillois and issued from South America: Church praised it even before its first appearance and then arranged for Stevens to receive it.[14] A regular feature of the journal, going under the heading "L'Actualité Littéraire," entreated readers like Stevens, otherwise unaffected but still absorbed by French writing, to follow actuality in bits of understated detail, literary war news with the French slant. In "L'Actualité Littéraire" rumors could be confirmed about the travails of the writers to whom Church regularly referred as endangered friends and colleagues. There Stevens could learn further of Wahl's and Paulhan's troubles with the Nazis,[15] of Wahl's subsequent release and arrival in the United States,[16] and of news of the first American *entretiens*.[17] The 1942 gathering at Mount Holyoke was organized by Gustave Cohen (he would be a dominant presence in 1943 also). At the 1942 conference, the anonymous voice of "L'Actualité" reported, Wahl gave a reading of "poems he composed in France during his time in a concentration camp"[18]—the very same poems Wahl would personally send Stevens in typescript.[19] Wahl's poems were especially horrifying to someone who had known of the camps only from the usual back-page newspaper reports, and who was certainly unaware of the deportations of French Jews through places like Drancy to killing centers in the east.[20] There is little chance that the man Stevens would meet at Mount Holyoke did not know that Drancy was being prepared to serve as "the Paris antechamber to Auschwitz,"[21] little chance, no matter what station the prisoner had fallen to in the camp, that he would not have heard, even in uncreditable rumors, that death lay ahead for most of the 67,000 French Jews who came to Drancy (all but twelve of the seventy-nine French trains went there), even though his release came before deportations had become systematic.[22] Though horror in such detail could not have reached Stevens's ears from so authoritative a source until the day of his talk, he had already prepared himself to know of the special pressures reality brought to bear on the writer in France. Church had recommended to Stevens an article by an American, in the March-April 1942 *Partisan Review*, called "Writers and Defeat." Here he learned of Gide's *Journal*, of the troubles at *NRF* between Paulhan and collaborationist Drieu la Rochelle. He may have been glad to see that Péguy, whose works he admired, was termed here a "hero of Catholic socialists" ("I shall refuse to obey," Péguy had once nobly insisted, "if justice and freedom require disobedience").[23] So too, in Caillois's *Lettres Françaises* Stevens could learn that Henri Focillon, whose book *Vie des Formes* (1934) he was now reading in English (1942)[24] and which would heavily influence him,[25] had arranged to have the Free French (and de Gaulle himself in London) confer upon the Ecole Libre des Hautes Etudes all rights of a university.[26] With these and other articles describing the writers' situation,[27] Stevens began with some specificity to distinguish one spot from another on the dense resistance-collaboration spectrum. Church recommended the *Partisan* article especially, because, he told Stevens, the "whole picture," thickly layered with politics, "is real and intense."[28]

The writer who described the French intellectual scene for *Partisan* was Frank Jones, the same young classicist who, several months after Church recommended the article, passed through Hartford and paid Stevens a visit. Jones noticed the *Lettres Françaises* circular lying on an end table in Stevens's house, and distinctly remembers discovering that Stevens already knew (we can be sure from Church) that Roger Caillois was planning to travel to New York to meet with American contributors and donors—the mark of an insider's information.[29] "I assumed from the way he talked about Paris that he had been there . . . at least several times."[30] Jones's ostensible reason for visiting Stevens at home was that he had been assigned to review *Parts of a World* for the *Nation*. Because that review followed such a friendly visit from a fellow-traveling *Partisan Review* writer whose additional claim on Stevens was an admirable currency in French literary affairs, it must have emboldened Stevens to consider himself a poet who could take a relatively precise measure of the political difficulties writers faced. Praising Stevens's decision not to build a tower for himself—although "he chiefly proclaims that he can"—Jones described in print the change that had come over the wartime Stevens. "[N]ow he seems to have swallowed his magical world for good, and [we] watch him sadly contemplate the darkening scene."[31] The confidence with which Jones asserted Stevens's willingness to contemplate the scene beyond the enclosed world of his early poems was obviously encouraged by Jones's experience in Hartford—by Stevens's close attention to the fate of the literary exiles.

Stevens's most fervent interest was reserved for the central figure in Church's prewar circle—Jean Paulhan. Stevens had followed Paulhan's ordeal after the fall of France through Church, who reported that Paulhan had retreated to the unoccupied zone with Gaston Gallimard and members of the *NRF* staff.[32] Church immediately began to arrange employment for Paulhan in the United States and asked Stevens's help. Stevens responded immediately by writing Robert Hillyer (*L* 379) and began to discuss with Church Paulhan's possible candidacy to become the first holder of the proposed Church poetry chair.[33] As Church and Stevens worked to find Paulhan a safe American appointment, Paulhan, meantime, was not content to remain in unoccupied France. He petitioned Jean Lebrau, a functionary in the prefecture at Carcassonne, to obtain a passport that would enable him to travel back into the occupied zone. To continue publishing *Mesures*, he contended, he must return "to retrieve the manuscripts in order to satisfy a request of Henry Church"—sure to mention that Church, director of the journal, was an American-born French resident now in the United States. Church, in other words, was someone whom a low-level official in the Vichy bureaucracy—whether a Pétainist or one of the many heel-dragging patriots—would not want to irritate, this having

been before the United States was an official belligerent. The rationale
Paulhan offered Lebrau is significant for what it tells us about the uses to
which Church's *Mesures* could be put for the sake of France:

> It seems to me concerning a review where a large portion was provided from
> the beginning for German literature (*Mesures* gave both original and transla-
> tions of selected texts) that the German authorities can only view this project
> favorably. I'm quite ready in the meantime to submit to the proper party, as
> soon as I come back, the run of *Mesures* (where there have never been, even by
> allusion, any current topics, where even the war has never been mentioned).[34]

Mesures had been impeccably nonpolitical, and even Paulhan, whom the
occupiers and their French friends may have already suspected as their
enemy, could function without risk under the banner of Church. This ploy
seems to have given him a passably urgent reason to get to Paris and time
to begin his active resistance work. He noted that it would be best if the
letter endorsing the travel request did not allude to his involvement with
NRF[35]—no simple matter as he was known among Otto Abetz's cultural
fifth-columnists for having dared to arrange publication of André Suarès's
criticism of the New Order.[36] He was asking for official endorsement at a
time when the pages of his *NRF* were being pulled seventy at a time and he
considered himself in enough danger to employ, in all seriousness, such
phrases as "as long as my life lasts."[37] He received and used his pass, and
(presumably as planned) did *not* republish *Mesures*, though as late as October 1940 Church in Princeton believed—at least he told Stevens this—that
Paulhan would indeed reestablish the journal.[38] It is not clear if Church, by
learning to read between the lines of Paulhan's letters, was piecing together the new literary-political puzzle: the apoliticism of *Mesures*, its having had the now-useful "foresight" to have published non-anti-Nazi German writers before September 1939, could serve as a convenient cover for
subversive travel. Perhaps because he knew that official approval of the
journey back to Paris would require a sum of money, Paulhan specifically
noted in his letter of request that 15,000 francs had been deposited in
Paulhan's name at the Morgan Bank; we can at least be certain that the
money had something to do with *Mesures*, but, more, it may well indicate
that Church was trying to help get Paulhan out of the country. In any case,
Church was kept closely enough informed to know that Paulhan had returned and was now in fact stuck in Paris, a fact Church reported to Stevens.[39] There Paulhan involved himself in the first resistance group organized by French intellectuals; they published a journal, *Résistance*, working
out of Paulhan's residence, which is where he was arrested by the Gestapo.
He had been wise enough to break up the duplicating machine used to
print the journal (he and a friend had tossed it into the Seine). But seven

other members of Paulhan's organization were caught with evidence of their activities and executed. When the group was dragnetted again in July 1941, two more editors were shot; a few months after that, when the group was rounded up a third time, six were shot, six were decapitated, and others were deported to concentration camps in Germany.[40]

Whatever the extent of Church's involvement in Paulhan's return to Paris, he knew enough to report his friend's arrest to Stevens not long after the United States got into the war. "Paulhan was taken up by the Gestapo for a few days," having been accused of possessing "British tracts," and "questioned for eight hours on end, standing au garde a vous, his *juges* being relayed every hour."[41] In point of fact Paulhan was interrogated for two extended periods and imprisoned for a full week, accused of no less than intimate involvement with people who, in the words of his Gestapo interrogators, "prepared . . . an armed group that wants to attack the Germans";[42] yet the information Church had gathered caught the basic horror of the situation. That Paulhan was not deterred by this experience was surely impressive to Stevens, who sensed from the way Church spoke and wrote that he felt it was his absolute obligation to help lift Paulhan's spirits; Church and Stevens may not have known it, but Paulhan's letters to others indicate that their pursuit of a *Mesures*-in-exile,[43] as well as what mail from Church got through in those chaotic months, had the intended effect. One letter successfully delivered bore the heartening news that Stevens was working to find a place for Paulhan at Harvard (it also mentioned Stevens's long *Mesures* memorandum);[44] two other notes, written by Barbara Church, reported the *Mesures* lectures in detail and included praise for Stevens's participation.[45] The Churches' "letters are beautiful and heartwarming," Paulhan wrote Suarès.[46] In sending out their encouragement—whether to do so was naive, undue or shrewd—the Churches gave essential, timely comfort to the writer who became one of the founding participants of the Comité National des Ecrivains, the famous CNE. Of course, Paulhan continued to work on his own writing, and what he managed to see into print in France Stevens diligently read in the United States, beginning with the remarkable work of 1941, *Les Fleurs des Tarbes*.

Through Church, in short, Paulhan and Wahl gave Stevens, as he would later remark of Paulhan's evocation of Tarbes, "pictures of something that has ceased to exist" (*L* 567). From this point on it would be characteristic of Stevens's complex relation to Europe that he felt closest to the "real and intense" situation there just as what he had seen of Europe sight unseen—for instance, through Anatole Vidal's agency—became truly endangered. He thrilled to read Paulhan's book about Tarbes *because* it described something "that has ceased to exist." Now, in other words, tragic actuality was reproducing for all the sort of view of Europe Stevens had maintained all along for himself, for what was passing out of view had never been in his sight in the first place. We must not draw the easy conclusion that this was a sign of Americanist gloating. If his attitude conformed to the neocolonialist view imagining an inevitable new American centrality—to the thesis naming and promoting an "American Century"—it was distinctly a sentimental version, no less inspired than horrified; indeed, the intact survival and consequent economic and cultural superiority of Stevens's United States never overtly served as justifications for his increasing desire to know in detail the losses suffered by people like Paulhan and Wahl. Henry Church's own lost perspective fascinated him too. When they corresponded and convened during this period, the underlying question was: If and when Church returned to France, how much would remain of what he loved to describe?

Stevens watched closely now as Church agonized over—and finally, sadly rejected—a proposal made by no less impressive a threesome than Malraux, Gide, and Claudel to restart *Mesures* (perhaps using *Mesures'*s former apoliticism as a cover, just as Paulhan apparently had done). They wanted Church to be "directeur d'honneur," which may have meant to Church, still sore from Tate's "panhandling," only that he would be required to provide all the funds and have no control as to content.[47] Stevens must have wondered what Church wrote to *them* about his own wartime ideas, curious, undoubtedly, about what Gide thought of the soldier epilogue to "Notes toward a Supreme Fiction" when he knew Church was ready to send Gide in Algiers a copy of the Cummington Press *Notes*.[48] Stevens was reading Gide's *Journal*, aware, probably, that it was "the most popular book in the occupied zone," and virtually "unobtainable."[49] Several weeks after Jean Wahl's invitation came for the *entretiens*, Church had settled on a plan to renew *Mesures* on his own, by arranging to have it published in Algiers; Church enthusiastically reported at the same time that Wahl had begun to translate some of the sections of "Notes."[50] Stevens was never more pleased than when he could imagine his ideas working in the French matrix; if Wahl translated sections of "Notes," they might well appear in a journal published by the Free French in North Africa, and from there be sent into France to "Give Pleasure" to the unfree. The thrill was vicarious, just as the news was secondhand but still shocking; yet at Mount Holyoke, after all, he would be meeting Wahl in person. His lecture would be a rare opportunity to give pleasure to people who would truly appreciate it, and he was only glad that his work could be associated with people like Wahl, who were, he might have said, the real thing. At the end of 1942, Wahl had finished working with "Notes" and wrote a letter to Church praising it; Church sent it on to Stevens. Returning Wahl's letter, Stevens wrote Church that he was "most *content*, in the French sense of that word, to have pleased Jean Wahl" (*L* 430).

Between the time of Wahl's invitation and the summer date of the Mount Holyoke conference itself, the war began to turn—at least insofar as the French were concerned. In mid-April the final Axis defense position in French North Africa was reached. Most of the French colonies were by now formally disassociated from Vichy and had declared themselves to be with the Free French (French Guiana did so, for example, on March 18). On May 21, a portion of the previously neutralized French fleet, docked in Alexandria, elected to join the Allies; even Darlan now turned. On June 3, in Algiers, anti-Vichy military and political leaders, finally able to unite, formed a Committee of National Liberation. By the time the Mount Holyoke conference began in late July, Mussolini had been overthrown (July 25), Roosevelt had broadcast terms of surrender to the Italians (July 28), and the Allies were poised to invade Europe from the south; after the meetings were underway, but before Stevens arrived to give his own talk, the French Committee of National Defense had been organized (August 1). Stevens was aware of the shift signified by these events; his descriptions during this period of the day-to-day doings of the war indicate his witting participation in the new general optimism.[51] What could not possibly have escaped him, in any case, was the resurgent confidence expressed by friends who hung on news of the French in particular. Mrs. Church exulted at Roosevelt's decision at the beginning of the year to travel to North Africa himself; calling a meeting on "French soil" made American policymakers especially "sympathetique."[52] The Churchill-Roosevelt communique was not merely, of course, a psychological lift to the French: the meeting indeed took place on "French soil" so that the French general Henri Honoré Giraud could be called on to confer with the Combined Chiefs of Staff.[53]

For the exiles and their companions, then, talk in the first six months of 1943 had turned dramatically from defeat to victory. The Entretiens des Pontigny brochure, mailed in the summer, and undoubtedly written by Wahl—a fact Stevens probably realized[54]—spoke in terms and with a tone that would have been impossible for French refugees only four months earlier. It was post-Liberation talk; to speak of permanence in a time of utter contingency, of renovation in a time of destruction, was now rhetorical commonplace. And Wahl's themes were indeed "the permanence of values and the renewal of methods." Discussions about a lasting restitution of "values" at Mount Holyoke were to be explicitly hopeful when they turned, even obliquely, toward the subject of Europe awaiting liberation: "Permanence of values," the brochure declared, "in the spirit as in man, and in the *free city*." The founding idea of Paul Desjardin, who had gathered around him the first *entretiens* in the Cistercian abbey of Pontigny before the war, had been to attach "*eternal* themes" to "*actual* circumstances." Desjardin had explained this in rhetoric now understood to be the language of *résistance*, using a figure that was, as Wahl pointed out, "dear to Shelley," that radical master of the permanence-change trope: "values, like flames, secure their identity under continually changing appearances."[55]

The *entretiens* talks would pick up precisely where Wahl's brochure left off: there was a world of solid values that in certain times were obscured; they could not merely be glimpsed on occasion but could be understood as truth, and once understood as truth would offer us strength during times when truths seemed vulnerable, unguarded. Stevens's lecture opened with just this idea. He began by noting what most people feel about "the truth," which he called, in a somewhat playful taunt to the philosophers gathered around him, "the official view of being," the accepted position. But this view, he noted, did not "expect much" of poetry; on the contrary, poetry might be called up to give much greater service than it had been expected to give at exactly such times when the official view concluded that poets had nothing to say (*NA* 40). By defining poetic truth as a matter of fact—as "factual truth"—Stevens made it evident that he had come to the conference prepared to challenge the official view of the separate spheres and to stimulate those who held poetry above the world of material force—and to propose, on the contrary, that poetry can extend to people the power of lightening the "leaden" heaviness of bad times. He questioned three views and began by quoting them—Valéry's, Henry Bradley's, and, to a lesser degree, William James's. All three had said, in some fashion, what Bradley once did—that the world is too vast to be comprehended, and that all we would ever have are " '*glimpses* of the real problems, perhaps even of the real solutions' " (emphasis added); when we have " 'formulated our questions' " about the world, we have tended merely to substitute " 'illusory problems for the real ones' " (*NA* 39). The rest of the talk offered itself as an alternative to this argument, suggesting, in short, that the poet's job in 1943 was to grasp—and not merely glimpse—"the real problems, perhaps even . . . the real solutions" when he or she interrogated the world. Indeed, Stevens argued that it was the poet's job to recognize the "obligation" to make "an agreement with reality." And, as I have already noted, he spoke of this as a form of *victory*, a matter of *eliminating* an unreasonable order and replacing it with a credible one (*NA* 53). Thus the poet "feels his own power to lift, or help to lift, that heaviness away" (*NA* 63). The poet can "help" the world in his own manner by recognizing the world as fact—by examining the world detail by detail (*NA* 59)—not as a metaphysician but as a regular member of society going about things in an ordinary, practical way. The poet who "can't sleep, can't make a decision, can't buy a horse" (this is Stevens quoting Williams James's self-criticism [*NA* 58]) is not likely to make a contribution during the crisis of the times.

In presenting these points about this obligation-seeking poet, Stevens perhaps knew he would please the French in his audience, and not merely by citing no fewer than twenty French figures in a sixty-minute talk: Bergson, Valéry, Focillon, Cézanne, Descartes, Voltaire, Mallarmé, Maritain, Gide, Emile Bernard, Claudel citing Rabelais, Madame de Staël citing Bossuet, Pascal, Fénelon, Buffon and Rousseau, Chateaubriand, and "even" Balzac. He would also please them by referring to a recent review of a book on Gide by Klaus Mann. The political implication of this reference alone would have struck Stevens's listeners as signs of his growing political keenness: Stevens cited Mann, a German refugee whose reputation as editor of *Decision* in New York and whose *Escape to Life* (1939), *The Other Germany* (1940), and *The Turning Point* (1942) had established him as perhaps the premier articulator of the antifascist exile's experience in America; it was common knowledge that as Mann was writing the last pages of *The Turning Point*, he had arranged to have his enlistment status reclassified and was now speaking in German through a loudspeaker to the retreating enemy from the Allied front lines in Italy. Especially among leftist exiles, Stevens's reference to Mann's new book on Gide[56] supplied an impressively contemporaneous suggestion of unity between defeated German and French intellectuals that was irresistibly forward-looking. "The character of the crisis through which we are passing," Stevens said, "the reason why we live in a leaden time, was summed up in a note on Klaus Mann's recent book on Gide, as follows: 'The main problem which Gide tries to solve—the crisis of our time—is the reconciliation of the inalienable rights of the individual to personal development and the necessity for the diminution of the misery of the masses' " (*NA* 64). It is at this point that the talk turned to Burckhardt, whose work and association with Nietzsche Stevens and Church were already discussing in their letters (*L* 452–53). Here Stevens described a specific form of "the historical consideration of poetry," and the mere mention of such a project clearly marks the distance he had come from the pre–Pearl Harbor lecture at Princeton. Poetry, some say, is as capable of historiography as history. Poetry might even be said to out-historicize history, since, as Burckhardt pointed out, its discerning ears truly hear, among other things, the voice of "national life" (*NA* 64). Stevens's use of Burckhardt, bound up with his response to Church's mania for a theoretical Nietzsche, is by no means straightforward—Stevens finally did prefer "poetry in the sense of poetry" (*L* 452–53)—but for the purposes of the Mount Holyoke talk the reference served to remind the group that in considering the status of poetry in the actual world, in "various epochs and among various peoples and classes," there are strong arguments urging that what we must ask of poetry is "*who* is singing or writing, and for *whom*" (*NA* 64; Stevens's emphasis). From this point, moreover, Stevens could movingly conclude that the poet who learns to accept his obligation to the world of fact, who knows enough of the world's heaviness to lighten it, even if he is distant from the crisis (as *both* Stevens and his refugee audience were at that moment), can put into poetic thought "exchanges of speech" in which singer or poet understands the intense experiences of his listener or reader. Such a poet "is thinking of those facts of experience . . . which all of us have felt with such intensity, and he says: . . . *I am the truth but the truth of that imagination of life in which with unfamiliar motion and manner you guide me in those exchanges of speech in which your words are mine, mine yours*" (*NA* 67; Stevens's emphasis).

Such a statement was not merely significant as a private, grateful nod to Henry Church. Participants in the *entretiens* were "affected by what Stevens had said"[57] and were provoked to carry on lengthy discussions into the night, long after the Churches had retired to their room at the inn and Stevens had gone home (the next day was to be a day at the office). The refugees apparently took memorable satisfaction if not a measure of courage from what Stevens had told them; years later "letters to Mount Holyoke College still ask for news of 'ce poète généreux, bon et genial,'" recalled Helen Patch, chair of Mount Holyoke's French department. "Should not a chapter of the definitive biography of Wallace Stevens perhaps bear the title: *The Poet as Statesman?*"[58] For the new, improved interaction—even equivalence—between European and American experience, the "exchanges of speech" between endangered and secure intellectuals respectively, a cultural transaction that was, after all, the guiding principle of the conference, carried Stevens directly to a theme he would take up with astonishing variety and confidence in "Esthétique du Mal" of 1944. The *entretiens* gave him a chance to express his feeling that "for the first time we have a sense that we live in the center of a physical poetry" in a geography that is only made possible by a "non-geography" that attempts to close intellectual and experiential distances. It is perhaps the most moving confession that Stevens would make, and it is really, at bottom, a claim against his 1939–1941 self: "The greatest poverty is not to live / In a physical world, to feel that one's desire / Is too difficult to tell from despair." Stevens seems a little surprised at himself here for saying such a thing. And so he also asks:

> [W]ho could have thought, to make
> So many selves, so many sensuous worlds,
> As if the air, the mid-day air, was swarming
> With the metaphysical changes that occur,
> Merely in living as and where we live[?]
>
> (*CP* 325–26)

He had delivered his paper while sitting behind a table next to the still-emaciated Wahl in front of the group gathered on a lawn at Mount Holyoke, a pleasing image Marianne Moore and Barbara Church remembered years later (see illustration).[59] When he had finished, Wahl summa-

Jean Wahl and Wallace Stevens at Mount Holyoke College in August 1943 (Holly Stevens).

rized Stevens's points in French. A discussion followed during which Stevens made his remarks in English (*L* 457), and despite recollections of several witnesses who judged him to have looked out of place and withdrawn,[60] he obviously relished the experience. He was meeting Moore personally for the first time, after years of correspondence—she delivered her paper, "Precision and Feeling," on another day—and enjoyed the company of James Rorty, whom he found "very agreeable" (*L* 457). Moore's reference to Stevens in her own paper might have served to reinforce his agreement with wartime reality: she reminded her listeners that Stevens believed of poetry that "It can kill a man"—a line from "Poetry Is a Destructive Force" (*CP* 193).[61]

Moore later decided that Stevens had already been impressed with Gustave Cohen before meeting him at the conference; she thought Stevens had taken from Cohen his figure of Eulalia for "Certain Phenomena of Sound" (1942).[62] During the afternoon discussion, scheduled to be given over to the politics of war, Cohen, a medievalist, proudly described his position on the contemporary French situation. Indeed, Cohen was "a bit too patriotard and larmoyant" even for Henry Church, as he later remarked to Stevens.[63] No less a figure than Pierre Cot, air minister in the prewar Popular Front government and then a delegate to the Provisional French Assembly, was present and spoke during the discussion Stevens witnessed. Cot was visiting the United States to promote American-Free French relations, and undoubtedly, at Mount Holyoke, repeated the general message delivered throughout his tour of goodwill, namely that "[t]here is no anti-Americanism inside France" even though decent Frenchmen had had trouble stomaching American support of the indefensible Darlan.[64] Church wrote Stevens afterward that Minister Cot's remarks showed that at this peculiar moment in French ideology "a frenchman can only be a Radical-Socialiste even if he be a reactionary."[65] It was probably Cot's official presence that provoked Gustave Cohen to announce to the group on the afternoon of Stevens's visit his ideas for "a Republic of the Rhine." The tone of such postwar planning seems to have struck Stevens as somewhat unwarranted, premature optimism on the part of the ever-expansive French thinkers; he said he found such talk "rather a nuisance." Yet, despite the French overconfidence, Stevens admitted to John Peale Bishop that he "can't help licking the feet of people like Professor Cohen."[66] He was obviously honored to have been part of the event, pleased that his paper provoked discussion among the refugees, and delighted to have helped create an environment Church so badly needed. Church wrote him afterward: "Mount Holyoke brought us back to a french atmosphere we know well."[67]

Bishop was planning to publish the Mount Holyoke talks in a collection of essays, and he understandably took Stevens's comment about the afternoon discussions to mean that such a collection should be careful to dissociate the theoretical talk about poetry from the practical talk about politics. Presuming (wrongly, I believe) that Stevens would want no part of a published symposium that brought together poetry and the politics of total war—that is precisely what his talk had done—Bishop wrote to reassure Stevens on the point: "I plan to refer to Pontigny only as the occasion of the talks. I have no intention of mixing myself in French politics. While I am strongly in favor of any faction which is both capable and willing to resist the Germans, I thought much of the political discussion at Mt[.]

Holyoke academic and futile."[68] Thus it must have finally pleased Stevens, if I am right in reading his new "agreement with reality" as I have, to find that in the introduction Bishop had chosen to come off as something of a new nationalist himself. But Bishop's apparent switch may have amused him or, possibly, angered him: he had felt that *Wahl* was the right person to write an introduction to the collection of the *entretiens* papers.[69] Rather suddenly, it seemed, Bishop was willing indeed, in an essay Tate described as "sensitive and beautiful" in spite of its evident nationalism,[70] to get mixed up "in French politics," and so Stevens's and Moore's essays as they appeared in the *Sewanee Review* were, after all, introduced by remarks from Bishop such as these:

> [O]ne could not do better in time of war than to provide a place where ideas could be exchanged on the immediate issues of the war, in so far as they are things of the mind. . . . France had fallen; we were surrounded by exiles from France. . . . [S]ome had come from . . . prisons and concentration camps; some had been deprived of their homes, robbed of their books . . . ; all had come from defeat. None had succumbed. They had kept their courage. . . . With maimed hands and without accustomed resources, they had gone on with the work. . . . And in doing this, they were guarding that France, whose greatness and glory has been for nine centuries to have maintained the values of man, in the sure knowledge that, however dire and dangerous the circumstances, that man alone is free who is obedient to his own laws.[71]

Bishop went so far in print as to describe how it did not matter to the discussants that their sessions were interrupted by "the noise of army planes passing overhead," or of the summer-semester trainees who marched around the campus while the outdoor seminars were underway: "Young men must be prepared for war."[72] Notwithstanding the relevant roar, the great subject of "the fate of countries and the future of peoples" was discussed.[73] The point of the conference, for Bishop's introduction as for Stevens's "The Figure of the Youth," was that in leaden times "there is a continuity of thought which must at all costs be maintained."[74]

Bishop's insistence on such continuity directly contradicted the thrust of his *own* Mount Holyoke paper, where in a point antithetical to Stevens's talk he had seen danger in the convergence of prose and poetry, the former with its subjugation to "conveying information that may be [only] temporarily true," the latter with its strong tradition of purity. Indeed, to make this point Bishop repeated a common between-the-wars analogy made ruder by recent events:[75] "There is a border line where poetry and prose merge into one. But the fact that there is a province called Alsace should not lead us into saying that France is the same country as Germany."[76] This was shrewd, as it suggested the ratio of Germany to France as prose to poetry, and who among his audience would argue that Alsace belonged to the prose-mongers? Yet one did not have to think about the analogy for very long to realize that Bishop was putting French admirers of French poetry in the position of defending a tradition that had long been "declared to stand outside contemporary morality."[77] Moreover, the tradition of pure poetry was not only particularly French, Bishop had contended, but *exclusively* French. While Baudelaire advanced into the antipoetry of daily life, this was also, somewhat, a retreat into "the confines of prose."[78] This has led to the total convergence that in turn led to the ceding of the Alsatian middle ground, and to poetry that moved indistinctly with the "enormous floods of words pour[ing] daily from the press, . . . persuading the vast numbers of the literate to opinions whose only significance is that they may one day lead to action."[79] Bishop was obviously aiming his criticism at the call-to-service verse of the social realists, such as Sandburg: when poetry and prose collapse onto that lost, once-contested ground between them, the result is "neither verse nor poetry. We get 'The People, Yes,' which claims our attention only as communication."[80] If Bishop praised Baudelaire's break from the French tradition of pure poetry, while Sandburg, following with extreme logic from poetry's advance into the prose of social life, was *not* the proper inheritor, who was? Bishop's answer was clear: T. S. Eliot and Allen Tate.[81]

Stevens would have been especially curious about the contradiction between the antinationalism of Bishop's lecture at the conference and his thoroughly patriotic introduction; this apparent change of heart revealed much about the relations of poetry and wartime politics because it was indeed Allen Tate to whom it was left to organize the publication of Bishop's introduction and the two essays, Bishop having by then died.[82] Tate did manage to put his distinct antinationalist mark on the selection, dumping James Rorty's lecture because, as he told Stevens, it "doesn't interest me,"[83] or, as he told Moore, it "seems to me to go a little far afield"[84]—which almost certainly meant also that Rorty's reputation as a left-winger irked him.[85] As for Wahl's lecture, Tate decided that Wahl's English was so poor that it "seriously limit[s] the value of his views."[86] And Tate chose this issue for a bitter reassertion of his hatred of the nationalists and their demand for "cultural activities": "The State of Letters" was such that "American anti-fascists give their case away to fascism in their loss of insight into the meaning of authority other than that of force."[87] For the *entretiens* participants, if not also for regular readers of *Sewanee*, Tate seemed to have stripped the much-talked-about conference of some of its excitement and most of its relevance.[88] After all, Wahl's Mount Holyoke talk, "On Poetry," did perfectly bear out the aims of the conference Bishop had identified: Wahl had described the work of *Fontaine* in Algiers as a special wartime experience, producing, like the Algerian exile itself, "this whirling mixture of activity and passivity."[89] To Stevens the omission was surely another sign of Tate's insensitivity to the actual world at war: fluent in English or not, Jean Wahl was one of the survivors whose writings, produced by the "maimed hands" that had touched even Tate's ally Bishop, deserved to be heard and read.

ODE TO THE DUTCH DEAD

[W]hat would a series of poems by Stevens accomplish if they were written in strict *terza rima*?
—*Tate, writing to Stevens*

Tell X that speech . . . / is more than an imitation
for the ear.
—*Stevens, in "The Creations of Sound"* (CP 311)

We ignore the present, which is momently translated into the past, and derive our standards from imaginative constructions of the future. The hard contingency of fact invariably breaks these standards down, leaving us the intellectual chaos which is the sore distress of American criticism.
—*Tate, in "Emily Dickinson"*

I became interested in . . . the desire to realize the past as it was. At the moment I am reading a history of the early settlements which in a perfectly effortless way recreates the political tensions and business activity of the 17th century in this country.
This is an extraordinary experience.
—*Stevens* (L 457)

There were other soldiers, other people,
Men came as the sun comes, early children
And late wanderers creeping under the barb of night,
Year, year and year, defeated at last and lost
In an ignorance of sleep with nothing won.
—*Stevens,*
"Dutch Graves in Bucks County" (CP 291)

After returning from Mount Holyoke, Stevens had a revitalized sense of the value of *Mesures*, if only as a poignant symbol: the little magazine, nonpolitical and modernist and never more typically French than now, an utterly innocent victim of the war. It seemed that *Mesures* had been doubly victimized by aggressive strategies: if Stevens knew anything about Ransom's and Tate's approach to Church, it was that Ransom thought he and Tate could entice Church to come along with *Kenyon* by comparing it to the beloved *Mesures*. Ransom might even claim that *Kenyon* was better at doing for letters what *Mesures* had done; discussing the best approach to Church with his fellow New Critics, Ransom reminded Tate about "the fact that we have more than 1,000 subscribers when *Mesures* never had over 300."[1]

There were a great many differences, actually, between *Mesures* and the *Kenyon Review*. In the fall of 1943, after meeting Wahl and having heard more about Paulhan's experience with the Gestapo, Stevens saw the differences more clearly than he had before. How could Ransom's solicitation of "war-gifts" to the *Kenyon Review*[2] be responsibly compared to Church's struggle not merely to save *Mesures* but to help keep its editors alive? Even then, in 1943, Church kept talking about reissuing his journal.[3] Soon he would hit upon that plan to make it *officially* part of the war effort: he would put out an all-American number, have it printed in Algiers under the auspices of the Office of War Information (to which Fernand Auberjonois was now attached). "[S]o I am deep in Psychological Warfare since this is the branch that takes care of it," Church wrote when explaining the operation to Stevens. "[T]he interest in american literature seems real" among the exiled and occupied French.[4]

Because of this desire to keep Wahl, Paulhan, and the other *Mesures* writers in print, even at great cost, Church eventually came to know something of Tate's recalcitrance on the issue of the writer's wartime role. In the last months of the war, Paulhan published his full account of the trouble he brought on himself by publishing *Résistance*, the interrogation and detention by the Germans. It was printed in Spanish (in *Sur*, in Buenos Aires);[5] "upset" by this piece and feeling it must immediately reach an American audience, Church began translating it into English and to look for an editor who would publish it in the United States. "I thought Paulhan's description of his experience very remarkable," he wrote Stevens, "so tense and dramatic, a style serré." The danger Paulhan had been in, Church said, had been even greater than he had realized. Would Tate consider publishing the translation of Paulhan's account? "I may send it to Tate" at the *Sewanee Review*, Church wrote, "but I am afraid he may not appreciate it. Perhaps the Partisan would be better . . . ?"[6] And Church did not keep his feelings about Tate's apparent inattention to wartime sacrifices between himself and Stevens. Feeling he had been hit up often enough for money to support *Sewanee*, he suggested to Tate directly that the editors ought to give up their salaries for the duration of the war. He reported the reply to Stevens: "Tate was aghast. . . . Yet if they went in to war work they would not be paid." Then Church mocked *Kenyon*'s claim to be "the last stand for American Letters, almost important as war work."[7]

Tate's miscalculation with Stevens was in presuming they held similar attitudes about how the American literary enterprise should remain apart from the huge "democratic" business of the war effort. Perhaps Stevens would have agreed with Tate if he had restricted his comments to that issue; Stevens knew it was indeed an overwhelming business and Tate was right to the extent that it did threaten to overtake everything fine and discriminating. But by relating such judgments to the fate of the Churches, Tate unwittingly pushed Stevens away from the Tate-Ransom position and reinforced the feeling, stronger in Stevens now than ever, that Church was a man of letters after his own style. Tate wrongly assumed that Stevens would agree that Church "is daily rotting in inactivity." Because the Churches "cherish the delusion that they will be able to return to France very soon, . . . a cruel piece of self-deception which promises to ruin interesting and valuable lives," Church ought to find some way, Tate wrote, to "commit himself to American life." Tate evidently meant that Stevens should now intercede, not on Tate's but on Church's own behalf, and convince him to go in with the Tate-Ransom group. Tate could not have known that Henry and Barbara Church had told Stevens everything and knew what Tate now really intended when he confided in Stevens about Church's need to "commit himself" to a real American project. "They both have great confidence in you," Tate observed, "and if ever the occasion offers, you could perform a real act of friendship by encouraging them to make something of their lives in America." And when Tate added that *he* had "tried to persuade him to publish *Mesures* over here,"[8] he of course was referring, without saying so, to his and Ransom's plan to absorb *Mesures* into *Kenyon*—to give over to Church a few pages of *Kenyon* for a "foreign" section in return for a donation large enough to replace the funds Ransom had lost to aeronautics classes during the curriculum "speed-up" at Kenyon College.[9] After the *entretiens*, with its vital Frenchness, Stevens was prepared to resist Tate's assumption that it was a delusion to think France would ever again be the sort of place where the Churches could take up a cultural life.[10]

It was at this moment—in speaking of Henry Church's self-delusion about the war's toll on France—that Tate asked Stevens to do him a favor by sending a poem to the new interim editor of the *Sewanee Review*, Andrew Lytle, novelist, history teacher, friend of the agrarians, whose work was closely associated with them. The result, "Dutch Graves in Bucks County" (*CP* 290–93), gave Stevens a chance to express some of his misgivings about Tate's position, and to allow himself to put into verse the new sense of reality he had set forth in his *entretiens* paper. He evidently felt that his new poems should also be part of an "agreement" with the reality of the present total war, and might even celebrate the fact "That a new glory of new men assembles" and that "An end must come in a merciless triumph," forcing a total peace "that is more than a refuge."

Such a reading of "Dutch Graves" is strengthened by the fact that Tate approached Stevens for a poem on behalf of Lytle's *Sewanee* by specifically relating the "very considerable favor" Stevens could do for them to the consideration that Lytle "is going to have great difficulty getting it through the war," and that, despite the crisis, *Sewanee* must "carry on the traditions" of the *Southern Review* and the late, great *Hound & Horn*.[11] Stevens was almost certainly aware that, in writing a poem for Lytle himself, he was also in some sense writing for Tate, as it was well known that Tate, in George Core's words, "had been campaigning for the editorship of the *Sewanee Review*" and was about to get it.[12] Tate had been quite openly saying to his friends that Lytle was "wholly unfit" to edit *Sewanee*; Tate felt he could not "beg" for contributions on Lytle's behalf with "much conviction," as he wrote Bishop a few days after begging Stevens.[13] Until Tate's appointment in the summer of 1944, a move supported by Ransom,[14] Tate essentially coedited the review.[15] Stevens knew this just as he prepared to mail "Dutch Graves in Bucks County" to Lytle;[16] he knew, that is, that Tate was "taking over."[17] He may have sensed that Tate's supporters, including Lytle, saw Tate's editorship as a means of fending off aesthetic compromises brought on by the war mentality, of "hold[ing] our profession together in these uncertain years."[18] Stevens also knew that the editorial rationale *Sewanee* used to convince readers and libraries to subscribe to yet another literary journal in a time of wartime budgets was based on Ransom's emergency program at *Kenyon*. Poetry, the logic of the appeal ran, ought to resist the descent into confusion; it was rather a proper stay against it. "Especially during this time of storm and stress," one wartime appeal from *Sewanee* ran, "should libraries take advantage of our people's serious mood to encourage steadiness, soberness, and selectiveness in their reading."[19] Stevens did not consider it quite such a danger as to require the rhetoric Tate used, but he did know what Tate feared: "Here we are all in the fever of contemporary life," Stevens wrote Church after the first two issues of *Sewanee* had appeared under Tate's supervision, "with everything that is fundamental turned upside down and in course of re-examination"; yet, while Stevens said he thought Tate was "the man to do it"—to endure the "fever" of upheaval—he also doubted Tate's temperamental capacity for forging the necessary agreement with reality. "I don't think that Tate is going to be content there [at *Sewanee*] in the face of what might be called the rising fury of the future." The future, Stevens thought, was more internationalist and politically heterodox than perhaps Tate could tolerate: the literary morrow was better met by reviews that would now be edited in Paris, or Vatican City—or even Moscow, Stevens quipped—places where the world had *actually* been "turned upside down"—in "the profound misery of Europe" (*L* 483). The American poetry of a world of "Angry men and furious machines" (the opening line of "Dutch Graves") had to be prepared to imagine its Europe from the United States. Stevens was thus willing to inscribe into his poetry, a year after Pearl Harbor—on December 8, 1942, Tate told Stevens that Lytle had received "Dutch Graves"[20]—his strongest opposition to the sort of skepticism Tate expressed in, say, the "Ode to the Confederate Dead," where he had commemorated the fallen Southern soldiers of the past in order to complain about "the fragmentary cosmos of today."[21] In contesting this sort of skepticism, what certainly seemed to many American intellectuals in late 1942 to be out-and-out defeatism—and in offering his "Dutch Graves in Bucks County" as his reply to Tate's famous "Ode"—Stevens came as close as he would to the new nationalism.[22]

Tate's hatred of the new nationalists focused most intensely on the liberal notion of the "historical method." The past signified, to these easy progressives, these authors of "ubiquitous Uplift," these " 'generalizers' upon history,"[23] whatever victory or social advance they wanted it to foretell. Tate's bitter words were these: "The 'historical method' has always been the anti-historical method. Its aim is to contemporize the past. Its real effect is to de-temporize it."[24] Tate's fierce, career-long opposition to "historical scholarship" with its positivistic assumption that the literary text "expresses its place and time" was never stronger than in wartime.[25] In direct contrast, the poem Stevens sent Tate *deliberately* contemporizes the past. It calls forth as comparable images his own Dutch ancestors, buried in eastern Pennsylvania graveyards, and the fallen Netherlanders of 1942.

The historical analogy is obvious from the beginning of the poem: the title and the first instance of the refrain conjure Stevens's "semblables," his ancestral likenesses, while the intervening stanza refers to the present war as the occasion for the meditation on the past:

Dutch Graves in Bucks County	*past*
Angry men and furious machines	*present*
Swarm from the little blue of the horizon	
To the great blue of the middle height.	
Men scatter throughout clouds,	
The wheels are too large for any noise.	
And you, my semblables, in sooty residence	*past framed in a*
Tap skeleton drums inaudibly.	*present tense*

That Stevens must turn *to* the long-dead Dutch in the refrain—"And *you*," he calls to them—indicates a sufficient difference between then and now as subject matter. Yet there is already a central relation established. Though unheard, the drum taps of the old Dutch seem to support the warring "Angry men" in their "furious machines" above. The second stanza and the next refrain confuse the relation a little, as the airy battle now seems to involve the old Dutch. It is not an air war, but an infantry war made airy. "There are men *shuffling on foot* in air. / Men are *moving* and *marching*."

> And you, my semblables—the *old* flag of Holland
> Flutters in tiny darkness.

Yet who in December 1942 could fail to see the double significance of "the old flag of Holland"—now that Stevens's ancestral home was occupied, a foreign flag flew, and any proud display of the "old flag of Holland," even in verse, was understood there to be a form of bold resistance? Thus the fourth refrain can stress the poem's historical method more overtly than before; it is attuned to the aim of finding inspiration in the losses of the past:

> And you, my semblables, are doubly killed
> To be buried in desert and deserted earth.

From here, and through the middle part of the poem, the refrains express some doubt about the easy historical analogy even as the stanzas continue to bang the old war drum for a modern war. So while the fifth refrain reads, "And you, my semblables, in the total / Of remembrance share nothing of ourselves," the sixth stanza assumes that "what is common to all men" is the prosecution of total war to bring "An end of evil"—in rhetoric that was, at the time of the poem, distinctly American:

> An end must come in a merciless triumph,
> An end of evil in a profounder logic,
> In a peace that is more than a refuge,
> In the will of what is common to all men,
> Spelled from spent living and spent dying.

By this point, Stevens has armed the poem with the rhetoric of total war. The fallen soldiers of the past legitimize what would perhaps otherwise seem a goal entailing needless brutality, the goal of "*merciless* triumph." They justify a common will to defeat an evil even at the expense of many dead.

But if the stanzas become progressively undisturbed by the historical analogy, the refrains continue to question its purpose. That is, until the tenth refrain:

> And you, my semblables, behold in blindness
> That a new glory of new men assembles.

From here the two formal elements in the poem unite, the vision of the blind dead is restored, the old Dutch enlivened by the recovery of the new. The last lines of the poem rush toward an unmistakable conclusion: a new sense of likeness between past and present supports "These violent marchers of the present" in their dramatic "March toward a generation's centre."

Stevens was attempting to reverse the dulling effect of the past in Tate's "Ode to the Confederate Dead," where the visit to the gravesite marking familial war dead deadens the visitor himself. In Stevens's *Sewanee* poem the men of the present enable the dead to "behold in blindness . . . *a new glory*" of a new army. In Tate's ode, of course, the effect of the buried soldiers is to disorient, to blind, the present visitor:

> The brute curiosity of an angel's stare,
> *Turns you, like them*, to stone,
> Transforms the heaving air
> Till plunged to a heavier world below
> You shift your sea-space blindly
> Heaving, turning like the blind crab.[26]

Tate had explained the poem, and specifically his compelling image of blindness, in an essay, "Narcissus as Narcissus," that was collected in *Reason in Madness*, the book Stevens had bought on his own before Tate sent him the inscribed copy. The essay removed all doubts as to what modern tendency Tate was criticizing; his essay, by interpreting the "Ode" as an attack on historical subjectivity framed in a political language—by excoriating the ideology of subjectivity "or any other *ism* that denotes the failure of the human personality to function objectively"[27]—certified the poem as illustrative of the New Criticism. "Narcissus as Narcissus," collected in *Reason in Madness* at the height of the nationalist-formalist dispute, helped make the power of the poem a critical power. In Tate's own view, the visitor to the war dead is incapable of historical insight because he is paralyzed by the modern trend toward "private, romantic illusion," by "solipsism, a philosophical doctrine which says that we create the world in the act of perceiving it."[28] "You hear the shout, the crazy hemlocks point / With troubled fingers to the silence which / Smothers you, a mummy, in time" ("Ode," ll. 53–55). Stevens's willingness to write about the present war by subjectivizing the past stands, then, not only in direct contrast to Tate's insistent call for the poem as "objective frame"; it also serves as a rejoinder to Tate's attack on subjectivity itself in the context of the New Critics' wartime literary politics. Clearly, the emotional validity of "Dutch Graves" derived from Stevens's personal identification with his *semblables*, versions of himself as Dutch soldier. Especially antagonistic to such validity was Tate's conclusion that moderns learn nothing from the past, that they return to the war dead for an emotional shudder and nothing more. The poet who had long believed verse capable of creating in the world something of what it sought always had reason enough to respond; but in the fall of 1942 Stevens was especially sensitive to the point, as at just this time his passion for his genealogy "became intense," as his daughter has recalled (*L* 397).

Stevens's obsession with genealogy served him in various ways at different times. After the initial investigations of late 1941, 1942, and 1943, poems reproducing some aspect of Stevens's genealogical research, "The Bed of Old John Zeller" (1944), "Analysis of a Theme" (1945), "Two Versions of the Same Poem" (1946), "Extraordinary References" (1946), and "Page from a Tale" (1948), range in concern from exploration to religious ardor to settlement folklore to Indian fighting and home defense. And once he had adjusted to the basic facts of the matter—particularly that his mother's family, the Zellers, were German—he could have some fun at the expense of Zeller family zealots who maintained through the war that the family was indeed French. In late 1944 he noted for one present-day Zeller that the copy of a Zeller will stipulated "Jean Henri" when "it is actually the will of Johann Heinrich." In the last weeks of the war he reminded a prominent member of the Zeller Family Association that pamphlets distributed by the contemporary Zellers contained the "typically loose statement" that the family came from Deux Ponts—"but," Stevens noted, "Deux Ponts is really a French name for a German town, Zweibrügge."[29] This sort of attitude may lead Stevens's readers to the conclusion that the interest in genealogy, especially as it so obsessed him in the war years, led him away from rather than toward the world at war.

Yet at the time he wrote "Dutch Graves in Bucks County," relatively new confirmation of several basic facts about his family caused him to ponder the effects of war in a serious and personal manner. His sister Elizabeth, writing him four days after Pearl Harbor, seemed to recoil at the reminder that their mother's grandparents were German and not Dutch; Margaretha Zeller Stevens, in order to join the Daughters of the American Revolution, had checked into her ancestry and turned up the Germans. (As for the contemporary Germans, Elizabeth added: "I am not even going to say one word on current events. They speak loud and strong for themselves.") Examining this letter from his sister, Stevens took a scratch sheet and sketched out what he had by then learned of his German roots: Sarah F. Kitting was his mother's mother; John Kitting, Sarah's father, had married Margaret Gries, daughter of Ernst Gries, a German, a soldier.[30] While in his immediate reply to Elizabeth he advised that they both simply face whatever unsavory truths they discover about the family—"I simply want to know the facts," he told her[31]—the research of 1942 was dominated by the Dutch on his father's side. He had established the route taken by his father's mother's family from Holland to Bucks County,[32] and when he wrote "Dutch Graves in Bucks County" he had gathered the information he would need to visit the graveyards for himself (he made at least three visits in the following three years). Obviously the poem imagines such a visit from the genealogists' descriptive letters, pamphlets, histories and photographs he had by then collected. In June he learned that his Harvard classmate Floyd DuBois would second his nomination for membership in the Saint Nicholas Society, a club of Dutch descendents, explicitly described by DuBois as a "patriotic societ[y]" designed not only to strengthen relations to the Netherlands but to support "American tradition and ideals."[33] Frank Jones, who spent his afternoon at Westerly Terrace in September, took notes after that visit and later informed Peter Brazeau that Stevens told him he had just read the entire two-volume history of the Dutch county from which his ancestors came—"the whole thing, the whole two volumes" (*WSR* 131). When Stevens wrote "Dutch Graves" in late November or early December, he was anticipating any day the arrival of Lila James Roney's long report on her investigation into the first American Dutch Stevenses.[34] What he had already learned about his Dutch forebears was that they had been forced to leave Holland because of war— "wars," he wrote his niece, "which involved the massacre of so many people for religious reasons." He also learned that such victimization became "one of the sources of the will that prompted people to leave Holland" and migrate to places like Bucks County.[35] Close work with histories of the early settlements, focusing his "desire to realize the past as it was," taught him how to discern "the political tensions" of a single moment in time; genealogy offered him not only a lesson in the content of these centuries-old political disputes, but also taught him a method of unraveling positions within positions (*L* 457). And far from allowing him to resist the American mind capable of knowing a war fought elsewhere, genealogy enabled him to imagine a home front, the sustenance of hard will under occupation. He would learn of Henry Melchior Muhlenberg, "whom the British in Philadelphia did not like a bit," living five miles from the edge of the occupied zone; yet Muhlenberg "never budged an inch" (*L* 479). He would also study the Palatine emigration, in an attempt to establish his mother's line, and learned in great detail how weary his ancestors had become when troops were quartered in their houses by order of the French king. Their own food was denied them by the occupiers; so they fled and ran right into the line of march of the French troops, "going and coming."[36] How, then, at precisely the time when Göring was threatening to use the Allied blockade to starve the people of the occupied Lowland nations,[37] could Stevens's genealogical imagination *not* be said to have led him to conclude that his own Dutch likenesses were now "doubly killed," or have enabled him to see soldiers "creeping under the barb of night"—even if that effort entailed emotionally, even loosely, contemporizing the past, and endorsing, in Tate's disparaging words, an "*ism* that denotes the failure of the human personality to function objectively"?

We see in "Dutch Graves" the progressive elimination in Stevens of doubts about the historical analogy. Finally the refrain harmonizes with the stanza. The use of the stars to bridge the ocean separating the American imagination from the actuality of the European tragedy, serving not too many months earlier as an affirmation of American distance and uniqueness, now gave way to cultural and historical heterogeneity, engaging observable images of an American home front (Bucks County) to conceive of the "marchers of the present" abroad.

> So that the stars, my semblables, chimeres,
> Shine on the very living of those alive.

Having suppressed those doubts and personalized a connection to the war, Stevens could end his poem for *Sewanee* without the slightest qualification limiting the poet's relation to war.

> These violent marchers of the present,
> Rumbling along the autumnal horizon,
> Under the arches, over the arches, in arcs
> Of a chaos composed in more than order,
> March toward a generation's centre.
>
> Time was not wasted in your subtle temples.
> No: nor divergence made too steep to follow down.

The "Time" of the ancestral Dutch "was not wasted," the poem insists. In it Stevens proclaimed a general willingness to follow them imaginatively down.

As Tate helped see "Dutch Graves" into print, he turned to another Stevens matter on his desk. Preparing Stevens's *entretiens* paper for publication gave Tate the opportunity to work through Stevens's points carefully. He was intrigued by a reference to an article by Raymond Mortimer. Tate asked Stevens where he had found the Mortimer quotation, and the exchange on this matter not only reminded Stevens of Tate's "hot quick temper"[38] but raised again the issue of the relation between poetry and history. Tate decided that the idea Stevens conveyed through Mortimer "so closely resembles something that I wrote years ago in an essay on Emily Dickinson that I am wondering whether I borrowed the point from Mortimer or he from me."[39] In his lecture Stevens was citing Mortimer's argument "that the 'thoughts' of Shakespeare or Raleigh or Spenser were in fact only contemporary commonplaces and that it was a Victorian habit to praise poets as thinkers, since their 'thoughts are usually borrowed or confused' " (*NA* 56). This referred to Mortimer's review of E.M.W. Tillyard's *Elizabethan World Picture* in the May 8, 1943, *New Statesman and Nation*; Stevens obliged Tate and mailed him the precise citation.[40] Tate, now suspicious that his idea had been stolen, shot back: "I shall look up Mortimer's article. I am beginning to feel that somebody in England is playing back to me a phonograph record that I made."[41] Tate's argument in his essay on

Emily Dickinson (1932) had been that "Shakespeare is a finer source of culture than Addison" even though Addison was certainly "more culti-vated" than Shakespeare.[42] In other words, for Tate, as for Mortimer, one does not read the great poet to locate extraordinary ideas about the histor-ical moment, and why would anyone want to read for *ordinary* ideas? While the scholar may be able to "unearth the elements of Shakespeare's culture," and then discuss how these elements are inscribed into Shakespeare's art, Shakespeare himself "would not know what our discussion is about."[43] Or, in the expression Stevens used to rebuke this position in his poem "The Creations of Sound," "there are words / Better without an author, without a poet, // . . . intelligent / Beyond intelligence" (*CP* 310–11). So, too, for Tate in his Dickinson essay, "not all the strenuous activity of this enlight-ened age" can reproduce as a matter of history the great poetic achieve-ment.[44] Here, then, was Tate's indirect way of doubting Stevens's attempt to relate his reality-imagination complex to a contemporary crisis, at the *entretiens* and elsewhere (as in "Dutch Graves"). As a matter of fact, at Mount Holyoke Stevens had cited Mortimer's point and then expressed his reservation in a question that followed immediately: "But do we come away from Shakespeare with the sense that we have been reading contem-porary commonplaces?" The suggestion was that one might indeed read the poet designated great for an "*extraordinary* actuality"—to borrow ap-propriately Stevens's phrase promoting Hemingway's suitability for *Me-sures*—even while the great poet himself considered his ideas to reflect "a life apart from politics" (*NA* 57). This was yet another wartime version of the dictum "We are preoccupied by events even when we do not observe them closely." Stevens's Mortimer, in other words, was a foil for the ideal wartime poetic figure who says, *I am myself a part of what is real*, and whose ideas, extraordinary in generating later senses of the commonplace, served the purpose of obliterating confusion (*NA* 63) and lightened a leaden time. Contrary to this, then, Tate's quibble about Mortimer's argument against Shakespeareans' historicism only clarified a stance Stevens already knew, if only because he knew the Dickinson piece from *Reactionary Essays*. Here, specifically, Tate's position against wartime obligation helped counteract the position toward which he saw Stevens leaning in "The Figure of the Youth" and "Dutch Graves." Tate was pointing out to Stevens that even in wartime the good poet

> has no opinions whatever; his peculiar merit—his potential for realizing his genius—is deeply involved in his failure to think about anything; his mean-ing is not in the content of his expression; it is in the tension of the dramatic relations of his characters. This kind of poetry is at the opposite of intellec-tualism.[45]

"The Creations of Sound" (1944) reveals such great familiarity with this anti-authorial position that it is a wonder Allen Tate has not been identified as the poet "X" in the poem before this.[46] Poet X underwrites the intentional fallacy, eschews author-centered readings, thereby denying his feelings any access to the poem. So he can only offer us a poetry of disembodied sound—sound severed from poetic will. In the first part of the poem the position is summarized and criticized; poet X, in decentering the poet, in believing that "there are words / Better without an author," is paradoxically both "an obstruction" and "a man / Too exactly himself." The second half of the poem attempts to suggest a distinction between the willful, poet-centered poet—the creator of "The Creations of Sound" itself, Stevens—and X. The second part begins at this turn toward a tone of instruction: "Tell X that speech is not dirty silence / Clarified." "It is more than an imitation for the ear" (*CP* 311)—more, in other words, than sound. Poetry must also contain ideas.[47]

"The Creations of Sound" (published in the Spring 1944 issue of Norman MacLeod's *Maryland Quarterly*) constitutes Stevens's response, I think, to Tate's poem "Seasons of the Soul," published in the Winter 1944 *Kenyon Review*. Tate had directed Stevens to the poem: "If you are a subscriber to *The Kenyon Review*," he wrote, "you will see in the current issue that I do not spend *all* my time at translations!"[48] Tate was referring to his translation *The Vigil of Venus*, published by the Cummington Press and written, as Tate admitted, in an "impossible meter in English," trochaic septenarii;[49] obviously Tate was sensitive to the criticism that toying with archaic (let alone "impossible") meters made him irrelevant. Stevens's reaction to the "Seasons of the Soul," first when it appeared in *Kenyon* and again when it was collected into *The Winter Sea*, incensed Tate; thirty years later he was still talking about how "naive" he had been to think Stevens would respond generously to that poem. "His sole response to *Seasons of the Soul*," Tate wrote in 1977, "was a feeble joke about the 'combustible juice' of Spring."[50] But there was more to it. If, as Tate "strongly suspect[ed]," Ransom would not like "Seasons of the Soul" because "the meter is eccentric,"[51] Stevens's response was actually the opposite: while these verses do not "impair one's sense of Tate's power," a poem must finally be more than its form; or, in the language of "The Creations of Sound," "It is more than an imitation for the ear." "After reading these," Stevens wrote Henry Church of "Seasons of the Soul," "I wonder whether there is enough of the peasant in Tate." While the new poem is formally "intricate" and "acute," and while Tate should be "proud of it," such is the pride of a man who gives us "poetry written under glass" (*L* 461). (My point has been precisely what is indicated here: at this important point, Stevens could charge another poet with writing "poetry . . . under glass" without granting that the complaint might be turned around.) When "Seasons of the Soul" was collected in *The Winter Sea* (Tate sent Stevens a copy),[52] Stevens confessed to liking it better the second time, but he reminded both Tate and Harry Duncan of the Cummington Press that he had not liked it in January 1944.[53] We have seen that Tate's image of the suffocating well of one's personal past, from the "Autumn" section of the poem, was still on Stevens's mind five years later, when he wrote his own "Things of August" and seemed to reverse the charges on Tate, suggesting that *Tate* "Break through" from a past that trapped him—that only then would Tate "Have liberty."

Stevens followed the reviews of *The Winter Sea* (*L* 509) and found his reasons for disliking "Seasons of the Soul" not only confirmed by the critics but put squarely into the middle of the war-poetry debate. Stevens could see from the poem Tate himself had recommended that, in the words of one critic, Tate "remains unreconciled to pretty much everything: our literature, our civilization, our wars."[54] Tate's poems reminded Alfred Kreymborg that "[s]ince the advent of World War II, there has been a good deal of argument regarding the theme of Mars as a subject for poetry, a battle waged between those who feel that the muse must disregard the war or regard nothing else but the war." Here is what irritated Kreymborg, then, no less than Stevens if I am right about "The Creations of Sound" in the context of the nationalist-formalist controversy: Tate's poems showed that he is "a battleground in himself" and that if it can be said at all that Tate brings his new poems "to the poetic front," it is a front opened on his own. How, after all, can poetry in a time of war, be so "[c]ompletely scornful of the factual or commonplace"?[55]

The criticism that underscored Stevens's reaction to Tate's poem was one Richard Blackmur formed of Tate's *Winter Sea* particularly and Robert Lowell formed of Tate's poetry generally: at its worst, Tate's poetry is all sound. Lowell once told Tate he disliked "The Buried Lake," a later poem, because "he found the sound of it like 'choking.' " While Tate, to Lowell and other admirers, was capable of the finest terza rima in English—so Lowell deemed "The Swimmers"—his readers too often choked on "Allenisms," the sort of contorted phrasing the critics of *The Winter Sea* noticed in "Seasons of the Soul."[56] Blackmur wrote in his comment on *The Winter Sea* (we know Stevens read this review [*L* 509]): "so many of Tate's poems have in them a commotion that agitates in obscurity without ever quite articulating through the surface"; that is why, "above all, Tate resorts to the traditional metres, forms, and allusions," writing "with the tenacity and rage that usually go with the lost cause."[57] For Louise Bogan, Tate's formal order in *The Winter Sea* proved he was "a conservative of what may be called the High Tradition."[58] When Stevens engaged a traditional stanza himself, such as in the astonishingly variable "Notes toward a Supreme Fiction" stanza, it was never with such rigor as Tate applied, neither involving rage nor invoking lost cause, nor designed to conserve a High Tradition. Because Stevens *had* no cause to be lost, Tate himself felt, he could make freer use of the order form brought: this is exactly what led Horace Gregory to use not Dante but modernism as the standard for judging "Mr. Stevens's employment of the *terza rima*" in "Notes," which was "equalled only by Dr. Williams in his poem 'The Yachts' "; Stevens, added Gregory, is "the master of a tradition in English verse" (the French symbolists).[59] Yet when Tate felt himself to be the master of a verse tradition, the critical response was very different; even Blackmur, a genuine admirer, was rather amazed that Tate would attempt to write a "willed dream" about Walt Whitman ("False Nightmare") and at the same time to comment, in "not quite eluctable images," on capitalism and the death of tradition in America—all in terza rima! It was simply too much. Blackmur attempted to comment on the opposing tendencies inherent in such uses of terza rima—no easy matter—"both its strictness as metric and its implied value as a complete structural ordering of emotion."[60] Even supposing that Stevens did not quite share Blackmur's feeling about the problems in Tate's formalism, still the epigraph of "Seasons of the Soul," taken from the thirteenth canto of the *Inferno*,[61] would surely have reminded Stevens of Tate's response, very unlike Gregory's, to "Notes." For Tate had written Stevens: "I posed to myself the academic question, what would a series of poems by Stevens accomplish if they were written in strict *terza rima*?"[62] Stevens's reply to Tate's new poem, then, in "The Creations of Sound," embeds its critical response—poems must have ideas as well as formal mastery—in the precise imprecision of its tercets. And so its *peculiar* horns play a *spontaneous* music, as it were: in the following tercet, for instance, its near-rhyme seeming to be deliberate in *not* conforming to the "strict *terza rima*" Tate wanted him to try:

> To see nor, reverberating, eke out the mind
> On peculiar horns, themselves eked out
> By the spontaneous particulars of sound.

Yet in "Seasons of the Soul," it is easy to see, even when Tate is attempting *not* to be "scornful of the factual or the commonplace" in another strict form—the difficult "little" canzone (*aba, cbd, ecde*)—that his commitment to the creation of sound as another lost cause undermines plain referentiality: if there is a real battleground here, it is (in Kreymborg's words) "a battleground in himself," Allen Tate's western front:

> It was a gentle sun
> When, at the June solstice
> Green France was overrun
> With caterpillar feet.
> No head knows where its rest is
> Or may lie down with reason
> When war's usurping claws

> Shall take the heart escheat—
> Green field in burning season
> To stain the weevil's jaws.

Even Tate's advocates felt that his point here was lost because of "a few Tate-isms," in Donald Davidson's phrase, "—words you are too fond of," for instance "escheat."[63]

The contemporary critics' response to such verse—and I suggest Stevens's as well—was to wonder why, if Tate wanted to further his critique of the new-nationalist fervor in favor of the war, he could not make it clearer. Blackmur, referring to "Ode to Our Young Pro-consuls of the Air," the poem Tate had written explicitly against the new nationalists, expressed this criticism best when he wrote: "The attitude is, to say the least of it, difficult, ironic, and has internal echoes that can be understood as one understands gesture, as at once formal, close with old meaning, and untoward, full of the unaccountable."[64] "Seasons of the Soul" ends with what must have seemed to Stevens, as he wrote "The Creations of Sound," a disingenuous call—to the old woman, mother of the sons "who have gone down / Into the burning cave" of Plato—to "Listen, while we confess / That we conceal our fear." "The Creations of Sound" responds, then, not merely by offering itself as a creation of sound, and by arguing about X's manner the *idea* that "We do not say ourselves like that in poems." While it perhaps does not effectively offer a solution to the problem of balancing cultural commitment against pure sound, the poem also served Stevens in forcefully rejecting Tate's intentional fallacy, to restore a sense of personality and emotion to the sound of words. Thus it allowed him to say, simply, We *do* say ourselves in poems:

> If the poetry of X was music,
> So that it came to him of its own,
> Without understanding, out of the wall
>
> Or in the ceiling, in sounds not chosen,
> Or chosen quickly, in a freedom
> That was their element, we should not know
>
> That X is an obstruction, a man
> Too exactly himself, and that there are words
> Better without an author, without a poet,
>
> Or having a separate author, a different poet,
> An accretion from ourselves, intelligent
> Beyond intelligence, an artificial man
>
> At a distance, a secondary expositor,
> A being of sound, whom one does not approach
> Through any exaggeration. From him, we collect.

Tell X that speech is not dirty silence
Clarified. It is silence made still dirtier.
It is more than an imitation for the ear.

He lacks this venerable complication. . . .

THE WAR-POEM BUSINESS

In the presence of extraordinary actuality, con-
sciousness takes the place of imagination.
—*Stevens quoted by Alvin Rosenfeld in*
A Double Dying:
Reflections on Holocaust Literature

This pitiful sound, which sometimes, goodness
knows how, reaches into the remotest prison cell,
is a concentrated expression of the last vestige of
human dignity. It is a man's way of leaving a trace.
. . . Silence is the real crime against humanity.
—*Sarah Berkowitz, a camp survivor, in*
Where Are My Brothers?

Having sometimes sensed a voice that comes from elsewhere
To dictate my verse in the middle of the night
I hear suddenly an interior speech
Saying to me: of these words none must be written.

Ayant parfois senti la voix qui vient d'ailleurs
Pour me dicter mes vers au milieu de la nuit
J'entends soudain en moi le verbe interieur
Qui me dit: de ces mots qu'aucun ne soit écrit.
—*Jean Wahl, "Inspiration and Silence,"*
a quatrain written at the concentration camp in Drancy

His firm stanzas hang like hives in hell. . . .
—*Stevens, "Esthétique du Mal" (1944)*

It was not unusual for poems emerging from Europe's concentration
camps to cling to traditional formal structures in much the way that the
imprisoned people themselves clung to the structures of habit, washing
methodically when the water was even dirtier than the body that needed
washing, eating with ritual care even when there was almost nothing to
eat.[1] A similar aesthetic urge toward accomplishment, precision, finitude,
even polish—toward formality as itself a satisfaction, as an essential exer-

cising of normal aesthetic desire—arose from the fact that many of the prisoners who turned to verse for solace were amateurs; in other words, writers who had never been professional, let alone experimental, would not likely turn from traditional rhyme and meter when first undertaking a poem as a stay against the chaos of the camps. There were others for whom formal writing *in extremis* represented a reversion from professional and academic modes of modern experiment, people already "modern" when incarcerated, who willingly gave up adherence to the exciting prewar revolt against tradition in order to take whatever relief might be gotten from the firmness, certainty, and sanity of convention at a time when the imagination fought its life-and-death battle against instability, caprice, and madness.[2] Jean Wahl had been one such poet-prisoner. It is not clear when Stevens received the typescript of Wahl's poems, fifty-eight of them clearly marked as having been written about camp life when Wahl was a prisoner at Drancy,[3] but it was almost certainly after Wahl and Stevens met at Mount Holyoke in August 1943 (though possibly later, in May of 1944 when Stevens was expressing renewed interest in Wahl's case and felt strongly that Alfred Knopf "ought to know about" him).[4] He had been one of six thousand Parisian Jews rounded up to form Drancy's first interned population; conditions actually improved somewhat after the Germans took over the administration of the camp in 1943, but during Wahl's earlier stay it fell between French bureaucratic cracks: when the first four thousand prisoners arrived, the camp had only twelve hundred wooden bunk-bed frames; fifty adults lived in a single room. Meals consisted almost entirely of cabbage soup. "A serious outbreak of dysentery made the inmates look like skeletons" at Drancy, and only then did the French call upon the Germans to investigate.[5] Wahl's "Witness Despite Myself," typical of the group of camp poems, emphasizes the means by which the verses themselves strengthen a resolve to resist in spite of such conditions. Such a will to bear witness is perhaps the most common theme in writing from the Nazi camps:[6]

> And here I am thrown in the middle of these struggles
> "It's just," "it's well," "it's right."
> I say like the others,
> Despite myself I bear witness.[7]

A stanza becomes a means of "leaving a trace," circumscribing silence, even if it means that the entire body of the writing is its very form (bearing witness, most commonly). If Stevens remembered Wahl's statements at Mount Holyoke, or read them in the Winter-Spring 1944 issue of Princeton's *Chimera*, the issue of silence would have been even clearer in the poems: "For whom does the poet write? He tells secrets," Wahl had said, "he tells things he ought not to tell."[8] No matter what filthy form the poem's noise may take—one of Wahl's poems, entitled "No Outcome," consists of a single line, "Frightful days, nauseating and no outcome"[9]— the stanza, as in Stevens's "stanza, my stone" (*CP* 203), gives rhetorical solidity to tenuous bodily life, exteriorizing the "interior speech" of Wahl's "Inspiration and Silence," which offers its paradoxical advice: draw stability from a simple old stanza to show yourself that *you* at least are civilized in the old ways, and do not forget to speak to the absolute uniqueness of your pain; yet "of these words," Wahl's interior speech tells him, "none must be written." Still, again, as Stevens could not fail to note (even if only by the look of some of Wahl's poems on the page), Wahl asked help from voices and structures not his own making. He translated Shakespeare's sonnets, for example, not so much for what Shakespeare said in them, but obviously for the tradition and stasis the sonnet form could signify.[10] So, too, with Keats. A perfect *abab* quatrain imitates a satisfying literary pattern and yet revises a famous literary sentiment: "Truth," this poem begins, "you are only beautiful when under threat."[11] As both Lawrence Langer and Alvin Rosenfeld have argued,[12] the "reversal of a familiar literary pattern" is nowhere more complex than in writing from the Nazi camps, with the doubled desire—affirmation yet repudiation—infecting even "the playfulness of rhyme," as Rosenfeld in particular has shown.[13] The generalization seems strongly confirmed by the experience of Primo Levi, then a chemist, making his way through the bleak Auschwitz workday by translating *The Divine Comedy* from recollected Italian into extemporaneous French (for a companion), working hard to retain every last terza rima ending.[14] At times in the poems Wahl gave Stevens, indeed, the severe pressure of rhyme—defiant *écrit* against dehumanizing *nuit*; *l'air transi* striving thematically to cancel *nuit de Drancy*—permits Wahl his most satisfying subversion and greatest hope: he has found a way to rhyme the very name of the camp, fixing it in sound, rendering it a poet's word, nothing but air itself. Yet the pained voice began as a bodily function, having undergone a process Elaine Scarry has described as "the transformation of body into voice."[15] So while Wahl's shrewd tactic of verbalizing the camp only calls us to attend more keenly to the physical pain the prisoner must constantly control in order to survive until morning, it also suggests the psychological acuity needed to hold on until then. Wahl's poems in this way suggest an effect of the sort that is, as Stevens put it, "part of the sublime / From which we shrink": "pain," to quote Stevens again, "torturing itself, / Pain killing pain on the very point of pain. / The volcano trembled in another ether, / As the body trembles at the end of life." The camps, Wahl showed, might not only provide documentary realism—though they did that amply—but also, in special instances (the academic philosopher imprisoned), a surprising self-reflexivity, poems whose power was formal and intrinsic and yet of the painful world: actual pain measurable only against itself. We have already seen the use of bodily pain (and the "Drancy"/ "transi" rhyme) in Wahl's "Drancy at Night": "Factory of death, Drancy at night, / Where the body, creaking, already feels the planks / The shoulders ache, I feel the hips groaning / But the mind remains supple and warm in the chilled air." Here outer discomfort created the occasion for the poem. It was as subversive as the supple manipulation of Drancy's assonance with air, with nothing. These and other poems in the group Wahl sent Stevens formed the basis of the "firm stanzas" of canto iii of Stevens's aesthetics of pain, as "Esthétique" strived to metaphorize the physically realized but vague death threat of war as a ubiquitously terrifying volcanic threat, and to thematize a reversion to formality in the poetry of pain. And so it was also a rejoinder to Tate's suggestion that Stevens try terza rima in a time of war in that it responded to an actual testimony of pain:

> His firm stanzas hang like hives in hell
> Or what hell was, since now both heaven and hell
> Are one, and here, O terra infidel.

That Stevens also inscribed into "Esthétique du Mal" several hints of indebtedness to Henry and Barbara Church further supports the idea that the formal hell of canto iii is dependent on Stevens's glimpse of Wahl's experience, a view for which he had only the Churches to thank—that, in short, "*his* firm stanzas" are Wahl's. Peter Brazeau's exhaustive work and Helen Church Minton's fine memory make it possible to approach what Stevens meant when he said he "got Mrs. Church's paratroopers in" the eleventh canto (*L* 472); Barbara Church had described for Stevens a dream she had had about military invasion in which "little men [were] coming down with lawn mowers" (*WSR* 223), the stimulus having evidently been her constant waking thoughts about the emancipation of France. "At dawn," Stevens wrote, "The paratroopers fall and as they fall / They mow the lawn"—an image of liberation awakening dormant tufts of flowers now "spring[ing] up from buried houses / Of poor, dishonest people" who had "Long since" allowed the steeple bells to go unrung (*CP* 322). This eleventh scene of Stevens's poem, however dreamlike (and to that extent private), is quite obviously, in the summer of 1944, an attempt to convey the scene of the Allied landings as depicted, in dreams and otherwise, by the Churches via Fernand Auberjonois of the intelligence corps, now himself crossing through retaken France toward Paulhan in Paris. Stevens imagined "A vessel [that] sinks in waves of people" coterminus with the surreal dawn of paratroopers. The poem also contains, less elaborately, what seems to be a private joke between Stevens and Henry Church, who had complained of Proosch's translation of Hölderlin. This had Hölderlin's ducks swimming in an ocean (*Meer*) instead of a lake (*See*).[16] Into "Esthétique" Stevens encoded a pithy assent: "Lakes are more reasonable than oceans" (*CP* 325).

Despite these personal messages, "Esthétique du Mal" forced Stevens to reckon with several major issues of the moment. When writing to the Churches about his new poem after it was finished, in August 1944, he apparently gave a hint of the sort of pain he meant. "I think of you pretty often," he wrote, "in the face of the news from France, but suppose that, even if it were possible for you to return tomorrow, you would not do so. There appears to be a good deal to be settled in France before the milkman begins to come round regularly again, and it is certain that it will not begin to be settled *until after the British and American forces are out of the place*" (*L* 472; emphasis added). Interesting that Stevens would be thinking not merely of victory but of a continental Europe once again disentangled from Anglo-American assistance; this sort of thinking had been unusual in 1939, when Stevens wrote for the *Partisan* symposium as an isolationist while astutely suggesting that the biggest problem facing the United States was how to prepare for the postwar world, after new American expectations of power had been raised. Even now, almost exactly five years later, the idea was uncommon outside circles of policymakers; most Americans were thinking about victory first and foremost, and not about Allied withdrawal, Allied incursion being then only weeks old.

"Esthétique du Mal" was written at the request of John Crowe Ransom, when that incursion was just nine days old. The poem Stevens wrote by that August conforms to Ransom's June 15, 1944, request for "a sizable poem, or set of poems" for his *Kenyon Review*.[17] Stevens got the idea for his poetics of pain from a scolding given *Kenyon* in a recent issue. It was a letter to the editor from a soldier, which Ransom quoted as part of his editorial comment for the Spring 1944 issue. The soldier found "the poetry in *Kenyon Review* lamentable in many ways *because it is cut off from pain*"—because, for one thing, it did not publish enough poetry about the war. But what kind of war poetry did the correspondent mean? First of all, the soldier made an *exception* of "poets of charming distemper *like Wallace Stevens* (for whom we all developed considerable passion)" (emphasis added). Yet he called upon Ransom to support poems of "muscle and nerve," and hoped to see more poetry of reality. "[I]t must communicate a lot of existence," the soldier wrote plainly; in response to the end of the war, it must reflect and satisfy "an overwhelming desire to go on."[18] This letter would not have inspired Stevens to write "Esthétique du Mal" had not Ransom replied to the soldier as dismissively as he did; he had bigger fish to fry, and used the enlisted man's unsophisticated sense of poetry to mount yet another counterattack on the new nationalists. He saw "little to gain [for

American poets] by pretending they were at the front," and decided that "normal literary activity" should continue unabated simply because it "could not occur at the front." He recalled what had happened at the *Nation* and the *New Republic* after the Great War; a commitment to battle-front reality "turned many first-rate literary men into commandos," the effect of which was to radicalize those two opinion weeklies through the thirties and beyond. Ransom even took the opportunity to plug Arthur Koestler's *Darkness at Noon*, providing us a foretaste of powerful literary-political alliances to come: Koestler, the disillusioned ex-communist, util-ized by Ransom to prove *Kenyon*'s point about the related failures of ideo-logical criticism and social realism—what Koestler's American compatriots would come to call "the end of ideology." Ransom came very close to mak-ing that designation himself in the 1944 editorial, recommending Koest-ler's book as a cure for the soldier's undistinguished craving for war poems because it "tells of the disillusionment of a political revolutionist whose ideals have been smashed, a sore situation." Then this practical problem: What would happen to the professional war poet when there was no more war? Ransom feared that if the war-poem business continued to boom "a poor soldier," aspiring again to good poetry, would be unable to "retire in good conscience" after the war. Ransom used the soldier's complaining letter demanding a poetry of pain to attack generally the "powerful illusion . . . that art is accountable as a public utility." *Kenyon* would remain op-posed to the idea that the poet should ever "enlist his art."[19]

As with Tate's most acrid counterarguments, Ransom's editorial seems to have struck Stevens as unfair and certainly impractical as an answer to a simple and reasonable, if clumsy, request from a soldier. Right then, the soldier had written, he needed a poetry that would not deliberately cut itself off from real suffering. "What particularly interested me," Stevens wrote Ransom, "was the letter from one of your correspondents about the relation between poetry and what he called pain. Whatever he may mean, it might be interesting to try to do an esth[é]tique du mal" (*L* 468). If Ransom rather abstractly announced that the soldier's "communication is still unanswered," and if his editorial, in Stevens's view, repeated the stan-dard formalist argument against war poetry without ever really responding to the issue raised by the soldier from the point of view of a witness to war, then the poem Stevens now sat down to write did form a response.

The obvious place to locate such a response in the poem, it would seem at first, would be the seventh of the fifteen cantos, the well-known section that begins "How red the rose that is the soldier's wound." It continues:

> The wounds of many soldiers, the wounds of all
> The soldiers that have fallen, red in blood,
> The soldier of time grown deathless in great size.

. . . .
In which his wound is good because life was.
No part of him was ever part of death.
A woman smoothes her forehead with her hand
And the soldier of time lies calm beneath that stroke.

This is an anthologizable war poem if ever Stevens wrote one. Yet I would argue that one searches more usefully for Stevens's response to the soldier's need for poetry about pain in the eighth canto, where a "shaken realist" who "First sees reality" arrives at an affirmation, an enabling new sense of the real that induces confidence despite the periodic deaths of the imagination: "In the yes of the realist . . . he must / Say yes, spoken because under every no / Lay a passion for yes that had never been broken." A response to Ransom's correspondent might also be found in the eleventh canto, notwithstanding its private nods to the Churches. The village steeple bells ring out victory. The speaker, recounting the story of paratroopers, finds his "tongue caress[ing] these exacerbations," relishing the task of reporting the events of an important dawn operation. Yet this canto provides evidence of the sort of verse the soldier criticized in his letter to Ransom: poets ought to scorn the "well-made" scene of war, for example "A ship that rolls on a confected ocean" in "pink," imaginary weather. The "exacerbations" of the tongue telling pain distinguish themselves from that tongue's "essential savor"—a new and bitterer taste, as it were, for verse "Like hunger that feeds on its own hungriness."

The final canto expresses Stevens's reply to poetry and pain perhaps most responsively of all. Here the recognition that the "greatest poverty is not to live in the physical world" leads Stevens directly to the conclusion that for the Western poet of the ninth canto—with his new distaste for cricketlike voices of naturalized indifference "Here in the West"—it suffices that he lives "Merely . . . as and where" he lives. New poetic self-doubts are in fact the result of solid contact with the real, connection to a world of pain that seemed otherwise to negate the very "thought" of such "sight." But now it does not prohibit poetic insight: "One might have thought of sight, but who could think / Of what it sees, for all the ill it sees?" Here we can measure the advance made in Stevens's wartime poetry in just the few months since "The Creations of Sound." Along the way, from "Creations" to "Esthétique," he discovered the paradoxes of testimony in "Repetitions of a Young Captain." If there the poet and the Young Captain joined in one voice to anticipate the objection that "these were only words," not the thing-at-war itself but a "repetition" of the thing, now Stevens could take the fate of retelling a crucial and liberating step further. The conclusion to "Esthétique du Mal" thematized just what war poetry "could *not* propound," and so it was left to tell movingly of the effort to replicate pain in verse formed "out of what one sees and hears and out / Of what one feels." It was not merely an acute modernist ear that heard and selected speech deemed appropriate, but externality that demanded a hearing, a "Speech [that] found the ear, for all the evil sound." Stevens would continue to consider the "metaphysical changes that occur," to be sure, but these were now "swarming" with a new knowledge of a physical reality, and a comprehension of the tremendous project entailed in living "merely"—in surviving with no other thought but surviving.

In contrast to these persuasive responses, in the eighth, eleventh, and fifteenth cantos, the anthologizable seventh served essentially the same purpose as the terza rima canto, the third ("His firm stanzas hang like hives in hell"), but with this key difference: in each, the third and seventh, the impulse is *exclusively* formal, but in the case of canto iii, formality itself sates a structural desire, feeds a formal habit as a means to survival (a lesson learned from Wahl's experience in the poetics of pain). Yet "How Red the Rose That Is the Soldier's Wound," from that perfectly regular line onward, was obviously, if only half-intentionally, more than a reaction to a poet's painful wartime experience; it was also, I think, a reaction to the war-poem business itself. It seems deliberately, again, a poem to be designated subgenerically, answering professionalized definitions of obliged response to reality. It can quite easily be removed and read separately, as no other canto in the poem can be—apart from the special mode of pain introduced in the first two cantos and then generally sustained in the rest of the poem. The pain of the other parts does not purport to be more than psychological or spiritual discomfort, a soreness or an ache, a severe disappointment; they do not attempt a bloody wounding.

"How Red the Rose" was indeed plucked from the other cantos and hailed as a "war poem" in the professional sense, and set out on a career all its own. Lieutenant Commander Richard Eberhart and Master Sergeant Selden Rodman reprinted it as "The Soldier's Wound" in *War and the Poet: An Anthology of Poetry Expressing Man's Attitudes to War from Ancient Times to the Present*.[20] And Oscar Williams used it in *The War Poets* of 1945, where it met with the editor's great praise.[21] How had Stevens's connection to the war-poem business come so far? The answer to this question gives a hint of the acclaim awaiting Stevens in the postwar years. By the time the war-poem business reached dead end— the publication of Williams's *War Poets* in June 1945 sufficiently dates it—the inclusion of Stevens's verse attracted notice for its inherent value and not for its status as war poetry. Vivienne Koch, thoroughly disgusted with Williams's selection by then, proclaimed "Repetitions of a Young Captain"—it had been segregated in the civilian section—"the best *war-poem* in the book." (Among the poems by "Men in the Armed Forces," she felt Reed Whittemore's "A Winter Shore" to be the best, but she was "willing to venture" that it was not "composed during Mr. Whittemore's service.")[22]

For *New Poems 1942* it had been quite enough for Oscar Williams to say that poets who generally recognized society as "fearfully complex"[23] would serve well as war poets. And since the planning and printing of his anthology awkwardly crossed the date of American entry—his introduction was written in March 1942, while many if not most of the poems collected were written before the previous December 7, including Stevens's contributions, "Metamorphosis," the two "Contrary Theses," "Phosphor Reading by His Own Light," "The Search for Sound Free from Motion," and "Jumbo"—Williams's definition of war poetry was created as much from an expedient sense of the changed market as from a coherent sense of the subgenre.[24] To the doubters' question "Where are the war poets?" Williams was armed with a book full of verse answers constituting a tradition unto themselves. Another logical form of Williams's nationalist rejoinder was this: so much good *new* poetry—not war poetry only but poetry in general—was being written that "[p]oetry is an unacknowledged war industry."[25] In all his war-poem anthologies Williams tried to play it both ways, but never more than here, in *New Poems 1942*: if his selections came to be considered "war poetry," then they would have found a general audience; yet if his readership did extend beyond the usual finite group of poetry lovers—and this was clearly his aim—it would consist of the very same public crying "for drum-beating patriotic rhymes" he criticized in his introduction. There is indeed a sampling of such poems in the selection, such as W. R. Rodgers's "End of a World,"[26] which Tate scorned along with the whole nationalist genre in his review of the 1942 anthology: "beyond the fact that it is a war poem," Tate wrote of Rodgers's contribution, "I do not know what it is."[27] Another rationale for the nationalist idea of the year's work in poetry as war verse was that the selection stood beyond the reach of ideology. To Williams, unity was not achievable as a reconciliation of *competing* views about the role of art in society; putting together war-poem anthologies was not a matter of either consensus or dissensus. Rather, they were constructed by "a purely personal choice." "If I have chosen poems from the 'regional' school or the 'left' school, I didn't look to see the name on the door." Nor had poems been chosen that "illustrate a critical theory," though Williams himself attempted to offer one.[28] Only one poem among Stevens's offering of six, going under the collective title "Six Discordant Songs," suggested any relation to the emerging war-poem business. (The exception was "Contrary Theses I.") To glean more about the business from the 1942 anthology, one turned rather to Jarrell's "90 North" or to Karl Shapiro's "Scyros,"[29] both of which *Tate* cited as fine war poems. Tate briefly acknowledged "good new work by Stevens"; but, he added, these poems were "not his best." Nor could he resist getting in a shot at MacLeish here, whose poem "The Spanish Dead" Williams included in the anthology: "Let us in kindness to MacLeish, hold the belief that although the poets are not *irresponsible*, his own verse has gone sour for a while" (emphasis added).[30]

New Poems 1943 kept apace the business Williams himself had helped start, defining the war-poem genre more enthusiastically (though no more specifically) than a year earlier. He now broadened the definition of war poetry, and Stevens's poetry was implicated in the effort to certify Williams's judgment that poets "are experiencing a great disruption" and that they "intensely felt the fact of war, whether their subject matter be swans or strawberries, rifles or love"—that they write "not of the movement of troops, the horror of the enemy or the mechanism of the tank, but of the state of the human organism in the emotion of now living"—and that the "poet is thus always at war."[31] Here Williams quoted the statement Stevens had appended to *Parts of a World* to make it seem a wartime book. Though Williams's rationale for citing Stevens's statement in 1943 was obviously designed to serve his own and not necessarily Stevens's interests, it did provide, however accidentally, just the right context for the three poems Stevens offered this collection, creating the strong impression that he had learned something about poetry's necessary participation in public relations, perhaps from having seen his "Six Discordant Songs" fare so poorly, by war-poem standards, against the poems in the 1942 volume by Jarrell, Auden, MacLeish, Spender, C. Day Lewis ("War Poem"), George Barker ("Requiem Anthem for the Austrian Constitution"), and by Karl Shapiro writing from the Pacific. Indeed, as I have argued, each of the three poems he submitted for the 1943 anthology, "Dutch Graves in Bucks County," "No Possum, No Sop, No Taters," and "Chocorua to Its Neighbor," arose from the same basic impulse that led Williams, however clumsily and for very different reasons, to speak of home-front verse as authenticated war poems. In other words, they could help in the editorial effort to affirm war poets' talent for writing of "a great disruption" without having to make troop movements or tank mechanisms the matter of poems. Each of these three works, characteristic of Stevens's national moment, seemed in context to be "doing its bit," as Williams put it.[32]

Yet even the Americanization of "Dutch Graves," "No Possum," and "Chocorua" was overshadowed (to judge from the reviews) by war poems more clearly fitting the new definitions. Such a poem was Marianne Moore's contribution, "In Distrust of Merits," which obviously outdid Stevens's effort to forge a poetry of the "inward" war of the home front, a quality critics then[33] and now[34] have noticed in praising Moore's willingness to assert that "There never was a war that was / not inward."[35] She was brilliantly appealing to both sides of the war-poem question—to Vivienne Koch, Oscar Williams's detractor, who found in Moore's poem attestation to a "strange and enriching humility,"[36] and to Williams himself, who was certain Moore "illustrate[d] my present thesis" (Williams's Moore gave "direct communication of honest feeling by one ready to search her own heart to discover the causes of war").[37] Still, for a few who knew to look closely for it—such as Koch, getting impatient with Williams's annual (and changing) dicta, and Frank Jones, with his particular political knowledge both of French writers and of Stevens's interest in their close calls and rescues—Stevens's "inward war" might also be discerned. "No Possum, No Sop, No Taters," with its hard-won sense that home-front belt-tightening forced one to feel the effect of total war in the absence of the heat, as it were, of battle; and "Chocorua to Its Neighbor," which democratized and denaturalized a combatant's heroism while Americanizing the sources of poetic inspiration at a time when European sources had dried up; and "Dutch Graves in Bucks County," with its historicist rationale for finding signs of the fallen at home and thus supporting total war—these also were poems deeply marked by signs of victorious "inward war," by an "enriching humility" certainly "strange" when put next to much of Stevens's other work.

Williams's 1944 volume, published in August of that year, presented still greater claims for the special interest in war poems than a year earlier. In reply, critical skepticism began to be expressed more bravely; and Stevens found his contribution, "Repetitions of a Young Captain," caught in the middle of the controversy. Rationalizing the division of the anthology into two sections—for the first time, "Poems from the Armed Services" were segregated from the noncombatants' poems—Williams asked his readers to set "Repetitions of a Young Captain" against the repetitions of F. T. Prince, "who is actually a young captain."[38] Did Williams's comparison of Stevens and Prince mean to suggest that one could really tell the difference between inexperience and experience with war, a detachment and a directness? In one there was the plain, brave speech of the soldier-poet:

> On a few words of what is real in the world
> I nourish myself. I defend myself against
> Whatever remains.

In the other, the noncombatant's cerebral contemplations on this war's destruction of high culture:

> He plays with death and animality;
> And reading in the shadows of his pallid flesh, I see
> The idea of Michelangelo's cartoon
> Of soldiers bathing.

Yes; but the lines quoted first are Stevens's (*CP* 308), and those quoted next are from Captain Prince's "Soldiers Bathing."[39] Williams's comparison hardly meant to disparage Stevens's poem, yet it did imply—wrongly, I hope it is clear—that Stevens's war poems merely advance his old self-reflexivity and that Prince's warriors glistened of earth's water, not of art's. At the same time, of course, Williams wanted to keep Stevens's hand in— wanted it to be evident that "the value of poetry does not of course come from the fact that poets suffer the action of life or of war." Yet he also announced a new idea, a great change from 1942: soldier-poets like Prince get us closer to war than home-front poets like Stevens; "work by men in the services, springing as it does from the actual scenery of war, cannot but have an extra emotional impact for anyone alive today. The validity of experience when touched by talent has a special interest and deserves a special respect."[40]

Insofar as there was now beginning to be a backlash against the war-poem business as a business,[41] it was also directed against Williams himself, who, as everyone now knew, had built a career from the timeliness of a subgenre.[42] Harry Roskolenko decided that Williams gathered his poet contributors as "a Hollywood director" gathers "handsome male actors."[43] Many sensed the decline by 1944—"Not All New, Some Good" was F. O. Matthiessen's qualified praise for the new annual[44]—and not only the re-viewers but also the soldier-poet readers. Sergeant Sam Morse, writing the Grolier Book Shop to order new books, wondered if he should bother with *New Poems 1944*: "I'm not sure there is very much worth reading in it," he wrote Gordon Cairnie, "*but there may be a Stevens poem or two*" (emphasis added).[45] Note, then, a shift in the way such books by diverse hands were being read: as readers and critics began to cringe at another big volume filled with war effort, Stevens's verse—here "Repetitions of a Young Cap-tain"—was drawing attention for its intrinsic value as *a Stevens poem*. We know, from Auberjonois's story, the irony of this particular use of Stevens, for "Repetitions" was at least one wartime poem that might be said to have been constructed from a witnessing of war; Stevens's poem, like Prince's, was grounded in the experiences of a man who was *actually a young captain*.

For Matthiessen, Stevens assisted in the overdue reproval of Williams's editorial rationale. In disagreeing strongly with Williams's decision to de-tach the mobilized poets from the civilians, and in ridiculing Williams's claim that the soldiers' poems "have an extra emotional impact," Mat-thiessen commented: "it must simply be said that unless they were in uni-form, they would not be in an anthology."[46] So Matthiessen was drawing Stevens back to the other side. Praising "Repetitions," the critic asserted that Stevens's poem was one of the "two most impressive reactions to the war" in the book.[47]

In her ground-breaking essay "Poetry in World War II," Vivienne Koch took Matthiessen's objection to the war-poetry business a significant and final step further. Koch vigorously attacked Williams's idea that " 'active participation in the jeopardy of war does enhance the validity of well-written verse.' " "If this is true," she observed, "it is certainly not borne out by many of the poems he has included." And here she stated her judgment that "Repetitions of a Young Captain" was simply the best poem among all those Williams selected.[48]

Returning to "Esthétique du Mal" now, with a sense of the shifting literary politics presiding over the professionalization of war poems, we find the pressure to conform to the genre distinctly impressed upon the poem's structure. From this it is but a small way toward an explanation as to why the poem must be formally fifteen different things in as many cantos. While this is a remarkable achievement of variety in itself, virtuosity alone does not describe the severe strain—a strain caused by the equal and opposite pulls of Williams's optimism and Tate's, Ransom's, and now Roskolenko's, Matthiessen's, Koch's, and others' doubts—that tends to pull the poem apart, even as such pulling reassures us that Stevens's mastery withstood a time of what he soon bitterly described as a "violent change" in aesthetic value (L 525). We note, however, that this virtuosity is most in evidence when the logically rigid categorizing of section xii ("He disposes the world in categories, thus") requires the disingenuous, muscular irrationalism of the anticommunist canto (the fourteenth, where Stevens merely repeats verbatim from Dwight MacDonald's *Politics* Victor Serge's claims against Konstantinov, postideological revisionism against murderous political orthodoxy)[49]—and threatens with its obvious counterbalancing to obscure the genuine pathos of the final canto, the fifteenth, with its striking confession, "The greatest poverty is not to live / In a physical world." So, too, the comparison between the third and seventh sections, made inevitable by the obvious quality of the seventh as a wartime set piece, works to undermine the motives for overt craft of the third section (the response to Tate's terza rima challenge and Wahl's pain).

In "Esthétique du Mal," as throughout the period of this agreement with reality (late 1941 through mid-1944), Stevens's war verse is most original *as* war verse when it reacts favorably to the new nationalism by reacting negatively to Tate's and others' antinationalism; more to the point here, Stevens had least to say when reacting plainly or positively to the nationalists. But this is not just another sign of his addiction to indirectness. I have tried to show how others' direct responses to the national call were full of double impulses as well and, conversely, how some—Kenneth Burke, for instance, succeeding in his *Mesures* talk and elsewhere—formulated a response the persuasiveness of which was indeed dependent on its indirectness (in Burke's case, also on its conciliatory tone). The three rare moments in which Stevens formed a *directly* favorable reaction to Williams's brand of nationalism help clarify the point: one came in "How Red the

Rose" of "Esthétique"; two others were the prose statement about poetry and war attached to *Parts of a World*, and the soldier epilogue to "Notes."

The soldier epilogue is not usefully considered part of the "Notes toward" Stevens's most important idea. We must assume that it causes an undeserved break between itself and the thirtieth canto of the poem proper, a far more appropriate conclusion to its argument.[50] The postscripted claim—that "The soldier is poor without the poet's lines"—sounds precisely like a working out of Oscar Williams's rules for war poetry, and understates, just as Williams annually did, the complexity and drama of Stevens's agitated and not-always-successful attempts to approach a concept of reality in the preceding climactic cantos of "Notes" itself. Such facile exclamations as "How simply the fictive hero becomes the real" hardly seem the invention of the particular muse of the final "It Must Give Pleasure" section, she who sits "Bent over work," "anxious" but finally triumphant after great formal effort, sustaining a "fiction that results from feeling" (*CP* 406). Evidence for such a view is to be found in a letter Stevens wrote in which he expressed a clear understanding of the problems the Cummington Press *Notes* would have finding its way among books of war poetry pouring off the presses just at the time he added his soldier epilogue. How could *Notes*, notwithstanding its epilogue, stay in the mind of any allegiant reviewer when there was also John Russell McCarthy's *At 10 P.M. the News*; W. R. Rodgers's *Awake! and Other Wartime Poems* ("Rodgers," wrote Ruth Lechlitner, "subscribes to the belief that this war is the End of the World");[51] Stephen Vincent Benét's *They Burned the Books*, a radio play in verse written for the Writers War Board; Muriel Rukeyser's *Wake Island* (the island's few gallant defenders were "PROOF OF AMERICA!");[52] and Mark van Doren's *Our Lady Peace and Other War Poems*? This last book led Northrop Frye to remind his readers that "[a]ll the average poet knows about war and Fascism is what he sees in the papers," and to quip that poets under the spell of the war-poem genre merely "communicate to one another in subtly cadenced murmurings the fact that they deprecate war and Fascism."[53] Not surprisingly, then, Stevens noticed a few months after he added the epilogue to his own poem that "there has been a change in the atmosphere that hasn't done the book any good."[54] Stevens appended the war poem just after May 19, 1942—much of "Notes" had been written in March and April—and he supervised the production of the book that emphasized it. Only at this precise point, then, did he explicitly direct the Cummington Press to design the back cover so that the war poem would be prominent (*L* 408). The first two and last two lines were arranged to form a rectangular border on the cover (see illustration). This design would convey the distinct impression that the address to the soldier was not merely to be read as an afterthought, but rather as providing a wartime frame for the whole project of the supreme fiction. "Soldier, there

The back cover of the Cummington Press edition of *Notes toward a Supreme Fiction*.

is a war between the mind / And sky, between thought and day and night. . . . How gladly with proper words the soldier dies, / If he must, or lives on the bread of faithful speech." Similarly, "How Red the Rose" of "Esthétique du Mal" called out for canonization in its own day; indeed, it was praised when Oscar Williams published it—omitting, of course, all else in "Esthétique"—in his greatest wartime effort yet, *The War Poets* of 1945.

At the end of 1944, to ballyhoo *The War Poets*, which was planned for release the next summer, Oscar Williams organized a symposium in which poets would get the chance to say how important their war poems had been to the war effort. Excerpts from the poets' replies would be published in *Harper's* and would form a special section in the book. Williams conducted his survey publicly as "a kind of Gallup poll of the soul." Such overt democratization of poetry was apparently too much for Stevens, especially as the volume would include two of his own poems. To Tate's pleasure, he and Stevens finally agreed on an essential point: the problem of the moment was less and less the war itself and increasingly the threat of organized labor in the United States and overseas. Tate wrote Stevens at the end of November: "Williams asked me for an article on this subject, but so far I haven't been able to think of anything that I haven't already put into certain poems."[55] Stevens's reply was in part a fib about his recent work (an exaggeration obviously designed for Tate's eye), and yet it was also a premonition of the ostensibly postideological moment to come:

> [Williams also] asked me for such an article, but I did not promise to send him one. After all, *I have nothing to say about the war*. The big thing+ in the world is not the war, but the rattle and bang on the left and in the labor movement.
>   + potentially[56]

He did, of course, have something to say about the war in his poems (as he clearly acknowledged later);[57] obviously, other matters were now on his mind, as evidenced by the letter he wrote Williams the same day, in which he repeated his idea that "the thing that really involves the future is not the war, but the leftist movement." The force of the postwar left, he predicted, a movement created by "the proletarian politics of the New Deal" and held at bay during the war, was now "as great as the force of war" and, moreover, "will survive the war." This idea would dictate Stevens's overt political positions in the late forties and early fifties. But as for the immediate future—for "Description without Place" of 1945—even more significant was his notion that the impact of the war on Americans' sense of place had already peaked and that if a new "abundant poetry" (*L* 495) was to arise out of this next troubling phase of the war it would reflect the common feeling that the United States was prepared for unprecedented reaching outward:

"From our point of view here at home, America has never been on the make, or on the grab, whatever people may have said of us elsewhere"; but, he added, "The Japanese war is likely to change all that" (*L* 507). As he began to discover, in end-of-war poems like "Debris of Life and Mind" (published July 1945), that a unified sense of the satisfyingly familiar became untenable, he began to wonder why "Speak[ing] of familiar things," things of the American home (*CP* 338), was so disconcertingly similar to extracting the foreign from a reemergent correspondent like Leonard van Geyzel in Ceylon or from a new, exciting one like José Rodríguez Feo in Cuba; Stevens would begin to investigate why, in James Clifford's words, "[t]he 'exotic' is uncannily close."[58] Indeed the shift from the "gathered-up forgetfulness" (*CP* 360) of an unchanged American hometown, which received the returning soldier as himself a kind of foreigner (in "A Woman Sings a Song for a Soldier Come Home"), to the animating idea that "One Must Sit Still To Discover the World"[59] entailed a more ethnographically sophisticated move than one might at first expect from a poet who had abandoned plans for travel. Despite his recognition that one must "extract" familiarity from the foreign (*L* 513), it is hardly less true of Stevens's sense of postwar culture-collecting than of Clifford's that "[d]ifference is encountered in the adjoining neighborhood, [while] the familiar turns up at the ends of the earth."[60]

As for Tate and Stevens, they were still jockeying for position even as Stevens was moving onto these new issues: in 1945 the two only reached agreement, apparently, for each other's benefit. As a matter of fact, Tate had *not* refused to submit a comment on war poetry to Williams for the last big anthology. He had only told Williams himself that he was "a little skeptical" because—he took the familiar stance—"[a]nything said ought to be said in the poetry." On that point, at least, Tate was being theoretically consistent. Still, among Oscar Williams's war-anthology papers at Harvard lies a letter from Tate promising at least this much: "I will try to make a statement about war & poetry" and "I will see what can be done."[61] My speculation is that Tate was then encouraged by Stevens's apparently adamant resistance to the idea of writing a prose statement, and in the end Tate did not submit one to Williams. When several weeks before V-J Day *The War Poets* appeared, with some fanfare,[62] it must have come as quite a shock to Tate to find *Stevens's* name listed among those who had contributed a statement on war poetry, Williams's "Gallup poll of the soul." Stevens had relented, permitting Williams to reprint the prose statement that had been appended to *Parts of a World*. So Wallace Stevens was right there among "The War Poets," seeming to contradict what in no uncertain terms he had told Tate he now believed. But in print he reiterated his brand of nationalism: "[I]n war, the desire to move in the direction of fact as we want it to be and to move quickly is overwhelming."

If Tate looked closely at the statement reprinted from *Parts*, on the other hand, he might have found the clue to the impermanence of Stevens's successive agreements with reality (once in the Popular Front days and now, in wartime): so long as these agreements held Stevens close to the world of pressing facts, he seemed to be saying "the yes of the realist . . . because he must / Say yes" (in the words of "Esthétique" [*CP* 320]), to be an affirmer of the American reality and strategy that he, with Tate at other times, mistrusted. But such agreements, it might have been equally evident, were special moments of convergence between Stevens and "the actual world"—moments that had every bit as much to do with movements in that world, its peculiar but measurable rhetorical confusions, as with movements in Stevens's poetic rhetoric. He was obviously about to emerge from this particular agreement, and yet the belated use of the 1942 statement seemed oddly to confirm that the movement from engagement to detachment was cyclical, and that Stevens would again return to reality after a time away: "We leave fact and *come back to it*," he is quoted as saying in *The War Poets*, published on June 19, 1945, "*come back to what we wanted fact to be*, not to what it was, not to what it has often remained. The poetry of a work of the imagination constantly illustrates the fundamental and endless struggle with fact" (*OP* 242; emphasis added).

Part Two

STEVENS AT THE END OF IDEOLOGY

CHAPTER 3

Description without a Sense of Place

His places are places visited on a vacation.
—*Robert Lowell, in a review*
of Stevens's Transport to Summer

From the depths of his distance from everything he
extracts, because he needs to extract.
—*Stevens, writing about Leonard van Geyzel (L 513)*

Because our "internationalism" lacks solid foundation it may be difficult for us to see in any consistent way just what is to our self-interest.
—*Hadley Cantril, "How Real Is America's*
Internationalism?" April 29, 1945

following
the crisis (at home)
peasant loyalties inspire
the avant-garde.
—*William Carlos Williams,*
"A Place (Any Place) to Transcend All Places,"
a poem written in reply to
Stevens's "Description without Place"

JUNE 27, 1945. Not surprisingly, when asked to give the oration for the Phi Beta Kappa exercises at Harvard on that date, Sumner Welles chose to refer to events of the moment. Former undersecretary of state, author of the polemical *Time for Decision* (1944), theorist of postwar balance of power, vociferous proponent of the nascent United Nations organization, Welles could offer the Harvard audience his "Vision of a World at Peace,"[1] a vision that enabled him to perceive "traditions of generations of isolationism" still working counterproductively though "subconsciously" in the minds of Americans.[2] Yet he also saw that the United States would not be the primary stumbling block to a postwar peace. If anything, "[w]e have too often refrained . . . from maintaining any firm position, even on questions of the highest principle, in problems in which the Soviet Union was primarily involved. This has been the case even though we ourselves are known to have no axe to grind."[3] Thus "we," unlike the Soviets, "have made it clear that we desire no territorial or material gain." Welles was giving the graduating class at Harvard its final and most important lesson in political science. "No student of the world's history" could deny at that moment that the American people would now make the decisions affecting "the destinies of the human race in the coming years." Nor, despite Americans' physical distance from the battle still raging, would such a twentieth-century historian deny in June of 1945 that the "tidal waves" of this second world war were "making their effects felt in every field of life."[4]

If Welles's decision to refer straightforwardly to recent events came as no surprise at Harvard, what should we make of Stevens's decision *not* to? The final point of Welles's speech itself suggests that the poet who shared the platform with the politician that morning at the Fogg Museum would also surely have something to say about prevailing circumstances, for the politician's way of speaking about the effects of the war "in *every* field of life" served to enlarge the relevance of his position from politics to politics-as-including-culture. Welles could easily sustain the wartime conception of art, too, as a war effort that must not relent in the postwar period, and in his Harvard speech he pushed that point by rhetorically creating a moment in which he acknowledged the situation of his fellow speaker. Traditionally, indeed, the annual PBK Oration and Poem—ritually capitalized in all correspondence files of the Harvard PBK chapter[5]—complemented each other. Yet Stevens's offering, a long poem called "Description without Place" (*CP* 339–46), evidently had nothing to say about the present situation.

The organizers of the occasion had not in fact given him much guidance. Theodore Morrison, chairman of the Literary Committee of the Phi Beta Kappa chapter and member of the Harvard English department, when inviting Stevens to read, informed him that while "no custom determines the kind of poem to be presented," it should be new and unpublished.[6] William C. Greene, secretary of the chapter and classics professor, wrote in mid-March to say that "no strict limits" had ever been placed on the length of the Poem; yet it had been held customarily to ten or fifteen minutes.[7] Stevens broke with this custom if not all others as well; "Description without Place" would grow to 152 lines in the next thirteen weeks and, at his sometimes exasperatingly slow pace of reading, would be twice or three times as long as his audience expected.[8] Morrison pointed out from the start that the world war had transformed the occasion to the extent that it had become "progressively more informal,"[9] and as Stevens looked through the newspapers in the late spring he must have realized that events surrounding university activities elsewhere had been less than traditionally festive, even subdued. Typically, commencement speakers that season took time to commemorate the dead and wounded among students and alumni.[10] Guest orators of all kinds were instructing the college and university classes of 1945 in "the struggle for domination, for power and gain," and urged competing factions among the nation's future leaders to cooperate now as never before to end the "cruel and murderous conflict" caused by nationalism. We must guard, another speaker argued, against "emotional lassitude in the years after the war." On the contrary, another said, by making postwar tasks "as personal and as concrete as you have made your war-work services," Americans can constructively and happily make the transition from "total war" to peaceful cooperation (although competition was still the key: "our youth must be as enthusiastically devoted to our way of life as the Russian youth is to theirs"). America's youth, said another, must exhibit utmost loyalty and yet somehow at the same time learn to resist the temptation to join a "hideous scheme" as German youth had done in the thirties. We can no longer "avoid all possible participation in public life," announced the commencement speaker at the University of Pennsylvania; students must learn to refer to a world of "political facts," he said, and recognize that they "can no longer dwell apart."[11]

Stevens may have finished his poem before he fully comprehended the oratorical custom of the season. And although the PBK exercises, as he himself said, were "in a general way part of" the college commencement (L 506), it is possible that he saw the two events as sufficiently distinct, so that the Poem would not be out of place if it departed from the usual topicality inherent to the commencement genre.[12] That Harvard's Phi Beta Kappa Poems before Stevens's had been explicitly topical and occasional, however, is a matter of record. They uniformly took as a subject the contemporary political theme, the American response to the war. The 1942 Poem, Christopher LaFarge's "The Great and Marching Words," was a patriotic marching song, its own language intended as active military steps taken: "These are the great words marching with high proud steps / Over the valleys of effort, pain and war: / Liberty, Democracy, Sacrifice." Theodore Spencer's "The Alumni," the Poem of 1943, profiled the quotidian lives of Harvard alumni and set them against regular martial refrains—such as "The footsteps heavily march, tramping on stone, / And down the darkened street march heavily on." The total effect of Spencer's Poem was to conjure a favorite new-nationalist image: every able, responsible Harvard man leaving the safeties of job and home for enlistment. In 1944 Winfield Townley Scott presented his Poem "Contradictions in an Ultimate Spring" guiltily, "as one / Too old and too preoccupied to go" to the front; yet Scott did his part, referring directly to the "one piece of news"—the Normandy landings—that would have been on everyone's mind by the late-June date of that year's exercises. Moreover, Scott's Poem had to consider the very moment of its recitation to be the "Ultimate" moment of all, supposing no future beyond its utterances. Thus the Poem immediately preceding Stevens's met the sense of crisis head-on: Scott's was overtly "Written for reading in a public place / Perhaps even after the terror has begun."[13]

Yet if Welles's 1945 Oration, by its rhetorical form of consensus politics, acknowledged the 1945 Poem, the Poem did not seem to return the acknowledgment in kind. In other ways, of course, Stevens was trying to concentrate on the world crisis, as we have seen in his letters and other poems. And even as he had begun to ponder the subject of his Phi Beta Kappa Poem, a few months earlier, his thoughts turned sympathetically toward Barbara Church's German family, whom he imagined trapped "in the area of the fighting." Still, it is hard to read the two main paragraphs of this April 4, 1945, letter to Henry Church without seeing some telling disparity between two distinct notions of place. (I have emphasized and lettered the contending notions.)

> The [A] *situation on the other side* must be terribly upsetting for Mrs. Church. . . . *People in Germany must be in an incredible predicament, in which even correctness is incorrect.* This makes it difficult to chatter about the things that interest me, but, in any case, I have only one piece of news, and that is that I am going to read a poem before the Phi Beta Kappa at Harvard [in] June.
>
> I am about to settle down to my subject: DESCRIPTION WITHOUT PLACE. Although this is the second or third subject that I have had in mind, unless it develops quickly and easily as I go along, I may change it. It seems to me to be an interesting idea: that is to say, the idea [B] *that we live in the description of a place and not in the place itself,* and in every vital sense we do. This ought to be a good subject for such an occasion. (L 494)

If we are to trust Stevens's compassion for Barbara Church in her awkward exile—and my argument in Chapter 5 is that we should trust it—we will also learn to accept his intention of imagining her ancestral "place" now on the front lines. Yet insofar as the notion of a German place provides a politically odd context for thoughts on a new, occasional poem about place in the abstract (B), the geopolitically precise sense of place (A) at this pivotal historical moment would seem to be the main exception to his otherwise unremarkable generalization that "in every vital sense" we do not live "in the place itself." For the very idea that actual places are not indeed *where we live* (B) would seem unnecessarily abstract, even silly, if meant as a genuine consolation (A) at an unbearably bad moment. And what is the "one piece of *news*" Stevens reports here, in the spring of 1945, when the nation's news was full of costly victory in Europe and strategies of attrition in the Pacific? An idea about place for a poem that was to *befit the time and place,* an occasion, a June 1945 commencement.

If a postwar context can be even partially recovered for Stevens's Harvard appearance, it will perhaps no longer seem so strange that a poem whose "rhetorical aim is a queerly hypnotic one . . . enclosed in a kind of baby talk" (as Helen Vendler has put it), "one of the most private of Stevens's poems" and "not likely to earn for [him] many admirers" for its "dangerous aridity" (Joseph Riddel), and one showing the poet "at his most arid" (Harold Bloom), should be indeed the poem Stevens chose to write for an occasion so dramatically *public*.[14] One recent critic, Michael Beehler, in an essay devoted to "Description without Place," examines a tendency even among Stevens's historicist critics to view a poem as "not refer[ring] to any system of meaning outside of itself" and as having "no referent beyond its own 'closed systems.' "[15] Beehler demonstrates that "Description without Place" continually plays on a double sense of referentiality, but in this instance the critic, when pointing out the poem's abdication of reference, merely assures us of the poem's own deconstructive work; that is, Beehler's words for Stevens's project best describe the critic's main operational assumption: "description, and language in general, 'cannot coincide' with its object."[16] Although convincing in its own terms, this sort of reading will not recognize that if there is a particular historical convergence inscribed in Stevens's very resistance to referentiality, it is what promoted that resistance in the first place; I shall argue here, in other words, that that situation is the emerging postwar moment, characterized by a newfound imaginative power in which American intellectuals, emerging from a period of partisanship, were presented with the apparently liberating idea that ideologies had exhausted themselves and that political writing was to be outmoded.[17] Vendler is right, then, to suggest of the manner of "Description without Place" that with its mere "appearance of logic" and "baby talk" it glances at the thirties. In its "lapsing back to the old dazzle of 'Owl's Clover' " and its "Blue Guitar"–like "hum of reiterated syllables"[18] it does entail a kind of total collapse of reference and apparent plain sense while at the same time it is also very shrewdly marked by the politics of 1945 and beyond, with a special, postpolitical reversion to outmoded styles of a bygone era of social realism in which Stevens tried to play the role of the poet as reliable commentator on events. In my reading, he was attempting to play such a role again, though the role had radically changed since the thirties and had been undergoing further change in recent wartime months. For this reason alone, Tate's response to the new poem will be instructive.

Despite Morrison's initial assertion that no custom had guided Phi Beta Kappa poets previously in their choice of topics, the annual Poem was in fact a stylized and narrowly defined genre—as the wartime contributions amply indicated; obviously the most important rules were unwritten and unspoken.[19] Stevens's "Description without Place" simply violated those rules, not only by excluding topical references to the war but by making a theme of resisting referentiality itself. This resistance characterizes its very point but also in the end suggests that some discerning reference is indeed being made. Given the overwhelmingly obvious concerns of the time, the poem's choice of abstraction deliberately incites controversy, or at least disappointment, as its point is to frustrate the usual effort to hear topicality in a poem recited on such an occasion, to contextualize the very decontextualization of the historical moment in the face of an overwhelmingly clear expectation that it would plainly describe that moment. The poem defies this expectation incessantly, the strongest variation of the point appearing in the seventh and final section: "Thus the theory of description matters most. / It is the theory of the word for those / For whom the word is the making of the world. . . . / It is a world of words to the end of it, / In which nothing solid is its solid self." On a morning when a programmatic former undersecretary of state put forth the point that we live in a period in which it will be the duty of Americans not only to help in "the task of reconstruction" but "to impose world order,"[20] the Poet's notions appeared to be politically perverse. The identity of an era "is merely a thing that seems" (*CP* 340). History, "the integrations of the past," is "so much" and also "*so little*, our affair" (342; emphasis added). What we "see, / Hear, feel and know" is in the actuality of seeming (340). If history is no less or more than history-writing, a "theory of description" that "matters most," then a past of men made out of words is description without place (345). If we think we are referring our experiences to our sense of seeming, then we must also know that knowledge derived from such experience is but "a knowledge / Incognito" (343). Being, in short, is constantly subject to seeming.

In this context of a world without context, great personages are not historical figures but random examples. The "green queen" of the first section is "*this* queen *or that*," a figure chosen casually, with a rhetorical informality that withstands historiographical exactitude. She remains unidentified. Paradoxically she has "the illustrious nothing of her name." The usual distance between us and historical figures like John Calvin, Queen Anne, Friedrich Nietzsche, and V. I. Lenin may be narrowed, as history may suddenly be reduced to a moment of temporary clarity and truth. As being is seeming, and history language, so the representative scenes of which political biography is constructed are fictional displacements of imagined personage onto imagined place. "*Things* are *as they seemed* to Calvin or to Anne / Of England, to Pablo Neruda in Ceylon, / To Nietzsche in Basel, to Lenin by a lake" (emphasis added).

But are these examples as random as they seem? And if they are not random, how must we modify the idea that they are set in representative scenes? The three modern displacements—Neruda *in Ceylon*, Nietzsche *in Basel*, and Lenin *by a lake*—bring to mind Nietzsche's own characterization of biographical truth: "Three well-chosen anecdotes," he said, "can achieve the portrait of a man." (The remark was once quoted by Paul Rosenfeld in a *Nation* review with the alluring title "History for Art's Sake.")[21] By just such a scenic method, Stevens offers densely allusive slices of three lives made seemingly unimportant, and removes them to sites apparently unconnected with their historical significance. Stevens is obviously less concerned to "achieve" portraits of Neruda, Nietzsche, and Lenin than to allude to the very idea of indicative portraiture. Nietzsche in Basel is probably the most densely allusive reference of the three, for, as Rosenfeld suggested, Nietzsche could be used to refer to the displacing impulse itself.

Urged by Henry Church to read Nietzsche all the way through, Stevens had trouble sticking with the theory, and came away only with an odd sense of place: "[W]hat I really got out of Nietzsche last winter was a sense of Basel and of Burckhardt living there. If the war was over I should fly to Basel this afternoon and perhaps buy a set of Burckhardt (in French) and a few photographs, and, possibly, an autograph letter or two. Then I should return by way of Paris."[22] But he wrote this letter in late June 1944, and his fanciful idea of sauntering across the Atlantic several weeks after D-Day to purchase a few rare odds and ends was clearly a message to Church, saying in effect: I crave not Nietzschean ideas but a taste of things far more remote at the moment—of Basel, Switzerland. That Stevens's fantasy included a "return by way of Paris," long a contested place, certifies the allusion to cool, neutral Basel as filling an uncontested zone with an untheoretical Nietzsche. When preparing his Mount Holyoke lecture, Stevens had decided at one point to scrap the idea of "provok[ing] a discussion of poetry as an academic subject" because he had just then read, as he told Church, "Jakob Burckhardt (who was a friend of Nietzsche's at Basel)"; as we have seen, he learned that Burckhardt, influencing the younger Nietzsche on this very point, had used poetry "as an aspect of history" (*L* 452–53). Church always regretted Stevens's inability to enjoy Nietzschean ideas for their own sake, feeling that his friend's error was perhaps in putting down *The Genealogy of Morals* before reading far enough into it. As a remedy for what he assumed was Stevens's indifference to Nietzsche's theories, Church decided to encourage his friend to continue with the anecdotal image of Nietzsche in Basel.[23] And when Stevens told Church of his plans for his Phi Beta Kappa Poem, in April 1945, Church's reply deliberately returned to the subject of Nietzsche; Church went out of his way to applaud Stevens's talent for reducing the abstract to a telling image. "I have by no means a philosophical mind," he admitted, envying Stevens his. "I have enough material in my head to write half a dozen books on Nietzsche and I don[']t know where to begin."[24] Stevens's starting point with his new poem was perhaps the intention of proving to Church and to himself that *he* knew where to begin. The allusion in "Description without Place" thus serves the double purpose of removing Nietzsche from the level of the abstract to that of the biographical—confirming Church's praise of Stevens's particular talent—and connecting just such a reduction to the very place (Basel) that he and Church associated with his own 1945 decision, *contra* the Burckhardt of 1943, not to speak of poetry explicitly in the sense of history.

The reference to Lenin traces a history of dehistoricizing in the same way. To strip Lenin of historical sense, meaning inevitably to deradicalize him, is clearly in itself an effort made within a historical context—postwar anticommunism—a context Sumner Welles was at that very moment helping to create. In other words, to depoliticize Lenin in just such a way is to politicize oneself; again, the stripping of context was now wholly in context, just as generally the poem can tell the story of how the postwar intellectuals, facing their objectivity crisis,[25] need not have forgotten that even that ultimate-seeming crisis had its basis in political fact and event. Here is the second half of the fourth section of the poem, the Nietzsche-Lenin canto:

> Lenin on a bench beside a lake disturbed
> The swans. He was not the man for swans.
>
> The slouch of his body and his look were not
> In suavest keeping. The shoes, the clothes, the hat
>
> Suited the decadence of those silences,
> In which he sat. All chariots were drowned. The swans
>
> Moved on the buried water where they lay.
> Lenin took bread from his pocket, scattered it—
>
> The swans fled outward to remoter reaches,
> As if they knew of distant beaches; and were
>
> Dissolved. The distances of space and time
> Were one and swans far off were swans to come.
>
> The eye of Lenin kept the far-off shapes.
> His mind raised up, down-drowned, the chariots.
>
> And reaches, beaches, tomorrow's regions became
> One thinking of apocalyptic legions.

I will eventually have something to say about the way in which Lenin's relation to the distant beaches both described and epitomized a perilous world-absorbing view. For now it will be sufficient to note how the end of this passage pays some respect to Lenin's attempt, even in his reduced state, to control "the far-off shapes" and to transform a harmless, local poetic observation of receding swans into advancing, transregional "apocalyptic legions." This qualified admiration carries the implied claim that the revolutionary imagination itself eschews a specific sense of time and place in order to do its exclusively forward-looking work—work done nonetheless in the name of history. But the initial image of Lenin is not nearly so serious. This biographical Lenin, poorly dressed, exiled to Zurich, sitting on a bench by a lake—ruminating, not causing trouble—"disturbed" no more than the swans he sees. He is without effect, feeling rather out of place: "He was not the man for swans."

The inspiration for this Lenin is to be found in Edmund Wilson's *To the Finland Station*. Knowing that van Geyzel admired the American intellectual left, Stevens mailed Wilson's book to Ceylon in 1941 as a gift. Van Geyzel's response probably sent Stevens to an issue of the *Partisan Review*; van Geyzel had found Wilson's book "admirable in the biographical parts—couldn't be better—but in the critical parts I agree with the man in P.R. who found fault not with his conclusions but his method."[26] The "man in P.R." was Meyer Schapiro, whose review of Wilson was called "The Revolutionary Personality." Schapiro chose Wilson's "artistic conception of Lenin as a man"[27]—presented by Wilson in a chapter attractively entitled "Lenin Identifies Himself with History"[28]—to criticize Wilson's idea that "the revolutionary movement, and *history in general*, is not only a product of reason and social conditions, but also of *the peculiarities of the men who led it*" (emphasis added).[29] Describing Lenin's power as a function of personality, Wilson set scenes that had the unintended effect, Schapiro decided, of trivializing radical thought. The result was just what Stevens presented in "Description without Place": "He wants us," Schapiro said of Wilson, "to read in a literal sense the images of writers whom he has already held up to us as poetic minds," and so "metaphysics [is] the poetry of abstract imaginations." Such a "mechanics of personality" leads to an unhistorical "improvised 'depth' psychology" that "encourages a purely analogical fancy."[30] Stevens's comment to van Geyzel about Wilson only partly reveals his interest in this analogical fancy. "Wilson's TO THE FINLAND STATION," he wrote, ". . . is thought particularly well of in respect to the portraits of the figures with which it deals. People are reaching a point where they are very much interested in the personalities of the Marxians, early and late. That is about as far as I myself go" (L 381). Stevens's Lenin in "Description without Place" took Schapiro's dissent from Wilson's revisionist story of Marx's inheritors a good bit further, pushing Wilson's novelistic, reductive method to the point of undoing Lenin's effectiveness entirely. By stuffing Lenin's pockets full of bread (not stones), dressing him in old clothes—he is punningly *suited* to such a state—Stevens ironized the Marxist cry of *decadence*, certainly a claim to be made against the poem that contained this irony. But the complaint would have to be made against Lenin. Here, then, Lenin himself participates in the decay of purely imaginative, inconsequential, rumination.

Even if the audience that morning at the Fogg Museum caught none of the points in the long poem Stevens read to them, they would surely have been astonished, nevertheless, by the contrasts between the manner of these dense dislocations (precise references having the contrary effect of abstraction) and Sumner Welles's straightforward references to people and places. As the politician held that at a moment when war was being won "the United States need not abstain from seeking the realization of its own objectives when the world knows that these objectives are neither selfish nor material,"[31] so the poet seemed to abstain from this new version of the well-worn story of consolidating power. To decline comment, as it were, on such a situation might be a repudiation, further, of a worldly force founded on conventional diplomatic knowledge. After all, according to Stevens's program for describing a place without a sense of place, one might find "the invention of a nation in a phrase" (*CP* 345). Welles's speech concluded with a line plainly scripted by the commencement-address genre: "[E]ven though the immediate present be darkened, we can look forward with confidence to the future." Stevens did not allow even this. "The future," he ominously intoned, "is description without place." And yet, at such moments, despite what must have been an overwhelming impression of difference, the exhortations of Welles and Stevens were basically one, for insofar as Welles articulated American benevolent assimilation, Stevens's conception of place embodied it. Welles, while describing places and urging an American knowledge of the foreign, implied no less than Stevens that the future entailed description without place.

If "Description without Place" proposed the paradoxical idea that a sense of place—of a nation—can be conveyed by a "text we should be born that we might read," it also offered its curious idea of the province of poetry. It thus challenges us to imagine how a "provincial," non-American but place-bound reader must respond to a characteristically American text whose two strongest claims are its evident status as autotelic and its audacious definition of describing a place. It can be said, then, that Leonard van Geyzel, living in faraway Ceylon, successfully created out of his own sense of dislocation a "text" to be read by his American friend Stevens, whom he knew to be an avid reader of Ceyloniana. The Stevens–van Geyzel friendship may be summarized in this way: one man's isolation inspired both to acquire a book-knowledge of the world. Periodically through this seventeen-year correspondence, Stevens admitted that he wanted to know the real Ceylon as a "background" of reality for the objects he arranged to purchase. He was delighted when boxes of tea shipped from the renowned Scrubbs Estates arrived with "a pile of postcards" that would enable the Hartford man to visualize the distant place where the tea had been grown. "These," he told van Geyzel with delight, "helped me to see what Nuwara Eliya is really like. There cannot be a moment's doubt about the interest of the place as a background for one's tea."[32] He meant not tea, of course, but himself; he wanted an exotic context for himself. He toyed further with this metonymy, commenting to one young poet who visited him at his office, as they sipped tea sent to Stevens from overseas by diplomatic pouch, "I would love to sail in a pouch."[33]

This is not to say Stevens took either van Geyzel or the correspondence lightly; he sensed it was an unusual ethnographic encounter, and he hung on every letter. During Frank Jones's 1942 visit Stevens recalled from memory pleasing details of the exchange (*WSR* 127). Indeed Stevens seems surely to have intended a benevolent relation between himself and the East to be established by his book- or postcard-knowledge of an otherwise (for him) unknowable place. After all, van Geyzel was well aware that his correspondent was engaged in a form of culture collecting; when he explained how he depended on imported texts to know the world, he knew that he was providing a "constructed domain of truth" in James Clifford's specific sense[34]—knew well that the roots of a tradition he often described as straight and deep had been many times cut and retied. To know van Geyzel's small world, in turn, just as deliberately as van Geyzel set out to know the world beyond, was a matter both of common sense and of constructed cultural interchanges of truths; and, despite the unevenness of the two projects, Stevens saw cultural truth-trading as a kind of balanced trade. At the same time, notwithstanding Stevens's best efforts, poems expressing a distant obligation do read, as Randall Jarrell decided, as the writings of "some *Travel-Diary of an Aesthetician*, who works more for pleasure than for truth"; in this view Stevens "turns out to be not Robinson Crusoe but Bernard Berenson,"[35] and the relationship with van Geyzel was *im*balanced. Stevens did feel that the need of a metropolitan Ceylonese person wanting things from the world beyond was keener than that of a person from the world beyond who wanted things from Ceylon. But again, this was an agreed-upon process; and van Geyzel understood that Stevens's interest in Ceylon was in part generated by the Eurasian's culturally mixed sense that the poems' mimetic claims were at bottom the issuance of social practice and that whatever bits of the U.S.-Ceylon relation got reproduced in poems would be based on an intentional though unwritten contract wherein poet and indigene, like the writer and reader of the text, temporarily shared an agreement about the conditions under which those texts can be composed and comprehended. I should not want to be understood, that is, as leaving van Geyzel unimplicated in what I will nevertheless describe as a relationship in which the American extracted and the Ceylonese produced. Stevens himself wanted to think of van Geyzel as the one extracting. His description of van Geyzel for José Rodríguez Feo revealed a great deal about the reversal: "In the depths of his distance from everything *he* extracts, because *he needs to extract*, from poetry and from reading generally *far more than you and I extract* from the things that we have in such plenty, or that we could have because they exist in such plenty near at hand" (*L* 513; emphasis added). Stevens did not quite acknowledge here that his own sense of Ceylon, in return, also confirmed the titular thesis of "Description without Place." Even when van Geyzel's letters provided firsthand information about the complex cultural differences and relations between the majority Sinhalese (Buddhist) and minority Tamil (Hindu) cultures, or suggested that descendents of the island's early European, mostly Portuguese and Dutch settlers (the latter called "Burghers") formed a class different from the Sinhalese and Tamil on the one hand and yet still quite distinct from the officially colonial British (the more purely European) on the other, Stevens mistakenly told van Geyzel: "I know that you regard yourself as English." Van Geyzel's sense of himself as a racially and culturally mixed, urban elite was not so reductive as that.[36] And Stevens clung to *British* representations of Ceylon from books designed for the Western coffee table, such as Ashley Gibson's *Cinnamon & Frangipanni* and Lord Holden's *Ceylon*. He thrilled to have the things van Geyzel packed in crates and shipped to the United States for the Stevenses at Christmas: brilliantly colored saris, cans of jaggery, milk punch, "beach" hats, a "simple and explicit" reclining Buddha for the poet's bedroom window, necklaces for Elsie, woodapple jelly, and five pounds of the very best tea. The tea, he had warned his Ceylonese friend, should be of a kind not procurable anywhere else (*L* 324, 327, 333, 337).

When Stevens received these things, he was elated to find that Gibson's book, *Cinnamon & Frangipanni*, which he assumed van Geyzel had read, spoke of the items his friend had sent him as truly representative of a place (*L* 327). These acquisitions, he thought, authenticated his picture of van Geyzel's place. Stevens did not apparently consider the possibility that van Geyzel had sent what he thought his new Western friend would want—to oblige Stevens or endorse his Western view of the exotic (a view that van Geyzel, the elite metropolitan, might somewhat share)—and that this would quite as easily explain why the saris, beach hats, and necklaces were all items to be found in Gibson's travel book in the first place. On the one hand, "It has always made Ceylon seem more *reasonable* to know someone *like oneself* out there" (*L* 838; emphasis added); too, the great difficulty of making contact with places as distant as Ceylon in an effort to get a true sense of "the actual thing" (*L* 327) was "to find people of taste" (*L* 328). Yet on the other hand, van Geyzel was sufficiently strange to Stevens—seemed foreign and cut off from culture—to have chosen for him "things most truly representative of Ceylon." Would not the happy discovery of a person "of taste," because it was considered rare by the Westerner whose sense of taste guided the search, disqualify rather than authenticate the things sent as "truly representative"? "It is, of course," Stevens admitted, "difficult for anyone on this side of the earth to realize with any definiteness just what Ceylon is like. But I think that your box, with your very interesting letter, together with a book or two, helps to create a pretty clear impression" (*L* 327). Thus Stevens retained rights, as it were, to the perspectives of both parties to the exchange. He wanted his foreign correspondent to be someone very much like himself, so that the foreign correspondent would know intuitively the sort of thing Stevens desired from so foreign a place. Yet he wanted van Geyzel to remain "difficult . . . to realize" (*L* 327), "faraway" (*L* 381), living "in an unchangeable center,"[37] or, as van Geyzel himself agreeably put it, "heavily assisted by Geography" in remaining unaffected by world events.[38]

In Stevens's effort to make Ceylon "reasonable" he either stressed a basic equation between the people of Ceylon and the people of Connecticut, and thus avoided confronting a radically new cultural disposition, such as that of the Sinhalese Buddhists in particular, or he ignored human culture entirely to emphasize the total domination of nature over will. He could thus conceive of the distant land as a natural, depictable *scene*, what Edward Said has called "the vision of the Orient as spectacle, or *tableau vivant*"[39]—wholly realizable in pictures and yet pleasingly unavailable to the distorting processes of political thought as well as inimical to poetic theory. (Stevens confessed to being astonished that the Sinhalese *had* a poetic theory and a critical tradition.)[40] When turning over the pages of a Ceylonese calendar van Geyzel had sent him in 1940, he was drawn to a photograph of villagers returning from the market at dusk and noted, "This sort of thing goes on, no doubt, even in the depths of the jungles"; a "shopping trip" was "exactly the same," no matter if the market were Colombo or Manhattan (*L* 353). Yet, at the same time, because he wanted to let Ceylon remain Ceylon, impervious and "unchangeable," he was more likely to overlook the people. Reading Leonard Woolf's novel *The Village in the Jungle*, the "Colonial Cloth" edition of which Stevens added to his growing collection of Ceyloniana,[41] surely endorsed the idea that the recuperative powers of the inhuman world of Ceylon far surpass any effort of will made by the people (as by Westerners observing those people) to endow local institutions with value. Watching helplessly as the jungle draws "its ring closer round the remaining huts,"[42] the poor villagers who have barely subsisted throughout the novel finally realize that the human idea of order is useless against the "impenetrable disorder" of timeless nature.[43] When Stevens wrote that Woolf's novel "is full of pictures of Ceylon and ideas about Ceylon" (*L* 332), he meant a Ceylon naturally inimitable, impenetrable to Western eyes, yet full of things that could be possessed; but most of all it had to be natural and *inhuman*, in his special sense of the word. And his reading relentlessly supports this double impression.[44] "Ceylon," he said, "is the sort of place with which one can come to grips and still be fascinated" (*L* 353).

Perhaps Stevens's rhetorical colonialisms were unintentional. If so, his attitudes were hardly less typically colonialist than those expressed by *The Village in the Jungle*, despite Woolf's obvious intentions to the contrary.[45] "Somehow," Stevens once wrote van Geyzel, "the presence of the English in a place of this kind has a way of turning what might be a steamy mess into something reasonably fastidious" (*L* 353). Given such remarks, I find it entirely unsurprising that van Geyzel, who enjoyed (and if Stevens was right, craved) contacts with educated Westerners, would obligingly if unconsciously defer to the extent that he must, offering up the "reasonable" version of his place Stevens seemed to want so badly—and to which he himself partly subscribed.[46]

At one point van Geyzel sent Stevens "The Essence of Buddha's Teaching," the transcript of a radio address by the Venerable Nyanatiloka Maha Thera, the German Buddhist scholar-monk, founder of the Island Hermitage of Dodanduwa in 1904, who was then, in October 1941, a prisoner in a British internment camp. Van Geyzel hoped Stevens would appreciate Nyanatiloka's pamphlet, the best "short statement on the subject" van Geyzel knew.[47] Stevens seems to have been impressed by it to some degree at least, finding "an exquisite poverty about the book's appearance" (*WSR* 127). "Montrachet-le-Jardin," a poem published in the January-February 1942 *Partisan Review*, reproduces elements of the pamphlet and seems to combine a Buddha figure (a "root-man," "tortured by his mass" as Nyanatiloka's Buddha fasts, becomes a "skeleton" and teaches himself "corporeality") with the interned scholar-monk: "Delivering the prisoner by his words, / So that the skeleton in the moonlight sings, / Sings of an heroic world beyond the cell, // No, not believing, but to make the cell / A hero's world in which he is the hero" (*CP* 261). And:

> Consider how the speechless, invisible gods
> *Ruled us before, from over Asia*, by
> Our merest apprehension of their will.
>
> *There must be mercy in Asia* and divine
> Shadows of scholars bent upon their books,
> Divine orations from lean sacristans

Of the good, speaking of good in the voice of men.
All men can speak of it in the voice of gods.

. . . .

A little while of Terra Paradise
I dreamed, of autumn rivers.

(*CP* 262–63; emphasis added)

Of special interest here is the resemblance between Stevens's imprisoned scholar and the dark rabbi-scholars of earlier poems, familiar to us
from "Le Monocle de Mon Oncle" (1918), "The Sun This March" (1930),
and "Life on a Battleship" (1939)—"scholars bent upon their books." For
Nyanatiloka's Buddhism is typical of some scholarship since the late nineteenth century of Western and urbanized Ceylonese Buddhists, who
tended to infuse original Buddhism with rationalistic European philosophy, somewhat disentangled from dogma, belief, and history, portraying it
as a straightforward, demystifying method. The source for Nyanatiloka's
presentation of Buddha is almost as much in Nietzsche as indeed in traditional South Asian belief. Thus it tends to underestimate the value of traditional Sinhalese Buddhism as practiced in rural Sri Lanka, where it has
been replete with mythology, worship, and prayer, and steeped in its own
history. Despite his references to his particularly *Asian* major man, Stevens's god, speaking in the voice of men in "Montrachet," endorses the
modern rationalization. Does man need to believe outright? "No," the
poem stresses, belief is rational and man understands by "*not believing*" but
studying the texts of pure will. Even if the poet got no further than the
pamphlet's second page, he would have found a Europeanized creed:
Nyanatiloka immediately lays stress on the "absolute soberness and clear-
ness of Buddhism," as Nietzsche is extensively quoted at the head of the
pamphlet, boldly insisting that "Buddhism is a hundred times *more realistic
than Christianity*," that "[t]he notion of 'god' is done away with," and that
"[p]rayer is out of the question" (emphasis added). Hence the Buddhism
Stevens saw in this pamphlet is not altogether as unfamiliar to the curious
Westerner as one might think.[48] Indeed it does little to challenge "those of
a different faith." Nyanatiloka accepts Nietzsche as gospel: "The teaching
of the Buddha is perhaps the only religious teaching that requires no belief
in traditions, or in certain historical events."[49] "Montrachet-le-Jardin"
does little to strain Stevens's imagination in its effort to absorb an abstract,
uncorporeal philosophy—South Asian in aesthetic form, undeniably, but
European in philosophical content. The replication of the foreign place,
an "inaccessible, pure sound"—like "Serendib" itself, the sound "Ceylon"
as a sweetness produced for the delighted foreign ear[50]—is thus quite easily
realized, in orientalized images of things; in Said's sense, these are item-
ized, decontextualized, and objectified:

Item: The green fish pensive in green reeds
Is an absolute. *Item*: The cataracts

As facts fall like rejuvenating rain,

. . . .

Item: Breathe, breathe upon the centre of
The breath life's latest, thousand senses.

(emphasis added)

The poem works its distant obligations handily into the typical Stevensean tropical meditation, not unlike the much earlier Florida-Cuba poems. And yet it denies a special past to a particular religion, rhetorically asking, "what good were yesterday's devotions?" (*CP* 264)

Such a denial seems inevitable when one considers the bits of Ceyloniana Stevens then had at hand. We have seen how the philosophy of "Montrachet" is borrowed from the rationalized Buddhism of Nyanatiloka's pamphlet. Similarly, the orientalized images-as-items themselves are surely derived from the delicious catalogings of Lord Holden's *Ceylon*, a book Stevens bought in 1939, the year it was first published. Holden's book consists of a series of standard views presented in writing and accompanying plates. These Stevens found stimulating, admiring "the photographs of the ruins and particularly of the statues" (*L* 337). But the views are refracted through the long lens of Holden's intense subjectivity, through his evident wish that the reality described and photographed might remain as still as the words and pictures freezing it along the described tour. Holden's *Ceylon* continually expresses the fantasy of the Ceylonese remaining unchanged. He deplores Western dress, "since no coloured race gains in either dignity or comfort by imitating the customs of Europe."[51] He encourages his Western readers to "do" Ceylon as he has, yet reinforces the naturalization of the Orient by quoting the "classic lines" penned by Amelia Heber, the wife of the Lord Bishop of Calcutta, who, Holden half-jokingly suggests, might have been pondering the irritation caused by the slowness of native hotel servants when she wrote: "What though the spicy breezes, / Blow soft on Ceylon's isle, / Though every prospect pleases, / *And only man is vile*" (emphasis added).[52] A century after Mrs. Heber, in Ashley Gibson's *Cinnamon & Frangipanni* (1923), the Sinhalese servants fare no better, "lurk[ing] slackly in corners . . . smirking and rather limp . . . masking their native boredom behind the inscrutable smile of the well-fed tom-cat." Yet these were the very same typical "boys," Gibson notes, who "failed on first acquaintance to make me feel at all Oriental"![53] Gibson's manner of apprehending Ceylonese reality is steeped in the rhetoric of sentimental imperialism:[54]

A writing man I knew once, who had never sailed those seas but in the ships of other people's fancy, but whose wit erupted sometimes in flashes intuitively illuminating, announced that the East was only an invention of the nineteenth century, an expression not of philosophy, of geography, but of temperament; a dream, in short, that had led many to leave their people for its people, their homes for its desert tents, in an effort, it might be, to turn its conventions into realities. It was a dream, he would have it, made possible by the discovery of local colour. Vulgarised by the rude touches of many fingers, its glamour has all but departed, but not before it has caught some of us and whisked us out of our proper orbit, leaving us writhing, like stranded starfish, in hot discomfort beneath alien rays. Bastard Orient though the modern capital of that Serendib may be, the tale of whose wonders kept even Scheherazade's lord from pondering on unpleasant matters, yet Colombo has its sights, its scents, its sounds, whose memory will be always with us albeit we contemned them before they had time to become familiar.[55]

Clearly *Cinnamon & Frangipanni* excludes itself, its own words, its incessant felicitations, from the category of the "rude touches of many fingers"; "stranded" on a foreign beach, under *"alien* rays," lamenting departed glamor, lost sights, gone scents and sounds, Gibson's "friend" evinces what Renato Rosaldo has called "imperialist nostalgia" ("where people mourn the passing of what they themselves have transformed").[56] The particular figure of Gibson's nostalgia—repeated rude touches by foreign fingers— makes reading the book a physical act of complicity; poring over this book, as one would an ethnographic collectors' catalogue, to see what new exotic-yet-truly-representative items he could ask van Geyzel to send him, Stevens did not apparently conclude that Gibson's mourning disqualified him from describing what purchases could still be made that were not typical of tourists but indeed of a fantastically unified "East." Stevens was delighted to note, for instance, that Gibson "puts a taboo on ebony elephants and the sort of thing that tourists pick up," so that when *Cinnamon & Frangipanni* goes on to speak "of precisely the things that you have sent as being things most truly representative of Ceylon" (*L* 327) a certain reality—Gibson's and now Stevens's—is endorsed. Here is the sort of passage Stevens read, then, in order to form a judgment as to the soundness of Gibson's advice to foreign collectors:

[Y]ou can buy quaint and not unattractive grass mats and baskets from Galle, and notably Kalutara hats woven also of grass [one of the items van Geyzel did send] . . . and . . . not lacking in artistic merit, the trade being a resuscitated and now thriving village industry which receives every encouragement from Government and private patronage. And you can get lovely things, from a complete dressing-table outfit downwards, in native tortoiseshell, though it is well to interview your workman to see that he executes his task exactly to your order, his own taste probably running to ungainly riveted shields and what-nots in gold and silver foil.[57]

Of course the taste of the native craftsman working in tortoiseshell runs to "riveted shields and whatnots" at least partly because he believes they are the things Westerners want to possess. Gibson himself, however, wants to buy those things the craftsman produced before the moment when indigenous values were altered to suit a Western market. This is what Stevens admired about Gibson's respect for the "taboo" that had been placed on the ebony elephants; it is the quintessence of an anticolonialism nevertheless imperial.[58] Such a logic endorses what Gibson and Holden finally present as true to the sentimentalized scenes they describe, their *anti*tourist credentials having been ostensibly affirmed. So when, on the day after Holden's book arrived in Hartford, Stevens wrote, "Ceylon has taken a strong hold on my imagination" (*L* 337), he obviously had in mind those special credentials. The Ceylon he imagined had specific origins: Holden's and Gibson's pictures of the jungle ruin, the lonely Tamil picking tea, the complacent elephant bathing in an ancient tank, the bullock cart pulled along a Colombo street, the indolent fisherman sitting on a pole.[59]

We find van Geyzel's Ceylon in Stevens's poetry almost immediately after he began consulting books like *Cinnamon & Frangipanni*. In "Connoisseur of Chaos" we are asked to imagine the hard-to-imagine, such as Englishmen living "without tea in Ceylon" (*CP* 215); in "Extracts from Addresses to the Academy of Fine Ideas" the same far-off place is somehow *so* far as to be "past apocalypse" (*CP* 257); and in "A Weak Mind in the Mountains" "the wind of Iceland and / The wind of Ceylon" improbably meet (*CP* 212). These references are much more than what George Lensing calls mere "playful interjections of geographical fancy," though they are that, and Lensing's reading of them is otherwise accurate and suggestive.[60] The meteorological improbability involved in the convergence of Icelandic and Ceylonese winds, for instance, occurs only in relation to a troubling butchery, a bloody grappling of North/West and South/East that requires far more indeed than a sense of Stevens's well-developed playfulness to explain it:

> There was the butcher's hand.
> He squeezed it and the blood
> Spurted from between the fingers
> And fell to the floor.
> And then the body fell.
>
> *So* afterward, at night,
> The wind of Iceland and

> The wind of Ceylon,
> Meeting, gripped my mind,
> Gripped it and grappled my thoughts.
>
> (*CP* 212)

One wants to know much more about the logic of "so," about the relation of time (before and "afterward"). Does Stevens believe that the convergence of North and South, as cold and hot, spare reality and steamy fantasy, really follows from (and masks) the violent climate, or does he believe such merging inspires the violence? "A Weak Mind in the Mountains" savagely comes to grips with a geographical sense that can only be imagined.

In "Notes toward a Supreme Fiction," a few years later, Ceylon is a little more definitely realized, though at moments the reference falls familiarly into the tourist's trap. Canto v of "It Must Be Abstract" (*CP* 384–85) is divided into two distinct parts. The first is given in reductive travel-book language, resembling—perhaps satirizing—Gibson's and Holden's stilted style of accumulation, with its compounded predicates. "The lion roars . . . / Reddens the sand . . . / Defies red emptiness," and so on.[61] Here, in turn, are depicted the lion roaring, the elephant trumpeting, the bear snarling. The second part of the canto, beginning with "But you, ephebe" in the fourth of seven triadic stanzas, turns from the seen and known to the view and the viewer framed by his Western window:

> But you, ephebe, look from your attic window,
> Your mansard with a rented piano. You lie
>
> In silence upon your bed. You clutch the corner
> Of the pillow in your hand. You writhe and press
> A bitter utterance from your writhing, dumb,
>
> Yet voluble dumb violence. You look
> Across the roofs as sigil and as ward
> And in your centre mark them and are cowed . . .
>
> These are the heroic children whom time breeds
> Against the first idea—to lash the lion,
> Caparison elephants, teach bears to juggle.

This adventure, we are to assume, is seen wishfully by the ephebe from his attic apartment furnished with rentals, a viewer's site as safe and civilized as the place he imagines is violent and rude. Struggling with his writing, pressing his face against his pillow, the ephebe emits "A bitter utterance" that is paradoxically "voluble dumb violence." The ephebe is one of many children, a generation deemed "heroic," with irony due a novice

going about the hard work of inventing "a nation in a phrase"—an appren-
tice whom only "time" trains (or "breeds"). But, over the course of time,
trained to do what? Trained to look across from hypercultural West to
inhuman East, from the "celestial ennui of apartments" ("Notes," I.ii; *CP*
381) to outlying deserts, jungles, and mountains, and to tame and then
possess in a verse circus the "supple challenger" of the Western imagination—"to lash the lion, / Caparison elephants, teach bears to juggle";
trained to be "ward" of such seen territory even though his status as immature is never questioned; fit now to turn "violence into circus play,"
as Vendler has put it.[62] The problem of caparisoning elephants (gussy-
ing them up for show) can be considered closely here, as it is an idea arising directly from Stevens's perceptions of Ceylon. In the first section of
the canto we learn that "The elephant / Breaches the darkness of Ceylon
with blares, // The glitter-goes on surfaces of tanks." Not long after finishing "Notes," Stevens remembered having imagined the scene precisely
enough to explain the image of the tanks to Hi Simons in such a way as to
suggest an insider's information. He admitted that the word "tanks" would
not be understood by those who did not know the usage in Ceylon, where
a tank is a water reservoir or pool with particular ritual significance, "a
basin which may have been . . . the excavation for an ancient building"
(*L* 434). Once again, the source of this image was probably *Cinnamon &
Frangipanni*, a chapter on the ritual capture and caparisoning of bull elephants, entitled "Beasts and Super-beasts." Here Gibson tells the story of
the big beast Billigamanaya, who, having escaped from his mahout, spends
an odd night in an abandoned bungalow, where he not only "Breaches
the darkness of Ceylon with blares"—in Gibson's excessive words, "a perfectly horrific blast of trumpeting set every piece of furniture in the place
a-rattle"—but then appropriates a nearby tank "for bathing purposes."[63]
The chapter is full of *objets sauvages* domesticated yet maintained for their
power to disconcert and delight. In the story of Old Bill, "[t]he childlike
fondness of the Sinhalese for 'dressing up' " is the reason for the elephant's
eventful escape in the first place; the mahout's "wonderful habiliments"
had frightened the big animal in his stall and drove him into a frenzy.[64] The
point of the chapter is not to describe the mature Ceylonese elephant in
the wild, but to narrate the most humorous aspects of their abduction and,
indeed, their "dressing up," childlike, for performance—to "caparison elephants" indeed. The subject-position of this orientalist travel narrative
overpowers the viewed, admired object. So, too, the purpose of "Notes
toward a Supreme Fiction" at this early point (in the fifth of thirty-one
cantos) is to teach the ephebe his first lesson about fulfilling the distant
obligations of the modern imagination. He need not be ashamed of his
too-obvious creative effects (juggling bears), much as they are "voluble

dumb violence" in the face of roaring, blaring, snarling actualities from places about which he admittedly knows nothing. If he is eventually to succeed in creating a fiction sufficient for making existence pleasurable, he must learn to bridge that distance only as he can, and to avoid obvious questions of heroism and cultural insight—and, in short, to "caparison" Ceylon itself.

Some of the pride lost in this bold and clever admission was regained, of course, when Stevens realized that he could explain with authority the Ceylonese use of the word "tank" to Hi Simons, for its connotation was determined exclusively by a knowledge Stevens had attained and which he believed was unavailable to his reader. Moreover, he realized he was explicating his poem for a critic who had a great deal invested in authorial intentions. Simons was by now mired in the critical biography he would never finish, an all-consuming " 'life's work.' "[65] Because it took him "an inordinate amount of time to analyze" Stevens's poems,[66] the critic came to depend greatly—sometimes emotionally—on the poet's explications. "It is always difficult for me to acknowledge the letters you send me," Simons once wrote, "because, to confess the literal truth, I get so excited over them that I don't sleep."[67] In a sense, then, the sleepless, intention-oriented Simons trying to understand the exotic, fluid Stevens is, for Stevens, as the ephebe is to the "tank" of Ceylon. When Stevens explained "tank" for Simons, in 1943, he had not worked out a coherent theoretical position to support inconsistently defended but perhaps visceral doubts about *explications de texte*.[68] Here he found himself caught between his desire to view his new poem as having spoken with special insight into the subtle formalities of language and an equally strong desire to write a major modernist poem (the thirty-two-page "Notes toward a Supreme Fiction") that would not require annotations and displays of source work of the sort provided by Eliot and Moore and evidently required by Pound. The allusiveness, he felt, must seem natural. These conflicting impulses carried over into the explanation he prepared for Simons:

> There are several things in the NOTES that would stand a little annotating. For instance, the fact that the Arabian is the moon [in "It Must Be Abstract," canto iii] is something that the reader could not possibly know. However, I did not think that it was necessary for him to know. Even without knowing ——— [Stevens's dashes] But in the line ...
> "The glitter-goes on the surfaces of tanks" the word tanks would be obscure to anyone not familiar with the use of that word in Ceylon. It was not an affectation on my part to leave the word unexplained. (*L* 434)

Only when he put into his poetry a final and still more difficult reference to Ceylon, in "Description without Place," where Pablo Neruda washes up on van Geyzel's distant shores, would Stevens be forced to articulate his position on the value of authorial intention and explanation. The "invention of a nation in a phrase" and the articulation of the critical attitude were in fact a single, pivotal occasion.

For seventeen years letters traveled back and forth between Colombo and Hartford. In that time two events threatened to cancel Ceylon's distance and difference and thus its basic attraction for Stevens. The first had been the coming of war. Growing international tensions in the late thirties had only encouraged van Geyzel's already well-developed cosmopolitan habit of following European and American cultural politics. The second event, far less dramatic, was the arrival and rapid institutionalization of a special form of academic criticism at the outposts of the British Empire, a critical and pedagogical practice recently described by some of its critics as having been itself a response to the political conditions that gave rise to war.[69] We do not know much for certain about Stevens's reaction to the first of these new challenges, the Ceylonese westernization in wartime, since van Geyzel's desire to know the United States began to emerge in the correspondence just as the mails stopped moving. We do, however, know Stevens's response to the idea of Practical Criticism arriving at the ends of the Empire, because this response is preserved in "Description without Place."

Van Geyzel's realization in 1941 that Ceylon was implicated in the world at war threatened Stevens's fantasy of having his Ceylonese friend remain isolated and abstracted from history. After all, to understand the United States, van Geyzel turned not to American commentators but, for instance, to Denis William Brogan's Oxbridge monograph on America, *U.S.A.* (1941), with its extraordinary generalizations about life in the United States in 123 small pages. Stevens was certain to resist such an attempt by van Geyzel to internationalize and modernize himself. Yet if Stevens could read British and French characterizations of Ceylon[70] and then declare to a Ceylonese man that he now knew a true Ceylon, surely van Geyzel could unapologetically read Brogan's British pamphlet on the United States and write Stevens exuberantly, "Yes, I am getting to know America pretty well."[71] Van Geyzel was also reading the Americans themselves, of course, a trend he made quite clear to Stevens, dropping in a single letter the names Steinbeck, Faulkner, Cather, McCullers, and Delmore Schwartz and knowingly referring to Wilson's *To the Finland Station.* Van Geyzel went quite a bit further than name-dropping, however. He proposed that T. S. Eliot was best suited of all living poets to translate the *Mahābhārata* and hatched the plan of commissioning Eliot to supplant Edwin Arnold's "sadly" outmoded English translation done "in a Hiawatha rhythm."[72] Being privy to such a bold scheme only gave Stevens further indication of van Geyzel's dependence on Western reproductions of the native literature available to him in his own world. (Van Geyzel, Stevens discovered, did not easily read Sinhalese, and could not write it.) That his isolated friend "would welcome greater American influence in the world than there has hitherto been" may have troubled Stevens, not because he had come to oppose Americanization but because van Geyzel's ambitious cosmopolitanism would hasten the end of the pure Serendib Stevens loved to imagine; in fact, it only demonstrates that van Geyzel, when pushed a little, was willing to make it clear that knowledge for him had to be a hybrid—that, in Clifford's terms, "[t]he concrete activity of representing a culture . . . is always strategic and selective" and that "[t]he world's societies are too systematically interconnected to permit any easy isolation of separate or independently functioning systems."[73] Making just this point, van Geyzel was perfectly capable of his own culture-collecting—not so unlike Stevens, in this respect, he collected paintings and "valuable Chinese vases," and his house was "aesthetically furnished" in the Victorian sense[74]—and thus could turn the collector's gaze on Stevens; van Geyzel professed to have a new understanding of "American politics which seemed up to now to be *a sort of esoteric cult*" (emphasis added).[75] Again, because the correspondence was cut off, we can only guess how Stevens responded to this shrewd ethnographic reversal, the Ceylonese studying *him* like an esoteric cult. Now *America* was itself one of those exotic places that could be made accessible and yet remain fascinating.

When the correspondence was firmly reestablished, in the spring of 1945, Stevens tested what he hoped was van Geyzel's renewed isolation—though he probably knew better.[76] He offered this challenging remark: "Ceylon, for all the distance between it and Connecticut, is almost a familiar place to me; I don't think that you can possibly say the same of Connecticut" (*L* 486). Interestingly, Stevens would soon say the same of postwar Europe. While many other places were forced by the world war to remain themselves, with certain recalcitrant political factions looking nationally inward and seeking to manage a return to premodern separation, or merely picking themselves up culturally among the ruins, America had extended its image and knowledge of the world far outward *to* the world, its international vision now sharpened, to use Sumner Welles's nascent cold-war trope. (One of the key elements in Welles's Spring 1945 lectures, in fact, and not only the Harvard speech, was the idea that U.S. policy must prevent the small nations from returning to separateness; he urged that Western policy be formulated to respond to "the rising forces of nationalism in the Near and Far East" so that these movements do not become culturally isolationist even as they become politically separatist.)[77] If van Geyzel no longer had easy access to the modern, international texts to be used in the effort to close the distance from the cultural powers that produced them, he and others among the Ceylonese elite did now have at hand a critical ideology that was deemed well suited to colonial students who had always struggled to find a context for Western literature read in the extremities.

Among van Geyzel's friends was a subscriber to this new critical practice, Professor Evelyn Frederick Charles Ludowyk, also a Christian-born Eurasian, a Burgher, and like van Geyzel one whose "interest in the folkways of Sri Lanka was insatiable."[78] Ludowyk's three books on Sri Lankan religious and cultural history, including *The Footprint of the Buddha*,[79] attest to the validity of the description provided me by Ludowyk's former colleague H.A.I. Goonetileke, who describes for his friend's case the difficult double game played by many of the Oxbridge-educated Eurasians in Ceylon: Ludowyk "yearned to enter the mainstream of Sri Lankan culture, rather than nourish the flickering flame of his Burgher inheritance."[80] Ludowyk taught literature at the University of Ceylon, and as the war was ending attempted to convey to his Ceylonese students, in their teacher's words, "the general subject of *the place in poetry of a cognitive or meaning aspect*, and the extent to which that must influence evaluation" (emphasis added)—a view of literary meaning and of pedagogy, and all expressed in a vocabulary, that was unquestionably shaped by I. A. Richards. When Ludowyk had studied at Cambridge in 1929 and 1930, with Leavis and then with Richards himself, "the reverberations of the lectures on which *Practical Criticism* (1929) was based still echoed not only in the lecture rooms of the English Faculty but throughout the University." After obtaining First Class Honours in the newly liberalized English Tripos, and claiming the Oldham Shakespeare prize, he returned triumphantly to Colombo, *Scrutiny* literally under his arm, with the intention of proselytizing the new antiphilological approaches and of reforming the curriculum there.[81]

Keenly sensitive to the failures of the colonial procedure by which members of the indigenous elite were educated in the Imperial Tongue and then trained in England to man the upper ranks of the Colonial Service,[82] Ludowyk apparently did not view the critical method he himself had brought back from England as itself part of the larger intellectual impression of West onto East. He did not see, apparently, how so illuminating and reformist a method as Richards's could itself fall prey to accusations of imperialism, for *it* held the power, if any educational method did, to "save" (that Richardian word) the otherwise dull Colonial Service students schooled in the unreformed Ceylonese curriculum.[83] Seeing Practical Criticism in the Third World as a rational yet redemptive liberating force, Ludowyk was its tireless promoter; by 1945, with his ground-breaking book *Marginal Comments*—its "Reading List" contains sixteen titles, no fewer than eleven of which are works by Richards, the Leavises, Eliot, or Brooks—he became closely associated with the new critical revolution.[84]

He went so far as to propose an analogy between the reforms of Practical Criticism, with its effort to illuminate a benighted world of literary study, and the effort the English and Americans *could* make (but probably would not) to comprehend the Ceylon they intellectually and culturally dominated. "Such a task as this"—that "[t]he West has to unlearn a great deal it has come to believe about the East"—had, he thought, its most recent and most powerful precedent in Practical Criticism. The task of de-imperializing the world, Ludowyk wrote, "might seem too vast a scheme for human imaginations fretted as they are with the frustrations of political misunderstandings. . . . Yet one cannot help remembering, and still being bewitched by, the clarity of analysis and the fervour of Dr. I. A. Richards. . . . [Given] the feeling engendered by the aftermath of global wars . . . he believed . . . that *if understanding could save*, then there was indeed something *practical* our universities could do" (emphasis added).[85] This practical educational procedure, Ludowyk had been taught, might be gotten underway with the intense study of a single poem. "The single-poem assessment," Ludowyk's colleague has recalled for me, "was one of his favorite gambits, and he relied a great deal on this method."[86]

It so happened, then, that at exactly the time Stevens and van Geyzel renewed their regular correspondence, Ludowyk decided to use a Stevens poem as a New Critical classroom experiment. Learning that his friend van Geyzel was a correspondent of the oft-anthologized American poet, Ludowyk presented van Geyzel with a detailed report of an assignment he asked his students to fulfill. Van Geyzel not only knew about Ludowyk's 1944–1945 project of compiling and evaluating student interpretations; he helped Ludowyk prepare *Marginal Comments*, a work largely taken up by descriptions of those results of the interpretive experiments.[87] Ludowyk's students were told to write out their responses—"I didn't want a paraphrase," he afterward insisted—to "The Emperor of Ice-Cream" (*CP* 64). Their teacher was attempting to assess in Ceylon what Richards had tried to measure years earlier at Cambridge and what he wrote up in *Practical Criticism*. Sample audiences read poems stripped of titles and authors' names, generating protocols; Richards's method, of course, had been to analyze in these responses various evaluative misdirections and then to identify the causes underlying students' inability to approach a poet's "mental condition." Van Geyzel enclosed Ludowyk's typewritten comments about his own students' responses to such a psychoaesthetic test with his March 18, 1945, letter to Stevens, certain that Stevens "would be interested to see what happens to . . . your poems . . . in unfamiliar circumstances." And despite the fact that Ludowyk's exercise was aimed at demonstrating to the Ceylonese, in Ludowyk's words, "exactly why they were using the poem as *something outside themselves not a private fantasy* of their own" (emphasis added), van Geyzel's own summary of the students' failure to understand the function of ice cream in the poem included a very clear warning. "The most serious obstacle to appreciation," he wrote, "would seem to be *provincialism.*" ("The Emperor gave quite a lot of trouble + when I met Ludowyk in Colombo a few days ago he told me that one ingenius person even suggested that it was addressed to a refrigerator.") It would seem that what had failed was the idea that if only "understanding poetry" were made more "practical" it could also become universally effective. Ludowyk himself admitted that "the difficulty was the too powerful draw of ice cream as a luxury here";[88] he was not unaware (as Mr. Goonetileke has recalled) of "the problems of teaching English literature at a sufficiently high level to undergraduate students whose cultural backgrounds and everyday experience were poles apart from the themes and spirit of Western thought."[89]

The only conclusion to draw from the students' failure to understand Stevens's poetry was that the cognitive value not of all poetic discourse but of particular words (the free American's inevitably ironic or unfamiliar use of "emperor," for instance) was contingent on place only when that place happened to be as extremely dislocated—in Stevens's *and* van Geyzel's view—as Ceylon. If Richards's demonstrations at Cambridge had sought to identify routines and customs of feeling that students brought with them to a text, deforming or blocking their responses to it, then Ludowyk had not only discovered that a culturally relative sign was likely to block non-Western students; his experience also evidently suggested to Stevens the specific conditions in which the central idea of even so basic a poem might be missed when so much attention is paid to psychophysiological response. The student protocols focused almost exclusively on the single image that attracted these readers because of *its*—and *Stevens's*—exoticism; this may have led them to ignore the relation between seeming and being, the poem's central idea, summed up in the famous line "Let be be finale of seem" (*CP* 64).[90]

When he received van Geyzel's letter and Ludowyk's report, in mid-May 1945, Stevens was just beginning to think about how the seeming-being question might inform his occasional poem about place, "Description without Place." Here, then, his poems ran up hard against "unfamiliar circumstances" in his own "true" Ceylon, and so his old sense of seeming had been lost in a site that had given *him* such a strong and apparently clear impression. "The occasion," Professor Ludowyk had written of his students' responses to Stevens, "was completely left out." Ludowyk asked van Geyzel to ask Stevens how far the idea that being is the "finale" of seeming could be taken. Convinced that a poem should not merely mean but be— he told his students to avoid denotation because it "becomes a kind of here we go round the synonym bush"[91]—the critic evidently introduced the poem by speaking hopefully of its relevance to his own methodological goals in such a way as to emphasize being. One response to the odd Ludowyk-Richards encounter was to take seeming to its extreme in the project of "Description without Place," updating the crux of "Emperor" to the postwar sense of place.

Van Geyzel's plain summary of Practical Criticism in Ceylon—he could not have known that Stevens had already read Richards at least twice[92]— takes up one page of a lively five-page letter that goes on to discuss things much more indigenous to Ceylon than Richards and "The Emperor of Ice-Cream." His discussions of an unusually dry spell of weather (on the third and fourth pages of this letter) and of Pablo Neruda's experience as Chilean consul in Ceylon (pages 4 and 5) were certainly more in keeping with the topical customs of the correspondence. Even van Geyzel's discussion of postwar politics here—despite his praise of the Russian contribution to the Allied war effort, and despite his engaging quasi-Marxist language about change—supported Stevens's notion that in Ceylon all change is natural and inhuman (I have emphasized two bits of dogmatic rhetoric): "If, as you say, socialism is disruptive, it may well be so because we are still *in the grip of forces that are imperfectly understood*, and any 'advance' that comes *can only do so convulsively*, like earthquakes, or the migration of birds."[93] So, too, in van Geyzel's description of the recent drought he was trying to point out that the unusual weather had not ruined but encouraged the exotic beauty of the island. He described the blossom of a fruit, waxing perhaps consciously poetic (just as José Rodríguez Feo sometimes did) because, having seen Ceylon appear in four poems already, he knew such gorgeous imagery might stir the poet to write about his place a fifth time: "It is really quite extraordinary how this delicate colouring produces an effect of coolness, almost of spring against the burnt grass and the hot purples, reds + yellows of bouga[i]nvilleas + poinsett[i]as." The urgent natural language here, in a letter that had begun with the importation of the Empire's latest form of critical power as an aid to reading "The Emperor of Ice-Cream," is itself derived from an importation: van Geyzel informed Stevens that the flower described in the passage just quoted (Madre) "is in fact a native of South America." This reminded the letter-writer of his interest in keeping up with the latest South American literature, and so brought him to the topic of Pablo Neruda, a poet who had actually traveled to, and lived in, the places he described in his poems. Van Geyzel was certain to observe, as if to reiterate his usually less subtle invitation to Stevens to come to Ceylon for a visit, that Neruda's work as consul had not been taxing; the Chilean government had been enlightened enough to "provide its artists" with easy access to the world. And the mere fact of Neruda's having once made his presence felt in Ceylon showed van Geyzel how his feelings of cultural isolation might occasionally abate: "Few people as interesting and attractive as Pablo Neruda," he wrote, "seem to get washed up on these unpropitious shores."[94]

In Stevens's polite but firm response to this long letter and its enclosure (the typewritten account of Ludowyk's protocols), he mostly rejected the critical practice. As for the search for cognition in poetry, he insisted, in theoretical language Richards's student could not have accepted, that "the cognitive element involves" not psychological astuteness so much as a plain sense of the real. "If poetry is limited to the vaticinations of the imagination," he continues, "it soon becomes worthless. The cognitive element involves the consciousness of reality" (*L* 500). Despite this apparent affirmation of the actual world, Stevens went on to speak of the "place of poetry." He explained that poetry "is simply the desire to contain the world," an idea that would seem to go against a positive identification "of the real," and against any assumption of limits to the imagination—against, in other words, the positing of objective conditions. Moreover, Stevens was bold enough here to implicate van Geyzel and Ludowyk (and by extension Richards) in this world-absorbing view, by assuming that at such a great distance from cultural centrality Ceylonese readers of "The Emperor of Ice-Cream" "share this need" to contain the world (*L* 500–501), a need identified by Welles (among many others) as the fresh American need. He may have sensed that the assumptions underlying Ludowyk's liberal enterprise were themselves hardly liberal. When Ludowyk lamented his students' misapprehension of "The Emperor of Ice-Cream," was he not, after all, complaining about "the known docility of the Ceylon schoolboy, and his inability, in spite of his natural dislike of the English, to measure things except by English values," and about "the bad English produced by the eccentric development of words in Ceylon"?[95]

"Description without Place" follows directly from Stevens's response to the van Geyzel–Ludowyk–Richards reading. Reacting specifically to van Geyzel's remark that it is rare to find so distinguished a figure as Pablo Neruda washing up on these "unpropitious shores," the poem offers its three biographical constructions—van Geyzel's Neruda in Ceylon, Henry Church's Nietzsche in Basel, and Edmund Wilson's Lenin sitting by a lake. Stevens's deradicalized Lenin, tossing bread to the receding shapes of the swans, reinforces the effect of obscuring the "distances of space and time," as in the postrevolutionary imagination these forms flee "outward to remoter reaches, / *as if they knew* of distant beaches" (emphasis added). How different really is this act of imaginative extension from Sumner Welles's vision of the new American hegemony, this conception of Western attitudes as reaching toward and defining "distant beaches," a new, innocent American "desire to contain the world wholly within one's own perception of it"? By creating a context in the act of generally eschewing context, the displacements of a neutralized (Swiss) Nietzsche, a shabby, harmless-seeming Lenin, and an ambassadorial (pre-Marxist) Neruda establish the extensive reach of the imagination as natural and harmonious with things as they are. In the Nietzsche-Lenin section of the poem, the fourth, the transitive *reaches* is made to rhyme simply with those remote *beaches* (Stevens's version of van Geyzel's phrase "unpropitious shores"). Thus here, in the poem evidently designed to resist reference to current events, an important reference is indeed made to contemporary cultural politics: the long arm of American poetry extends itself outward, hardly unlike Welles's thesis allowing Americans who share his internationalist "Vision" to see and seize a near future shaped by a United States that "desire[s] no territorial or material gain." "Regions," a grammatical object of reaching rhyming with advancing "legions," brings to formal completion the poem's densest lines: "And reaches, beaches, tomorrow's regions became / One thinking of apocalyptic legions." These words help us to follow Stevens's nontemporal, nongeographical swans in their flight from historically significant, human figures. Perhaps the swans know what Lenin, theorist of "convulsive . . . forces that are imperfectly understood," does not himself know, that change comes naturally (to revise van Geyzel's dogmatic language)—not "convulsively," like earthquakes, but beautifully and imperceptibly, "like the migration of birds." The Harvard poem takes its theme of extensiveness seriously, and even the humorous scene of Lenin sitting on a bench in old hat, shoes, and clothes serves the generally grim procedure of satisfying the desire to contain and naturalize even the most resistant elements of the actual world. If Lenin at first "disturbed" the swans, finally the silence in which he sits is described by "decadence"; so the swans' smooth path away from him remains unblocked by his presence.

To be sure, when it was presented to him in an extreme form, Stevens was capable of recognizing imperial imposition on a world that resisted American knowing. It happened that at about the time he received Professor Ludowyk's report on Ceylonese difficulty with ice cream, he also received a letter from an association of American ice cream manufacturers, who wanted the poet to explain the role of ice cream in the same poem that had caused the tropical islanders to view it not as a universal image producing a measurable response but as an actual American product. Apparently these ice cream executives hoped the famous businessman-poet would explicate the poem in a manner they could use to advertise their product. Putting the two dislocated readings of his old poem together, Stevens wrote Alfred Knopf about this strange request and joked that the delectables of *Harmonium* created out of the East a new market for the West. He now saw that Ludowyk's students' readings, expressing the Ceylonese craving for ice cream, provided "an interesting business vista" for the manufacturers. His own ample imagination had identified a strong colonial demand; now others were asking him to explain the American supply. For Knopf's amusement, he quoted a brief portion of E.F.C. Ludowyk's letter, and added: "It is entirely possible that the Secretary of the Almagamated [Ice Cream] Association would have the edge on even Buddha in Ceylon" (*L* 502).

On June 27, 1945, a few hours after the Harvard reading, Stevens scrawled Allen Tate a note from Boston, on Hotel Statler stationery, and enclosed the Phi Beta Kappa invitation card.[96] We know that Tate appreciated "Description without Place," if only enough to be willing to publish it. He wanted the autumn issue of the *Sewanee Review* to contain a poem by Stevens to accompany Hi Simons's critical essay "The Genre of Wallace Stevens." The apparently barren abstractions of the poem seemed nicely to confirm Simons's earnest effort to prove that Stevens was a philosophical poet; Simons was trying to counter Horace Gregory's 1942 essay in *Accent* that had asked, point-blank, "Is Mr. Stevens a philosopher?" Gregory's answer there had been: "Mr. Stevens is not an intellectual, and . . . the value of his poetry cannot be measured in intellectual terms."[97] It is safe to assume that the new poem, even if like Simons's essay it was motivated by an effort to offer poetry "measured in intellectual terms," suited Tate's taste for Stevens's abstractions, just as the choosy editor of *Sewanee* was rejecting some of Theodore Roethke's experimental greenhouse poems on the grounds that they were all imagery and no intellectual structure. ("Serves you right," William Carlos Williams jabbed Roethke, "fer trying to play around with them Taters.")[98] The new Stevens poem was, in comparison with what Kenneth Burke would soon (in the *Sewanee* itself) call Roethke's "vegetal radicalism," all intellectual structure and no imagery.[99] Others' difficulties with Stevens were exactly what Ransom and Tate, though Ransom more than Tate, liked best: the tendency to render subject matter "trifling" and to take no "moral, political, *sociological* or religious" position. It was precisely that Stevens's poems were not—so it seemed— suited to be "about 'res publica,' the public thing," that made Stevens attractive.[100] If Tate now had those sorts of problems with "Description without Place"—much later he wrote that "one gets tired of being told in almost every poem how ingenious [Stevens] is *in not knowing anything*"[101]— the *Sewanee* editor chose for the moment to focus his criticism on the *reticence* with which Stevens had presented the poem in public at this moment of crisis. In Tate's view, once the poet chose to make his poem "the public thing," then he always deserved time equal to that given over to the politician, certainly to one of Roosevelt's old programmatic cronies and at a time when a rollback of New Deal thinking was finally possible (the 1946 congressional elections would bring just that). "I can't let the little card to the Phi Beta Kappa literary exercises pass," Tate replied to Stevens on

July 3, "without an obvious sociological comment. I observe that the orator was the *Honorable* Sumner Welles while the poet was not even *Mr.* Wallace Stevens." Tate recommended that Stevens consult Ransom's early poem "Amphibious Crocodile,"[102] obviously because he wanted to suggest, with the help of Ransom's boorish *Mr.* Crocodile, so recently emergent from the primeval slime and already claiming a stake in the world's high culture, that opportunistic politicians like Welles, with their persistent reptilian instincts, frustrate the true citizen-poet's efforts to do the properly human things.[103] Stevens's letter in response to Tate's criticism does not apparently survive,[104] but from Tate's next note we may infer that Stevens, in the lost reply, simply would not allow Tate to get away with saying through Ransom's Crocodile or otherwise that the poet's point of view had been slighted at Harvard in favor of the politician's. In his earlier note, posted from Boston, Stevens had written: "Mr. Welles on the new World Charter sounded more like a poet than I did."[105] And Tate replied: "I can see that the honorary Phi Beta Kappa was a way of compensating you for the 'Honorable' prefixed to the name of Sumner Welles. I am not sure that statesmen should be quite as honest *as you seem to think Mr. Welles is*" (emphasis added). Tate could not resist ironizing still further the political implications of the occasion. The postscript of his letter reads: "Anything addressed to the Hon. Allen Tate at Sewanee, Tennessee, will reach me."[106]

If Tate was amused or perhaps a bit irritated by Stevens's willingness to distinguish the poet from the politician in "Description without Place," Williams was furious. Not long after reading the poem in the November issue of Tate's *Sewanee*, Williams sent to Ransom's *Kenyon Review* a long riposte, "A Place (Any Place) to Transcend All Places," a new work about a specific place. On November 11 Williams wrote Byron Vazakas, a young poet from Stevens's hometown, Reading, Pennsylvania (a coincidence Williams relished), informing Vazakas that Ransom had accepted his piece, adding: "It is a reply to Wallace Stevens' poem in the last Sewanee Review which I didn't like at all."[107] At this very moment Williams was revising proofs of *Paterson 1*. The main idea of the first book of *Paterson* was that the poem about place not only had to be rooted in a real, referred-to place, but that it should figuratively be peopled by place, as Dr. P embodies Paterson itself; the poem would underscore Williams's ethnographic modernism, the "perpetual veering between local attachments and general possibilities" that Clifford and others admire, in which "local cultural breakdown" leads the American poet to believe he shares the fate of the impure American product.[108] Stevens, in apparent contrast, staked his own claim to a theory of locality, the Connecticut poet whose conception of modern, heterogeneous urban life, insofar as it extended into Williams's territory, included Jersey City but only condescendingly: "Polacks that pass in their motors / And play concertinas all night. / They think that things are all right" ("Loneliness in Jersey City," *CP* 210). Williams would theorize about place only through concrete particulars, he insisted, following the idea he had long nourished. Consistent with Williams's addiction to reality, *Paterson*, his grand poem about place, had been delayed by the war; in 1944 he had written Walter Arensberg, his and Stevens's mutual friend from their New York days, "I am working like mad at my [medical] practice largely because it is a necessary war effort and I . . . find the war an essential devotion. But after the war, if I live, the related work of literary composition will go on."[109] Now the war was over and the first part of the masterwork of locality was nearly ready, a few months after V-J Day; yet here was Stevens, whose "war effort," the "related work" of poetry or business, had never been obvious to Williams, and whose poetic career seemed impervious to the crisis: Stevens had put out three wartime volumes! Worse, this was the person who now proposed to contain the complexities of the postwar world in a single abstract poem, officially—at Harvard—making clean theoretical work of Williams's hard-earned, grounded sense of place. Stevens knew how passionately Williams believed in the local, for Williams had made a point in 1944 of telling Stevens how important the postwar project of reconstructing American poetry would be. He had praised Stevens's willingness to write an introduction for Sergeant Sam Morse's *Time of Year*, putting Stevens and himself in a select "elder group" of writers who must oversee the transition to peace and who together would encourage "an art that is slowly acquiring reality here in our God forsaken territory."[110]

Because Williams's anger at "Description without Place" took the form of a poem in reply, we may read the poem to reconstruct, in turn, a valuable contemporary reading of "Description without Place." Williams evidently interpreted the seventh and last section of the poem (beginning, "Thus the theory of description matters most") as an attack directed at him. Williams himself was the Spaniard, he thought, the figure whom Stevens saw as limited by its devotion to locality, playing the subaltern role Williams was certain others wanted him to perform, as "Carlos the wild Spaniard."[111] Setting aside the Spaniard of section vii, however, we can still see that Stevens's theory of place contested every earthy thing Williams had ever said on the issue—that American poets should, in the words of the old *Contact* group, "seek only contact with the local conditions that confront us." "Description without Place," by displacing people, violates an idea Williams now brought prominently into *Paterson*: poetry should situate the individual in his primary relation to place.[112]

The riposte contains the valuable idea that "Description without Place" could suggest to a poet like Williams the new importance of the American poet who *really* lived to describe his local context, whose verses excavated the real, down to the sewers if possible, "draining places from which New

York / is dignified, created." Williams contests the American poet's sense
of place with a new vengeance.

> New York is built of
> such grass and weeds: a modern
> tuberculin-tested herd
> white-faced. . . .
>   Sweatshops
> and railroad yards at dusk
> (*puffed up by fantasy*
> *to seem real*).

(emphasis added)

The poem-reply posits this reading of Stevens's first postwar poem: as
place is the basis of all things, so poems-about-places should contain not
ideas about place in the abstract but a detailed, fundamental sense of the
place itself. The appearance of Stevens's poem about place in Tate's *Sewanee* seems only to have strengthened Williams's critical reading; it is of
special interest here that this context confirmed for Williams Stevens's
betrayal of a postwar poetry that would return to the American scene and
encourage the otherwise unrewarding work of "slowly acquiring reality."
The Harvard poem clinched for Williams the postwar alliance between
Stevens and the Tate-Ransom group, an irony in this case since Tate did
not entirely sympathize with the original political context of the poem he
saw into print. Williams objected that the Tate-Ransom group, named
"Southern writers" in his poem-reply, had uncritically absorbed Eliot's
ideas of impersonality and habits of abstraction, which meant that poets
who wanted to respond to actual American experience had no chance once
the Tate-Ransom formalism held sway over the magazines.[113]

We may generalize further about the broad, controversial claim made in
"Description without Place" by associating the new readings formed by
Williams and Richards's colonial student Ludowyk, and adding the implied significance of Sumner Welles's political speech—a point brought
home by Tate's comment on Welles's relation to the postideological politics of the occasional poem. The result of such a combination is a clearer
sense of Stevens's new notion of historiography, offered at precisely a time
when Americans were being urged to have an enlightened, internationalist
view of the historical moment and to situate America's new, undeniable
centrality within that moment. A "revisionist" reading of Welles's apparently liberal speech, with its One World utopianism, would suggest that its
main goal was indeed to prepare Americans rhetorically for policies of unprecedented economic expansion and political neocolonialism.[114] "Description without Place" depends on two ideas that are likely to be seen as
contradictory in such a revisionist approach. The point of the strongest

language in the poem, in section iii, is that in a moment of intense change, a temporary state of complete, superideological observation, the world "shrinks to an immediate whole, / *That we do not need to understand.*" Yet in the seventh section, the portion Williams found especially offensive, Stevens argues that provincial people live in the character of their speech. Can he have it both ways? Stripped deliberately of a sense of place, description is thus reduced to describing its own functions. But the poet still cannot reduce difference to a "whole," eschew the conventional desire to "understand" a world of basic cultural distinctions, and still, finally, in section vii, celebrate its linguistic vividness by citing the mountain of men in Spain who merely reproduce a local speech (ll. 7–11)—like Carlos Williams himself in Williams's anxious view. It is left to section iv, the only section of Stevens's Harvard poem in which vivid description is sustained, to resolve this dilemma. The dilemma is recognizable from Stevens's struggle to see in his Ceylonese contact a "reasonable" man, a man *like* himself, and yet to sustain distance from and imperviousness to the "longed-for lands" ("An Ordinary Evening in New Haven," canto xxviii) as different. By placing historical thinkers out of time and place—or, in Williams's reading, by disconnecting the individual life from its primary site, whence the imagination springs—and by testing, as van Geyzel noted about Ludowyk's use of Richards in Ceylon, a familiar poetic idea in unfamiliar circumstances, Stevens stipulates a definition of time and place at the end of ideology. This new, powerfully disarming definition substitutes the expectation of cooperative rhetoric about things for the things themselves. So he may argue (generally in section v) that description *without* a "solid" sense of place is actually proficient in the business of acknowledging difference: description without place is "The difference that we make in what we see, / And our memorials of that difference." "Description without Place" does more than save the cognitivist from his failure to entice exotic, ill-prepared readers of American poems beyond meanings overdetermined by provincialism, produced by classics of modernism like "The Emperor of Ice-Cream." More, it accomplishes this feat by tipping the seeming-being scale irrevocably toward seeming, by pushing points Professor Ludowyk's benevolent dogma prevented him from emphasizing to his students: that being cannot be an end in itself; that actuality, the world of reference, must become, rather, the goal or end point (the finale) of seeming. To be envisioned as being, this new world must be described as becoming. Significantly, again, such an idea finally endorses rather than resists Secretary Welles's official American notion of a reconstructive moment. The resulting American "Description" of a place, then, would indeed be the postwar description Stevens proposed at Harvard, a text "we should be born that we might read," a text whose possible significance for history, it argues deceptively, can be known without any sense of time or place, in a whole world of texts that "we do not need to understand."

Van Geyzel's letter to Stevens dated August 30, 1945, marked a change in their relationship. It inscribes a coda to the story of Stevens's first postwar poem, for here van Geyzel withdrew his support from the critical formalism that had partly suggested the poem in the first place. Bowing to Stevens's strong language about Ludowyk in the letter the poet had written while he was composing his Harvard poem, van Geyzel now made an important admission. "The business of nitpicking poems has I think been taken too far," he confessed. "To note all its possible meanings is to relieve a poem of vital overtones, even though the critic's intention is to present a poem not merely as an integration of a number of ideas." From his post in Ceylon, from this point on, he would rather resist the temptation to interpret, would rather leave a Stevens poem unexplicated, would rather be its *source* than its *expositor*—its stable, knowable object than act in concert with Stevens as the constantly shifting subject. In effect van Geyzel apologized for having forced Stevens to speak of his poetry at all in his letters to Ceylon. And he somewhat timidly retreated into the image Stevens had originally suggested was most pleasurable, that of the isolated but cultured man extracting reality in small doses by reading modern poetry and criticism, knowing and being known at an "unchangeable center." This was precisely the relation between knowledge and power set out in "Description without Place." "Knowledge means rising above immediacy," Said has argued, "beyond self, into the foreign and distant. The object of such knowledge is inherently vulnerable to scrutiny; this object is a 'fact' which, if it develops, changes, or otherwise transforms itself in the way that civilizations frequently do, nevertheless is fundamentally, even ontologically stable."[115] Thus "Description without Place" must seem abstract to a fault. Said observes that when the orientalist, viewing his peripheral object-influx as an unchangeable center, tends to gather his thoughts beneath the binary, exclusive labels West and East, "reasonable" and inscrutable, "reasonably fastidious" and "a steamy mess," he has left himself no choice but to "conceive humanity either in large collective terms or in abstract generalities."[116] It is important to note that this postcolonial idea would not have been unfamiliar to van Geyzel, as E.F.C. Ludowyk often drew very similar conclusions: "[I]t is surely ironical that fixed entities with antithetical adjectives . . . should designate what used to be regarded as East and West. Wherever in the geographer's world of our acquaintance the West has come up *against* the East—the preposition slips in so readily that it is worth noting—the more ancient culture has been rebuked, and practically all its values have been thrown into the discard."[117]

Yet in reexplaining how and why he liked Stevens's poems, van Geyzel retreated somewhat from Ludowyk's and others' harder line, suggesting finally that to read Stevens's poetic observations on Ceylon was to involve oneself in a "continual process of discovery," as if each new Stevens poem he received was itself a staker of claims establishing beachheads on the unpropitious shores of Ceylon. Van Geyzel withdrew into a passive understanding, a mode of receiving poetry from afar embodied in the postwar American poem that served as its own cultural diplomacy; he would praise · ambiguity and yet be careful to deny that in Stevens's case ambiguity ever amounted to obscurity. He cited the pink and white flowers of "The Poems of Our Climate" (1938) in this letter, noting that his reading of that poem "finds endorsement" in the line "The imperfect is our paradise" (*CP* 194). Acknowledging his own desire to contain the world, and referring to Stevens's response to Professor Ludowyk, where there was outlined a project for locating "the place of poetry in thought," the foreign correspondent expressed the hope that Stevens "will undertake the job" of describing, in some new poem, "the genuine difficulty that arises out of the enigmatic quality that is so essential a part of the satisfaction that a good poem gives."[118] Stevens evidently wrote the poem van Geyzel suggested. In "Man Carrying Thing," composed soon after van Geyzel's letter, and beginning, "The poem must resist the intelligence / Almost successfully" (*CP* 350), Stevens did "undertake the job."

Van Geyzel never showed a sharper awareness of Stevens's desire to receive by air mail descriptions of exotic places than here, in this long and at times morose letter, where he hoped for a new discovery of the imperfect paradise of poetry. At least for Stevens's sake, Leonard van Geyzel, cosmopolitan, urban, culturally and racially heterogeneous, was willing to retreat into a role he never actually played in Ceylon, that of the guileless islander. Despite once having made a strong case in favor of *greater* American influence, now he readily acknowledged his desire to have the Western military defenders depart quickly, "and let us revert once more to being just a small island." And despite having used a good deal of internationalist language in earlier exchanges, he declared that Ceylon's "status of 'a bastion of freedom' or whatever it was we were supposed to be . . . is altogether too exalted for a little place like this."[119] He now wanted no part of the effort to position him politically in the postwar world and, having deeply internalized the strong desires of his American friend, learned to wish to remain innocent of history.

CHAPTER 4

Cuba Should Be Full of Cuban Things

> The fact that [Hemingway] has had such a success
> makes me fear for that hierarchy of values which
> must reign in a nation if its culture is not going to
> fall into the most slappiest of arrangements.
> —*José Rodríguez Feo from Havana to Stevens*
> *in Hartford, February 13, 1945 (SM 41)*

> He was provoking me, saying and always insisting
> about me being this Cuban who was too American-
> ized. And I can remember too that we had a politi-
> cal discussion that day, because when he said this I
> said, "Well, don't forget that we are an American
> colony." I said, "Don't forget that you Americans
> still regard us as a colony. You still have th[e] idea
> that we Latins are inferior." He said, "No, no.
> How can you say that, José? Do you think that I
> consider you an inferior person to me?" I said,
> "Maybe you don't consider me an inferior person
> because you're a poet. I'm a literary critic, so on an
> intellectual basis that is sort of above this idea. But
> I sometimes wonder, when you're so nice to me—
> you write me here and you write me there—if
> you're not a little patronizing." Then he became
> very sad, [saying,] "Oh, you don't really think
> that." And I said, "Well, I don't know. The Ameri-
> cans are a very strange people."
> —*José Rodríguez Feo in 1978, in an unpublished*
> *portion of an interview with Peter Brazeau*

THE YOUNG Cuban committed his mother to the asylum several times. At her sanest she deemed herself to be all intuition. She had not read a book since leaving school, a nunnery in Pou. Once, when she convinced herself of the wonderful, preposterous idea that her son's famous correspondent, Wallace Stevens, raised chickens in his yard in Connecticut, her son did not try to dissuade her. One afternoon he brought to the house two friends who were members of the Cuban Communist party, and the talk came around to the inevitable subject of Stalin. The mother, overhearing this, asked if he had finally married Chencha, the mulatto girl who lived in the neighborhood. While his radical friends gave his mother dirty looks, José Rodríguez Feo found himself momentarily taken in by the notion that Stalin was to marry a poor Cuban girl, until he realized that his mother had thought he had said "Balin," the name given a young man "who had been running after Chencha for a long time." Rodríguez Feo discovered his mother's error too late. By then his radical friends had left the house in disgust. "I had to give mother a lesson in modern history to avoid further complications," he wrote. The next day he decided to locate a single reference to Stalin in an American newspaper to prove to her that such a man really existed, and indeed found the Soviet leader "mentioned rather ungraciously." But his mother, faced with the evidence in black and white, merely asked her son why the Americans "called him certain names," and Rodríguez Feo "had to give up" attempting a serious explanation. He concluded for Stevens that his mother knew a great deal about "cows, horses and chickens." But if one "mention[ed] strange, exotic names in front of her," he continued, "one never knows where they are going to pop up again" (*SM* 129–30).

For the charming Cubans who peopled Rodríguez Feo's letters, "Stalin" was an exotic name. But for Stevens by this time Stalin was merely the dull daily fare. The exotic inhered, rather, in the appellations José and his mother invented for the family colt ("Platon") and the family cow ("Lucera"). A colt named after Plato! It is not in the mother's ramblings, however, but rather in Stevens's poems, at least four of them written directly in response to Rodríguez Feo's letters, where incidentally mentioned exotic things are more likely to "pop up again." To Stevens, Balin's possible relation to Stalin was as telling, as delightfully ironic, as the mother's fool-wise refusal to sanction the taking of sides in political controversies raging everywhere else but in her apparently happy Cuba, even as such partisanship was beginning to be important to many Cubans of Rodríguez Feo's generation who would live to see a wholly new day. Although Rodríguez Feo was genuinely distressed that his mother's miscues jeopardized his friendships with young communists and if, in spite of his attempts to explain to her why Americans were unlikely to refer to Stalin without calling him "certain names," he really did hope such scenes would not be repeated, to Stevens, on the other hand, the political causes or interpretations of these domestic scenes were not what mattered. Quite to the contrary, he wanted from these Cuban letters more of Balin and less of Stalin. In response to this particular charming anecdote, Stevens endorsed the mother's local coloring, admired her unwillingness to comprehend let alone take sides, and thus resisted his young correspondent's anxiety about political correctness. "How much more this mother knows than her son who reads Milosz and Svevo," Stevens wrote Barbara Church, immediately after receiving the letter containing the account of the Stalin-Balin incident. "She is controlled by the force that attaches; he by the force that detaches"—the "force that attaches" being a charitable force. "[A]nd both are puppets on the strings of their relationship to reality. She shrinks from leaving home; he from remaining there" (*L* 602).

Stevens added, however, as usual, a note of qualification: "The *Stevenses* shrink from everything." Still, he did feel the urge to instruct his Cuban correspondent in the rules of living in an exotic place. Such instruction, often kindly and qualified but sometimes harsh, recurs throughout their ten-year exchange of letters. Stevens's concept of a natural Cuba (at those very times when Rodríguez Feo's letters incited Stevens's poems) kept it from being much more than an ample place of sapodillas, cigars, and sweet drinks. In his harshest criticism Stevens refigured himself as the strong force that attaches, the puppeteer, in his metaphor, controlling the strings of his Cuban's relationship to reality. "Your job is to help to create the spirit of Cuba," he once insisted.

> Every one of your friends who writes a poem, whether or not it is about Cuba which nevertheless is a thing of the place, and every one of your friends who does a painting which in a perfectly natural way is a particular thing as a sapodilla is, or a good fat cigar or a glass of piña fria is, is doing just what you ought to be doing somehow or other. (*SM* 166–67)

When writing here of Rodríguez Feo's poet and painter "friends," Stevens was referring knowingly to the group associated with *Orígenes: Revista de arte y literatura*, the magazine Rodríguez Feo founded and initially funded after returning to Havana from Harvard in 1943. The life of *Orígenes* and Rodríguez Feo's correspondence with Stevens span exactly the same eventful decade, 1944 to 1954, and their stories are closely connected. Not long after Rodríguez Feo wrote Stevens for the first time (*SM* 33–34), asking for permission to translate "Esthétique du Mal," *Orígenes* contained first appearances of four of Stevens's new poems, in Spanish translations by the *origenista* Oscar Rodríguez Felíu.[1] In total, Rodríguez Feo and his colleagues put out thirty-six handsome outsized numbers of *Orígenes* in Stevens's last decade. More than perhaps any literary journal of its day, *Orígenes* was the organ of a group. The "Orígenes Group" consisted of Rodríguez Feo, the poets Eliseo Diego, Cintio Vitier, José Lezama Lima, Angel Gaztelu (a priest), Fiña García Marruz, and Lorenzo García Vega, and the painter Mariano Rodríguez. Rodríguez Feo was a competent and energetic editor, with astonishingly extensive contacts. He solicited contributions from F. O. Matthiessen and Harry Levin (both of whom he had known at Harvard), T. S. Eliot, Stephen Spender, and Allen

Tate (he met all three), Katherine Anne Porter, Elizabeth Bishop, Alfonso Reyes, W. H. Auden, Albert Camus, Thomas Merton, and Anaïs Nin, and Stevens's friends Walter Pach and James Johnson Sweeney. Rodríguez Feo himself contributed essays on Santayana, Gide, and Melville; a baroque short story called "The Closed Door"; and translations of poetry by Stevens, Williams, Aragon, Spender, and Eliot ("East Coker" and "Burnt Norton," both with Eliot's urging). He also translated James on Balzac, Camus on Nietzsche, Levin on Joyce, Auden on Lawrence, Theodore Spencer on Stephen Hero, Matthiessen on Eliot, and Santayana on himself.

In a statement of purpose introducing the first number of *Orígenes*, the editors explained the name of the journal by defining their goal of soliciting and publishing work that reveals the artist in the act of formulating his ideas, "those moments of creation in which the seed becomes a being and the unknown becomes possessed insofar as is possible and does not engender an unfortunate arrogance."[2] In this sense the Orígenes Group *did* dismiss pure poetry right from the start, though they would still soon be accused of loving it. They would also be accused—in a judgment surely made severer by time, given changes in the literary-political climate in Cuba since then—of offering the critical and creative writings printed in *Orígenes* as "universalizations," descriptions without place.[3] "For the first time among us," José Lezama Lima claimed in a retrospective of *Orígenes* in 1952, "the modern is not a provincial nostalgia."[4] Among the *origenistas* Rodríguez Feo was valued for his efforts to bridge the wide waters between national cultures. Lezama Lima singled out for praise Rodríguez Feo's having inspired a poem by the revered Wallace Stevens, "A Word with José Rodríguez-Feo" (1945), in which fine details, "the unthought-of groupings," "the far-off poetic imagination," are also "unmistakable signs of *universalization*" (emphasis added),[5] fully in spite of Stevens's deeply seated Americanness and the poem's gross assumptions about Cuba. For his part, Stevens deemed the *origenistas'* notion of universalization naive, and continued to be frustrated in his effort to find something intrinsically Cuban arising from the *Orígenes* project, exactly as he was thwarted when Rodríguez Feo's letters were not full of cows, chickens, and colts, fruit and cigars, resorts and white beaches—descriptions thick with place.

The *origenistas* soon formed their own publishing house, Ediciones Orígenes, and of the seventeen books of poetry they published between 1945 and 1954, no fewer than twelve were by members of the inner circle. The most important of these publications was Cintio Vitier's *Ten Cuban Poets, 1937–1947* (1948), which for the first time clearly identified the group's purposes, not by proclamation but by poetry: an antiregional, international modern art. Because Stevens wanted local color from Rodríguez Feo, he was able to see a contradiction in the *Orígenes* project, and almost immediately he articulated the criticism he would eventually assign to Rodríguez Feo personally. On one hand the group promoted its universalism, and on the other it was utterly sequestered, devoted to self-enclosure. Rodríguez Feo's talented young friends wrote and painted as if untroubled by the very set of conditions that should trouble universalists most, an attitude only reinforced by the fact that they referred to each other and their magazine so often as to be subject still more specifically to the charge of hermeticism. And hermeticism was the very thing they had formed the journal to avoid. The fresh, young Mariano Rodríguez painted oils *about* his friends and his aesthetic, such as one he entitled *Reading Orígenes* and allowed to be reproduced in the magazine.[6] But even this unapologetically programmatic work led Lezama Lima to the naive conclusion that the group was never derivative and never "surrendered to flattery," that Mariano wished only, in Picasso's words, "[t]o express what was within ourselves."[7]

Rodríguez Feo made a similarly innocent claim in writing to Stevens, in part, surely, to test the warmth of the waters between Havana and Hartford. He knew Stevens shared his anxieties about the cultural uses of art, and so he attempted to convince his American friend that the *Orígenes* poets were writing for others and not for themselves—for the postwar literary world and not for Cuba. Nationalism and not aestheticism, he implied often in the first years of the correspondence, was the root of decadence in modern art. Later, when *Ten Cuban Poets* was coming off the press, and obviously with his group's program in mind, he wrote Stevens: "I saw the Mexican show here. I finally came to the conclusion . . . that Rivera, Orozco and Siqueiros are all terribly overrated and are really now embarked upon an academic stage which reveals their decadence. The Cubans are less pretentious, more charming and some have produced works which surpassed the bloody, screaming, *cultural and nationalistic propaganda* of the mejicanos" (*SM* 123; emphasis added).

After Rodríguez Feo made him a gift of two Mariano watercolors, both depicting Cuban scenes,[8] Stevens understandably began searching his copies of *Orígenes* for more about this young painter. He not only found Mariano and the others mentioned there, but he also found a myriad of cross-references: *Orígenes* printed Angel Gaztelu's poem to Mariano; Rodríguez Feo and Lezama Lima both wrote essays about Mariano's painting; Lezama Lima's poem "Ronda sin Fanal—Para Mariano" describes one of Mariano's oils in heavily symbolic but still obviously homosexual language.[9] There were also Eliseo Diego's poems dedicated to Lezama Lima, Lezama Lima's to García Vega, García Vega's to Lezama Lima, and Lezama Lima's to Diego. The Winter 1949 number would devote almost all of its pages to poems by *origenistas* about each other or about the magazine itself. Could the *origenistas* long maintain their universalism and yet be so utterly self-involved? At first Stevens was mildly amused to discover how seemingly detached from Cuba these Cubans were. For Church, who knew a good deal about an ambiguous sense of place and had edited the journal of his own coterie, Stevens described how Rodríguez Feo detested "the taste" of his countrymen even though "it is Cuba that has been his own matrix" (*L* 508). When Rodríguez Feo got up the nerve to respond to Stevens on this point, he was engaging an already well-developed strategy. The *origenistas* were prepared for such attacks and held a clearly marked line. In a statement defending his all-*origenista* anthology, Vitier felt he could defend *Orígenes* with the following words: "We are . . . very far from building that exquisite species of escapists that some imagine," he wrote, despising the "accusation of coldness, of obscurity and hermeticism [that] falls, more or less vaguely, over . . . the centrality of our poetic attitude."[10] Vitier, Lezama Lima, and Rodríguez Feo decided together, editorially, on the best line of defense: *Orígenes*, they declared, stood at once for "a poetry of exile and fidelity."[11]

Such a relation between exile and fidelity, however strategically shrewd, was culturally and politically tenuous, its elaboration in *Orígenes* vague. *Orígenes* raised the sort of question Stevens otherwise loved to put to his foreign correspondents: Did these islanders mean exile *from* or *to* the real world? Whereas Stevens craved fidelity, as small but satisfyingly familiar truths, "Cuban things" that were felt to be indigenous because they were inscribed into letters and sent *from* Cuba, José on the other hand believed that what Stevens really wanted was a sense of exile, of foreignness within Cuba itself—Cuba *not* as a home so much as a writer's exotic retreat, a place to come to.[12] If Stevens was not careful and fell into his usual habit of traveling great distances in a single wishful sentence, Rodríguez Feo was likely in his reply to further the imagined tour with a special vengeance. When on March 19, 1945, Stevens whimsically likened Walter Pach's Washington Square studio to Paris, Dresden, and Mexico City (*L* 491), Rodríguez Feo responded explosively four days later by deleting his own Cuba almost entirely from the literary map, energetically inserting into one 614-word letter the non-Cuban names Chesterton, Shaw, Valéry, Mallarmé, Góngora, Pierre Brantôme, J. Malcolm Brinnin, Harry Levin, Alfonso Reyes (Mexican, of course, not Cuban), Cyril Connolly, Henry Miller, Church's friend Roger Caillois, and Pach. (The letter does mention the Cuban artist George Valdés, but only insofar as his work was filtered through the lens of an observing North American, Elizabeth Bishop.)[13] "My dear Mr. Wallace Stevens," it began (*SM* 47–49),

> I wanted to publish ["A Word with José Rodríguez-Feo" and "Paisant Chronicle"] in this Spring number, but fear it shall have to be postponed for the Summer. There are already two Americans in this issue—Brinnin and Levin—and there are already accusations of IMPERIALISM in the air.

... Chesterton has kept me from [looking out] the window. I find him a most humorous, charming old fellow. . . . I have always disliked however his ultimate defense of the Catholic Faith; although it sustained for a longwhile his famous debates with Shaw and other sceptics. Today came a letter from Elizabeth Bishop, "la poetisa de Cayo Hueso," who has been very kind and offers an article on Valdés. . . . Also, Mr. Pach wrote. . . . By the way, I hope you have received the Caillois book. . . . Yes, Brinnin admires you very much. . . . I think Reyes will bore you. . . . [H]is poetry is only a competent combination of Spanish classical modes and Val[é]ry (with a little Mallarmé to cap it all). His best works are critical like . . . his essay on Góngora, Mallarmé, etc. . . . Reading now a most daring but charming book, *Les Dames Galantes*, by Monsieur Brantôme. This pornographic book tells the inside stories of the great princes and princesses of the age of Francis the First and really puts to shame Mr. Connolly and Mr. Miller's attempts.

I hope you will have interesting remarks sur Monsieur Caillois. . . . I wish you could come across the Channel and stay a while with us.

Yours sincerely,
José

This single exchange is representative of the whole. During ten years of long letters, Stevens's eclecticism was in every case the cause of Rodríguez Feo's. It is clear from the March 23 reply, as from many others, that his name-dropping was an attempt to please and impress. But he was mistaken if he thought Stevens would prefer to discuss *literary* matters as energetically as this.

Stevens's response to such letters could be quite merciless, even while good intentions seemed guaranteed by the nice last touch of self-deprecation: "What I really like to have from you is not your tears on the death of Bernanos, say, but news about chickens raised on red peppers and homesick rhapsodies of the Sienese look of far away Havana and news about people I don't know, who are more fascinating to me than all the characters in all the novels of Spain, which I am unable to read" (*L* 622). Rodríguez Feo understood that this American poet, when he wrote in such a manner, was protesting too much. He knew full well by then—1948— that Stevens would have loved, actually, to find and buy and read all the books of Spain, and that his notion of the proper description of Havana was itself derivative. Far less physically adventurous than his Cuban friend, Stevens could be assuaged, as Rodríguez Feo eventually learned, by words detailing "the *Sienese* look of far away Havana," despite his knowing even less of Italy than of Cuba. After a certain point, then, Rodríguez Feo began to learn how to respond obligingly. He told another story about his mother's wonderful fears: if her son accepted an offer to live in Paris—he had been offered a job at UNESCO—he would freeze in an unheated hotel, just as another aspiring artist and voracious reader had frozen in Argentina, book in hand. Rodríguez Feo could not really have been surprised, after telling this truly delicious tale, to find it retold in Stevens's poem "The Novel," where Stevens quotes nine lines verbatim from Rodríguez Feo's letter. This was too alluring a story about the mother's provincialism at war with the son's internationalism. Here are the lines from Rodríguez Feo's letter as they appear in Stevens's poem:

> *Mother was afraid I should freeze in the Parisian hotels.*
> *She had heard of the fate of an Argentine writer. At night,*
> *He would go to bed, cover himself with blankets—*
>
> *Protruding from the pile of wool, a hand,*
> *In a black glove, holds a novel by Camus. She begged*
> *That I stay away.*[14]

Nor could Rodríguez Feo have been very surprised to receive Stevens's hilarious letter—two full pages of single-spaced elite typewriting—about the farm animals. "I take the greatest pride in knowing Pompilio," Stevens wrote here of the Cuban's mule, "who does not have to divest himself of anything to see things as they are. Do please give him a bunch of carrots with my regards." But Stevens meant to make a point here: "This is much more serious than you are likely to think from the first reading of this letter." What ought to be taken seriously, he went on to explain, was Rodríguez Feo's mostly unmet potential for realizing the primitive element in his surroundings. To push the lesson, Stevens described a fellow who regularly came to The Hartford headquarters, an unskilled man who wandered the polished corridors of that great building, office to office, dispensing with his shoeshine invariably primitive figures of speech Stevens found irresistible. He delighted in the bootblack's homely similes and paratactic constructions, and offered this example: "I was tired and laid down under a tree like a dog." And despite the fact that the image of Rodríguez Feo's family farm in this letter was a bucolic scene of unaffected animals-imagined-as-peasants surrounding a lonely, hyperintellectual, cosmopolitan reader, Stevens expressed his desire to make Rodríguez Feo less like his correspondent, the severe poet-attorney whose language was over-subordinated and whose manner over-civilized—with his own loneliness and devotion to reading—and *much more like* the harmless, semiliterate bootblack. The Hartford bootblack, Stevens urged, "is pretty much the same thing as you, yourself, seated under a tree at the Villa Olga and realizing that the world is as Pompilio sees it, except for you, or that the world is as the Negro sees it because he probably sees it exactly as Pompilio sees it."[15] (The "Negro" mentioned here was a cook who served Rodríguez Feo's family at the Villa Olga, and whom Rodríguez Feo described as continually "silent" [*SM* 69–70].) Thus the image of José reading in his room changed according to the strength of Stevens's wish to maneuver his Cuban friend into the bootblack's supposedly mindless position (lying down under the tree, dog-tired, *like an animal*), as into the cow's animal station (staring in from outside at a reader indoors). "Somehow I do not care much about Lucera," Stevens wrote of the cow outside the window. "I imagine her standing in the bushes at night watching your lamp a little way off and wondering what in the world you are doing."

The long letter, deconstructing the project of reading as an inexplicable, irrelevant act (seen by preconscious beings, it appears to be indistinguishable from the act of eating), became an impressive counternarrative against reading and thinking in the tropics, against "intellectual isolation." The quality of this letter itself as an enchantment, making resistance against its assumptions difficult, served Stevens much as the bootblack's folkloric, monosyllabic incantation ("I was tired and laid down under a tree like a dog") induced an apt linguistic lethargy; that is, the letter was itself meant to transform the insufficiently bucolic scene into a properly primitive state. Stevens's point was first introduced, tellingly, with a reference to van Geyzel as a man aspiring to be the intellectual center who is "actually," essentially, a farmer on the periphery:

> Of yourself you say that you read and write and cultivate your garden. You like to write to people far away and about such unreal things as books. It is a common case. I have a man in Ceylon with whom I have been exchanging letters for some years. He is an Englishman, an Oxford man and a lawyer, I believe, but actually he makes his living and the living of his family by growing coconuts. (*L* 512–13)

Rodríguez Feo seemed impervious to such pressures against literary discourse and literary reference at first. In 1945 Stevens's arguments against reading—that he had not read Robert Lowell's first book because a writer should not "nourish [himself] on the work of other people" (March 19; *SM* 46), and that he read "less of everything than most people" because "[i]t is more interesting to sit round and look out of the window" (March 2; *SM* 43)—could not yet bring Rodríguez Feo to throw his Milosz and Svévò away. "I like what you said about reading," the young man replied. "I am getting to prefer looking out of the window, also. *Nevertheless*, Chesterton has kept me from the window" (*SM* 47). So begins the delirious bibliography of March 23. Such imperviousness to Stevens was charming, even the Cuban's willingness to contradict himself in the act of trying to please.[16]

But the pressure from the north would not abate. Stevens made a special point of praising Rodríguez Feo's story of the kidnapping of the family Great Dane, Linda, and the tale of his vengeful neighbor, Consuelo, whom

Rodríguez Feo's conspiracy-minded mother suspected to be Linda's kidnapper (*SM* 140). Stevens not only joked wickedly about this incident, once imagining a new "Linda brand" of frankfurters (*SM* 148), but also used the occasion to reiterate his yearning to hear more about Cuba and less about poetry. "Literature nowadays is largely about nothing by nobodies," he wrote. "Is it not so? What kind of book would that dazzling human animal Consuelo sit down to read after she had finished washing the blood off her hands and had hidden once more her machete in the piano?" (*L* 624). The answer to his question is, of course: She reads no book at all.

Finally, all the book-talk flowing from Cuba made Stevens restate the reductive life-literature opposition and repeat his request for tales of the primitive life. "One writes about [life] when it is one's own life provided one is a good barbarian, a true Cuban, or a true Pennsylvania Dutchman, in the linguistics of that soul which propriety, like another Consuelo, has converted into nothingness" (*L* 624–25). Equating the Cuban and himself as barbarians—"barbarians" is a word Stevens probably would not have used had not Rodríguez Feo himself defined the term as a uniquely Cuban form of compliment (*SM* 141)[17]—makes the two men similarly "true" to what they essentially are, gives them a sense of ethnic and national origin that was just then strong in Stevens (at the height of his genealogical interest), even as the equation of a Cuban in impoverished, dependent Cuba and a many-generations-removed Pennsylvania Dutchman in suburban Connecticut may seem disingenuous, even absurd, to us now. Here Stevens was struggling to make a major point about his own poetic writing, which resists being read as the record of a life. When should one write about one's own life? Only when one recognizes the "primitive" in oneself can one create out of one's words a "linguistics of the soul," which social rules eventually diminish to nil. He and the Cuban, he claims, similarly have such a "soul."

In response to Rodríguez Feo's name-dropping letter of March 23, 1945, Stevens wrote again on April 6. He used Rodríguez Feo's request for a comment on Caillois's *Les Impostures de la poesie* as an occasion for criticizing *Orígenes*. Caillois's problem, Stevens decided, was that he attenuated and then ridiculed a taste for pure poetry that no longer existed, setting up a straw dandy, as it were. Caillois misread the trend toward the postwar mode that would deal with people, places, and things. "I think the feeling today very definitely is for an abundant poetry, concerned with everything and everybody" (*L* 495). This assessment gave Stevens the opportunity to measure the extent to which *Orígenes* reproduced the abundance of Cuba. He had just finished looking over the recent number of *Orígenes* containing María Rosa Lida's long article on Chaucer, hardly the sort of regional-ism with which to refresh himself after finishing with Caillois's lyric strangeness.

> There is something else that you have spoken of on which I should like to say a word or two, and that is the risk you run in respect to accusations of imperi-alism. I should say that the risk is not a risk in respect to imperialism but in respect to eclecticism. For instance, that article on Chaucer. The act of edit-ing a review is a creative act and, in general, the power of literature is that in describing the world it creates what it describes. Those things that are not described do not exist, so that in putting together a review like ORIGENES you are really putting together a world. You are describing a world and by describ-ing it you are creating it. Assuming that you have a passion for Cuba, you cannot have, or at least you cannot indulge in, a passion for Brinnin and Levin, and so on, at the same time. This is not a question of nationalism, but it is a question of expressing the genius of your country, disengaging it from the mere mass of things, and doing this by means of every poem, every essay, every short story which you publish—and every drawing by Mariano, or any-one else. The job of the editor of ORIGENES is to disengage the identity of Cuba. I hope you won't mind my saying this. After all, I am not saying it *for your sake, or for the sake of Cuba, but for my own sake.* I agree with Caillois in this, at least, that there should be many things in the world: that Cuba should be full of Cuban things and not of essays on Chaucer. (*L* 495; emphasis added)

The rhetorical tradition of imperialism here is quite distinct (though surely unconscious): "We are in Egypt," Arthur Balfour declared to the House of Commons, "not merely for the sake of the Egyptians, though we are there for their sake; we are there also for the sake of Europe."[18] Ste-vens's letter masterfully substituted eclecticism for imperialism, and thus rationalized an intercultural force as the natural result of reading widely and experimentally. This strategy enabled Stevens to present a criticism that minimized national power. He read "the force that attaches" as "*dis*engagement." He could say directly that by publishing Brinnin's poems and Levin's essays *Orígenes* was being more impressed by American critical values than it ought to be. But to see this as primarily a political matter, Stevens urged, was to underestimate an editor's capacity for creating a world by including it and denying a world by omitting it. It was within the young Cuban's power to create the world he desired. The irony of invent-ing a world in this sense was just that shared by Stevens's "Description without Place" and Sumner Welles's "Vision of a World at Peace," each promoting postwar reconstruction, or "creating a world," in terms that must mask their necessary association with the cultural desire to—in Jo-seph Conrad's figure—put one's denoting finger on the still-unnamed part of the map.[19] In drawing attention to this process of imagining a world, Stevens charged Rodríguez Feo with the thankless, unimaginative task of being Cuban for the sake of the writer who wanted to have continuous access to Cuban things—things legitimized *as* Cuban by the native editor who, taking such paternal instruction well, found himself choosing consciously to describe an unfamiliar place in familiar terms. Once Rodríguez Feo understood the irony of Stevens's special wished-for scene of instruction, then Stevens's attempt to maintain the segregation of political from creative forces might be said to have collapsed along with many other false distinctions, such as "This is not a question of *nationalism,* but it is a question of expressing *the genius of your country.*" Stevens's anticipation of an "abundant" poetry, postwar writing that would reproduce the extrinsic plenitude of the real, the "many things in the world" that emerged from the war, paradoxically became a call for restricted access. He had schooled the Cuban in what Cuba should *not* be full of.

How could the Cuban respond? First there was the matter of Stevens's having turned the accusation of imperialism inside out. The *origenistas* were not willingly the friends of cultural imperialists, in fact. On the contrary, Rodríguez Feo and his colleagues decried the influence of the United States. *Orígenes,* wrote Vitier, fortified Cuban art at a time when all Caribbean artists were in danger of being overwhelmed by the most powerful nation in the hemisphere.[20] At times Rodríguez Feo made it clear to Stevens that he abhorred America's proficiency at delivering the cultural goods:

> Amazing how mediocre taste will pervade when the nation who backs it up is powerful enough. The world will in time be inundated by vulgar, detestable American products, because America is all powerful and can deliver the goods. Example: *The Readers' Digest* is the best selling magazine in Latin America, *Red Amber* is a best seller to the South, everybody says Thank you, O.K., never gracias, Muy Bien, and the movies? Well, let's skip that one. (*SM* 63–64)

He also told Stevens he deplored North American criticism, by which he meant Yvor Winters in particular (*SM* 36). Winters's "Wallace Stevens, or the Hedonist's Progress" (1943) argued that Stevens's style had degenerated after "Sunday Morning." Rodríguez Feo in 1983 recalled that what particularly upset him about Winters's attack was the characteristically American—and, to him, mistaken—notion that a poem is bad if the victim of its irony is small game.[21] No surprise that Rodríguez Feo should think so, as it was not out of character for him to offer himself up as small game if the effect would be to encourage what he considered Stevens's strength as a poet—his irony—and thus to prove to Stevens himself his point about the flaw in American criticism. Such self-sacrifice was never a conscious strategy, but it is clear now to Rodríguez Feo that his letters—disorganized, presumptuous, provocative, irrational at times, and often confessional—created their powerfully disarming effects because they challenged the "hierarchy of values" (*SM* 41) that prevented new American writing from manifesting such qualities. In the letter he wrote that immediately prompted Stevens to compose "A Word with José Rodríguez-Feo," Rodríguez Feo presumed to characterize Stevens's own house as gloomy, asked why Stevens had been called the Whistler of American poetry,[22] related Hemingway's sexual obsession to his being a North American, and asked Stevens to explain the "major man" of the war years, a central concept Stevens had virtually refused to explain to Simons, whose letters full of similarly basic questions were so comparatively methodical. And particularly with Rodríguez Feo's scrawled, nearly indecipherable postscript questioning the grotesque in the Spanish tradition, Stevens's poem-reply found a great deal to respond to. Here is Rodríguez Feo's letter (*SM* 41–42):

My dear Mr. Wallace Stevens:

It was grand to hear from you again and to know that [Mariano's] watercolors are cheering your rather gloomy house. I was surprised to learn that your visit to Cuba was of twenty years ago, for your poetry always has had for me a certain evocation of tropical light and colors which I find quite charming and most unusual. Of course, you know that Hemingway has lived among us for a long time; but I have always maintained that the milieu has not affected him at all. I cannot see how anybody could not be impressed by certain *things* which I find completely absent in his most "Spanishied" works. Of course, I have never quite come to admire Hemingway: I mean that if you are a real blood and bone latino, you find absurd and a bit of an affectation those "virile problems" which seem to bother him so much. I sincerely think him an Illinois Puritan hunting for exotic sensations in the places and things which are naturally empty of all possibilities of adventure. I should not have said PURITAN, because he is really more of a bourgeois and his dislike of certain authors condemns him in my eyes. The fact that he has had such a success makes me fear for that hierarchy of values which must reign in a nation if its culture is not going to fall into the most slappiest of arrangements. You are dead right, as you Americans would put it, about Winters. . . .

You will pardon my stupidity but I don't quite get what you mean by "major men." What do you mean by some "arbitrary object of belief"? I think it was more exact to call them a "source of poetry," but that too is rather ambiguous, eh? Is the intention mythological at all? Why do critics insist in calling you the Whistler of Amer. poetry? What do you think of Brinnin's poetry and Penn Warren?

I am very grateful for the promised volume of poetry. I will have all your poems here with me then. Are you ever returning to our lovely Habana?

Yours modestly,

José

About Hemingway—Picasso's "Guernica" and Dali's mystifying stories are Sp[anish] treatments of the same subject[,] not Romantic but macabre[,] in the tradition of Goya in the case of Guernica——Hemingway has not exploited the grotesque in our lives. Who has?

Stevens wrote "Paisant Chronicle" (*CP* 334–35) to answer one of the questions posed by this tantalizing letter, and with characteristic under-statement observed to Rodríguez Feo that in the new poem he "defined major men for you" (*L* 489). Stevens's second poem-reply was equally swift and public, sent to the journal *Voices* within a week of receipt of Rodríguez Feo's letter, along with "Paisant Chronicle" and three other poems.[23] He mailed a copy of the typescript to Cuba:

A Word with José Rodríguez-Feo

As one of the secretaries of the moon,
The queen of ignorance, you have deplored
How she presides over imbeciles. The night
Makes everything grotesque. Is it because
Night is the nature of man's interior world?
Is lunar Habana the Cuba of the self?

We must enter boldly that interior world
To pick up relaxations of the known.
For example, this old man selling oranges
Sleeps by his basket. He snores. His bloated breath
Bursts back. What not quite realized transit
Of ideas moves wrinkled in a motion like

The cry of an embryo? The spirit tires,
It has, long since, grown tired, of such ideas.
It says there is an absolute grotesque.
There is a nature that is grotesque within
The boulevards of the generals. Why should
We say that it is man's interior world

Or seeing the spent, unconscious shapes of night,
Pretend they are shapes of another consciousness?
The grotesque is not a visitation. It is
Not apparition but appearance, part

Of that simplified geography, in which
The sun comes up like news from Africa.

(*CP* 333–34)

By way of an abashed "Thank you," Rodríguez Feo decided to express his regret that this poem was not for publication in *Orígenes*, rather than fully reveal his excitement over its being a special "Word" for him. Ironically, he had as much trouble understanding it as anyone else, although Stevens did offer a little help to him alone. "The point of the poem," he explained, ". . . is that, although the grotesque has taken possession of the sub-conscious, this is not because there is any particular relationship between the two things" (*L* 489). If we go on this alone, it would seem that Stevens missed entirely the point of Rodríguez Feo's postscript, which had not tried to make a case for the relation between the grotesque and "the subconscious."

The play in the title of this poem of instruction moves Stevens from the idiomatic (*I would like to have a word with José*) to the literal (*I would like to take up the problem of a single word—the "grotesque"—with him*). The poem addresses itself to Rodríguez Feo just as if it were one of Stevens's letters, saluting him as one of the secret-keepers of the moon, one who acknowledges her reign over ignorance but deplores her for not drawing the line at imbeciles. If the Cuban has asked his North American friend why the moon makes everything grotesque, as the poem supposes, he must also wonder if this is because there are special *provinces* for certain experiences. Night, for instance, seems the special province of man's interior world—as is the steamy night of the tropics in particular. Night offers special entrance into that world—that is, into "Cuba," the Roman household goddess who escorts children into the world of sleep. The answer to the North American's rhetorical question—"Is lunar Habana the Cuba of the self?"—apprehends the Cuban as provincial in any case, because it is the same as asking, tautologically, "Are you yourself?" Insofar as you indeed are yourself, you cannot help but reproduce the relaxations of the human, the local color of, "for example," the old man selling oranges. That one can choose "this" old man—*this* man as casually distinguished from *that*—suggests the abundance that the "*particular* José" addressed apparently tries to deny in his own special province.

Once the cultural type seems no more malicious than a random reduction—this point comes as the third stanza begins—the "spirit tires" of the effort to generalize from the regional. Such exhaustion inevitably follows presentations of the real. For even the utterly casual "example" leads us to ask theoretical questions about poetics. Such a spirit, weary of these sorts of questions and craving local fecundities such as things the orangeman sells, proposes the ignorance of indigence as an "absolute grotesque," an untransformed externality. And so this tired spirit finally rejects José's interest in the interior world of places like Havana where the extrinsic life is sufficiently abundant to command every bit of one's attention. The grotesque is actual, visible, "not apparition but appearance"—a part of (the poem admits) "that simplified geography" of the North American imagination thinking *of* and also *for* the Caribbean. In a simplified geography the weary world is freshened just as the oldest trope (the sun) crosses over from the category of "weather" to that of "news." The sun-trope emerges from anywhere and thus from *nowhere in particular*, from places analogous and interchangeable, from *this* primitive place or *that*, from *Africa*, "for example." So the poem suggests in closing: "The sun comes up like *news* from *Africa*."

After several years of letters in which he felt he was being urged to be isolated and suitably provincial, to resist Americanization, Rodríguez Feo submitted, significantly if temporarily, in playing the role of Stevens's Cuban primitive, by agreeing to console himself with the task of describing the bougainvillaeas and reproducing the banana vendor's song. "Attempt to Discover Life" (*CP* 370), the poem that prompted this confession of limits, thus had an effect quite the opposite of the discovery offered Rodríguez Feo in the title. "Attempt to Discover Life" was created out of the Cuban's failed effort to alter the unwritten rules of the relationship. The "Attempt" was made rather suddenly in 1946: Rodríguez Feo invited himself to Hartford for a visit. The letters had become a little more intimate than before, certainly for Rodríguez Feo, who wrote on May 10, 1946, in response to Stevens's gift of *Esthétique du Mal* (*SM* 83–84):

> All the admiration and longing for a more personal friendship could be expressed by my telling you how delighted and grateful I am to you. Reading, caressing (it almost comes to that) your marvelous "Esthétique" has been a benediction. . . . It comes to exclaiming that it is the most regaling present I have ever received and from a poet I don't even know personally. What a pity circumstances keep me so far away and prohibit a more intimate colloquy! . . . Do let me know of yourself and what you are doing in Hartford. Are the trees all green and the wild-flowers inciting young men into the woods?
>
> Your fu*rr*iously admiring Antillean,
> José

Rodríguez Feo has recalled for Beverly Coyle and me two important functions of this first face-to-face encounter: it would enable him to be explicit about his presumption that he might get to know Stevens's life in Hartford in the same way as Stevens wanted so urgently to know the particulars of his in Cuba; and it might, if planned just so, provide him an

occasion to be honest about his homosexuality.[24] Unfortunately, Rodríguez Feo's departure for the United States was ill-timed; he just missed
Stevens's response to the idea of the visit, insisting that they meet in Manhattan instead of on Stevens's own ground. What followed was a month-
long comedy of errors involving an exchange of four letters, at least one
phone call, and no fewer than three near misses.

As planned, Rodríguez Feo proceeded first to Vermont to assist in a
summer language program at Middlebury College. From there he wrote to
Stevens on August 25 that he would stop briefly in Boston before heading
in Stevens's direction. By the time Stevens received this message, there
would be no way to head off the young man. Two days later, on the
twenty-seventh, Rodríguez Feo wrote again that he planned to visit Stevens at his office in the next week. Despite its pretense of being business-
like and precise, the note captures the spirit of his other letters—playful,
inexact (he forgets to name the *day* of the visit), and comically meditative:
"[I]t shall be at *exactly* noon so as to trap the poet as he exits from the
walled citadel of the insurances. . . . I am motoring; . . . I shall detail *precisely* the route so as not to confirm the old Gothic invention of mañana
and retarded overtures. What a triumph; to immortalize with the twelve
bells the fame of my timeliness" (*SM* 87–88; emphasis added). This letter
would almost certainly have reached the offices of The Hartford by Friday,
August 30, and Stevens may or may not have comprehended its message.
He and his wife, planning a brief vacation, intended to be away from that
Friday until the next Monday (only five workdays away from the desk), and
he would have plenty of time to return home and travel back by train to
Manhattan to meet up with Rodríguez Feo, which, he had said in a letter
sent to Cuba, he very much wanted to do. Later correspondence reveals
that he knew Rodríguez Feo would be staying at the Stanhope and would
not leave the country until September 23.

Rodríguez Feo tried everything possible when he arrived at "twelve
bells" and found the poet gone. His effort included an abortive long-
distance call to Stevens's resort in Hershey. Through a bad telephone connection the two men apparently had difficulty sorting out the matter. On
this particular visit to Hershey, Stevens became involved in new genealogical research into his mother's family.[25] He extended this rare vacation with
Elsie from ten to twenty-five days, arriving in Manhattan on September
24, the day after Rodríguez Feo had left. "I called up the Stanhope, which
confirmed your departure" (emphasis added). He did seem to regret missing
Rodríguez Feo, but wrote to say so a week later in over-apologetic tones.
The letter is unnecessarily repetitious, and for the first time Stevens speaks
in a protective plural: "[W]e had one of the happiest holidays we have ever
had." A paragraph later, he adds: "But, after all, we had one of the happiest
times of our lives" (*SM* 88–89).

Rodríguez Feo received Stevens's explanation along with another new poem, "Attempt to Discover Life," which refers to the sulfur-bath resort Rodríguez Feo frequented, San Miguel de los Baños.[26] Here is the first stanza:

> At San Miguel de los Baños,
> The waitress heaped up black Hermosas
> In the magnificence of a volcano.
> Round them she spilled the roses
> Of the place, blue and green, both streaked.
> And white roses shaded emerald on petals
> Out of the deadliest heat.

Whether Stevens meant it as such, Rodríguez Feo accepted the poem as a gift—as the much warmer part of Stevens's apology. As consolation for having missed the poet in his element, here was fresh proof that Stevens could intimately imagine Rodríguez Feo in *his*. The Cuban was humbly and effusively grateful: "How very fine of you, to pay homage to our *little local villages.* . . . How magical the *discovery*!" (*SM* 89–90). Stevens's "discovery" is that the Cuban scene, the resort café, is so thickly abundant— flowers are "heaped," "spilled," colors "streaked," and so on—that it naturally dispels the poor woman who enters and stands by an occupied table, apparently waiting for bits of the patrons' excess wealth to be left behind. In the end, the cadaverousness of the poor is overcome by the natural richness of the place. "The green roses drifted up from the table / In smoke. The blue petals became / The yellowing fomentation of effulgence." And so "The cadaverous persons were dispelled." Next to the table where they had stood "were lying—dos centavos." The poem ends with an inconsequential tip and its obvious message: How easily are such social differences resolved in so natural a retreat.

Yet Rodríguez Feo, interpreting this poem for himself after returning from his trip, did not concentrate on the way in which it suggests the wealthy young Cuban's resort as the site for such a dismissal. He seemed to think the poem carried some message not generally on the differences between their two cultures but on the sentiment shared between them—on their friendship, as a sign of compensation for his failed "Attempt" to know Stevens more intimately. In Rodríguez Feo's view, the final two pennies "were pathetic, not condescending."[27] He wrote, "How come you see from so far-off those touching scenes?" (*SM* 90). Now, then, moved by what he read as tenderness on Stevens's part, Rodríguez Feo translated the poem for *Orígenes* himself (rather than have another *origenista* undertake the job as before).[28] In his letter of November 30 he thanked Stevens and seems to have submitted to the "simplified geography" of the earlier poem by speaking of his new willingness to settle for knowing the "little things" around him. He referred to his loneliness now in such a way as perhaps to suggest his homosexuality, in case Stevens knew how to take such a hint:

> My life flows as usual. I write, read and frequent the company of a few and selected amigos. I am as lonely as ever and yet quite happy in my isolation. All the vines are in bloom now, and looking across its flowery branches I see the sky remains blue and shining up there. What more can you ask of life? To open one's eyes in the morning and see only flowers and the open spaces blue and white above. And to read kind, friendly messages from our friends below. It doesn't signify that we avert suffering and misery, all that is within us, but we must remain platonic and make the best of the little things the gods so kindly offer us every day: be it the vision of a violet bouganville or the song of a banana vendor. I think that is wisdom, not cowardice. I prefer to be foolish in those little things; not be made a fool reaching for the stars. (*SM* 90–91)

Stevens's brief reply to these sentiments must have been at least temporarily another disappointment. Answering a direct question about the poem—Rodríguez Feo had asked, "[W]hat are hermosas?" (*SM* 90)—Stevens postponed his response to the more difficult issues raised in the letter concerning the meaning of the poem in the context of their relationship. He simply answered: "Hermosas are a variety of roses," as if it had been Hi Simons, and not José Rodríguez Feo, who had asked for explication. Even in his very generous letter of December 19, he takes up none of the issues Rodríguez Feo raised about his loneliness, his possible consolation offered by his "platonism," the disappointments of his visit to the United States. The image of Rodríguez Feo's resort, San Miguel de los Baños, Stevens now wrote, had not been intended to record his physical response to specific people, to a Cuban as opposed, say, to a Mexican or Argentine. On the contrary, he argued, his poem referred to an entirely unreal place, a description without a necessary sense of place.

From this point in a decade of letters, if Rodríguez Feo was to criticize "that hierarchy of values"—values which, to be sure, he more than once suggested Stevens represented—it had to be embedded, and thus formally qualified, in the letters-of-travel subgenre, a *pensée sauvage* Stevens had desired in the Cuban's letters. Even the politically radical suggestion that the world be "Cubanized" rather than Americanized—that the "civilized" nations ought not prepare for atomic attacks, and thus refuse to acknowledge the survivability of a nuclear exchange—had to be qualified by the idea that Cubanizing the world would actually mean simplifying and primitivizing it:

> [R]eading the paper tonight I felt a little sad. Why don't we "cubanize" a little the world? Then everybody would take it easier, would live for today, leave things for *mañana*, and get along better with their neighbors. I see N.Y. is ready

for an atomic attack. From here, my dear friend, everything you read sounds a bit fantastical and absurd. Maybe we are (the Spaniards and Cubans) a race of retarded mortals. We still live by norms of other centuries and will not recognize completely the mechanical urge. Just to prove this point: in Habana the new *cafetera* (little engine that makes coffee) are called (as advertisement) *La Bomba Atómica*. That sense of humour has saved us from the madness and nonsense that threatens to end your more "civilized" histories. (*SM* 184)

From "here," from this point in time and place, Rodríguez Feo's Cuba, where cold-war fears of nuclear annihilation seem "fantastical" and "absurd," North American political anxieties are resisted exactly as they are naturalized—Cubanized—in terms powerfully managed by Stevens throughout the correspondence. To resist the anxieties of politics, to go unbothered by what one reads in the newspapers even while still reading them—to make Stalin Balin while remaining well aware of Stalin—was to move the subject to a position where Stevens had wanted to locate it all along: to a place existing not prior to but beyond the mechanical urge, resistant to civilization after having known it utterly.

CHAPTER 5

The Postcard Imagination

[H]e steeped himself in Europe, gathering postcards, catalogues of art exhibitions, books, magazines, photographs, and correspondents there, so that he knew the parts that interested him as if he had been there. Perhaps, toward the very end of his life, he might have gone—except that he felt World War II had changed everything. Or was it that Europe might not have been what it was in his imagination?
—Holly Stevens, in "Bits of Remembered Time"

I believe, very sincerely, that we in the U. S. during all those [war] years knew nothing of the realities—even now I keep thinking and talking in terms of the privileged one on the other side of the ocean and each time I feel and know that I am wrong. But I keep telling the Europeans that we must learn from America too.
—Barbara Church, writing to Stevens from France

Out of the silence of oppressed peoples, out of the despair of those who have lost freedom, there comes to us an expression of longing.
*—Harry Truman, the Jefferson Day Dinner speech,
April 5, 1947*

Lugano has been more or less of a spot for me this summer. Early in the summer I wrote to the Villa Favorita at Castagnola, which is either in or about Lugano. . . . They sent me a catalogue and a lot of reproductions and postcards. It must have been an extraordinary experience to live in Lugano.
*—Wallace Stevens, in an unpublished letter to Barbara Church
mailed from Hartford after she had visited Lugano*

Great travellers / Are bourgeois too / Nevertheless. They . . . make rules, stick to habits . . . And find of course / That the new world / Has grown older / And that the old one / Returns.
*—An unpublished poem by Barbara Church,
sent to Marianne Moore*

Poetry is a renovation of experience.
—Stevens (OP 202)

AS HE BEGAN to write a series of poems that would be published together in "The Rock" section of *Collected Poems* of 1954, Stevens proposed a new agreement with what he again called the "actual world." This decision to face reality can be dated at late summer 1952; in so dating it, I want to suggest that the person for whom he described his new knowledge of reality, Barbara Church, was the one friend whose thinking about Europe indicated to him that there did exist strong outside forces operating upon his late career. Yet at the same time he came to know that these outside forces moved at cross-purposes. Barbara Church's eyewitness accounts of unabated European misery, in the postcards, letters, and snapshots she mailed him, tended to contradict the optimistic American election rhetoric Stevens was just then hearing and reading. In the dominant political metaphors of the day, accepted by both major political parties and, remarkably, by two otherwise very different presidential candidates, *reconstruction* (of the physical Europe) was supposed to endorse, not contradict, *containment* (of antidemocratic ideology in Europe and elsewhere).[1] In two poems that I think follow directly from Stevens's new resolve to approach the actual world, "St. Armorer's Church from the Outside" (*CP* 529–30) and "The Green Plant" (*CP* 506), these political metaphors contend. The first of the two poems, "St. Armorer's Church from the Outside," struggles to recognize these apparently complementary but actually conflicting American metaphors, briefly but brilliantly discloses the opposition as a social and international issue, but finally naturalizes the political contention by falling back on a genius-theory of the individual poet and his reconstructive power; in other words, American "[p]oetry is a renovation of experience." Here is the poem in full:

> 1 St. Armorer's was once an immense success.
> It rose loftily and stood massively; and to lie
> In its church-yard, in the province of St. Armorer's,
> Fixed one for good in geranium-colored day.
>
> 5 What is left has the foreign smell of plaster,
> The closed-in smell of hay. A sumac grows
> On the altar, growing toward the lights, inside.
> Reverberations leak and lack among holes . . .
>
> Its chapel rises from Terre Ensevelie,
> 10 An ember yes among its cindery noes,
> His own: a chapel of breath, an appearance made
> For a sign of meaning in the meaningless,
>
> No radiance of dead blaze, but something seen
> In a mystic eye, no sign of life but life,

15 Itself, the presence of the intelligible
In that which is created as its symbol.

It is like a new account of everything old,
Matisse at Vence and a great deal more than that,
A new-colored sun, say, that will soon change forms
20 And spread hallucinations on every leaf.

The chapel rises, his own, his period,
A civilization formed from the outward blank,
A sacred syllable rising from sacked speech,
The first car out of a tunnel en voyage

25 Into lands of ruddy-ruby fruits, achieved
Not merely desired, for sale, and market things
That press, strong peasants in a peasant world,
Their purports to a final seriousness—

Final for him, the acceptance of such prose,
30 Time's given perfections made to seem like less
Than the need of each generation to be itself,
The need to be actual and as it is.

St. Armorer's has nothing of this present,
This *vif*, this dizzle-dazzle of being new
35 And of becoming, for which the chapel spreads out
Its arches in its vivid element,

In the air of newness of that element,
In an air of freshness, clearness, greenness, blueness,
That which is always beginning because it is part
40 Of that which is always beginning, over and over.

The chapel underneath St. Armorer's walls,
Stands in a light, its natural light and day,
The origin and keep of its health and his own.
And there he walks and does as he lives and likes.

The second and better-known poem, "The Green Plant," begins at the point where the hard work of the first poem left off—at exactly the point where the terms of containing and reconstructing the world collapse into a single, uncontroversial poetic impulse. The second poem then turns toward reality without apparent forthrightness, just as if this realization came after a genuine struggle *against* reality. "The Green Plant" assumes and then affirms the poet's new determination to face that reality boldly:

1 Silence is a shape that has passed.
  Otu-bre's lion-roses have turned to paper
  And the shadows of the trees
  Are like wrecked umbrellas.

5 The effete vocabulary of summer
  No longer says anything.
  The brown at the bottom of red
  The orange far down in yellow,

  Are falsifications from a sun
10 In a mirror, without heat,
  In a constant secondariness,
  A turning down toward finality—

  Except that a green plant glares, as you look
  At the legend of the maroon and olive forest,
15 Glares, outside of the legend, with the barbarous green
  Of the harsh reality of which it is part.

The resolution of this second poem does seem convincing. After the turn at "Except," the last stanza does claim that the speaker faces a *"harsh reality."* But it is the sort of natural claim that can be understood only if it is measured against *both* the apparent failure of the preceding poem, "St. Armorer's Church," to sustain its resistant, corrosive relation to the actual world and Stevens's subtle response to American policies of reconstruction as they were distorted by nonmilitary or "cultural" conflict, by "cold" war. In this unexpected context, I want to describe an American poet's crisis of direction, of motion through two poems—from "St. Armorer's Church," published in the October 1952 issue of *Poetry*, to "The Green Plant," published that December in the *Nation*[2]—as having been settled in the facile reconciliation of the second poem. The language in that reconciliation develops a deliberately overstated strategy for facing "harsh" reality from the apparent failure in "St. Armorer's Church" to know how present realities must indeed be faced. Nevertheless, along the way toward this new recognition of self-assurance and mastery in "The Green Plant," Stevens's career, as well as its relation to American ideas, has been slightly but significantly redefined in "St. Armorer's Church"—its motion redirected, its aims politically tested, and a certain lack of awareness about a previous tendency now partially acknowledged: namely, the tendency to underestimate the extent to which the idea that the American imagination had arrived at the end of ideology was itself ideological, that seeming indifference to politics was itself a new, powerful form of cultural politics. Insofar as Stevens in his last years remained unaware that he adopted one explicitly partisan metaphor of the actual world (containment) while shrewdly criticizing another ostensibly natural or nonideological one (reconstruction), it is left to the literary historian, measuring the poems against such cultural shifts, to trace an unwritten motion of the story.

Between 1948 and 1952 Stevens took special pleasure in the letters he received from a largely unreconstructed Europe. The lively exchange with Thomas McGreevy during 1948 and 1949 made it clear that there were Irishmen at least who resented the competing entreaties of the Russians and the Americans. This excitable friend equally criticized George Marshall's and Joseph Stalin's bearing postwar gifts of aid.[3] At the same time, a renewed exchange with a Swedish professor of literature, Ebba Dalin, an Americanist who had published translations of Stevens's poems, taught him that a feeling of purity or impartiality had finally been reached in some icy, peaceful zone in the northern extremities, that the world war had been entirely gotten over in some otherworldly place. Paule Vidal, successor to her father as Stevens's Parisian art and book dealer, might worry that one of her painters had disappeared behind the iron curtain; reporting this possibility to Stevens, she used Churchill's metaphor in French.[4] Yet, no less nonpartisan about the cold war than McGreevy, Vidal could also observe to Stevens that her most faithful customers came from the Russian embassy. These communists really did retain a passion for fine books, she wrote him two days after the Korean War broke out. Of course she hastened to note that her American friend was the exception to her otherwise provocative generalization that the Soviets were becoming her faithful clients.[5]

Stevens's most sustained contact with Europe in these years was with Henry Church's widow, Barbara, whose elaborate automobile tours, particularly in the summers of 1949 and 1952, offered him a knowledge, albeit a postcard-knowledge, of cultural, political, and religious survival. Her 1949 trip made its way into "An Ordinary Evening in New Haven" (*CP* 465–89), and the 1952 trip produced "St. Armorer's Church from the Outside."

Stevens's efforts at sympathizing with Barbara Church's laments about the ruins of Europe were always qualified. His analysis of political conditions in Europe, he invariably apologized, was "the view of a total outsider." Yet this remark, for instance, only followed directly from his endorsement of the notion, increasingly fashionable among American conservatives, that Pétain had been after all a man of dignity, his scheme for French capitulation a sensible one, and that the French had been helpless under occupation. Stevens's interest in this form of political revisionism was rather presumptuous, I think, for his retrospective assessment of the Vichy regime was offered, in a revealing letter, to the one correspondent who would be particularly sensitive to this point—Mrs. Church, who had herself been a wartime exile and whose estate at Ville d'Avray had been occupied and partly destroyed by German troops. Moreover, Stevens was writing her *about Jean Paulhan*, who had risked his life to publish a resistance journal out of his own Paris home. "The French were universally helpless and that great, vengeful France of the resistance simply did not exist. . . . I don't think that Americans ever in general felt that P[é]tain was guilty of treason" (*L* 748). When he wrote those words, Stevens had been reading Paulhan's *Lettre aux Directeurs de la Résistance* a second time;[6] this pamphlet retrospectively criticized the relations between the Resistance and the communists and intensified the debate already raging about French wartime behavior, perhaps itself provoking a still-further rightward realignment of post-Resistance cultural politics. Notwithstanding the reasons for Paulhan's own shifting alliances, Stevens's notion that "the loyal character of Jean Paulhan will *speak for most of us* as respects communism"—no matter how qualified by such comments as "This is the view of a total outsider"—is indeed a presumptuous generalization (*L* 748; emphasis added).[7] To borrow, to reproduce selectively, always to qualify, and, without realizing it, to Americanize whatever positions on the complexities of postwar European life he happened by chance to read; to try earnestly to view the inside of a foreign scene from the outside, and in what he believed was his own language to try and get it right: these were the habits of Stevens's writing about the world during this transitional period.

Stevens's habitual use of his European sources was not confined to his personal letters. "St. Armorer's Church from the Outside," as I read it, repeats the pattern of borrowing, reproducing, qualifying, and Americanizing European turmoil. Borrowing from the observations, the insights, and even the phrasing of postcards and letters he received from Mrs. Church during her summer 1952 journeys, the language of the poem, in ten of its eleven stanzas, keeps to the clear promise of the title that its perspective would remain "from the Outside." In a general sense, the poem does reproduce Barbara Church's perspective—she wrote him that she saw the church from outside. It raises "Outside" to the level of a political trope. Here, as with the qualified anticommunism of his remarks on Paulhan's post-Resistance politics, "outside"—"This is the view of a total outsider"—signifies American innocence perceived as an impartial and therefore inarguable view. It is the perspective of the American Stevens looking politically over as well as psychologically in. But from this second sense of "Outside" the poem reformulates Barbara Church's descriptions of the continuing European misery in two important ways.

The particular holy site Barbara Church described for him—renamed in the poem, we may initially assume, for its outer resistance to destruction—had *survived* wartime bombing largely intact, according to the plain facts she reported from a journey into Italy. Stevens's poem—or, rather, the church constructed there, as "his own" (l. 21)—modifies her report tell-ingly. The structural aspirations of the church she saw ("It rose loftily" [l. 2]) have degenerated in the poem; only the poet's breathings will restore natural freshness to it. By the last lines, the poem has amended its source by applying restoration with a lyric insistence, in "an air of freshness, clear-ness, greenness, blueness" (l. 38).

The second reformulation is in Stevens's assessment of the effort made by European generations to renew their world. Mrs. Church described in one of her letters the way in which the survivors of both Allied and Axis bombings were now forced to collect themselves after the latest round of destruction, "rebuilding each generation after war and devastation have passed."[8] The difference between this eyewitness report and Stevens's ver-sion of such efforts at renewal is an important one: to Stevens these efforts were not cyclical (as they were to Mrs. Church, who observed "rebuilding *each* generation") but straightforward, a direct program, a poetic policy of reconstruction. There must be, he seems finally to argue, a direct, though slow, return to health, to nature, to direct light, to individual creativity. Here, then, the reference to Henri Matisse's *Chapel of the Rosary of the Dominicans at Vence* (1948–1952) in lines 17 and 18 begins to make sense. Matisse's work, Stevens implies, serves both poorly and admirably as an example of the experimental reconstruction he himself would impose on the destroyed forms. His St. Armorer's Church "is like a new account of everything old, / Matisse at Vence *and a great deal more than that*" (empha-sis added). For Matisse's wall drawings and stained glass made a modernist masterwork of an entirely new chapel; Stevens, on the other hand, wants to involve degenerated structures of the past in a responsive restoration of history itself, new constructive words breathed into a "sacked speech" (l. 23), the "new *account* of everything old" (l. 17)—where, in his well-seasoned trope, an old sun renewed could spread new colors (ll. 19–20) and contribute to reconstruction ("will soon change forms" [l. 19]). Thus the reconstructed chapel will itself "rise"—be built up and also aspire up-wards—like a new source of light and life, let naturally in from without.[9]

The poem ends with sunshine that predicates true liberty—the actual "weather" taking precedence over the actual "news," to use Stevens's fa-vorite antinomies representing the natural outstripping the political. "And there," inside the chapel underneath the ruined church, "he walks and does as he lives and likes" (l. 44). Despite all descriptions of ruins, the church may be very rapidly restored. But first the imagination generally, and not the war specifically, must be credited as a force of disbelief capable of having destroyed the structure. Over "Time's given perfections," the poem contends (l. 30), generations rebuild themselves. Lost culture is nat-urally recoverable. "Poetry," and not a Marshall Plan, "is the renovation of experience."

This is a strong and positive idea, of course—renovation by poetic breathing. Yet it was not at all the reality Barbara Church had meant to report when, struck by the apparent willingness of Europe's peasants to await reconstruction planned by outsiders, she wrote Stevens to describe how Europeans were forced by elements beyond them to begin anew. She was referring specifically to agriculture here—to agricultural production that fails or succeeds as a result of the political and not merely the natural climate. But Stevens's attention is focused on the natural sense of renewed culture, on the weather or climate of renewal, as it were, growth that occurs without the intervention of human or state planning. When Mrs. Church spoke of the peasants continually starting over, she meant to indicate an endless cycle of destruction, hunger, misery, and more destruction as specific historical, human facts. For her, the new postwar form of history was not a moving forward but an endless return. That the poem, then, concludes with a restorative self-reliance and generally suggests an idea about renewal that is Stevens's American figuration, and speaks of degeneration with an assurance absent from Barbara Church's firsthand reports, tells us not only how Stevens's political unconscious managed poetic sources. It also shows us how he might deftly overstate his role as a poet in the business of remaking the world. For at bottom he was responding to physical destruction by presuming that a renovation through American rhetoric would be sufficient; that is, "his own" reconstruction of the church rested on a "sacred syllable" restored to significance from a cultural "speech" that had been "sacked" along with the towns and buildings.

Despite her wealth and leisure, Barbara Church continued to feel the effects of the war's destruction. She conveyed this feeling to her American friend repeatedly. During the harsh winter of 1946–1947—notorious now for having intensified calls, such as Dean Acheson's famous Cleveland, Mississippi, speech, for a massive American aid program—she confessed she could not keep her mind off "the millions of Europeans freezing," especially as the oil furnace at Ville d'Avray worked well.[10] Stevens had fully expected that on their return the Churches would find Europe "pretty much of a cavern"; so he confided to Tate.[11] But for their sake, Stevens expressed full confidence that things would return to normal. In fact, however, Barbara Church's sense of what had been destroyed in the war increased rather than decreased as time passed. This certainly challenged Stevens's feeling, in late 1945 and throughout 1946, that it was not merely time to "pick up" where "we" had left off but that total European recovery was a matter of course.[12]

What was his feeling, then, when three eventful years later Mrs. Church was still writing him about homelessness? Her sister's German family, whose houses had been destroyed during Allied bombing, still lived all together under one roof, in the farmhouse Barbara Church owned in Bavaria. (She had given the farmhouse to her sister to prevent it from falling into the hands of the Nazis, who might otherwise have seized it, she being a German expatriate wed to an American residing in France.)[13] Now she spent much of her annual time in Europe visiting half-destroyed churches and villages; that seemed to be her obligation,[14] and she felt similarly about traveling with and befriending people of the lower classes.[15] Rarely did she fail to point out for Stevens the fervor of the pious poor, who prayed inside ruins if necessary. She told him about her sister, who brought home bricks from the toppled tower of one little fifteenth-century Bavarian church, cherishing them, somewhat pitifully, "like the Chinese keep the bones of their ancestors in a shrine."[16] On the back of a postcard depicting a crowd of peasant women, costumed in black, praying and pressing at the doors of an old church, she wrote, "it gets harder and harder for me to look at ruins—we are a sad lot, we humans after all—we destroy and cannot bear the sight of it."[17] Returning to the haven of Ville d'Avray after this trip, which had included an emotional return to a mostly intact Mont Saint Michel, she concluded that "Europe, the hard breathing, shattered Europe is again in one of her critical hours—but she will survive in spite of all the isms."[18]

The Marshall Plan, named after the secretary of state who announced it in a brilliantly disarming speech at Harvard in June 1947, was rhetorically designed to transcend "all the isms." Barbara Church's final assurance in her letter of September 30, 1948, that Europe "will survive" undoubtedly refers to the exciting news that the first installments of thirteen billion American dollars were just then flowing into the ruined societies she toured. Secretary Marshall's plan, the "European Recovery Program" (ERP), passed through the U.S. Congress in early April 1948; by early autumn, as Mrs. Church was writing Stevens about "shattered Europe," short-term effects of the new money were to be felt and seen in Italy, England, France, the Lowlands, and particularly in the western zones of Germany. Seventy percent of France's harbors had been destroyed during the war; only a year after Marshall aid was approved, every one had been reconstructed. Food-ration tickets were also unnecessary in France by 1949.[19] The program of reconstruction was initially designed to last four years, until 1952, and would be directed principally at repairing physical structures, restoring industry, and encouraging agriculture. It would and did alter physical facts. Yet the "by-products" of the ERP were also intended to be powerfully "psychological."[20] When first describing conditions in Europe, Marshall's staff planners prepared memoranda that closely resemble Mrs. Church's reports of the spiritual devastation; they noted, just as she did for Stevens, the "psychic exhaustion of people everywhere" and "feelings of disillusionment, insecurity and apathy" as well as the more obvious "social and economic dislocation."[21] When Stevens referred to "the exhaustion of Europe" in one of his later letters, the cold-war connotation of the phrase is clearly derived from the language invented by the first planners of American foreign aid. "The exhaustion of Europe is a great menace to both Europe and ourselves," he wrote.[22]

In spite of the psychological thesis having the effect of making American assistance seem therapeutic for both the giving and the receiving parties, some policy planners themselves privately admitted—notably George Kennan, who had invented the political metaphor "containment" in the famous "Long" State Department telegram of 1946—that the ERP did not actually transcend "all the isms."[23] The planning memo that spoke of the need to relieve Europeans' spiritual exhaustion at the same time proposed massive aid to Europe as a way of combatting the psychopolitical "maladjustment" that "makes European society vulnerable to exploitation by any and all totalitarian movements"—meaning the Soviets. The plan actually signified containment through reconstruction—or, to be more exact, reconstruction rhetorically confused with containment. It seemed a welfare program palatable to many American conservatives because it could be described, for instance by Truman and Acheson, in the language of anti-communism. And it was a strong defense against European communism acceptable to most American liberals because it could be described, for instance by Marshall himself, in the language of charity and enlightened internationalism.[24]

Stevens's responses to his correspondent's descriptions of misery in the first years after the war are generally sympathetic; his letters do engage the subject, even if briefly. So, too, his understanding of the relation between the economic fact of Western European misery and the political thesis of Russian expansion is quite clear by 1946. "The world is full of poverty and misfortune," he wrote Henry Church then, "and it seems to take little or no effort to convince people that communism means an escape from poverty and a refuge from misfortune." This observation was connected to his comment on the news of the day, renewed foreign requests for economic assistance, which he mistrusted. His analysis of this news reveals that *eleven months prior to the popularization of Marshall Plan rhetoric and a full year before George Kennan went public with the metaphor of containment* Stevens was fully versed in the language of containment-through-reconstruction. "It may be," he wrote, "that with her aggressive attitude [Russia] is making progress toward her goal a good deal more rapidly than we are toward our goal, but, surely, we are not afraid. Nevertheless, we have the sense that Russian antagonism is growing stronger and more widespread and we are bound to meet it everywhere." He also wrote: "England is trying to commit us to her welfare. The Jews are trying to commit us to their welfare. It is hard to understand Russia. One English weekly says that we made the loan to England because we were afraid of Russia. . . . We are not afraid of Russia" (L 531–32).[25]

Mrs. Church's continued emphasis on the effects of destruction, in 1949, and indeed through 1952, when the ERP was supposed to have completed its restorative work, must have taken him somewhat by surprise, for her pessimism must have seemed to contradict regular reports in the American press highlighting the success of reconstruction.[26] Stevens's responses to her letters during this period stress not the destruction of the town or church she had described, but the assurance she derived from the patience and piety of the people who carried on with life. He picked up the hopeful points. Surely he did not discount her reports of unrelieved misery; they consisted of undeniable and fully imaginable details. Yet these details continued to preoccupy her fully despite the huge American commitment, which Stevens felt himself in the burden of his rising personal income taxes, a condition he noted regularly between 1948 and 1952.[27] He must have considered the possibility that for personal and not political reasons Mrs. Church was reading inner, spiritual misery (the interrupted lives she described) into the outward, physical devastation she saw (homes and churches). It was possible that these outward signs of destruction shielded her from the fact that, as isolationist critics of the ERP suggested all along, much of the actual reconstruction was after a certain point unnecessary and that the massive size of the aid program had been designed by partisan politicians to fulfill the Kennan-Truman goal of *psychological* "adjustment" (read: Americanization) well beyond physical rebuilding.[28] "To be sure," writes one commentator, summarizing the impression of American occupiers, "as one toured German cities and farmlands the destruction looked dreadful. Piles of brick and stone, bomb craters, twisted steel girders rising from the rubble, children in rags: all presented a vision of destruction. And yet, once the ruins were cleared away, it turned out that much of the industrial capacity of Germany was intact."[29] While Stevens, too, might be skeptical of the actual value of such vast amounts of American aid, in analyzing the domestic political reasons for it he did not of course have the firsthand view these officials had; he had literally to *read* the situation through the descriptions, postcards, and snapshots of his correspondent. Moreover, he did at least "recognize," even after almost certainly voting for Thomas Dewey (who was misperceived as anti-ERP) in November 1948, "that the vast altruism of the Truman party is probably the greatest single force for good in the world today" (L 623).[30] Yet he made it known to Mrs. Church in several ways that in his analysis of the situation the need for American internationalism may have been deliberately overestimated. The result of this double thinking was a curious version of the sentimental imperialism he had already applied to van Geyzel's Ceylon and Rodríguez Feo's Cuba—curious because here the "primitive" culture was no less than civilized Europe itself, laid low. If Europe could somehow be kept European, even if that meant encouraging it to resist American reconstruction (and so, for instance, naturalizing ruins as both sublime and inevitable or "periodical"), the poet could then "have" his Europe in its truest form: exotic, foreign, and yet decayed—that is, *not* American and thus desired ("longed-for"). Yet was *that* Europe, in effect, not also a Europe to be Americanized, a vacuum to be filled?[31] Stevens's attitudes toward war-torn Europe were perhaps not quite as discernible as those he held toward Ceylon and Cuba, outlying places he had much less trouble conceiving as steamy messes. One manifestation of the new attitude toward a ruined, exoticized Europe, however, was his half-joking assertion that the poor were probably not so poor after all. Simplicity was not necessarily poverty. He could imply as much by distinguishing between those living in poverty and those with genuine ambition, describing these as if they were exclusive categories, and specifically borrowing from the language of the modern American conservative opposed to forms of welfare on ideological grounds. "It is true there are great masses of poverty and misfortune in the United States itself," he wrote, "but there are great masses of the opposite: there are great masses of happy, hopeful and ambitious people who expect to make something of themselves and of the world in which they live" (*L* 532).

Another manifestation of Stevens's desire to have Europe remain unimpressed by the gregarious American reconstructionists was his doubtful assessment of the domestic political motives generating Marshall aid. Such a criticism makes the following otherwise unremarkable observations about the cold war remarkable indeed:

> I think that the general feeling is that while no one wants war with Russia or with anyone else, nevertheless, considering the incessant provocations, we cannot permit Russia to have its way merely because it might be fateful to stand up to it. It would be fatal not to stand up to it. Moreover, our domestic politics is very much involved in what we do. The present [Democratic] administration feels most pious about prosperity, full employment, high wages. The Marshall Plan is in part a plan to advance these objectives. War, too, would advance them even though it bankrupted the country as a country and the wealthier classes as a class. But there is a vast element opposed to all this. At the moment, too, in mid-summer, when everyone is interested in having a holiday, there is a vast element that is simply not interested one way or the other: that wants to lie in the sun or sleep in the shade. This last element, I am afraid, is the one to which I really belong. (*L* 686–87)[32]

He casually proposed three camps here: one supporting containment, one opposing it, and a third party, politically indifferent. The effort in this statement to sustain a moderate tone ("I think that the general feeling is . . .") only helped to affirm general declarations about what "we," Americans *and* Europeans multilaterally, could and could not "permit Russia" to do unilaterally, and seems to indicate Stevens's membership in the first party, coolly endorsing containment. Then there was the sizable "element" opposed to containment in Europe and Korea; while endorsing internationalism (for example, the United Nations), this "vast" second group—in fact, it was not at all "vast"—might criticize as economic imperialism the aspect of the Marshall Plan that expressed the wish to remake European markets in the American image. Yet what is most interesting in the statement is the playful suggestion of an indifferent third element. Did Stevens not humorously imply here, in a typical postscript to a serious political observation that qualifies it almost entirely, that he belonged to the third party as well as to the first? The connection between the lethargy induced by unusual or "inhuman" weather, as he might have put it, and this third, ostensibly impartial or postideological element (not "interested one way or the other") keenly characterizes the special qualified assertions of the poetic language of Stevens's last period (1945–1955)—a language impressed by the realities of this postwar decade in this apparently neutral, indolent manner, by pointedly being disinterested as a means of being an *interested* third party to the more conventionally oppositional politics of the other two.

Stevens's comment on the ERP generally shows, then, that he *was* both knowledgeable and interested, despite the very profession of indifference. His uncritical absorption of the rhetoric of containment (regarding Soviet aggression) was attached to his shrewd, critical reading of the rhetoric of reconstruction. The contradictions that resulted from this mix of approbation and criticism, I would argue, were essentially those of the verse responding to Barbara Church's laments about European deprivations. While accepting containment as the postwar fate, Stevens evidently saw the political presentation of the ERP as a masterstroke of domestic political language disguising economic integration as generosity and effective anticommunism ("The Marshall Plan is in part a plan to advance" Truman's political agenda). The ERP's billions in credit for reconstruction, if also motivated by altruism or fear, seemed to guarantee diplomatic indebtedness and economic addiction abroad and permanently high tax rates at home.[33] Yet the idea of the plan was publicly unveiled in an inarguable, nonpolitical, natural rhetoric. "Our policy," declared George Marshall at Harvard, "is directed not against any country or doctrine but against hunger, poverty, desperation, and chaos."[34] When "St. Armorer's Church" adopted an American rhetorical strategy—when it was designed to create a durable climate of acceptance for the poet's power to reconstruct, and when it engaged the European church as a point of continuity between explanatory and exhortatory schemes—it did not serve simply as a reply to

Barbara Church's sympathies for the poor; it responded to an ascendant cultural language and shows Stevens to have been a sensitive reader of the new, confusing text of American policy. So, given the documented range of Americans' reactions to Marshall's plan, established by contemporary pollsters, we might finally place Stevens within his second, or dissident, element, along with the apparently few Americans in whose view the ERP was *not* merely designed as an act of charity.[35] Still it is not as important to know exactly where Stevens finally stood on the official rhetoric of the ERP as that he came at the critical second position through the indifferent third.

For all his astuteness about the politics of American benevolence, when writing more generally about the European scene during this period Stevens could speak of restoration as an ambitious goal that could be met by fresh inhalations, a supremely poetic remedy well beyond politics. So, too, while "St. Armorer's Church from the Outside" attempted to comprehend Barbara Church's view of a civilization still then only minimally restored, it inevitably inscribed, or breathed, an inward, spiritual freshness into the "outward blank"—onto the cultural blank page of Europe. As such it was hardly different from the project Stephen Spender urged on American intellectuals: "the Marshall Plan . . . alone will not persuade Europeans" that they need American reconstruction, he argued; cultural aid—paintings, sculpture, plays, and poems, as weapons in the arsenal of "spiritual freedom"—was no less materially important than dollars.[36] In a letter of August 1947 (three months after Marshall's announcement), thoughts about the "misery of so many" led Stevens to discuss the total psychological "conflict" in which the other side aimed finally at taking our property from us—not a conflict *between* forms of mutual subversion (Western political differences) but a struggle *against* a single subversion (communism). Was he aware as he was writing this letter, then, how it moved from this barely hidden anxiety about holding on to his own property to the idea of a "restoration" in defeated Germany that could be accomplished merely by breathing "woods-coolness"? "I am glad to have your letters," he begins, encouragingly:

> For you, they are a form of exteriorization, which is, I suppose, what you need—what all of us need. How nice it would be if everyone for the next month or two could frequent les terrasses du soleil or (to do it in a big way) des soleils, forgetting about the misery of so many, the great conflict going on between ideas for the possession of men's minds—and ultimately of their property. . . . As scepticism becomes both complete and profound, *we face either a true civilization or a blank; and literature ought to be one of the factors to determine the choice.* Certainly, if civilization is to consist only of man himself, and it is, the arts must take the place of divinity, at least as a stage in whatever general principle or progress is involved. . . . I walked in the little park near

us, before starting in town, this morning. There is a good enough woods there
and I inhaled the deep woods-coolness as I used to at home. Don't you look
forward to *some such restoration* if you visit Germany again, regardless of its
being Germany? Here in the trance of midsummer all things come together
again and one is happy to be alive. (*L* 563–64; emphasis added)

This series of loosely related observations is held together by a typical
postwar urge: the letter as a whole works extremely hard to rationalize a
"great conflict going on" in Europe in order to restore optimism and to
induce Mrs. Church to breathe easily. The observations are as follows: her
letters to him beneficially "exteriorize" her troubles; an associated way of
forgetting about the current conflict, thus (ironically) of forgetting our
fears of losing our property during a time of great political upheaval, is to
relax on sunny terraces, the sunnier the better; poems, being similar therapeutic restorations (like the writing of exteriorizing letters), having their
own inspirations, must replace the now-destroyed structures of divinity;
thus, surprisingly, one might "look forward" to returning to Germany in
August 1947, "regardless of its being Germany"—that is, the home or root
of the destruction—for in this naturalizing logic the restoration of war-
torn Europe is to be understood as a matter of inhaling "the deep woods-
coolness." Thus, strangely, at such a moment of crisis—one might even say
naively—the usually doubtful Stevens could conclude that "one is happy to
be alive"; obviously there was a point to this uncalled-for optimism. To
make his point about a therapeutic indifference to political extremities—
about "[h]ow nice it would be . . . [to forget] about the misery of so many,
the great conflict going on"—Stevens neatly borrowed from his poems
some of their strongest moments of renewed confidence. He suggested
assurance as "Credences of Summer" urgently had at the end of the war:
"Here in the trance of midsummer all things come together again." He
called for order in a time of great disorder, in the unusual if-then cadence
of "Connoisseur of Chaos," written just before the war: "if civilization is to
consist only of man himself, and it is." And he relied on the idea of the
restored church of the imagination that had been provided by the Santayana thesis and registered in the early poems: "the arts must take the
place of divinity."

As Barbara Church prepared to leave New York for her summer 1949 trip,
Stevens wrote her one of his long bon voyage messages. In it he unwittingly set his sedentary self in relation to a peripatetic other. He announced
that he had finished writing "one long thing." This was "An Ordinary Evening in New Haven." He would go on to add a few more cantos, including
the twenty-eighth, which is marked by an ironic mix of images of European war-related misery and postwar tourism.[37] He also announced his

plans to send Alfred Knopf the manuscript of *The Auroras of Autumn,* a collection full of figures of grand decline that would win him the National Book Award. Recognition would be coming to him, he sensed—perhaps a sign of the end. He wrote:

> [I]t is interesting to plan ahead for a long period of thinking and writing and, for me, it is something new because I have always done that sort of thing casually and as part of the experience of living. One of the drawbacks of going about it in this casual and intermittent way is that every fresh beginning is a beginning over: one is always beginning. One of the really significant reasons for devoting one's whole life to poetry in the same way that people devote their whole lives to music or painting is that this steady application brings about a general moving forward. I shall know a little more about this sort of thing by the end of the year. In the case of the painter, his career is a career of making progress.

This complex definition of career, especially when put in full context (I have quoted from the second paragraph of a five-paragraph letter, printed in its entirety in *L* 638–40), was obviously as much an encouragement to Barbara Church, the widow existing in Europe from month to month apparently without a plan, as a description of the poet's own design for the end of his poetic course. A career in poetry, like the long poem itself, was to be made by steady application—"a general moving forward," part plan, part improvisation. It is true generally of Stevens's letters to Barbara Church after Henry's death in April 1947 (and especially those he sent her just before and during her trips to Europe) that they were as much for her benefit as for his. An idea that might understandably have seemed paradoxical, then—that one always made a fresh beginning, yet one thus generally moved forward—found resolution if only by Stevens's characteristic insistence on conventional forms of getting on, or in other words by old-fashioned hard work. This had always been his way of saying, first to Henry and then to Barbara Church, that he was simply not capable of their sort of existence. He meant, of course, a life without a steady office job. He had noted to Henry Church that, as he was rising to get ready for a day at the office, Church was just switching off his reading lamp (*L* 431). He generally associated the fact that he had never toured Europe with his perpetual work at The Hartford. His "career" there was specifically the excuse he gave many times for staying "in a single spot," as he once put it (*L* 644). At his most despondent, he saw the job as circular, a habit of living that got him slowly nowhere, that served only "to keep . . . the wheels of the baby's chariot turning," as he told Williams (*L* 246). Mixing those two early metaphors for Stevens's work, then, we arrive at a central paradox of the late career. It is diachronic to sustain its synchronicity, a general moving forward somehow designed to keep the wheels turning. The new long poem about poetry, if it would replicate the career itself, must be planned and improvised both, repetitive and yet probing, straightfoward yet a spinning of his wheels. So, if the subtext of this particular encouragement to his widowed friend was to urge *her* to form a personal reconstructive plan, not to wander excessively from a goal, not merely (in a favorite phrase he learned from his business-minded father) "to knock about" in Europe,[38] Barbara Church herself seems not to have read the letter in this manner. And insofar as "An Ordinary Evening" records these American-European differences in perception, Stevens did take a very special interest in her series of snapshots and postcards tracing the outlines of her latest wanderings. At times he told her straight out: in her travels, and in her writings about them, she extemporized "for" him because he could not find the time to be so free.

From France she responded skillfully. She wrote that she was happy to hear how much pleasure he took in going nowhere, in composing poems while "sit[ting] in one's room and watch[ing] fireflies." She urged him to continue seeking the "fresh beginnings" *he* had described for *her*, and to stay at home in order to be himself.[39] Referring to his gloss of the overall plan of "Ordinary Evening," she implied that in his poetic language he might demonstrate how going nowhere can itself be the subject of poetry. Here is canto xxviii in full:

> 1 If it should be true that reality exists
> In the mind: the tin plate, the loaf of bread on it,
> The long-bladed knife, the little to drink and her
>
> Misericordia, it follows that
> 5 Real and unreal are two in one: New Haven
> Before and after one arrives or, say,
>
> Bergamo on a postcard, Rome after dark,
> Sweden described, Salzburg with shaded eyes
> Or Paris in conversation at a café.
>
> 10 This endlessly elaborating poem
> Displays the theory of poetry,
> As the life of poetry. A more severe,
>
> More harassing master would extemporize
> Subtler, more urgent proof that the theory
> 15 Of poetry is the theory of life,
>
> As it is, in the intricate evasions of as,
> In things seen and unseen, created from nothingness,
> The heavens, the hells, the worlds, the longed-for lands.

(*CP* 485–86)

In the middle of her 1949 journey Mrs. Church had elaborated Stevens's idea that a career may paradoxically go nowhere, combining his notion of fresh beginnings in poetry with her own interest in the actual processes of rebuilding—which she now called "remaking"—Europe. In a note enclosed with a series of snapshots she wrote: "I think I like living in an atmosphere of making, remaking things and places—le changement—et plus ça change, plus c'est la même chose—says the french cynic."[40] This came as a reply to his letter, written a few weeks earlier, in which he told her he continued to work on "An Ordinary Evening" and argued that its goal was to seek "normal life" and "insight into the commonplace" (L 643). Canto xxviii accordingly asks what Mrs. Church might have asked, in response to such an argument: Which is "commonplace" here? Idealized postcard and snapshot views, however directly they arrive from the European cavern? Or imagined unseen misery, however Americanized? "New Haven / Before and after one arrives"? Or, on the other hand, "Bergamo on a postcard, Rome after dark / Sweden described, Salzburg with shaded eyes / . . . Paris in conversation at a café"? Real or unreal? The poem does not answer these questions. It treats the disparities it describes with a touch of guilt left unexplained; to me, however, the typical American response to the new foreign policy of "generosity" does help explain it: "[T]o the great majority," one historian has written of the Marshall Plan, official American policies toward Europe "brought a sense of relief. . . . [T]he plan for . . . aid tended to assuage the abashment an American felt in comparing his own growing abundance with the chaotic and still desperate conditions in Europe."[41] "Abundance" was surely the key concept in reconstruction, for in spreading American abundance the United States affirmed one of the operative axioms guiding the end of ideology: "The American free-enterprise system," Geoffrey Hodgson has paraphrased it, "is different from the old capitalism. It is democratic. It creates abundance. It has a revolutionary potential for social justice."[42] When Stevens wrote Rodríguez Feo, "I think the feeling today very definitely is for an abundant poetry" (L 495), he was playing upon the real in the key of his time.

That is why the sources for the "unreal" list in his poem barely transformed materials sent to him by Barbara Church; in this way, Europe could be savory, abundant, and thus visitable, and its images could be derived unaltered from a sincere, unimpeachable source. The poem contains almost exactly what Mrs. Church sent Stevens: she had sent a snapshot of her standing in front of the Palazzo de la Ragione in Bergamo;[43] she had described Sweden as seen from her Scandinavian Airlines flight, from which she glimpsed, below, the bonfires of St. John's night, when sunset and sunrise meet;[44] not far from Salzburg, she was photographed while she shaded her eyes, not because of the sun but because she felt "afraid," as she mysteriously wrote on the back of that photo;[45] and a letter from France described a "good dinner . . . in a little café near Notre Dame on the sidewalk overlooking the Seine."[46] Taken together, her reports, postcards, and snapshots provided him with an experience in itself: the time he took merely to read the letters, view the cards and pictures, was itself full of the activity of a traveler. "What a *busy* morning I have had with all this!" he wrote. "It has quite set me up."[47]

The poem begins by testing the essence of this busyness—the notion that reality exists in the mind—and proposes this in order to reunite the real (of Connecticut) and the unreal (of unseen Europe). Thus "unreal" means a postcard-knowledge of the real, as postcards are idealizations of another real that the touring sender has seen and wants to convey in the combination of picture and words. The unseen places, the postcard-inscribed "experiences in themselves" (*L* 486) that somehow "follow" from New Haven in the logic of the poem—scenes in Bergamo, Rome, Sweden, Salzburg, and Paris—are so attractive, so strongly imagined, that it also logically "follows that / Real and unreal are two in one." The truth of the then-clause (real equals unreal) must in lines 4 through 9 suggest, belatedly, the truth of the opening if-clause (reality exists in the mind) of lines 1 through 4. Thus, encouraged to work backwards from the catalogue of Barbara Church's toured places, and despite the opening qualification of "If," we are asked to assume as truth the proposition that images of poverty are realities existing only or primarily in the mind. By setting up antithetical images of poverty and of tourism, the canto conveys the double-sidedness of Barbara Church's postcards and snapshots: on the front, tourist views; on the obverse, jotted words, signs of justification as well as description, installments of an insider's story of the new Europe, sometimes conveying a sense of the reality of impoverishment as a background of the tour. Yet the list of images of poverty in the poem—"the tin plate, the loaf of bread on it, / The long-bladed knife, the little to drink"—is hardly persuasive in denoting such a background of reality. These stock images of the common life actually conform more to the conventions of the front of the postcard (ideal view) than to the reverse (descriptions of or pointings to things seen in the world). This part of the poem is a set piece, a *view* in an outmoded sense, an idealized scene of *simplicity*, not necessarily of poverty, a still life of peasant things arranged as a modest and purely symbolic relief from fasting ("her Misericordia"). Bread should have been *absent* from the scene if the disparity between imagined tour and poverty was to seem truly great, as shortages of bread in Europe by this time were perhaps the most common image Americans had of the misery their dollars were helping to relieve—the famous "posters showing fat livestock eating wheat in the U.S. when the hungry people in Europe are in terrible need." (These were Henry Wallace's words. His criticism of such ERP poster-propaganda is pertinent to the claims of "Ordinary Evening": the public-relations campaign, inspired by former president Herbert Hoover, who conservatively supported *relief* but not comprehensive *reconstruction*, only contributed to Americans' lack of awareness that bread voluntarily saved here and there "for the hungry people of Europe . . . will add up to very little.")[48] The poem's bread may seem to simulate realism, but it is actually constructed of types: *the* (typical) plate, *the* (typical) loaf of bread, and so on. It does not depict the observed scene. Definite articles stand for the universal; "the," rather than pointing to misery, points away.

These images seem even less persuasive as commonplaces when the attractive list appropriated directly from Barbara Church's tour "follows" from them. In the overdetermined logic of the first three stanzas of canto xxviii, the universal images make it seem reasonably certain that real and unreal can be equated. Poverty is no more specifically real—in the sense of "commonplace" or "ugly," Stevens's programmatic terms for "An Ordinary Evening"—than the wealthy European tourist's Europe. Yet the poem ends with so profound a sense of qualification and self-doubt that a more profound loss than the sufficiency of images of poverty must have been suffered by the poet if the pathos of these last lines is to be justified. A better poem, he cries, would have served as "more urgent proof that the theory / Of poetry is the theory of life, // As it is, in the intricate evasions of as, / *In things seen and unseen, created from nothingness,* / The heavens, the hells, the worlds, the longed-for lands." The "more severe, // More harassing master" would have "extemporize[d] / subtler," more subtly than *this* canto as it stood, and would seem to have offered Stevens "more urgent proof" that his poetry and his life were integrated only insofar as he could first address the differences between unreal and real, tourism and poverty. If the hypothesized, more masterful canto would be about freedom, as freedom in this instance was the power to imagine an integration of the commonplace and the Grand Tour, then what was the toughest imaginable test of such freedom? The counteracting power to imagine an *unvisited* place without submitting to tourist standards that had been lowered by postwar American access—a particular obsession with Stevens.[49] As Robert von Hallberg has shown, the lure of travel in the late forties and fifties was checked in American poets by a disapproval of travel-writing clichés, "English gardens, French boulevards, and Italian piazzas"; yet unlike Olson, Merwin, Lowell, Bishop, Viereck, Hecht, Merrill, Wright, Howard, Rich, Creeley, Wilbur, Ashbery, and Tate, who traveled abroad in this period, Stevens stayed home to ponder the crucial related matters of freedom and constraint.[50] Freedom in this sense meant the ultimate freedom of—but also the greatest challenge to—the unmoving poetic master whose work had always depended on a harmony between extemporaneousness and discipline; Stevens freely realized that he *was here* because he could write so convincingly that he *was not there*. Thus limited, freedom was only possible "*before* one arrives" imaginatively in the place being nevertheless described. To remain free to imagine "his" Europe, in short, the poet did not go; he retained the postcard-knowledge. The risk was that he would also remain innocent of actual conditions, "the misery of so many" (to use his phrase in the letter about the politics of aid quoted earlier). He would have to depend upon tropes emerging from "the great conflict going on between ideas and the possession of men's minds," the cultural cold war itself, in order to propose that the essential battle was really one between reality and mind, between life and poetry.

Such a "great conflict" was only to be resolved, then, by a new theoretical policy of openness, a warming in the relations between poetry and life, by "urgent proof that the theory / Of poetry is the theory of life." In suggesting this equation as a way of negotiating the great conflict, "An Ordinary Evening" specifically furthered the argument Stevens had put forth in his contribution to a *Partisan Review* symposium on the state of American poetry a year earlier. "[I]t is natural," Stevens wrote in his response to seven questions put to him (and to eight other American writers) by Delmore Schwartz, "to project the idea of a theory of poetry that would be *pretty much the same thing as* a theory of the world" (emphasis added). He also wrote: "[T]here probably is available in reality something accessible through a theory of poetry which would make *a profound difference in our sense of the world*" (emphasis added). It sounds as if Stevens was making an argument for improved relations between poetry and politics: some extrinsic things existed; such realities could and would be approached by the appropriate poetic theory; and this approach could and would change "our" sense of the world and thus the world itself. Note, however, the questions proposed by the *Partisan Review* editors to which these remarks were responsive: "What is the effect on American writing of the growing tension between Soviet Communism and the democratic countries?" and "How are cultural interests affected by this struggle?" and "[D]o you think a writer should involve himself in it (as writer? as person?) to the point of commitment?"[51] Since for Stevens the Soviet position was to insist that life and reality were the *same* as politics, he felt he must argue oppositely. For all "one's interest" in negotiating the discrepancies between life and reality, and fully in spite of the liberal critics' belief that reality might be "accessible through" literature so as to change the world profoundly, politics still remained distinct from reality *and* life. For the *Partisan* symposium, he was adamant on the point: "[T]he basic meaning of the effort of any man to record his experience as poet is to produce poetry, not politics." Although the terms of Stevens's refusal to identify a poet's interest in life and reality as political were determined by the necessary opposition to what the Soviets did, a total conflict between the Soviets and writers "of the democratic countries" remained the undisturbed assumption in his response.

Interestingly, then, the conflict Stevens chose to define and explain here was not taking place between westerners and Russians but *among* western-ers, poets and poet-politicians with competing ideas as to how American writing ought to have responded unilaterally to the threat from outside. An essential opposition was presumed, and the rhetoric of opposition was re-served for parties contending for the strongest position on the same side: "In the conflict between the *poet* and the *politician* the chief honor the poet can hope for is that of remaining himself" (emphasis added).[52]

Taking a cue from what in his *Partisan Review* statement Stevens seems unwilling or unable to admit—that there could be an "abundant" poetry that would not necessarily strengthen the Russian position—we return to the version of the argument advanced in "An Ordinary Evening," search-ing for such an admission. But here too there was much the poet was un-willing or unable to admit. What the poet-speaker of canto xxviii does not understand about his own writing is the way in which images of poverty and images of tourism can be said to be mediated, thus reducing the cold war between poetry and life. If poverty, in images of poverty, can be "cre-ated from nothingness," can remain a sight unseen and yet be absorbed wholly into poetry—especially poetry claiming a relationship with com-monplace life, as Stevens claims nowhere in all his poetry more passion-ately than in canto xxviii of this poem—then the program of restoring that impoverished real might be no great program at all, but rather a call merely for subtler *extemporizing*. Moreover, this American poet, temporarily re-jecting the equivalence of reality and politics in the *Partisan* symposium, chooses to "remain himself" with a vengeance, to belong as and where he is. So he effectively opposes both the Russians *and* those dissenting Ameri-can writers (such as Robert Gorham Davis, an ex-radical contributor to the symposium) whose mistake, in Stevens's view, was to hope that American poetry would explicitly take sides and thus challenge the Russians to a po-litical argument—to deal with them, that is, in their language and on their terms.[53] Yet in this context the refusal to engage in political argument is just such an argument. Poetry and politics "are not the same thing," Ste-vens's statement concludes, "whatever the Russians may pretend." (If the Russians like to mediate poetry and politics, then to do so, no matter by what form of mediation, is to play politics their way.) Subject to this doubt, canto xxviii tries to imagine a better version of itself that would call for greater subtlety as a rhetorical means of smoothing over, just as his *Partisan* statement did, more substantial, conservative postwar arguments that sepa-rated poetry and politics entirely. Such outright conservatism, unusual for Stevens in the poems, was presented briefly in "Imago," a poem written soon after the Marshall Plan was announced. There the major question of the day was answered antipolitically, and as such it should remind us of the isolationist question posed by "Martial Cadenza": "What had this star to do with the world it lit, / With the blank skies over England, over France / And above the German camps?" Yet "Imago" was as political a poem as Stevens would write; it was finally another of his poems about poetry, but it began by asking: What actual force could resolve "the great conflict" going on—could reconstruct Europe? The answer: the self-image of the universal poet insistently remaining himself.

> Who can pick up the weight of Britain
> Who can move the German load
> Or say to the French here is France again?
> Imago. Imago. Imago.

> > (*CP* 439)

For his epistemological vocabulary here Stevens plainly drew on diplomatic language. "An Ordinary Evening" only adorned and qualified this plainer version of the idea—epistemological by design, to be sure, but politically assertive in effect—that American images of poverty were invented, images of conditions that were likely to be exaggerated by partisan forces of internationalism and by promoters of the fashion for an abundant postwar American poetry that would both feed and be fed on such images. If "Ordinary Evening" is understood as a response to this literary-political trend, then how was Stevens merely "remaining himself," staying clear of the new politics and remaining "Here in Hartford," when he wrote Rodríguez Feo, "I cannot believe that the world would not be a better world if we reflected on it after a really advantageous dinner"? (Pushing hard on this irony by using the word "empty" to suggest both hunger and stupidity and a little more explicitly mocking the literary left, Stevens added: "How much misery the aphorisms of empty people have caused!") And to what degree a jest, given his poetic appropriation of Barbara Church's 1949 tour, was his later prediction for her that the 1952 presidential election would be based "on the idea that the poorer people were never so well off as they are now" (*L* 760)?

Preparing her trip into Italy in late summer 1952, Mrs. Church went to the expense of shipping a red Cadillac from the United States. She reported to Stevens that she and her chauffeur and this big, bright American car—one can just imagine how ostentatious it seemed—made it safely through the mountains into Italy. In "St. Armorer's Church" this alluring scene has become:

> The first car out of a tunnel en voyage
>
> Into lands of ruddy-ruby fruits, achieved
> Not merely desired, for sale, and market things

That press, strong peasants in a peasant world,
Their purports to a final seriousness—

Final for him, the acceptance of such prose,
Time's given perfections made to seem like less
Than the need of each generation to be itself,
The need to be actual and as it is.

This may be compared further to Barbara Church's account. After she announced the emergence of the big American car into agricultural Italy, her letter continued: "It is astonishing to see long stretches of apparently fertile ground without villages, only here and there ... poor wretched houses—the peasants did not return to their farms, people get tired of rebuilding each generation after war and devastation have passed." Where have the Italian peasants gone? "[T]he towns and factories," she observed, "seem more attractive and pay better."[54]

Stevens's long reply, dated September 10 (fully reprinted in *L* 760), made a series of related promises that the poem impressed by Barbara Church's trip tries to keep but finally cannot. First, the poem nicely restores to coolness the "first summer that I have ever disliked," the heat of which, as in 1950, has been repeatedly equated with that spent, "third" party of postwar apoliticism. Formalizing its response to the real "heat" of figurative "cold" conflict, the poem revives itself from summer's political lethargy by shifting perspective from outside in and down, to cool "Terre Ensevelie" (l. 9), a buried, subterranean zone within the main religious site, a deep chapel within a broad church, in an effort to get at the source of renewal and create out of this dankness "an air of newness," with "natural light." The restoration achieved here is for the sake of Europe but also for "his own" sake, in just the logic of "generous self-interest" provided by contemporary descriptions of American assistance—the "origin and keep of *its* health and [thus] *his* own" (ll. 37, 42, 43). "Keep" is no less the maintenance of than a hold or recessed repository for his own reconstructive experience.

A second promise was made in this letter, arising from Stevens's critical analysis of 1952 election rhetoric. Since the poor were not as poor as certain politicians have led us to believe, a new poetics of the commonplace was in order; in 1953 and 1954 this idea would develop into his "new knowledge of reality." The pro-reconstruction platform, updating old (Wilsonian) internationalism and thus in effect defending New Deal social and economic spending programs for the domestic poor by now applying them abroad to depressed Europe, tended to romanticize the richness of impoverishment—a tendency of the literary liberal-left Stevens had satirized in the thirties in the first, second, and fourth parts of "Owl's Clover" and in the first third of "The Man with the Blue Guitar." Such a platform later committed the strategic error of the by-then outworn idealization of the lower classes. This promise of a new poetics of poverty might be met in a timely 1952 poem by a willful conception of *restored* "ruddy-ruby fruits" grown by "*strong* peasants"—"for sale" as "market things" in a *plentiful* "peasant world." The distinction Stevens makes in lines 25–28, then, measures an important advance, small as it might seem, for the poet of desire severed from its object: this produce is "achieved / Not merely desired," hard-earned, not merely wished-for—constructed out of nothingness by strong will and accomplishment, not only brought into being by the pathetic cry of want. The marketable vegetable world does survive, the poem suggests, along with the healthy peasants necessary to tend it. Notwithstanding the advance, this conception counters Mrs. Church's firsthand report of "apparently fertile ground" *unattended* by farmers, still economically ruined, withdrawn to cities, unaffected by American aid that at least one branch of cold-war historiography has concluded was not in the long run designed to trickle down to the lower classes.[55]

But a further point of Stevens's September 10 letter reacted against this logic. Whereas the United States itself faced bankruptcy during and because of the recent war (L 687)—a point made vaguely, I think, because Stevens must have known it to be generally untrue from his experience in the insurance business—and now the nation faced the awesome choice of becoming "a true civilization *or* a blank" (L 564), his own recent poems were striking him as detached from this crisis and thus sadly irrelevant. He confessed this feeling of irrelevance to Barbara Church, much as he had in 1946 to Rodríguez Feo when he had reread a group of "academic and unreal" poems then belatedly appearing in *Orígenes* (L 525). And he promised in his new writing to make a renewed contact with "our actual world." A group of six new poems would be sent out to a journal shortly after he made this statement; that this journal was the liberal-left *Nation*—one of the very few weeklies to question the great project of American reconstruction—is surely to the point.[56]

> There is going to be a *Selected Poems*. . . . The book seemed rather slight and small to me—and unbelievably irrelevant to our actual world. It may be that all poetry has seemed like that at all times and always will. The close approach to reality has always been the supreme difficulty of any art: the communication of actuality, as poetry, has been not only impossible, but has never appeared to be worth while because it loses identity as the event passes. Nothing in the world is deader than yesterday's political (or realistic) poetry. *Nevertheless* the desire to combine the two things, poetry and reality, is a constant desire. (L 760; emphasis added)

To the extent that the six new poems would fulfill this last great promise, they could do so only by including some acknowledgment that they indeed pointed to "our actual world." The letter, to Mrs. Church, of course, contained this qualification. But these new poems must make their close approach to reality in such a way, he argued, so as not also to confine themselves to some contemporary political meaning that would pass from relevance as the event to which they refer passed. So special a category of a new "political (or realistic) poetry," satisfying the desire to bring poetic thought in line with the actual world, marked the limits inside which "St. Armorer's Church" did its difficult work of referring.

Promises of poems combining poetry and reality also led Stevens to face a small crisis about the use of his friends as source-gatherers. As one grows older, Stevens wrote Mrs. Church, one's poems seem increasingly to borrow images from others. Now, in offering an example of this new attitude toward the restrictions imposed by fidelity to actual sources, Stevens cited a corresponding feeling of freedom. Apparently he wanted to make it clear to her that a loss of poetic individuality did *not* necessarily result from such acknowledged cribbing. Viewed similarly, "St. Armorer's Church" begins by vaguely alluding to the private source but ends with what I have been arguing is an unnecessarily strong restoration of poetic self-reliance. Stevens wrote of his sources:

> As one grows older, one's own poems begin to read like the poems of some one else. Jack [John L.] Sweeney (the Boston Sweeney) sent me a post-card from County Clare the other day—the worn cliffs towering up over the Atlantic. It was like a gust of freedom, a return to the spacious solitary world *in which we used to exist.* (emphasis added)

The nostalgia provided by this postcard—the explicitly acknowledged, untransformed postcard-source of "The Irish Cliffs of Moher" (*CP* 501–2), published in the *Nation* that December—depended on a wholly ambiguous "it." If "*it* was like a gust of freedom," was "it" the pleasant feeling of receiving the postcard from afar that made the new *Nation* poem possible? Or the postcard-picturing itself? Or generally the act of borrowing? Why was "it" not similarly the "freedom" of using Barbara Church's snaps and cards as the basis for "St. Armorer's Church"? In that poem, after all, the poet removes himself to a resistant, underground world (the chapel) in which he can be individually free; the poem would seem itself to support the freedom of borrowing. "[H]e walks and does as he lives and likes"—in a strong, regular line that ought to remind us, as it surely did Stevens, of the temporary but rhetorically assured self-idealizations of "It Must Give Pleasure" in "Notes toward a Supreme Fiction."

Having just returned from the trip anticipated in Stevens's September 10 letter—he mailed it to Ville d'Avray expecting then that "the cloud of dust over Italy is the dust of your car: as I remember it, you are now in

Italy"—Barbara Church wrote about the chapels and towers of San Gimignano on the backs of four postcards inserted into one envelope. Here,
then, is the scene that impressed Stevens:

> San Gimignano is the place most people were afraid of being destroyed by
> shells in the last war but nothing happened, the 13 towers—in the middle ages
> there were 67—are still there—we went there on a Sunday with all the men
> standing and talking in front of the Church while the women were praying
> inside—one more Catholic custom—we walked around, were duly looked at
> with smiles and bows.[57]

One of the postcards depicts these undestroyed towers (see illustration).
In Stevens's poem what is left of the church is the smell of plaster (l. 5),
sumac growing on the altar (ll. 6–7), a chapel rising from buried earth (l. 9),
a chapel "of breath" emptied of meaning, except for the meaning to be
assumed in life's newest growth—"no *sign* of life but life" (ll. 11–14). The
"vif," the liveliness, associated with viewing the church—as a physical
structure, from the "Outside"—lies only in the process of inner reconstruction, "of becoming."

A postcard Barbara Church sent Stevens, depicting the undestroyed towers of San
Gimignano.

In the air of newness of that element,
In an air of freshness, clearness, greenness, blueness,
That which is always beginning because it is part
Of that which is always beginning, over and over.

The chapel underneath St. Armorer's walls,
Stands in a light, its natural light and day,
The origin and keep of its health and his own.
And there he walks and does as he lives and likes.

The poem adapted the scene described by the European traveler to the political assertions and qualifications of the poet's promises to write a new kind of realistic poetry. Now he would record trends in the actual world even if he must cover his sources for such observations out of the anxiety that if they referred too exactly to the world they would be dead as rapidly as "yesterday's" political poetry.

Such reasoning, however, fails to explain the way in which the poem counteracts many of the points made by his correspondent. Why did he not acknowledge Barbara Church, even privately, even in 1949 when he obviously borrowed for "Ordinary Evening"? After all, the source provided by Jack Sweeney at the Irish cliffs was subjected to no such transformation. Why did Mrs. Church not receive a little note of acknowledgment as Sweeney did, saying "I wanted to write to you ... to say ... that your postcard picture of the Cliffs of Moher eventually became a poem which was included in a group in the *Nation* of December 6"—and, more important, that he was sorry that he had risked distorting the sender's purer apprehension of the scene depicted in the postcard ("I hope I haven't made another lampshade out of the Cliffs")?[58] Perhaps Stevens directly acknowledged Sweeney because the Irish source for "The Irish Cliffs of Moher" was self-consciously mythical, spacious, nonhistorical; not contemporary, "realistic," and specific, as with the Church source.[59] By dismantling the one cultural form Barbara Church visited that had in fact resisted destruction, Stevens had his Europe both ways. He could sympathize generally with the European's lamentation and support the call for reconstruction. At the same time he could disarm his friend's liberal internationalism. To her willingness to remain outside and yet describe and respect the labor ritually divided, the poem responds by remaining impervious to a difference that was essential in Barbara Church's view—a view she freely shared with Marianne Moore but not with Stevens.[60] She, a woman sympathetic to the plight of women, and a religionist sympathetic to the challenged faithful, accepts her own exclusion: the men talked while the women prayed inside, yet she, respecting cultural and class differences between her and the native women, remained outside. In the poem Stevens boldly presumes to enter and tread upon the realm his source had specified as excluding men: "In . . . / That which is always beginning because it is part . . . // He walks and *does as he . . . likes.*" His new-found freedom only blurs differences noted specifically and left unquestioned there by Mrs. Church as a matter of proper perspective, a perspective Stevens abandons despite the title of the poem.[61]

Imposing its own poetic recovery plan on his correspondent's sincere descriptions of devastation, yet restoring not an entire needy generation but an individualist poetic, "St. Armorer's Church" must be read finally as a postwar rewriting of "A Postcard from the Volcano" (*CP* 158–59). As such it begins to posit a thirties for the fifties, recognizing the limitations of "yesterday's political (or realistic) poetry" in its attempt to address political (now partly veiled as "cultural") issues by redirecting social themes away from American society itself; it recognizes the assumption that ideology itself had been expended by 1952, that an American intellectual could urge New Deal–style pump priming for Europe while living comfortably in a politically altered society where it was "politically possible . . . to damn the New Deal as a Communist-front organization."[62] Stevens's new poem modified the earlier one: an American spirit now stormed in Europe's outwardly blank walls. Several points, developed from the Depression-era poem, testify to Stevens's comprehension of the shift between the thirties and the fifties in the forces that impelled the motion of an American's poetry through twentieth-century history. The decay of human structures was now given its specifically foreign and apparently nonpartisan context. "A Postcard from the Volcano" (1936) had clearly borne the mark of the domestic economic depression: it pictured and symbolized the decaying American "house." "Children . . . / Will say of the mansion that it seems / As if he that lived there left behind / A spirit storming in blank walls, // A dirty house in a gutted world" (*CP* 159, ll. 16, 19–22). But in these subsequent boom years, boom largely contingent on others' bust, the idea that the American house might be declining was no longer the anxiety it once was. The later poem protected the American "house" from a foreign collapse by directing its lyric energy at, and optimizing, the decay of the European "Church," by which Americans like Stevens, he admits, are largely unaffected. Plotting his course from the thirties through wartime to the fifties by these two works, we find Stevens bearing out in the 1952 poem a contemporary internationalist conception of American foreign aid as a New Deal for the world.[63]

The remarkable thing about Barbara Church's letters and postcards describing scenes she knew Stevens would enjoy seeing is that their language was uninvited. She offered him vistas of Europe, postcards as "experiences in themselves," not because she hoped they were of the kind that would then reappear in one of her famous friend's poems, but because she took real pleasure in helping him see what he had not seen. If ever her writings did cry out to be read as occasions for poetry, Stevens did not discourage it. Typical is his comment, "The postcards from Ville d'Avray came the other day. They did me a lot of good. In fact, I survive on postcards from Europe" (L 797). Several generalizations about his need for her European journeys—that his poems begin to sound as if others, from other countries, were writing them (L 760), and that she does his traveling "for" him[64]— were quite enough to send the signal without requiring the sort of responses he received from Rodríguez Feo, Thomas McGreevy, and Ebba Dalin, all of whom, at one time or another, wrote him to suggest that the foreign images they reported in their letters would do well to serve as pretexts for poetry.

We do not know if Professor Dalin read "The Green Plant," which was set in motion by a newspaper clipping she sent Stevens in October 1952. But when she read *Ideas of Order*, although its publication preceded her first letters to Stevens by a decade, she wrote of one of the poems in that book: "Perhaps the line in *Botanist on Alp (I)* 'Stockholm slender in a slender light' has its origins in the pictures I once sent you. A very moving description and very revealing."[65] Actually she sent those pictures of Stockholm in 1947, along with a "piece of art" delivered by her sister-in-law (I have not identified this, but it is certainly not the van Gogh she had been seeking for him), in return for some American books Stevens had sent her that she needed for her university teaching. The correspondence was revived in 1952, when on a visit to New York she herself brought him a Swedish tapestry.

Stevens's exchanges with Professor Dalin, similar in these respects to the Stevens–van Geyzel letters, amounted to both parties' descriptions of the local weather, Stevens's reiteration of his need to discover like-minded people abroad ("There is nothing quite the same as knowing civilized people here and there around the world," he told Dalin),[66] his alluring claim that such contacts excited his poetic mind ("You stimulate my imagination, as you see," he wrote her),[67] and, most important, his various requests for "something I should like to pick up . . . now and then."[68] So he forthrightly told Professor Dalin in his first exchanges with her in 1947, after she had introduced herself as someone who would like to translate into Swedish "How Red the Rose" from "Esthétique du Mal," his well-known war poem. "I have often wanted to know someone in Sweden with whom it would be possible for me to exchange letters in English," Stevens wrote her. "Some years ago I tried to correspond with a weaver at Landskroner with pathetic results."[69] Several long letters complained about the heat of the summer of 1952 and, as I have noted, he associated it with political discontent; as he also associated Sweden with a sparkling clarity and coldness—another effort to locate a zone beyond the reach of American policy (Sweden's contemplation of *staying out* of NATO was a significant deviation from Allied response to U.S. plans)[70]—where better a place to pick up a correspondence during the intensest heat of the bad seasons of cold war?[71] "I suppose that if there is ever a war with Russia," he wrote Barbara Church, "I shall look back on July, 1952, and consider it worse. The heat has been ungodly" (*L* 758). He again wanted to compare the American and European situations at least on the basis of the unusual weather. As he began to write some of the seven new poems for the *Nation*—of these, "An Old Man Asleep," "The Plain Sense of Things," "Lebensweisheitspielerei," and "The Green Plant" all express some aspect of the malaise induced by the summer—a letter from Professor Dalin arrived announcing the strange early-October weather in Sweden. Snow had preceded the falling of the leaves. The language unapologetically suggested this as a perfect source-image for a new Stevens poem; the letter was deliberately vivid, beginning with the opening image, which she evidently borrowed from "the first autumnal inhalations" of Stevens's "Credences of Summer" (*CP* 372):

> Dear Mr. Stevens:
>   The fall in Sweden has been so strange that I have wished you were here to record its sensations and inhalations in a poem. The winter has arrived ahead of schedule. Cold winds blow while autumn colors rage around the hills, contrasting with the deep blue-green of the fir trees. . . . Red, green, and yellow leaves falling. . . . "The leaves have always before fallen *before* the snow comes."

This last line was quoted in translation from the newspaper clipping she enclosed with the letter. At the top of the clipping was a photograph of a man walking a dog in the unusual weather. "The sun shone from a clear-blue sky on brilliant white mountains bedecked with forests still in full foliage. It was a magnificent sight," the newspaper report ran, "brilliant fall colors in red, orange, yellow and green."[72]

As it happened, Stevens did not require Ebba Dalin's account of the Swedish situation to record the "sensations and inhalations" of the odd weather in a poem. After the hot, hateful summer, the same early signs of winter descended on the U.S. Northeast. On October 21 he wrote her:

> Your note and the little picture in the newspaper clipping were nice to have. Only yesterday I went to New York for the first time in months. Between Bridgeport and New York there was a driving snowstorm, the first of its kind at such an early date since 1909. It is often said that an exceptionally hot summer (such as we had this year) brings on an exceptionally long and cold

winter. However that may be, there is so much about the weather on the radio and most of it is so much worse than it is that I prefer to take it as it comes. Today is a true October day.[73]

Three days later he wrote McGreevy:

[A]t this very time of year when we are in the midst of autumn and well aware that the cold is coming on, I keep thinking that I would like to go South. Who doesn't? Then a day or so ago I received a note from Sweden with a little picture showing the ground covered with snow before the leaves had fallen (a sign, if not a proof, of a long winter), and a man walking across country with his dog, and I'd like that too. (*L* 763)

In its last stanza, "The Green Plant" sharply turns toward the forests that defy the disruption of the natural cycle, forests "still in full foliage" (in the words of the Swedish account), in just the way the programmatic September 10 letter to Barbara Church promised a turn toward the real. Now this "true October" put the heat of the summer of 1952 so far behind Stevens that it seems to have knocked the breath out of his weakened poetic language—so "The effete vocabulary of summer / No longer says anything" (ll. 5–6). Ironically this moved the poet so far in the direction of the "irrelevant" (not the news but the weather) that to fulfill his promise of a new knowledge of the real he now strategically chose to make contact with a "*harsh* reality" (l. 16), in a poem that did not envision Europe's human devastation but recorded the violations of its record-breaking weather— weather-as-news could be devastatingly important, surely, but remained utterly uncontroversial. So his own true October day easily shared in Sweden's. With very little of the exertion of "St. Armorer's Church," "The Green Plant" could absorb its European source and claim to generate Stevens's approach to harsh reality:

> Silence is a shape that has passed.
> Otu-bre's lion-roses have turned to paper
>
> . . . .
>
> The brown at the bottom of red
> The orange far down in yellow,
>
> Are falsifications from a sun
>
> . . . .
>
> A turning down toward finality—
>
> Except that a green plant glares, as you look
> At the legend of the maroon and olive forest,
> Glares, outside of the legend, with the barbarous green
> Of the harsh reality of which it is part.

Here the poet countered other pessimistic reports of degeneration (a "turning down toward finality") by associating Sweden, through Dalin, with the natural resourcefulness of the weather. The most violent intrusions into human life were meteorological. Weather was the nonpartisan force of reality that might overpower Hartford or New Haven and Stockholm, Paris, Bergamo, or Rome similarly. In its effort to suggest the weather as the real news, the poem implied by its facile conclusion that great poems do not argue, they exfoliate.

Other poems written in this season plotted similar moves, making turns toward the real as sharp as the turn here in line 13 at "Except." "The Plain Sense of Things," part of the *Nation* group with "The Green Plant," turns similarly—on the strong, well-known line "Yet the absence of the imagination had / Itself to be imagined" (*CP* 503). These and other poems in "The Rock" group (1950–1954) reconceive the imagination as a direct confrontation with the extrinsic, but it would take several final steps into public American life before the last poems could finally establish a direction from imagination to reality as programmatic terms (a movement some important critics would resist, as I will show). For now, however, the new knowledge of the real followed only from the definition given it in the letter to Mrs. Church, which had led to "St. Armorer's Church." It was reality stripped of historical reference only and exactly to the point where the identity of its connection to actuality might be deemed merely personal, and any potentially disturbing contact with the world might still be somewhat deferred.

For all their differences, "St. Armorer's Church from the Outside" and "The Green Plant" are alike in that they at first admit a postcard-knowledge and then move past major qualifications to the idea of poetic mastery, such as that "one's poems begin to read like the poems of someone else." In "St. Armorer's Church" this mastery is achieved by Americanizing the acceptance of history as it is reproducible in natural terms, in "The Green Plant" by displaying the poet's great talent for drawing on some anomalous American reality—freak weather, a "periodical" disturbance of weather as a kind of news—exactly matching the European. Each poem then turns toward a presumed "inside" understanding of a harsh reality as a matter of shared experience, of friendship, correspondence, apparent social equation. We may consider "The Green Plant" the more successful poem—by which we mean it rhetorically typifies "The Rock" poems—offering as a reason that Stevens's shift follows beautifully from his confession of limits and thus makes for a poem that does not struggle as "St. Armorer's Church" does in forming a mixed attitude toward regeneration. We speak in such a way about the poem only because, following critical consensus in the late forties and fifties, we assume that it was primarily or solely Stevens's early work that taught us to read his late career self-referentially. But forces beyond Stevens's control are obviously also at work, both generally with respect to the way in which Stevens's imagination-reality complex would be distorted by postwar criticism and specifically in this instance. Holly Stevens is right, I think, to conclude that World War II "changed everything" in her father's Europe. At the beginning of that hot cold-war summer, and incidentally at a time when, for once, he was seriously considering a trip to France in connection with a Twentieth Century Work gathering, he wrote Paule Vidal:

> There seems to be only one place left in the world, and that, of course, is Paris, in which, *notwithstanding all the talk of war and all the difficulties of politics*, something fundamentally gay and beautiful still survives. I rode in town to my office this morning with a man who has just returned from Paris. When he had finished telling me about it, I sighed to think that it must forever remain terra incognita for me. (*L 755*; emphasis added)

Why would an American with Stevens's talent for imagining Europe want to go there in these times of terrible crisis? The one jarring qualification—"notwithstanding all the talk of war and all the difficulties of politics"—invites an ironic reading of the entire statement and almost wholly counteracts the apparently sincere point about the survival of Western Europe as a cultural center. The irony would suggest that what has survived of Europe lies principally in the (American) imagination. Many of the postwar poems work in this manner; some, like "Description without Place," attempt to make a whole aesthetic principle out of such a manner. It is easy for us to say that for Stevens postwar Europe remained terra incognita because this judgment sustains our belief in Stevens's uniqueness, in his devotion to imagination unspoiled by reality. But the judgment does not do justice to the complexity of his specific and hopeful—his characteristically American—relations with an actual world he was certain could be renewed.

Renewing these relations did involve denying to a certain extent the plain fact that everything in his Europe existed only by comparison, and repressing the idea that his literature was essentially comparative. "The poet in a time of disbelief [who] . . . shares the disbelief of his time," he said in a 1951 lecture, ". . . does not turn to Paris or Rome for relief from the monotony of reality. He turns to himself and he denies that reality was ever monotonous except in comparison. He asserts that the source of comparison having been eliminated, reality is returned" ("Two or Three Ideas," *OP 264*). Thus, even though he believed he understood Europe's "cindery noes" and in his poetry could optimize them into an "ember yes," to use the language of "St. Armorer's Church," he could only have done so by depreciating the source of comparison. Similarly, in his rather willful conception, peasantless lands his correspondent saw with her own eyes could be refigured to give forth the ruddy fruits of his own comparing labor. To read Stevens this way is not at all to show how his concept of "the imagination" finally reasserted itself at the expense of "reality," but to learn how primarily he felt the need to breathe easily again in the postwar years—and indeed how far into great contemporary issues he was willing to go to remain right at home. A general conclusion may also be drawn from this new special agreement with reality: if in the diplomatic rhetoric institutionalized by American aid the postwar imagination (in Stephen Spender's view, a cultural imagination) was explicitly tied to the new importance of foreign markets, then Stevens's sense of "market things / That press" surely participated in the same "great conflict going on" in which Spender was only more famously involved.

CHAPTER 6.

Last American Occasions

Every now and then I notice that somebody is supposed to have been influenced by me but, personally, I have never been able to recognize the influence. And, of course, I am no more interested in
influencing people than you are. My interest is to
write my own poetry just as yours is to write your
own poetry.
—*Stevens to Richard Eberhart,*
January 20, 1954 (L 815)

. . . be happy then,
That you shall never understand that radiant
Mastery. It is gone as soon as known. . . .

. . . .

Great nature is our master.
All our will and our flushed, enticed brains
Cannot unmake the world.
—*Richard Eberhart, "Formative Mastership"*

Master of the world and of himself,
He came to this by knowledge or
Will come.
—*Stevens, "The Sail of Ulysses" (OP 128–29)*

It is rather dangerous for me to read Wallace Stevens in 1976; it would have been better in 1956. I
felt him to be the large general mentor of the
times, whom I looked up to as commanding the
scene. I took comfort in this. . . . I thought he
represented America at its best.
—*Richard Eberhart, "Reflections on*
Wallace Stevens in 1976"

A FRIENDLY disagreement between Stevens and Richard Eberhart in 1953
and 1954 raised the related issues of Stevens's originality, authority, and
celebrity, and sent him further in the direction of what he finally posited as

"a new knowledge of reality." Originality framed this vexing question: Was it true that the greater a poet's recognized authority and celebrity—and adjudged representativeness—the less truly original he seemed? The Eberhart-Stevens exchange, in conjunction with a few last American occasions that were possible only because Stevens was indeed deemed culturally representative, supported the anomalous critical judgment of a young critic who wrote in 1951, in an essay Stevens read, that "acceptance of reality" was "[t]he final condition" of Stevens's career.[1]

Later, when Henry Kissinger invited Stevens—along with McGeorge Bundy, Arthur Schlesinger, Jr., Edwin Canham (editor of the *Christian Science Monitor*), and James Burnham (the former radical, then CIA "researcher"[2] who was arguing that "the only alternative to the communist World Empire is an American Empire")[3]—to participate in an "International Seminar" at Harvard, Stevens's status as a cultural authority (if not also as a celebrity) was surely confirmed; for the goal of Kissinger's seminar was to introduce a group of carefully selected future leaders from European and "developing" countries to "as wide and representative a segment of American life as possible."[4] Stevens was in fact forced to decline this alluring invitation; he wanted to accept, but even his voice, he wrote Kissinger, had not recovered from an operation weeks earlier (the procedure had been halted at the exploratory stage, having disclosed an inoperable cancer that would kill the patient that summer).[5] This did not prevent the issue of his representativeness from surfacing a final time in Kissinger's appeal; looking over the program materials, Stevens need have taken only a moment to consider them in the context of his status as a cultural figure. Who were these young people assembled by Dr. Kissinger, to be met by the likes of Canham and Burnham, and described by him as "on the verge of reaching positions of leadership in their countries"? The list staked out an indisputable political boundary: among the seminar participants were an exiled Nationalist Chinese, author of *How the Chinese Communists Treat Students*; a German who had begun work in the (West) German Foreign Service; a young Iranian short-story writer who had already been given charge of "distribution" in the National Iranian Oil Company. The way in which Kissinger described them, as members of a "generation which matured during the war and witnessed the despair and destruction of its aftermath"[6]—note, not the "despair and destruction" of the *war* but of *its aftermath*, meaning the period of communist consolidation—made it evident that the underlying goal of the program was precisely what George Kennan explained to an audience at the Museum of Modern Art almost exactly as Kissinger's invitation arrived in Hartford: "to correct a number of impressions that the outside world entertains of us, impressions that are beginning to affect our international position in very important ways." Kennan's, Kissinger's, and many others' notion of "International Exchange in the Arts" (the title of Kennan's MOMA talk) called for prominent American intellectuals to recognize their responsibilities in the project of reversing "negative conceptions about us prevail[ing] to one degree or another abroad," and of discovering how "negative feelings *are related to cultural rather than to political conditions*" (emphasis added).[7] Kissinger's invitation clearly recognized Stevens as one of those cultural diplomats, similarly—and obviously—displacing political onto cultural strategies.

If Stevens had gone to Harvard to help "reverse negative conceptions" of the United States, it would not have been inconsistent with a general willingness in his last few years to make public appearances that stipulated official American themes—a disposition made possible by the "close approach" to reality promised in a moment of self-criticism (for Barbara Church during the 1952 elections) and carried out in projects undertaken in 1953 and 1954. He accepted an invitation to read and record his poems at the University of Massachusetts, knowing that the series theme was "the American conception of the free man." He wrote an occasional poem for the Columbia University bicentennial, following the prescribed theme of American rights, knowledge, and freedom, and recited his poem on the climactic day of a yearlong celebration that took on great political significance and (later the same day) involved the president of the United States. And he readily agreed to write an essay for the Voice of America, following an arrangement managed by John Pauker, an undertaking thick with fifties-style cultural diplomacy and inspired by the great esteem that had been given Stevens within a well-connected group: Pauker, who had been a student of Norman Holmes Pearson, Yale's premier OSS-CIA contact, was a close friend and collaborator of James Jesus Angleton, later chief of counterintelligence for the CIA, the brilliant "poet-spy"; with Pauker and Reed Whittemore at Yale, Angleton prized Stevens's poems and had published five of them in the little magazine *Furioso*; Pauker himself had risen to the position of section chief at the United States Information Agency when the agency turned to Stevens.[8]

It might seem that all this attention would show him that he was finally being accepted as a poet of reality; yet just the opposite was true. For cultural representativeness now necessitated the imagination, not reality, as a *raison d'être*, and this is what would continue to separate Stevens's association with postwar cultural politics and his critics'. Even in the case of the Yale counterintelligence group: the Stevens they had always loved best— about which Pauker himself published an essay—was the Stevens of "Sea Surface Full of Clouds," the poet (and the very poem) Ransom relished as having "no moral, political, religious or sociological values."[9] It was one of the many great ironies of the time that the Stevens whose truly *national* reputation was emerging was specifically *not* going to be the sleepless figure worrying over the Spanish Civil War in "The Men That Are Falling," nor the isolationist of "Martial Cadenza," nor the home-front belt-tightener of "No Possum, No Sop, No Taters," nor, certainly, the skeptic of European aid in "Imago"—nor even the contented realist of "Credences of Summer" who urged, "Let's see the very thing and nothing else." Rather, the Stevens "seized upon and exaggerated" in the fifties was the poet who had "presented the exotic view of the world" in the teens and twenties, as Hayden Carruth, one of the few dissenters on this issue, phrased it in 1951.[10]

In his last few years Stevens saw the imagination in his imagination-reality postulate increasingly featured—even misused, he sometimes felt—to the general exclusion of reality. At times he pointed out to friends and correspondents how the first term was being pushed too hard, and could at least joke about the mistaken emphasis,[11] while at other times he submitted to it. The bias emerged for many and complex reasons, not the least of which was that Stevens inconsistently discouraged it; however, such a mercurial attitude on so central a point was doubtless itself, in turn, a response to a critical urge not easily stilled: a few critics had found in the Stevensean idea of imagination a means of purging American intellectual life of the "fact worship" of the realist thirties, a mode, as we have seen, that then divided writers in wartime but could not be honestly debated in that time of "essential" unanimity. There were other critics, neither overtly conservative nor consciously setting out to repudiate America's recent political past, who recognized a fortunate postwar convergence: Stevens's rising reputation as a poet whose commitment to worldliness could not be discerned and an era in which distinct ideologies were said to have been spent. This critical position, celebrating the convergence of Stevens and "The Age" in a way that fully characterizes cold-war liberalism,[12] was finally more effective than outright thirties-bashing in canonizing Stevens for the fifties (and well beyond); it was most clearly articulated by Randall Jarrell in an influential 1951 essay for the *Partisan Review*. The other, more conscientiously anticommunist position, less influential finally than Jarrell's but setting a cold-war Stevens in starker relief, was presented in the work of William Van O'Connor. What was perhaps not evident in the fifties is surely now: Stevens's idea of the imagination was itself becoming caught up in the general rightward realignment of American literary politics.

Recognition as a culturally representative and intellectually countenanced "American poet" likewise established, even in the very mention of the name "Stevens," a connotation of literary-political stability. The 1949 Bollingen Prize was not only an acknowledgment of a lifetime of work and of the great achievement of *The Auroras of Autumn*; it also signified an attempt to stabilize the prize itself in its having been an inarguably sensible, uncontroversial choice, a safe check against the great political chaos caused by the selection of Pound for the 1948 award.[13] "If there was less notice taken of this second Bollingen award than of the first to Ezra Pound," wrote Richard Wilbur with obvious relief, "it was proof not of indifference [to Stevens] but of a less troubled and more general satisfaction."[14] Stevens's credentials for playing the role Wilbur admired—causing less distress and providing "general" contentment—were impeccable: for one thing, Stevens had continually refused to state his position on Pound publicly. Though he did not "suppose there is the slightest doubt that [Pound] did what he is said to have done," at the same time Stevens did not "believe that the law of treason should apply to chatter on the radio *when it is recognizably chatter*" (*L* 516; emphasis added). Asked by Tate to sign a letter to the *Saturday Review of Literature* for the purpose of protesting Robert Hillyer's charges against the Bollingen Committee's selection of Pound (and concomitantly against the New Criticism),[15] Stevens wrote: "1. I know nothing about this; 2. care less; 3. do not believe that the Saturday Review . . . or Hillyer . . . could possibly harm the cause of letters; 4. prefer to keep out of this; and 5. intend to do just that."[16] Tate's indignant reply asserted that "Hillyer's smear . . . *has* done damage" and suggested that while "[i]n terms of the ages the incident is nothing . . . it seems to be that the ages are made up of incidents."[17] As we have seen, Stevens knew quite as well as Tate the importance of "incidents," yet the perception of Stevens, by well-placed people like Norman Pearson, was that Stevens's poetry bespoke ages and not incidents. As late as the early seventies, Pearson could respond to a request by Stanley Burnshaw that a certain poetry prize be awarded Norman Macleod, an ex-radical with a long and varied career of writing and editing, by suggesting firmly to Burnshaw that the selection committee "[f]ollow . . . the lead of Wallace Stevens with the Bollingen Prize . . . to establish the status of the prize." (Only after bracing themselves with a solid, Stevens-like awardee, Pearson advised Burnshaw, should the committee then "go to the Macleods of this world.")[18] Eberhart, looking back on Stevens in the fifties from the seventies, wrote: "I knew my man and believed in the excellence and *durability* of his stance. To me it was a high artistic position comporting with *an acceptance of an America it represented*. . . . There was this *secure* moment . . . when Stevens *satisfied* the capacity to live with belief within a sophisticated poetry" (emphasis added).[19] Stevens knew the political significance of the Bollingen, could take measure of "durability" and national "security," as it were, in political terms: when the selection committee was pondering whether to give the 1952 prize to Williams,[20] Stevens had sense enough of Williams's past radical affiliations, and also of McCarthyism, to observe that "if something has been discovered and if his record is not clear, one wonders what effect this may have on the Bollingen Prize which is already involved on Pound's account" (*L* 768). Of course Stevens was worried about Williams; yet he seemed hardly less concerned for the reputation of the Bollingen Foundation itself, even while having put off all efforts by foundation emissaries to get him involved on behalf of the Bollingen in the Pound affair. It would be hard to overstate the cultural significance of the choice of Stevens for 1949: it was precisely his refusal to state his position for Tate that created his uniquely strong (and rewarding) position. No matter what one thought of Hillyer's description of the crisis—"*Nothing can be salvaged* from the disgrace of the Bollingen Award" given Pound, and "It would be well for the Library of Congress to withdraw the prize, for *no decent poet* in the country would accept it" (emphasis added)[21]—decency had been redefined to betoken nonpartisanship.

Stevens sensed that in this period others gained official recognition as the result of a strategy of *not* seeking it—an idea he suggested to Pearson as a way of explaining why Williams was having "troubles in Washington" with McCarthyites. "I don't see why [Williams] doesn't withdraw his name" from consideration for the position at the Library of Congress, he wrote. "Not to want anything is still a practical as well as a philosophical way of getting in."[22] "He didn't try to play the game," Richard Eberhart later observed of Stevens, "as Williams did, trying to be better known" (*WSR* 150). It is true; one cannot describe Stevens, especially at this very late point in his career, as wanting or trying to "get in" by way of his Columbia bicentennial poem, his reading on the theme of "freedom" at the University of Massachusetts, or even by way of his Voice of America essay. Yet these last American occasions do demonstrate how Stevens could speak through and in the "voice" of America, if that were his agreed-to function.

We can be certain that Stevens knew about the political purposes—and the troubles—of the Voice of America before he agreed to write for its "This Is America" program. When NBC transferred its international section to the State Department, Fernand Auberjonois found himself working for the USIA, which was established under the United States Information and Education Exchange Act of 1948 to "counter attempts to distort the objectives and policies of the United States."[23] "I was doing out-and-out propaganda," Auberjonois recalls, "[yet others] regarded me as incredibly lax, not hard enough as a propagandist. . . . These are things I discussed with Wallace Stevens slightly."[24] Then, in February 1953, Senator McCarthy announced that he would prove the Voice of America was harboring communists; McCarthy and Roy Cohn elicited from Nancy Lenkeith, who had been a VOA book reviewer in the French section, the claim that there was a direct link between her dismissal and the favorable review of Whittaker Chambers's *Witness* she had written for broadcast. The accused was Fernand Auberjonois, who denied the charges for the *New York Times* on February 21[25] and, on February 28, for McCarthy and Cohn in executive session of the Senate Subcommittee on Internal Security.[26] Five weeks after this stressful event, Auberjonois met Stevens again at one of Barbara Church's parties.[27] "We became the section that McCarthy attacked first in the government." What were the accusations generally? "Well, you know, soft on Communism. Misuse of funds. Why so much entertainment? Why do you have John Houseman [a former radical] doing programs for you?"[28] Perhaps for Auberjonois the most disappointing aspect of the VOA purge was the difference between his own denial of McCarthy's charges and those of his colleagues. Their denials insisted on the very thing McCarthy had set out to reaffirm—that, in the words of one of the accused, the VOA would always "show a strong anti-Communist slant." "I have handled thousands of words daily," another guaranteed, "with the objective of exposing the Communist threat, which I regard as aimed at the enslavement of free men everywhere and particularly at the subversion of America's free institutions."[29] That Auberjonois could publicly stand by his position—Chambers's *Witness*, he had felt, was a confusing work and did not contain "the most effective material for broadcasts to a foreign audience"[30]—demonstrated that one could resist McCarthy's "degradation ceremonies," in Victor Navasky's apt phrase,[31] by answering questions narrowly without contributing further to the atmosphere of intolerance. At the early-April party, "we [he and Stevens] talked about this business of McCarthy. . . . He looked upon it as something rather stupid."[32]

What, then, did Stevens intend by agreeing to write for the Voice of America a little later? After Auberjonois quit the State Department, having labored under a cloud for a year following his congressional testimony, John Pauker of the USIA's Talks and Features Branch had the idea of involving Stevens in a new VOA project. Theodore Streibert, USIA director, wrote on March 9, 1955, inviting Stevens to do "a job that calls for direct insight into the people and places of the United States." Streibert explained that the mission of "the Voice of America is to give international audiences a sense of the quality and variety of American life."[33] Stevens's essay, "Connecticut Composed," after 335 of its 1,115 words were deleted by Pauker, appeared as "This Is Connecticut" in the state's newspapers, including Hartford's *Courant*,[34] in the VOA's overseas English-language transmissions, and in as many as thirty-seven other languages. If the rhetoric provided by the USIA for use with Stevens's piece in the newspapers was affirmative in the usual cold-war context ("This new Voice of America series seeks to present this country as it is—much as the visiting Soviet farm experts are now discovering the Corn Belt for themselves"),[35] then Stevens's rhetoric was hardly less Americanized. Indeed, his language was never more officially optimistic than here—nor plainer, nor less qualified. Was this the result of discomfort with the assignment? Or compliance with the expected civics-lesson style? Here is a sample:

> One could say in a few words simply that Connecticut is an industrial and business center.... There are only some two million people living in the state, which is the third smallest state in the country. Of these a quarter of a million are foreign-born. Of those who were born in the state, many are the children of parents who were themselves foreign-born, or of parents whose parents, generation back of generation, were foreign-born. All of us together constitute the existing community. Those who descend from earlier generations know that the forces that moulded them are today moulding those who descend from later generations. The children look alike. There are no foreigners in Connecticut. Once you are here you are or you are on your way to become a Yankee.[36]

The clichés of melting-pot pluralism—the common trope of domestic cold-war rhetoric, consensus through complexity[37]—presented in a series of uncharacteristically short and barely altered Americanisms (there are unelaborated references to thrift, frugality, hardihood, good faith, and goodwill), perhaps show Stevens poking a bit of fun at the assignment he had readily accepted. Surely one such point is an assertion made in spite of the fact that a majority of Connecticut citizens are "foreign-born": they are all most assuredly, nevertheless, on their way to becoming Yankees. Indeed now, Stevens observes, "The children look alike." Yet he is not, as it turns out, speaking of the emphatic American assimilation of "foreigners" in the sense that almost anyone reading the essay would assume, for at the end of the same paragraph it becomes clear that by "foreign-born" Stevens has meant those, *like him*, who had *emigrated from nearby states*. It is entirely possible that Pauker at the USIA, an admirer of modern poetry trained and practiced as a close reader,[38] sensed this half-suppressed joke about the American community's painfully slow way of protecting the "foreign-born" from their own threatening difference. In any case Pauker and not Stevens deleted the brief sentence about the look-alike children. The preceding sentence was deleted as well: with its easily misunderstood description of coercive democratic forces that bend even slight difference into sameness, it may have caused some small worry that the Stevens piece would give the wrong impression about "the forces" newcomers to America must endure. "Those who descend from earlier generations," the deleted sentence ran, "know that the forces that moulded them are today moulding those who descend from later generations" (*OP* 304). To the VOA and the USIA—as embodied in Pauker's editorial hand—the centrist idea, "All of us together [including those "different"] constitute the existing community," should remain unqualified by any un-American-sounding "forces" "moulding" sameness. While the VOA's intention to have its "This Is America" writers speak of pluralism in the moderate sense was hinted at from the beginning, not as a rationalization of force but as a sign of American freedom—Streibert wanted, he had written, "a sense of the quality *and variety* of American life"—the attempt to make the contributions all of an ideological piece, the real rules of the game, would be applied later, in the process of screening and editing.

Of course what the Voice of America really wanted would not need saying—particularly for Stevens, who knew from Auberjonois of the new McCarthyite pressures to conform within the VOA itself. If Streibert or Pauker had been specific in requesting their Americanist essay, had spelled out the vocabulary that must govern such occasional writing at such a moment, Stevens's response would probably have been to decline the invitation. That quite to the contrary he felt free to write what he wished made his VOA piece the cry of its occasion in offering what he evidently regarded as spontaneous judgments about American life in his time.

He had significantly more trouble with Columbia's and Massachusetts' requests for poems about freedom. In these two instances the professors in charge of committees set up for the occasions—very unlike Pauker and Streibert in seeing themselves as serving no political function at all, and in fact, as I have learned, deeming themselves to be academic liberals—ran up against Stevens's at least initial discomfort with having his poetry recast as an officially optimistic American language.

The Columbia poem was supposed to be attuned to the theme of the university's bicentennial, "Man's Right to Knowledge and the Free Use Thereof," according to a letter inviting Stevens to read at the public "Class Day" ceremonies following a conference to be held the day before on "National Policy for Economic Welfare at Home and Abroad." The man who extended the invitation, Horace Taylor, a Columbia economist, was chairing the conference on economic policy, which would involve such major figures as Arthur F. Burns, then advisor to Eisenhower, and Averell Harriman, then director of Mutual Security. Materials Taylor enclosed, describing his conference as covering topics such as "Toward a More Integrated Free-World Economy" and discussions of "mutual security"—meaning economic links only between nations of the Free World[39]—had nothing ostensibly to do with the poem Stevens was being asked to write, save that Taylor just happened to be associated with both the conference and the Stevens invitation. While the letter and its enclosures were confusing, they already suggested the importance and political density of the event and gave a hint of the bicentennial theme in action. Stevens responded to Taylor by asking for clarification, though he also indicated that he would try and compose such a poem; after all, he would have from that point (November 3, 1953—the invitation had come in October) until the last day of the following May to learn more about the bicentennial and write the piece. But he did express some basic reservations: "An assigned theme, *particularly a theme as broad* as the one of which you have spoken, is always a difficulty" (emphasis added).[40] Taylor replied immediately that he was "greatly embarrassed" by any misunderstanding caused by his invitation; he then attempted to explain how he was not as zealous about the designated topic of rights, knowledge, and freedom as his first letter might have indicated; yet, in his apology he rather narrowly delineated the *freedom* of the "creative artist"—"I realize that I am guilty of something that I would never do to a creative artist"—as something quite distinct from the sort of demands one routinely placed on guest economists. It would not be out of character for Stevens to try harder to meet the requirement of the occasion after sensing that the "freedom" of the artist to choose was a special condition of his irrelevance as a "creative artist" among policymakers—on an occasion that was otherwise planned around the well-defined and very serious business of dealing with the monetary integration of the free world. "The fact is," Taylor wrote in his apology,

> that we want you to prepare *any poem you may choose to write* that in your judgment will be *appropriate to the occasion*. If this should fall somewhere within the very large area of our Bicentennial theme, we should be most happy. We will, however, be equally so if you prepare anything that you may choose. I certainly did not intend to invite you to deal with a subject as broad as the theme itself, *but* I had in mind a possible poem pertaining to "man," "right," "knowledge," "free," "use" or any combination or permutation thereof. (emphasis added)[41]

As Stevens began thinking of his Columbia poem in response to simultaneously broad and narrow interpretations of Columbia's theme, another request came in that led to an oddly similar exchange. The Literary Society at the University of Massachusetts at Amherst had just won a grant from the National Association of Education Broadcasters (NAEB), a division of the Ford Foundation's Fund for Adult Education. A group of English professors had thought to put on a series of radio programs entitled "New England Authors," which, as specified in their proposal for funding, took as its theme "the expression in poetry of the American concept of the free man."[42] A year later Stevens would agree to write for the Voice of America partly because, as I have argued, that request only implied its officially optimistic theme and mentioned no guidelines; but at the specification of the Massachusetts theme Stevens initially balked. The contract he was about to sign stipulated that "Mr. Stevens agrees to provide the Project Supervisor [Professor of English Robert G. Tucker] with a list of poems which pertain to the series theme of freedom."[43] Stevens wrote Tucker:

There are two things that I did not gather from our discussion.[44] The first is that freedom was to be the theme of the poems. While you showed me the proposed contract, nevertheless that did not catch my eye. I do not have any poems on the theme of freedom. . . . While there are a few poems on the subject of war, I think that I must say that if it is required that the poems be on the theme of freedom I shall have to give up the idea of reading. The appearance of this theme in the matter suggests to me that you may really be thinking of a much younger audience than I have had in mind. I have been thinking of a normal, mature audience.

The second thing that I had not realized is that you expected me to comment on each of the poems. I could not do this in terms of freedom because the poems do not relate to the subject. It might be possible for me to say a word or two before each poem as, for example, in the case of A Pastoral Nun: the first poem that I shall read presents a theory of poetry; as to The Idea of Order at Key West: the next poem was designed to show how man gives his own order to the world about him; as to Credences of Summer[:] while it would be forcing the point, I could say the next poem shows the free man in his freedom.

From his experience negotiating the Columbia theme, Stevens seems to have predicted the reasonable response to his qualms, saying, in effect, that of course he *does* have poems that can *somehow* be understood as addressing the issue of freedom—in particular "Credences of Summer," one of the poems he proposed to record. At first, then, he insisted: "I do not have any poems on the theme of freedom." Yet in trying then to anticipate what was supposed to be an entirely different objection, concerning the comments he had been asked to make about each poem after reciting it, he agreed that in offering such a comment about "Credences" he could after all make the poem befit freedom.[45]

Stevens was recognizing the way in which one played fast and loose with two competing (and perhaps contradictory) senses of freedom: one was the specifically "American" freedom that the Fund for Adult Education had funded the program to protect, a theme to which the applicants for the grant knew they had, ironically, to conform; the other, of course, was the freedom to write, select, and recite one's poetry exactly as one chose. When the two freedoms were confused—and it was the general effect of postwar criticism to confuse them—the apparent political effort entailed in "the *freedom* of the artist" could be said to be thoroughly nonideological; it was no coincidence, I would contend, that one of the most obvious forms of this confusion appeared in the work of William Van O'Connor, an energetic canonizer of Stevens: "[T]hose concerned with maintaining the freedom of the artist to create his vision of the world," O'Connor wrote in 1951, "have no inevitable allegiance either to the Right or to the Left," a postideological remark extolled as such by W. K. Wimsatt.[46] Willing as Stevens was, in "Imago," "St. Armorer's Church," and elsewhere, to mark the distance traveled from the thirties—it was one of O'Connor's central objectives to reveal the movement from radicalism to (cold-war) liberalism—there was a crucial difference between the poet and his critic on this main point: Stevens was familiar with the two meanings of freedom *and with their confusion*; and he neither appreciated nor accepted the way in which "freedom" was being bandied about. In writing Barbara Church about the popular acceptance of modernism in painting, he saw the failure of liberalism hinging on the kind of "[f]ree thought, free art, free poetry" that had "produced this sort of tyranny"—how liberalism, by insisting on its version of freedom to the exclusion of everything else (and without knowing itself to be a *version* of freedom), actually "destroyed free thought" (*L* 573–74). "The total freedom *that now endangers us*," he said, "has never existed before" (*L* 620; emphasis added). Such a postliberal analysis was liberating in itself, I take it, as it helped Stevens stand apart from his cold-war critics; it also helped him interpret the patriotic assertions put out by an art world adjusting its rhetoric in the scramble for funding. Stevens was aware early, as Alfred Barr at MOMA would put it only later, that projects entailing freedom as a theme really meant "freedom in a world in which freedom connotes a political attitude."[47]

Just such a connotation had obviously led the organizers of the Massachusetts program to assure the granting agency that "we will ask each poet to read at least one poem in which he speaks . . . about his confidence and faith in the American concept of the free man."[48] It also led Stevens to quip that the sort of "freedom" funded by the educational foundation, the NAEB, seemed to him a theme designed for the indoctrination of schoolchildren, and to imply that in recruiting him, by no means a children's poet, there had been some sort of mistake—a criticism that partly displays Stevens's understanding of the way in which grants of this sort, consciously repeating nationalistic truisms straight out of the high-school civics class, funded otherwise wholly "mature" academic projects. David Clark, one of Robert Tucker's collaborators, recalled in 1989 that American freedom "may have been one of [the] themes suggested by the NAEB in their application form. Definitely we hoped, I at least, that the 'freedom' theme would win the grant."[49] Richard Haven recalls that "[t]he theme of freedom . . . was largely or wholly an attempt to conform to the language of the NAEB announcement."[50] Stevens's initial reservations about freedom were in fact mild compared to E. E. Cummings's, who reacted as if, in Clark's words, "we were jingoists beating the patriotic drum."[51] Cummings finally did record his poems for the program, but only after Tucker and the others agreed to allow him to produce his own recording, which opened with "as freedom is a breakfast food" and also included "a politician is an arse."

When the Cummings tape arrived in Amherst, some among the program's organizers were "thrilled"; but it "scared others." "It was, after all," Clark has noted, "the McCarthy period."[52] Haven learned later that officials of the Ford Foundation division overseeing the NAEB reviewed Cummings's tape and decided that it "abused the freedom promised";[53] it was never broadcast.[54]

These politically charged associations, inextricably tied to NAEB dollars, extended well beyond the general patriotic purposes of the Fund for Adult Education; Stevens and the other poets, in recording poems that would be played over 240 Ford Foundation–supported radio stations across the United States and overseas,[55] would help convey the very same idea as the cultural programs designed by Kissinger and urged by Kennan: "A free society will prosper in direct relation to the ability of its citizens to think independently."[56] Still, the Massachusetts program, and Stevens's involvement with it, came at a particularly sensitive moment, as the Ford Foundation was under attack from the right; its associate director, famous as an academic liberal, faced this main charge when summoned to testify before a congressional committee: while foundation trustees were of course loyal and politically acceptable, they remained woefully ignorant of programs "being used for subversive purposes" endorsed and funded by crafty underlings with "regrettable left-wing emphasis."[57] One result of the crisis, from this point in late 1952 on—and just prior to the time when the Massachusetts group made its application—was a special new obsession with "total accountability" in all funded programs from the top down. Indeed the grant-in-aid contract Tucker signed on behalf of the "New England Authors" program committed him to close scrutiny from above of all "promotion and descriptive material."[58]

It is no wonder, then, that the promotional material for "New England Authors" carefully balanced Archibald MacLeish's liberalism[59] and Cummings's "uncompromising advoca[cy] of individual freedom"[60] with Peter Viereck's indisputable loyalty. Viereck, who would read his poems in the third program, was identified clearly as "an advocate of a return to conservatism."[61] And then there was Stevens, also a stable symbol of the successful American compromise with the hurly-burly of capitalist life. Described as suppressing the usual poet's urge to "reject or defy the world inimical to art," he was said here to have made his peace with the America most (liberal) poets liked to hate—"with technological and commercial values."[62]

The political meanings of the "freedom" theme and the foundation's sensitivity to red-baiting were on the minds of all involved—Stevens included, I am arguing—and this was quite obviously in spite of the fact that Tucker and Clark were themselves progressives and that, in Haven's words, "the series . . . was in opposition to rather than a reflection of Mc-Carthyism."[63] As Stevens began to realize, and as Tucker twice tried to explain, the goal was really to record good poems read aloud by the poets and not consciously at least to serve the interests of the American state. Tucker wrote Stevens a long letter of clarification in which Tucker all but admitted the double game necessitated by the wording of the NAEB contract that had set Stevens going. As Tucker's explanation played off allegiant against liberal senses of freedom, it produced stimulating ironies:

> As for the freedom theme, we do not insist upon it—certainly not an immature conception of freedom. . . . Indeed, I find no insuperable contradiction between the idea of freedom and imaginative form in poetry. Your comment on The Idea of Order at Key West of "how man gives his own order to the world about him" strikes me as the kind of freedom meant. I take it that the poet is free to give imaginative order, shape, form, meaning to experience, to make a new order of reality. In any case, we very much want what you consider representative poems and, if *freedom* seems to you a stumbling block, we're willing to leave you *free* to select what poems you will. (emphasis added).[64]

By the end of this letter, freedom has dissolved into a double entendre even the earnest project director could not resist: freedom might itself become a stumbling block, so Stevens was urged to feel free to ignore freedom.

Notwithstanding all the assurances that "the American concept of the free man" did not mean to them what it obviously meant to the funding agencies, Stevens was ready to take what came next in the self-scrutinizing spirit of the times. Two faculty members on Tucker's committee, Professors Haven and H. L. Varley, having examined the chronological list of poems Stevens chose for the reading, wondered if Stevens would reconsider his selection of "Credences of Summer." They had decided that "Credences" did not prepare the way smoothly enough for the "picture of 'reality' " presented in "Large Red Man Reading" and "This Solitude of Cataracts"—which meant, evidently, that the brimming, physical real of "Credences" did not match the august imagination in the two later poems. This set Stevens wondering: Had his definition of the imagination moved so obviously away from reality? What was inappropriate to the 1948 poems about the axiom "Let's see the very thing and nothing else" written just a few years earlier (*CP* 373)? Tucker's colleagues felt that "It Must Change" from "Notes toward a Supreme Fiction" would better set up the later Stevens. The suggested alteration in the list, they wrote, would give the reading "a *free* movement of the *imagination*."[65]

Stevens had never read the sections of "It Must Change" in public before. So, pondering two problems—the time it would take to read all ten cantos for the recording session, and the relation between this old version of the imagination and the recent one—Stevens spent part of his evening on Tuesday, February 23, 1954, reading aloud from "Notes." He found that it took him three minutes to read a single section; thirty minutes for all of "It Must Change" would be too long for the session.[66] We do not know if the rereading caused him to disagree with Tucker's colleagues as to how well the conception of imagination in this group of "Notes" cantos fit with the later conceptions, though he did finally keep to his original list, including "Credences." There is a sign of his disagreement in a new poem he wrote at this time, "Not Ideas about the Thing but the Thing Itself." The poem responded to "It Must Change" so adroitly, and in particular to the "Bethou me" canto, that it is reasonable to propose what might seem at first an uncharacteristic position in the new poem as in fact a conscious and logical reassessment of the place of the real in the oeuvre. Here, then, is one of the poems of 1942 he read again in late February 1954:

> Bethou me, said sparrow, to the crackled blade,
> And you, and you, bethou me as you blow,
> When in my coppice you behold me be.
>
> Ah, ké! the bloody wren, the felon jay,
> Ké-ké, the jug-throated robin pouring out,
> Bethou, bethou, bethou me in my glade.
>
> There was such idiot minstrelsy in rain. . . .
> . . . .
> One voice repeating, one tireless chorister,
> The phrases of a single phrase, ké-ké,
> A single text, granite monotony,
>
> . . . .
> These are of minstrels lacking minstrelsy,
> Of an earth in which the first leaf is the tale
> Of leaves, in which the sparrow is a bird
>
> Of stone, that never changes. Bethou him, you
> And you, bethou him and bethou. It is
> A sound like any other. It will end.

(*CP* 393–94)

And here is the new poem Stevens wrote:

> At the earliest ending of winter,
> In March, a scrawny cry from outside
> Seemed like a sound in his mind.
>
> He knew that he heard it,
> A bird's cry, at daylight or before,
> In the early March wind.

The sun was rising at six,
No longer a battered panache above snow . . .
It would have been outside.

It was not from the vast ventriloquism
Of sleep's faded papier-mâché . . .
The sun was coming from outside.

That scrawny cry—it was
A chorister whose c preceded the choir.
It was part of the colossal sun,

Surrounded by its choral rings,
Still far away. It was like
A new knowledge of reality.

(CP 534)

Insofar as the "new knowledge of reality" was a response to the "picture of reality" Tucker's associates had wanted him to provide for "New England Authors," and as such a reaction to "It Must Change," it was also for Stevens more emphatically a reaffirmation than might be otherwise indicated by the understated last line of the new poem. Stevens really did mean a *new* knowledge of the extrinsic; he was reorganizing his aesthetic to shore up a sense of final commitment to the real in a specific context, a commitment, that is, that seemed to have been deteriorating in an atmosphere disproportionately rewarding reality-as-imagination. The originality of the "Bethou me" canto was obviously not to be found in birds' "one voice repeating," in "phrases of a single phrase," in "minstrels lacking minstrelsy," for whatever minstrelsy was demonstrated there was supplied obviously by the poet who had had an *idea* about their "single text," an idea hardly itself idiotic: such external sounds "cannot be transformed into the living dialogue of change that exists between humans," as Harold Bloom has put it.[67] Now, when a "living dialogue" was to be craved, it was important to conceive of meaning as issuing from an exoteric order that had only *seemed* wholly esoteric before. The discovery that the poetic substance came from beyond the poet as a form of originality—and most important, that it should be described positively and commonly if sparely—was in itself "A new knowledge of reality." Thus the old programmatic invective against the incessant birds threatening poetic monotony (bloody wren, felon jay, tirelessly bethouing sparrow) gave way in 1954 to a somewhat limited ("scrawny") but in any case underived being. The stupid, familiarizing repetitions in the early version are now *not* part of a "vast ventriloquism." In "It Must Change," "Change," the poem's means to "Pleasure," was itself threatened by sounds like any other that "will *end*." But the perpetual chorister of "Notes" is *not* "a chorister whose c preceded the choir" as the bird of "Not Ideas" was. The latter bird, like the later Stevens, cries out scrawnily a new central note distinct from any aesthetic idea, an utterance potentially independent of the imagination.

Tucker's approach on the issue of freedom coincided almost precisely with the fascinating exchange between Stevens and Eberhart in the fall of 1953 and the winter and early spring of 1954; early in the new year, when Tucker's colleagues' suggestions about "Credences" drove Stevens back to "Notes" and provoked the revisionist rhetorical realism of "Not Ideas about the Thing," Eberhart's observations similarly sent Stevens in the direction of the new poem. Eberhart wondered, in short: if the poetic master induced younger admirers to repeat him even in the act of gaining distance and independent voice, had the master's originality been diminished? Or was he merely a serviceable representative of his time? The issue was framed in just such a way as to suggest strongly that the last lesson of the master ought to be the renewed discovery of a world outside him; he must discern, in other words, if his poems were not, as it were, the only imaginative assertions under the sun. Once this problem had been much discussed, the terms of the argument had shifted a number of times, and the real of "Credences" affirmed at Amherst—and "Not Ideas" written— Stevens then turned toward his Columbia poem.

Eberhart and Stevens had first met in 1936. Later, especially after 1950, they carried on a friendly correspondence, attended college football games together, and (often with Samuel French Morse) dined at the Canoe Club and other nearby restaurants.[68] Eberhart's move to the University of Connecticut at Storrs, in September 1953, enabled him and Stevens to interact regularly. They planned an autumn luncheon after Stevens agreed on September 2 to "toss off something" for *New World Writing*. Stevens asked Morse to join them, and the three met on October 19. This was one of those long sessions, as Morse later recalled for me,[69] during which they drank pitchers of martinis and talked about poetry; here Stevens exchanged his own "Farewell without a Guitar" (*OP* 125) for two of Eberhart's poems in handwritten copies. By October 22 Stevens had read these carefully.

The two poems Eberhart gave Stevens were "Closing Off the View" and "The Meaning of Indian Summer." These were in fact written "for" Stevens, as I think he realized. If the special dedication was not made explicit during the long October 19 "luncheon" (though Morse was almost certain it had been),[70] it was confirmed later when the poems appeared in the May 1954 all-Stevens issue of Morse's *Trinity Review*. There they went under the heading "Two Poems (*For Wallace Stevens*)."[71] But the poems made themselves clear as expressions of admiration for Stevens's work and examples of its influence.

"The truth was always his will," begins "Closing Off the View," referring to a poet overcommitted to the idea of authorial centrality. In spite of this poet's self-mastery, there are indeed things "beyond him still." The rest of the poem proceeds from that mild but basic criticism: there are things even the master does not know about the world beyond him and thus may never know about himself. When this truth-knowing poet is thwarted by a new kind of reality for which he is evidently unprepared—a reality that makes a poet's consciousness incidental, a small part of the worldly whole—he responds by "closing off the view"; when the independence of things contradicts him, he surrounds them with his self-knowledge and so "reality" loses its independent status and becomes merely another aspect of the imagination. Here are three of the poem's seven stanzas:

> He saw them as he wished to see them.
> Whenever there was a world offense
> He effected Closing Off the View,
> Primordial recompense.

> He could not, in other words, pretend
> To a knowledge not himself,
> Dazzled by decades of appearances
> Centered in his senses.

> He willed to paint the world one way;
> When the world intruded
> With lofty peak, or noisome slough,
> He exercised Closing Off the View.

In "Not Ideas about the Thing" Stevens responded to the gift-poem. Compare Eberhart's claim against the poet who closes off the view—"He could not, in other words, pretend / To a knowledge not himself"—to "Not Ideas": "a scrawny cry from outside" only "*Seemed* like a sound in his mind" yet "It *was like* / A new knowledge of reality"—"the most tentative of rejoicings" but a rejoicing still.[72] The poetic habit of "Closing Off the View," a strategy for dodging "a world offense," was not unlike Stevens's own tropes for holding off the stressful public world of the arts—for instance, "The blinds are down" (a figure made for Tate).[73] Eberhart's attempt to identify the psychosocial basis of Stevens's aesthetic may have struck the latter somewhat as did various recent theses, some published and all gossiped, explaining his personal reticence; a published one was O'Connor's biographical chapter on the "Legend" of Stevens as the friendless, aloof executive in his "Hartford fortress."[74] ("The only part of it that was difficult for me was the first chapter," Stevens wrote O'Connor about his book. "[W]e shall just have to forget about the legend" [L 677].) The difference between Eberhart's effort to measure the proximity of the personality to the poetry and efforts like O'Connor's was that Eberhart had obviously read this pattern of repression in the verse itself, not in "the businessman's life," and, more important, was now responding to Stevens *in kind*. (O'Connor's unpublished papers reveal, incidentally, that his "Legend" chapter was added only at the insistence of antiformalist readers' reports at Henry Regnery.)[75] Eberhart, as he explained to Peter Brazeau, would not write "a poem against Stevens" (*WSR* 150); their personal relations were exceptionally good and their poetic sensibilities were basically congenial, a point Stevens made without prodding.[76] Indeed, Eberhart's idea that Stevens closed off the view when confronted by a challenge to his sense of reality had all along constituted not so much specifically a personal as generally a political reproach, even though it only seemed to have been such a thing with hindsight sharpened by the expiration of McCarthy, the activist sixties, and Watergate: "[I]t seems to me poetry has to be vitally associated with the commonweal," Eberhart told Brazeau in 1976, "with what people do and with what goes on in the world" (*WSR* 150). The reasonable implication here was that he had not been in a position to make such a criticism fully evident in the fifties. In part, however, he was underestimating his original insight, for in a review of *The Necessary Angel*, in 1952, Eberhart had worried that Stevens too readily abandoned his effort to "realiz[e] the violence of our times" and observed that even when Stevens devalued the poet's social responsibility he still claimed to " 'help people to live their lives' " (quoting *NA* 29). If he is to "help" in this way, "He can hardly have his poet without sociological or political obligation." While there was nothing wrong, Eberhart wrote, with Stevens "as exquisite abstracter of and coper with violent reality," he found disconcerting the "evasive" or "recalcitrant" way in which Stevens "abstracts, after all, the sociological and the political considerations from the view."[77] It was but another short step, then, from this 1952 review to the October 1953 poem, handed to Stevens personally, making just that charge: he closed off the view. Stevens would reply in a hail of subsequent letters and then finally, in "Not Ideas," in verse.

Eberhart followed his visit with a letter written two days later (October 21) in which he thanked Stevens for delivering "Farewell without a Guitar" and enclosed a typewritten version of a third poem of his own, "Formative Mastership." Though that poem assumes the same general position on mastery as "Closing Off the View," it puts the point positively; it might have belatedly occurred to Eberhart as a more appropriate homage than "Closing Off the View." "Great nature is our master," it asserts; individuals "cannot unmake the world." When the poet's meanings "prick" a world exterior to him, and enable him to gain a knowledge of a reality excluding the imagination, it becomes a kind of "mating time" for poetic words and worldly meaning.[78]

A response to Eberhart's poetic ideas came just a week later. Stevens decided that in arguing against the will of the poet in "Closing Off the View" Eberhart had sided with Herbert Read, whose essay on "Originality" had just appeared in "the current number" of the *Sewanee Review*. Read's article "describes the point of view stated by you in Closing Off the View," Stevens wrote: "It is not the will of the poet that counts." "I have never been quite sure about Herbert Read," he went on. "Apparently he is a tremendous reader rather than a tremendous scholar. He seems to have all the synthesis of a reader and not of an individual self. But the paper to which I have referred is well done."[79]

Stevens's shrewd use of Read's essay as a means of interpreting Eberhart's poetic homages did not, however, really address Eberhart's main charge. Stevens understood the theoretical "point of view," contending, in Read's words, that there was no "reason for crediting the artist with the creation of a work of art he spontaneously delivers."[80] He was right to think that Read's essay summarized for Eberhart a formalist's tenet. But several other main points in Read's essay modified the author-decentered argument of "Closing Off the View," and these were evidently the points that particularly attracted Stevens. Read did not abandon the genius theory of creation (his example, not surprisingly, was Shakespeare)[81] so much as he attacked "*influential* verse" (Eliot's in particular), poetry that played morally, socially, and politically to the tenor of the *Zeitgeist*, speaking in a "particular idiom" passed off as "personal" and having pretensions to universalizing poetic discourse of an age while merely reflecting the language of faddists.[82] This distinction would not refute but indeed sustain Eberhart's desire to resist Stevens's poetic influence even in the act of writing poems to and for him.

Read's other thesis in the essay was that great artists are not people of great ideas, an issue Stevens and Tate had thrashed out ten years earlier. Art results, Read contended, from the extrapersonal localization of ideas into "some concrete and factual material."[83] Paul Cézanne, he argued, was neither a humanist nor a Christian. "An *idea* hardly ever entered his head (except those he got from the newspapers)." And: "I would suggest that this is true of all great artists."[84]

Eberhart next sent Stevens a signed copy of his new book, *Undercliff*, conjuring in the inscription "joyful Canoe Club memories / 11/53."[85] Stevens wrote Eberhart twice about his reaction to the book, once to announce its arrival (*L* 802) and again, on December 7, with qualified praise (*L* 803). The second letter was extremely polite; yet it cleverly advanced the argument already underway. After pronouncing himself struck by the pure "sincerity" of *Undercliff*, Stevens suggested that he and Eberhart fundamentally agreed that their ideas had some value in their own right; this much, he noted, could not be said of much generally accepted poetry, like

Williams's, in which substance was relatively unimportant and the poem made its primary impact formally "as a structure of little blocks." Cannily, Stevens now paired himself and Eberhart as poets of ideas and substance remaining calm during a new formalist rage. Quite aside from the misreading of Williams, there was an obvious problem with this latest strategy, for Stevens had once again ingeniously closed off the view: not a month earlier the two had fundamentally disagreed about the poetic will.

By January 15, 1954, they had evidently been in touch again, perhaps by telephone, for on that date Stevens wrote to "sympathize with your denial of any influence on my part." Picking up several points Read had made in his attack on Eliot, Stevens explained that he too wrestled with the problem of influence and that his own solution was to avoid reading "highly mannered people like Eliot and Pound so that I should not absorb anything, even unconsciously" (*L* 813). Five days later he felt he had not explained himself clearly enough. "Why do poets in particular," he now plainly asked, "resent the attribution of the influence of other poets?" The point of this new note was to apologize for seeming in the previous letter to have claimed personal influence on Eberhart, or "for that matter, on anyone else." Yet he concluded by restating the argument he had once devised to counter Tate—and now notwithstanding Read—that "[t]he good writers are the good thinkers" (*L* 815). The enigma of his own representativeness, exacerbated by this four-month-old discussion on influence, mastery, and will, really agitated him at this point; he wrote Eberhart yet again on January 25 to say that he "ran across" still two more clippings "that may interest you in connection with the subject of influences," and he enclosed them.[86]

To these latest bits of evidence that good poets are good thinkers, Eberhart immediately responded. Here was an enclosure of his own, he wrote, "[b]earing on our discussion": a "perceptive full Catholic report of my work" in a review of *Undercliff* in *Commonweal* by Gerald Weales, who paired Stevens and Eberhart as "tightly intellectual," comparable poets of ideas. "At his best, like Stevens," Weales observed, "Eberhart gives poetic flesh to the processes of thought." Unfortunately there were occasions in Eberhart's Stevensean poems when "the workings of the mind banish the poet's vision"—the old complaint against Stevens (it was Tate's in particular).[87] Mailing the Weales clipping perhaps constituted Eberhart's admission that Stevens *had* been right after all to match them against, say, Williams. Still, Eberhart challenged Stevens's expression of the outmoded critical axiom that one may prefer ideas in the poem to the texture of the poem itself and the intuition that gave rise to it: "You say the best poets are the best thinkers or vice versa. *This is an old notion*, seems to leave out the whole world of the intensity of the feelings.... Shakespeare [Tate's and Read's example] is a better feeler than he is a thinker" (emphasis added).[88]

What more masterful way could there have been for Stevens to respond once and for all to the related issues of externality and poetic ideas—issues once raised by Tate via Raymond Mortimer and now by Eberhart via Read—than in the very idea of "Not Ideas"? Stevens's new poem offered itself as a final word on the "discussion," replying succinctly to the two related arguments—that the master did not know about himself that a new knowledge lay outside him (in "Closing Off the View") and that he could not hear outer sounds (in "Formative Mastership," ll. 2–3). What, then, constituted the originality of this extrinsic cry? "Not Ideas" posed just that question, though unpretentiously. Even such a minimal recognition, such a limited venture outward, credited the real. In other words, there was indeed something new under the sun of a poem designating things beyond the imagination. The idea echoed the opening line of the essay that had done most to stir the controversy, in which Read summarized his quarrel with the conventional theory of influence by expressing doubts about the old aesthetic adage "There is nothing new under the sun."[89] What was "new" under the bleak six-o'clock sun of March 1954 was a knowledge of reality finally answering the accusation that the great private poet had closed himself off from the world. In reasserting a rhetoric of reality, "Not Ideas" took into full account both Eberhart's complaint against the repressions of the poet seized as the advocate of the imagination, and Tucker's colleagues' conventional desire for more of the same famous Stevens, to bring him to the point in April and May of 1954 where he was prepared to respond as a poet of externalities at Columbia.

As he was savoring the "rich chocolate cake" of the all-Stevens *Trinity Review* in May—which included, along with Eberhart's two verse homages and "Not Ideas," prose tributes by Norman Pearson and the chair of Mount Holyoke's French department, who hailed the great poet-statesman of the 1943 *entretiens*—Stevens finished composing his Columbia bicentennial poem. Tied to the broad theme of knowledge, rights, and freedom, and "coupled with birthdays and commencements," "The Sail of Ulysses" "becomes a force of intolerable generalities," as Stevens himself admitted just three days after delivering it (*L* 834). He declined proposals from Babette Deutsch and Horace Taylor, the Columbia economist, to have it published, telling Deutsch that he would not use it "in its present form, nor allow anyone to see a copy of it" (*L* 835). Adam Pryce-Jones's June 3 request from the *Times Literary Supplement* Stevens deferred for most of the summer, finally sending a drastically cut version of the bicentennial poem on August 17.[90] Until 1957 it was in print only in this radically reduced form.[91]

Stevens presumed that Deutsch had herself experienced similar difficulties in writing public verse. He wanted to believe after the fact that his generalizations had been the inevitable result of limitations inherent to the celebratory occasion. His effort to broaden the theme to the point of ostensible abstraction perhaps followed from the qualm he had expressed in 1952 to Barbara Church—a concern that the significance of poems referring to specific political events would inevitably be lost when the collective public memory of the event was lost (*L* 760). In fact, as we have seen, Professor Taylor at Columbia, very much like Professor Tucker at Massachusetts, had not wanted freedom to constrain; in describing the arrangement afterward for Deutsch, Stevens somewhat exaggerated the restrictions. Deutsch sensed this and replied that she was "astonished" by "[w]hat you said about its having been written 'on an assigned theme.' " "[W]hen I was asked to be P.B.K. poet at Columbia," she wrote, "I was left quite free as to the theme of the poem." Nevertheless, that was "years ago"; times had changed greatly, and she too saw the irony in any poetic encumbrance incited by freedom: "[I]n view of the stress on 'man's right to knowledge and the free use thereof,' " she wrote, "it seems as if a poet should be left quite literally to his own devices."[92] The result of Stevens's somewhat willful confusion of freedom and occasional verse was a poem that, while seeming to him a failure in retrospect, succeeded in making him an integral part of an event peopled by the biggest political celebrities of the day (Dwight Eisenhower himself would speak a few hours after Stevens delivered his poem). Like "Description without Place," the Columbia poem bears few obvious markings of such an urge for representation; and yet, again like the earlier postwar poem, the urge was nonetheless great.

Thinking back on how he had gotten into this difficulty, Stevens recited for Deutsch the history of the arrangement. He had complained to Taylor that writing on the bicentennial theme "would create a difficulty," and the economist's response had been, as it was summarized for Deutsch, that "it would be all right if I would use some of the words" in the topic. What he did not say to Deutsch was that his attempt to use "*some* of the words" and to deal with "*one* aspect of the birthday theme" had not been nearly so casual. In point of fact he aimed so strategically at topicality, at incorporating the words in the thematic phrase and meeting the demands of the public genre, that that and nothing else was why the result seemed later, even to him, a perfect "confusion." His Columbia poem was indeed so energetically the cry *for* if not *of* its occasion that to understand why is precisely, I think, to learn something about Stevens's final *positive* attitude toward poetry "of the commonweal," to use Eberhart's later phrase describing an interest Stevens seemed then to lack but did not. Such a talent was again hidden by his embarrassed reactions to the civic moment; if he could come to believe he had been pushed in the direction of occasional reference, he could decide that he had responded with deliberate abstraction and could justify the poem's "confusion"—again, his word (*L* 835)—as generically inherent. "I *deliberately* wrote an abstract poem," he wrote Taylor ten days after the reading (emphasis added).[93]

How, then, did Stevens actually reckon with Taylor's assertion that the bicentennial committee had not necessarily meant to "invite you to deal with a subject as broad as the theme itself, but" that the economist and others did have "in mind a possible poem pertaining to 'man,' 'right,' 'knowledge,' 'free,' 'use' or any combination or permutation thereof"? Stevens answered literally with a permutation of those words. After having used *any* form of the noun "right" just four times in the previous forty years of poetry, and only once (*OP* 107) in the sense indicated by the bicentennial theme, he uses the word fourteen times in this one poem. "Knowledge" appears six times, "knowing" three, "know" ten, "known" four. And "free" or "freedom" four times. Indeed the concept of knowing is so strongly appropriative here that the phrase "A life beyond this present *grieving*," in the fifth and strongest section, could be revised, at a very late stage in the process of composition, to read: "A life beyond this present *knowing*."[94] Knowing was operative: to the extent that Stevens's willingness to refer to the history of Columbia University is traceable—quite aside from a crowd-pleasing line about "Eden conceived on Morningside"—it is revealed in his use of the phrase "the right to know."

"The right to know," it must be clear, was a term of overwhelming significance at precisely this moment, both nationally and at Columbia; in almost all bicentennial events the phrase referred more to responsibilities than indeed to rights. In the spring of 1954, "the right to know" was quite distinct from "the right to be," Stevens's other key phrase. The prologue of the poem establishes "the right to be" as an individual right: the right of the individual to be free to live, work, associate with others, and take aesthetic pleasure—to *be*, in short—as he or she wishes. Stevens's Ulysses, while a "Symbol of the seeker," assumes knowing in order to express concern about being; he annunciates this preference with the sort of insistence of one whose right to be is in question: "*He said, 'As I know, I am and have / The right to be'* " (*OP* 126). "The right to know," on the other hand, was then understood as a majoritarian's "right" of active national (or governmental) knowing. Because the Roy Cohn–David Shine disclosures were bringing Joseph McCarthy's incessant claim of the congressional right to know back to the front pages just then (April and May of 1954), the two rights tended in politically opposite directions, one toward the Bill of Rights, the other toward a broadly defined right of the state (via its obligation to defend democracy under threat). In late May, as Stevens prepared to read at Columbia, McCarthy confused the issue a good deal in his effort to prevent the release of transcribed phone conversations between himself and the army that had been monitored by an army clerk; McCarthy's supporters, suddenly sensitive about privacy, claimed that the "right to know" had violated McCarthy's individual rights.[95] In a twist no stranger, McCarthy went on the stump to announce that his aides, Cohn and Shine, had been "denied the right to know who the[ir accusers] are."[96]

The heated debate about "the right to know," the terms of which were largely set by McCarthy and his adherents, had preoccupied Columbia for months before Wallace Stevens arrived on the scene; the right to be and the right to know seemed sadly irreconcilable in ways the Columbia audience would have understood perfectly after a winter and spring of national events—the army-McCarthy hearings and a new wave of academic dismissals—had created the context for widely publicized bicentennial events that made the paradox distinct. When Stevens decided it would be one of the tasks of his poem to attempt at least a provisional reconciliation of contending concepts of rights, he was advancing a position in an important public argument—an argument he had doubtless been hearing.[97]

Grayson Kirk, Eisenhower's successor as Columbia's president, was perhaps the most prominent figure among those who hoped the bicentennial theme would support civil liberties unambiguously—to oppose, not endorse, the atmosphere of McCarthyism and to assert an unqualified right to be. "A university that fears to espouse a sound but unpopular view is not a true university at all," Kirk announced;[98] for him the theme phrase restated the First Amendment. "This is the ideal of full freedom of scholarly inquiry and expression," he said, "the right of mankind to knowledge and the free use thereof."[99] Kirk's and others' liberal intentions promoted a share of bicentennial events that stressed the mutual dependence of knowledge and individuality[100]—much as Stevens's Ulysses uses knowing at first to propound being ("*As I know, I am and have / The right to be*").

Yet the right to know was preeminent, never more strongly contended than at bicentennial events and by their organizers; and this connotation of the theme received far greater attention. Arthur Hays Sulzberger, president and publisher of the *New York Times* and overall chairman of the bicentennial, made it clear in his interpretation of the theme that "knowledge" was to be equated with "freedom" only insofar as freedom meant "[r]eal security, which [in turn] means the perpetuation of *our kind of* democracy" (emphasis added). "Freedom" was by no means individual freedom for all: "There may be some who are unfit to be trusted with the privilege of academic freedom. They should be eliminated by faculty . . . and not . . . by any group that would destroy the milieu of academic freedom"—a concept Sulzberger evidently did not feel compromised that milieu.[101] The regular *Bicentennial Clipsheet*, offering "Suggested Editorials" for newspapers willing to promote bicentennial events, defined "The 'Right' to Know": there are individual rights, it proclaimed, "[b]ut 'rights' also involve responsibilities," and this was "the real point of Columbia's bicentennial theme."[102] "Knowledge," then, was always to be associated with responsibility; it checked "freedom." In order to preserve the right to be, Sulzberger felt, one must feel the responsibility to know that "[t]he present adversary—communism—is ruthless and we cannot leave the ramparts unguarded for a single moment."[103] Freedom in this sense meant more the recognition of a responsibility to learn about the American version of freedom than the freedom to choose what to learn. "The right to knowledge . . . constitute[s] major responsibilities which each claimant to freedom must respect," namely security of the nation and protection against foreign threat.[104] For Eisenhower himself, in the keynote speech that took the Columbia theme as its own, "the right to know" signified not only the freedom of inquiry but vigilance against subversion from within: "[R]emembering that America includes also the protection of every American in his American rights, . . . [l]et us provide any additional laws or machinery necessary to protect America."[105]

"Knowing" thus meant knowing the triumphant truth of the American form of government. Coming to learn about American freedom implicated every knower, young and old, in a desperate, even armed, struggle. An issue of the *Bicentennial Clipsheet*, under a photo of a grade-school student studying American civics and thus "armed with knowledge," in Eisenhower's phrase, against what the president also described as the communists' "relentless and highly organized world campaign of deceit,"[106] reiterated Columbia's " 'Right to Know' Drive" with this caption: "Never need we fear the destruction of our liberties if our youth knows and understands that on the preservation of 'Man's Right to Knowledge and the Free Use Thereof' rests the survival of democracy" (see illustration). In Stevens's effort to reconcile being with knowing at Columbia—the right to be stands unabridged in the prologue but is increasingly offset as the poem goes on—he added to the equation a "democratic" sense of freedom that would have served well as a caption for the photo of the earnestly loyal student: "In the generations of thought, man's sons / And heirs are powers of the mind, / His only testament and estate. / He has nothing but the truth to leave. / How then shall the mind be less than free / Since only to know is to be free?" (*OP* 129). His right to be having been thoroughly constrained by the right to know (as by the progenitors' legacy of the truth), this "heir" himself becomes a figurative American Ulysses sailing after knowledge that may be discovered without leaving home, at "Eden conceived on Morningside, / The center of the self, the self / Of the future" (*OP* 127)—that is, at Columbia, where American traditions are secure. There being may be suitably balanced by knowing, and the young "heir" can teach himself to be not only the master "of himself" but "Master of the world" (*OP* 128). The problem engendered by such mastery is evident from the poem as well as from the bicentennial's programmatic sense of the knowledge the grade-schooler needs. Only section i gives a hint of the problem: when "knowledge" is considered "the only life"—"The only access to true ease, / The deep comfort of the world and fate"—then such knowledge is based on a limitation not apparent to the knowledgeable. "[I]f one's sense of a *single*

A pupil does his lesson in front of one of the panels in Columbia University's bicentennial exhibit "Man's Right to Knowledge and the Free Use Thereof." The quotation from the *Indiana Law Journal* reads: "Just as secrecy and democracy are incompatible, so totalitarianism and an informed public cannot coexist."

spot / Is what one knows of the universe" (*OP* 126), in other words, how far will the world extend when this knower is indeed "Master of the world"?

In the end "The Sail of Ulysses" proposed, somewhat as the president of the United States did a few hours later, that the right to know and the right to be could be understood as one. But for Stevens, unlike Eisenhower, who simply reasserted contradictory political axioms as if they were not discrepant in American social practice, the alignment of opposites was never intended to force a theoretical congruity. The poet's strategy could remain dependent on and yet be set to defuse the charged atmosphere and operative connotations of the moment. Thus the evident "confusions" encumbering his idea as to what then constituted knowledge of the world, American forms of truth-seeking: "abstractions" of the sort that could still cause him to slip into the predicament of "description without place." Yet the "abstractions" incited in Stevens's verse by the situation at Columbia are untenable only when read rhetorically as if they were part of a casual mid-to-late-Stevens improvisation; this is surely a plausible approach to several flat spots in the poem when the speaker loses the energy I have attributed to the effort of affirming a "right to be" as a defining form of a "right to know." Moreover, the poet as a figurative Ulysses ceaselessly sailing after knowledge is neither new nor remarkable. What does make the effort remarkable, I think, is that the context driving the knowing-being equation as a public matter produced in Steven's verse an answer to a cultural question that needed no asking at the moment of delivery. Insofar as the poem's venturer realized how sailing after knowledge *was* a ceaseless search for political direction, a journey's last leg made hazardous by the "litter of truths" bobbing about him, he began to know how a convergence of claims to rights could possibly occur. Liberation, he tentatively posits, would come only as the result of accepted limitations; sections ii through iv of Ulysses' speech mark three such courses: section ii attempts to accommodate loneliness with a sense of *inner* direction; section iii returns to the outmoded image of a fiction-maker's *self*-illumination (much in the manner of the earlier poem, "Phosphor Reading by His Own Light"); and in section iv Ulysses proposes a deliverance from constraining myths.

Section v then returns to the issue of rights. Following from the equation that seemed forced in section i after the prologue, in v "the right to know / And the right to be are one." Ulysses proposes a heaven vaguely political, in which the deep oppositions of individual privacy and collective knowing are permanently resolved, when "the right / To know [is finally] established as the right to be." At the cessation of all the politically symbolic chatter—the sort of language that set these ideas against each other at a time when conservatives' right to know and liberals' right to be were locked in what truly seemed a death grip—"the litter of truths" becomes desymbolized while good unreductive sense and common understanding return at last. This and nothing else is what

> sustains
> The eloquence of right, since knowing
> And being are one: the right to know
> And the right to be are one. We come
> To knowledge when we come to life.

Yet always there is another life,
A life beyond this present knowing,

. . . .

Not to be reached but to be known,

. . . .

The great Omnium descends on us
As a free race. We know it, one
By one, in the right of all. Each man
Is an approach to the vigilance
In which the litter of truths becomes
A whole, [with]

. . . .
                    . . . the right
To know established as the right to be.

(OP 128)

It is easy to see why Stevens's critics do not agree about this poem; Lucy Beckett cannot herself decide if it is bad because it is "certainly somewhat stiff and *public*" or if it fits neatly with similar epistemological meditations and should be designated Stevens's "final *soliloquy*" (emphasis added).[107] Beckett is right in implying that to learn the poem's handling of private and public issues one must know something of the relation between Ulysses' extended soliloquizing and the public bearing of the poet-speaker outside the frame.[108] The problem of the poem's reputation began with Stevens himself and was merely sustained by assessments like Beckett's; yet in the great effort Stevens actually made to situate his poem in an important public dialogue, he was coming to terms with an argument moderates like Kirk at Columbia were anticipating: he and they made passionate assertions of rights that were first antagonized by responsibilities and *only then* attuned to them. This effort served well to add to "Not Ideas" another rejoinder to the "Bethou me" canto, for here, to turn Bloom's terms, poetry *can* "be transformed into the living dialogue . . . that exists between humans." Stevens's immediate decision to slaughter the poem—to cut 152 lines out of 176 for the *TLS* version that summer—does not at all mean, *contra* Beckett, that "it is an occasional poem *on an unpromising subject*." In fact, issues of knowledge and freedom, mutually abridged rights, were just then so utterly promising as subjects for public oration that, if anything, Stevens was disappointed that he could not meet the matter's great potential *and* offer a poem to be deemed Stevensean.

As Stevens was discovering the poetic problems that arose when he engaged in the latest dialogue between contentions right and left, and when he comprehended them as such, his critics were realizing that the end of ideological difference meant an opportunity for his poems to receive a reading they could not have gotten during the contentious eras that had passed. Looking back from 1960, and clearly in a mood of decade-naming, Willard Thorp was able to observe that Stevens in the fifties "had a following among the young which can only be compared to the Eliot cult of the 1920's." (Thorp drew a clear line through 1950, dividing the "poet's and critic's poet" from the poet of wider cultural appeal.)[109] Several such efforts to canonize Stevens, undertaken in the early fifties, had everything to do with the critical revision Thorp would later describe as a matter of fact, most notably among them Randall Jarrell's "Reflections on Wallace Stevens" of 1951, where it was strongly implied that Stevens was a disengaged poet whose time had come. The year 1951 was, in other words, the perfect time for Stevens's poems to be *criticized* as "lack[ing] . . . immediate contact with lives," as tending always to "abstract" and "philosophize," as keeping readers "thinking that he needs to be possessed by subjects," *and yet at the same time* for Stevens to be named "one of the great poets of our century" and for the claim to be made that "[h]is best poems are the poetry of a man *fully human.*"[110] "Fully human" and yet "lacking an immediate contact with lives"? How could a single essay contain these opposites? Jarrell's terrifically ambiguous judgment, published in the *Partisan Review* just at the height of its deradicalization,[111] was possible only because the era he so adeptly characterized was one in which the late-modern avant-garde excoriated realism while insisting on retaining a commitment to social realities; the implication was that reality in the old sense only dragged one into others' fights no longer worth fighting. The old real having been defeated, one turned, then, with a sense and tone of coming finally home, to the poet of an "accustomed mastery" that now especially suited an age, to the poet who (it seemed) had all along confined his talk of reality to abstractions.[112] Despite his criticism, then, Jarrell genuinely admired Stevens for his synthesis of a world-weary sensibility fashionable among end-of-ideology ideologues, and for the aesthetic contemporaneousness that was expected of the postwar artist in the know (I have emphasized words and phrases lending themselves to the tone of exhaustion or supermature dispassion):

> As one feels the elevation and sweep and *disinterestedness,* the *thoughtful truthfulness* of the best sections of a poem like "Esthétique du Mal," one is grateful for, *overawed* by, this poetry *that knows so well the size and age of the world*: that reminds us, as we sit in chairs procured from the furniture exhibitions of the Museum of Modern Art, of that *immemorial order and disorder* upon which our present scheme of things is a *monomolecular film.* . . . Many of the poems look *grayly* out at "the *immense detritus of a world / That is completely waste, that moves from waste / To waste, out of the hopeless waste of the past / Into a hopeful waste to come.*"[113]

Hope and confidence (even "glory," Jarrell went on to say)[114] would emerge only as they superseded a sense of the "hopeless waste of the past." Jarrell did not have to state that he meant the failure of the *less* disinterested, *less* "thoughtful truthfulness" of those in previous years—the thirties—who had dared to think of order and disorder not as cyclical and immemorial but as answerable, who had dared to look at the future not as built upon "waste" but as a reason for the clean break. Jarrell, again, did not *say* that Stevens captured the sense of exhaustion with which thirties political idealism was deemed a dereliction—as a more energetic canonizer, William Van O'Connor, would say explicitly. Nor did Richard Wilbur, whose first book, *The Beautiful Changes*, James Breslin has helpfully put with "The New Rear Guard" of poets influenced both by New Critical formalism and by the end-of-ideologists,[115] say outright that Stevens's ascendancy was to be linked to the rejection of radical verse: "But," Wilbur wrote when reviewing O'Connor's *The Shaping Spirit*—the appearance of which, coupled with the Bollingen award, he took to indicate a final, deserved ascent—"we should expect from poetry not so much answers as *savors* and realizations: the *taste* of the world, a *sense* of our predicament" (emphasis added).[116] Jarrell, for his part, made obvious his longing for the Stevens prior to the thirties in such a way as to suggest that an open admiration for America had been lost forever afterward, now that writers had to reconcile with the United States after having reveled in alienation from it.[117] Stevens, however, had never reveled and so now was being celebrated for his maturity. "In *Harmonium*," Jarrell observed, "he still loves America best when he can think of it as wilderness, naturalness, pure potentiality." The Stevens of the twenties, reinvented by the fifties' disavowal of the thirties,[118] was to Jarrell in essence an allegiant poet whose work exemplified America's range and diversity, even including a noble concern for its minorities: by this logic Jarrell could claim retrospectively that *Harmonium* "treats with especial sympathy, Negroes [and] Mexican Indians."[119] Yet can poems like "The Cuban Doctor" (1921) really be said to be even sentimentally sympathetic to the figure of the Indian? He is undeniably a stale old type there, stalking, attacking, intruding dramatically but powerlessly on the imagination seeking to contain him: "The Indian struck and disappeared. / I knew my enemy was near" (*CP* 65).[120] But Jarrell was not stopping to consider the precise validity of his judgment at such a small example as this. He was busy establishing a critical commonplace, directly (and not incidentally) following Tate's earlier judgment: one wished, as Tate did in 1940, but now in 1951 for reasons much less straightforward, that Stevens had never passed through the era of social pressure. The fifties' *Harmonium* would be a book "one remembers longingly,"[121] exactly as the fifties yearned for a half-invented prepolitical twenties—being certain, in short, to bypass what Bell in *The End of Ideology* called "The Loss of

Innocence in the Thirties."[122] Hard as Tate had tried in wartime to bring Stevens and his poetry in line with New Critical thinking, that effort to circumvent *Stevens's* thirties had been premature; but Jarrell's Stevens could embody what Bell meant when he described for Sidney Hook, James Farrell, Richard Wright, Max Lerner, Lionel Trilling, and Edmund Wilson a common descent from "intense, hor[t]atory, naive, simplistic, and passionate" rhetoric (the thirties) to writing at the end of ideology (the fifties): "disenchanted and reflective[,] . . . from *them* and *their* experiences [*not* Tate's and Ransom's] we have inherited the key terms which dominate discourse today: irony, paradox, ambiguity and complexity" (emphasis added).[123]

William Van O'Connor, suffering a more intense dislike of the Red Decade than Jarrell, had even less trouble seeing a Stevens moving with the current of the new deradicalized era. Though O'Connor's case for Stevens, with Elizabeth Green's, Peter Viereck's, and several others', was more openly political than Jarrell's, the effect was basically the same: in this postideological moment, Stevens could only now be read all the way through, in Green's words, as "reject[ing] the ideology of Communists"[124] or, in O'Connor's words, as "ridiculing the pretentiousness of those who have set up the false antitheses."[125] As ideology itself disbanded, it was said, political options and oppositions collapsed, as Bell observed, into "complexity"; and "comity" and "civility" were qualities ascendant.[126] O'Connor presented Stevens's "complexity" and "difficulty" as identically the reason he had been attacked by the left in the thirties *and* the reason he was to be celebrated and intellectually befriended in the late forties and fifties.[127] In Stevens we were to see that "the ground of argument is no longer 'between Reason and Imagination . . . but between integration of thought and feeling and their dissociation.' "[128] Note how, by this logic, a semblance of opposition is maintained even while opposition itself becomes one side of a new opposition denying oppositions: the contention between Reason on one side and Imagination on the other has given way to "integration" (good) on the one side and "dissociation" itself (bad) on the other; that is, opposition has been reduced to the status of one term in a disagreement that was resisted only by resisting disagreement itself. The assumption of an irresistible consensus helped revise the possibility of Stevens's engagement with world crises for the sake of the later period. O'Connor saw in "Owl's Clover" especially how Stevens had recognized early what most intellectuals discovered only later—that the ideological oppositions insisted upon by prewar and wartime radical antifascists were part of an effort to reject any reconciliation but the total, cataclysmic one.

In an essay that would become a chapter in the very first book-length treatment of Stevens, *The Shaping Spirit* of 1950, O'Connor read "Owl's Clover" as repudiating the agonistic discourse of the left. It was but a short step from that point to a reading of Stevens through a series of anticommunist poems. Taking up "Forces, the Will & the Weather" (1939), O'Connor merely quoted two lines out of context: "There was not an idea / This side of Moscow." Of "A Dish of Peaches in Russia" he decided that Stevens was attacking "the unnaturalness of attempting to give one's allegiance to an abstract system." The image of Lenin on a bench in "Description without Place" supported the idea (from "Botanist on Alp," ten years earlier) that "Marx has ruined Nature"—even though, as we have seen, the effect is just the reverse: nature has ruined Lenin. O'Connor read the line "The Future must bear within it every past," from the fourth poem in "Owl's Clover," as thoroughly ironic, confirming the critic's sense of Stevens's notion that "[t]he 'envoi to the past' was certainly one of the most preposterous planks in the political platform that foretold the brave new world. Even now, some years after its break with the 'bourgeois past' the Soviet is rediscovering that certain institutions are human rather than bourgeois."[129] And to certify the point, O'Connor footnoted Alexander Werth's discussion of "Marriage in Russia," marriage being one of those human institutions whose survival in the Soviet Union refuted materialist predictions.[130] In a review of *The Necessary Angel* published at the end of 1951, O'Connor clearly defined the fifties' thirties and implied that new appreciations of Stevens were finally catching up to a tendency that was always there to be discovered in the work. Where fifteen years earlier Stevens's stress on the imagination had been deemed an escape, it was now to be hailed as heroic; O'Connor's review is titled "He *Dared* to Speak for the Imagination":

> Wallace Stevens has moved against the intellectual currents of his time to produce his poetry. That more recently the currents have tended to shift, so that to some extent he now is moving with them, in no way lessens his achievement. In a world that has had its chief pride in objectivity, documentary realism, statistics, and unadorned facts, he dared to speak for the virtues of the imagination. . . . It is a useful, if slightly over-extended generalization to say that American intellectual life in the Nineteen Twenties and Nineteen Thirties gave itself too wholeheartedly to the kind of fact worship, practicality and rationalism that the nineteenth century in England had witnessed with Macaulay, Bentham, Huxley and Spencer. And a very considerable part of American fiction, poetry and criticism moved in its wake.[131]

O'Connor generally associated with the New Critics;[132] the readings of poems in *The Shaping Spirit* have that odd mix of cold-war values and devotion to New Critical complexity then characteristic of literary end-of-ideologists (the intellectual and methodological convergence Bell savored).[133] Peter Viereck, on the other hand, standing unambiguously to the right of this ever-inclusive center, was known by all as "an advocate of a return to conservatism," in the phrase effectively used by the Massachusetts group. Yet Viereck's version of the fifties' thirties only added to the burgeoning critical consensus. The author of *Conservatism Revisited* (1949), with its bold subtitle, *The Revolt against Revolt*, found that readers of Steven's post-*Harmonium* work had "attached too much significance to what critics would call his 'increasing concern with social problems.' " This observation was followed by the usual postideological turn of the screw: "Never is Stevens deeper in dreamland and more detached from material realities than when, as a would-be concession to 'reality,' he refers to economics"—never less real, in other words, than when he commits himself to the real. The " 'true' Stevens," Viereck insisted, "is still the sentimental and unsocial one."[134] Thus, for both Viereck on the anticommunist right[135] and O'Connor in the anticommunist center,[136] Stevens could be mined for arguments refuting a political position (on the left) that had conspired in the thirties to misread Stevens as an ally. At the same time, both Viereck and O'Connor plainly asserted that Stevens's poetry *must not be read politically*: after compiling a poem-by-poem case for Stevens's anticommunism, O'Connor observed: "These poems, fairly numerous though they are, should not be taken to indicate that Stevens believes, as do some of his contemporaries, that politics must play a necessary part in the role of the poet."[137] And after making the astonishing claim that "Owl's Clover" was "one of the most successful long poems in our half century"—not because of but in spite of Stanley Burnshaw, the *New Masses*, and literary radicalism—O'Connor observed: "That Stevens succeeded in releasing [the poem] not merely from such connections *but even from the political decade itself* is clearly evident now" (emphasis added).[138]

As Stevens's most appreciative critics in the five or six years before his death in 1955 could not appreciate a notion that actually went back to 1946—that to him the poet "absorbs the general life: the public life" and that he "never wanted to understand . . . the world . . . more nor needed to like it more" (*OP* 311)—it should hardly surprise us that his final forays out into the American political experience, and generally his readiness to be taken up into "the public life," were left undescribed. "Think of the difference between Stevens and Frost in that regard," Eberhart told Peter Brazeau twenty years later. "Stevens would never have demeaned himself to want to go to a presidential inauguration and read a poem. Now that doesn't mean he was a snob. He had a much more private idea of what art was" (*WSR* 150). After Columbia's bicentennial, where Stevens kept to the letter of the public theme, even at the cost of producing a poem he felt required evisceration, he himself probably would not have challenged Eberhart's idea of privacy as his ideal poetic condition. Yet the view that Stevens's art is therefore best read as private expression is, I have urged, subject to both doubt and modification, just as the fifties deemed it private for reasons admirers and detractors alike then thought kept art from politics but which actually formed an emphatic political criticism. Whatever desire Stevens had for "getting in" publicly as an American poet was a good deal greater than Eberhart realized then, or even in 1976; while Stevens did not, it is true, "woo college presidents, college audiences, or a President of the United States,"[139] he made himself part of an occasion that had Eisenhower, the favorite son and keynote speaker, very much on its collective mind. And he did know enough about becoming a poet engaged in the national dialogue, after all, to say to Norman Pearson, with *his* connections to the powerful insiders, that one had to keep a somewhat low profile—"not to want something"—in order to be called upon for national distinction; such acceptance by denial surely summed up the age. Williams had not kept quiet about his craving for political reform in the thirties, nor about Pound in the forties, and so his appointment to the Library of Congress was jeopardized by McCarthyism in the fifties.

Another public display of Stevens was planned for the autumn of 1954, the poet's last fall. An exhibit was set up at Yale to show the few scraps he had saved from the composition of poems. Pearson, Morse, and others had managed to locate some drafts and typescripts; Stevens even lent them some of his specially bound editions to be put in display cases. He must have felt a bit as if he himself was being sealed, somewhat prematurely, in glass. By the time Eberhart explained why he could not conveniently make the trip to see the Stevens exhibit in New Haven—he was no longer in Storrs—he was already turning the corner away from Stevens, and, concurrently, his ideas about authorship and poetic influence were firmer than they had been the previous winter. On October 19, 1954, exactly a year after their exchange of poems over cocktails, Eberhart wrote to say that he knew Stevens's writing so well that he did not have to "look at your incunabular frettings, your be-all end-all holographs." He had once, he confessed, hoped to "get the smell off" Keats's death mask, as he noted for the seventy-six-year-old Stevens. But now Eberhart too was converting from biographical and historical fallacies. "It was an error of youth. One should read the poems. . . . The hand lifting the cocktail is life, yet insignificant if it did not write the poem. And so on."[140]

Thus even Eberhart, who helped shape Stevens's final thoughts about the role of the eminent American, did not fully feel the strength of Stevens's desire to understand and like the actual world more, not less, than he had before—nor, if one can judge from "Closing Off the View," did he see Stevens advancing toward that final assertion of reality. There was at least one young critic who observed these trends, and his effort to restore a sense of the real to Stevens criticism was then a dissenting strain. In "Wallace Stevens: The Life of the Imagination," an essay that appeared in the

September 1951 issue of *PMLA*, Roy Harvey Pearce saw in Stevens's poetic career not a circling back to imagination but a progression from the imagination to reality. He discovered in the recent poems a reaching out toward "a reality which is not part of th[e] self," and judged the older Stevens to be insisting that "[w]e can believe only in a reality so known."[141] This was certainly a discordant critical voice in the early fifties—contending that the later work was not merely a "triumph" but one that made the earlier poems "literally a 'prologue' " to the new knowledge of reality.[142] Stevens wrote a letter to Pearce soon after "The Life of the Imagination" appeared in *PMLA*, describing the piece as intelligent and sensitive; we know no more of his reaction to the revisionist suggestions there than that the poet undergoing revision read them (*L* 733).

One wonders if Stevens did not take Pearce's terms to heart ("The reward," for Stevens as for James, "is knowledge and individuality—and a measure of freedom"), for these are certainly terms that became central to him during his last American occasions. Pearce's "James" is of course Henry James—an unlikely citation, it would seem, for someone trying energetically to restore a sense of reality to a growing number of critics who were pitching the imagination hard. But Pearce's nascent sense of Stevens's availability to historicism—at least theoretically and methodologically—was supported by what James had written in the preface to *The Golden Bowl*, which was quoted in the *PMLA* piece: "We are condemned . . . if only because the traces, records, connexions, and the very memorials we would fain preserve, are practically impossible to rescue for that purpose from the general mixture. We give them up even when we wouldn't— it is not a question of choice." Still, urged a new sort of Stevens critic through a somewhat new James, suggesting a critical practice then untried for Stevens's hard case, "Our relation to them"—to these "traces"—"is essentially traceable."[143] If Pearce's idea that the poems' rhetoric of reality preserved " 'traces, records, connexions' " of and to an actual world was not itself much of an encouragement to Stevens as he wrote his last poems, it would nonetheless describe him in the end.

Notes

Preface

1. Stevens himself long implied such a reading, though in the most general terms. He once wanted his first book to be called *The Grand Poem: Preliminary Minutiae* (L 237) and later preferred *The Whole of Harmonium* to *The Collected Poems of Wallace Stevens* (L 834).

2. But see Alan Filreis, "Wallace Stevens and the Crisis of Authority," *American Literature* 58 (December 1984): 560–78.

3. Walter Laqueur, *Europe Since Hitler: The Rebirth of Europe*, 2nd ed. (London: Penguin, 1970), p. 212.

4. See Joyce and Gabriel Kolko, *The Limits of Power: The World and the United States Foreign Policy, 1945–54* (New York: Harper and Row, 1972), p. 359; and also Charles L. Mee, Jr., *The Marshall Plan: The Launching of the Pax Americana* (New York: Simon and Schuster, 1984), p. 92.

5. Letter from Stevens to Barbara Church, November 9, 1948 (Huntington, WAS3705).

6. Delmore Schwartz, "The Ultimate Plato with Picasso's Guitar," *Harvard Advocate* 127 (December 1940): 14.

7. William Van O'Connor, "He Dared to Speak for the Imagination," *New York Times Book Review*, December 2, 1951, p. 7.

8. Examples of a clipping and relocating a friend, respectively: letter from Stevens to Leonard C. van Geyzel, January 31, 1940 (Huntington, WAS2479); letter from Stevens to Herbert Pope, October 10, 1940 (WAS1468).

9. See below, pp. 247–48.

1. Playing Checkers under the Maginot Line

1. Letter from van Geyzel to Stevens, March 18, 1945 (Huntington, WAS2457).

2. Basic information about Amiot's military assignment may be gleaned from his 1939 Christmas card (Huntington, WAS376). On the unfortunate station of Le Mans, see Noel Barber, *The Week France Fell* (New York: Stein and Day, 1976), p. 178.

3. See Glen MacLeod, *Wallace Stevens and Company: The "Harmonium" Years, 1913–1923* (Ann Arbor: UMI Research Press, 1983), p. 22.

4. From an interview Glen MacLeod conducted with Rebecca Reyher on April 8, 1980.

5. James K. Lyon, in *Bertolt Brecht's American Cicerone* (Bonn: Bouvier Verlag, Herbert Grundmann, 1978), quotes both of these unpublished letters (pp. 60, 23); they were apparently in the possession of the late Ernst Halberstadt (and not, that is, among the Reyher-Stevens materials at the McKeldin Library, University of Maryland). I am grateful to Professor Lyon and to Faith R. Jackson, Reyher's

daughter, for providing information about Reyher's assistance to Brecht in 1939 and his appeal to Stevens.

6. Their arrival is confirmed in a letter from Fernand Auberjonois to Jean Paulhan, July 11, 1939 (Société Paulhan).

7. Even recently arriving exiles, Church lamented, "have lost immediate contact" (letter to Jean Paulhan, November 11, 1940 [Société Paulhan]).

8. Willard Thorp, interview with author, Princeton, New Jersey, May 7, 1986.

9. Wallace Stevens, "The Situation in American Writing: Seven Questions," *Partisan Review* 4, 4 (Summer 1939): 39–40; his and others' responses were later reprinted in *The Partisan Reader: Ten Years of Partisan Review, 1934–1944*, ed. William Phillips and Phillip Rahv (New York: Dial Press, 1946). Stevens's comment is now available in *OP* 308–10; I have quoted from *OP* 310.

10. Stevens, "The Situation in American Writing," in *The Partisan Reader*, p. 623.

11. Ibid., pp. 598, 617.

12. Joan Givner, *Katherine Anne Porter: A Life* (New York: Simon and Schuster, 1982), pp. 260–61.

13. Stevens, "The Situation in American Writing," p. 613.

14. Ibid., p. 610.

15. Ibid., p. 623.

16. For a characterization of he zigzagging communist line and the response of the noncommunist left, see Alan M. Wald, *The New York Intellectuals: The Rise and Decline of the Anti-Stalinist Left from the 1930s to the 1980s* (Chapel Hill: University of North Carolina Press, 1987), pp. 193–210.

17. Stevens, "The Situation in American Writing," p. 620.

18. Ibid., p. 605.

19. Ibid., p. 601.

20. In the course of writing *The Isolationist Impulse*, Selig Adler investigated the records of a local America First unit and was somewhat surprised to find how many of its members were not conservatives; they included unionists, pacifists, and veterans of the Great War, as well as members of the antifascist Women's International League for Peace and Freedom (*The Isolationist Impulse in Twentieth Century Reaction* [London: Abelard-Schuman, 1957], pp. 300–301).

21. See, for instance, various quotations offered by James T. Patterson in *Mr. Republican: A Biography of Robert A. Taft* (Boston: Houghton Mifflin, 1972), pp. 240, 242–50.

22. Klaus Mann, *The Turning Point* (New York: L. B. Fischer, 1942), p. 295.

23. In the interviews Brazeau gathered in his book under the heading "At the Hartford" (*WSR* 3–93), and in many hours of unexcerpted, partly transcribed tape recordings now at the Huntington Library, I find a significant social history and many helpful insights into Stevens's acute if easily disturbed sense of a workplace society, a corporate rhetoric reproducing national rhetoric, and the effect of social trends and issues on day-to-day business matters. Brazeau conducted interviews with a young home-office underwriter, several "field men," Stevens's fellow insurance attorneys, his mailboy, four of his legal assistants, and his "executive manservant" (John Rogers, later a professor of African-American history).

24. I have in mind here the much-discussed group of historians following William Appleman Williams's *The Tragedy of American Diplomacy* (New York: World Publishing, 1959). See, for instance, James C. Thomson, Jr., Peter W. Stanley, and John Curtis Perry, *Sentimental Imperialism: The American Experience in East Asia* (New York: Harper and Row, 1981). Williams's own preferred phrases are "imperial anti-colonialism" and "open-door imperialism," the latter usefully indicating the conflict between American intention and effect, the former suggesting the way in which Americans have thought of their own "internationalism" as postcolonial, liberated from the baseness of traditional colonialist presumptions. The term "benevolent assimilation" was coined by American policymakers within the McKinley administration (in the notorious "Benevolent Assimilation Proclamation") to disguise a military disposition in the Philippines that led directly to a brutal policy of counterinsurgency: this was rhetorically masked as "protect[ing] the natives in their homes" (McKinley's words, quoted in Bonifacio S. Salamanca, *The Filipino Reaction to American Rule, 1901–1913* [Quezon City, Philippines: New Day Publishers, 1984], p. 23). That the idea of "benevolent assimilation" or the American experience in the Philippines during and immediately after the 1898 war that gave the United States its only formal colony could have anything to do with Wallace Stevens's "coming of age as a poet" is the controversial suggestion of Frank Lentricchia, *Ariel and the Police: Michel Foucault, William James, Wallace Stevens* (Madison: University of Wisconsin Press, 1988), pp. 20–22.

25. Harold Bloom, *The Poems of Our Climate* (Ithaca: Cornell University Press, 1977), p. 168.

26. Marjorie Perloff, "Revolving in Crystal: The Supreme Fiction and the Impasse of Modernist Lyric," in *Wallace Stevens: The Poetics of Modernism*, ed. Albert Gelpi (Cambridge: Cambridge University Press, 1985), pp. 41–64.

27. "DeForest Sees Radio as a Weapon in War," *New York Times*, September 20, 1939, p. 2.

28. *New York Times*, September 20, 1939, pp. 15, 21, 11.

29. See, for instance, T. R. Fehrenbach, *F.D.R.'s Undeclared War, 1939 to 1941* (New York: David McKay Co., 1967), p. 187.

30. For a description of the raising and lowering of "the American fear of the consequences of a possible German victory" between September 1939 and April 1940 as a measure of conflicting attitudes toward neutrality and partisanship (or "partiality"), see Donald F. Drummond, *The Passing of American Neutrality, 1937–1941* (Ann Arbor: University of Michigan Press, 1955), especially the chapter "The Growth of Partiality," pp. 112–51.

31. Letter from Anatole Vidal to Stevens, September 17, 1939 (Huntington, WAS2665).

32. "sont parfaitement arrivées sans incident" (letter from Vidal to Stevens, November 18, 1939 [Huntington, WAS2666]).

33. "Ayant eu des rapports amicaux prolongés, vers 1900, avec des Allemands, puis des rapports commerciaux en Amérique-Sud avec des industriels de cette nationalité et aussi comme correspondant d'une Banque allemande à São Paulo et à Rio Grande do Sul—voici comment je juge le conflit actuel, le plus objectivement qu'il m'est possible de le faire."

34. "nous, Français, les plus exposés aux périls de l'esclavage, nous combattons d'abord."

35. "L'Allemagne est un grand peuple par son labeur, son organisation, sa ténacité, qui serait devenu le maître de l'Europe dans une atmosph[è]re de paix et de liberté."

36. "Contrairement à ce que vous pensez, je crains que cette guerre soit très longue. J'incline donc à croire, qu'il faut s'installer moralement et matériellement en cet état, aussi instable qu'il soit."

37. Letter from Stevens to Amiot, March 20, 1945 (Huntington, WAS380).

38. "si au point de vue biologique, l'homme n'a guère changé (massacres, tortures, guerre d'Espagne, Pologne), le seul bien véritable, qu'il doit s'efforcer d'atteindre, c'est la liberté ... qui lui permette ... d'agir suivant ... les atavismes de la race."

39. I am grateful to Professor Weber for his analysis of Vidal's statements (letter to author, December 17, 1987). Weber observed that "business as usual was the order of the day" when he himself passed through Paris in April 1940, some months after Vidal's letter. I have also relied on helpful advice from Gerhard L. Weinberg, Philip Nord, and Paul Fussell. Following their suggestive political readings of Vidal's November 18 letter, I note, additionally, that the influence of Emmanuel Mounier's "personalist" rhetoric seems inscribed in it: "The Europe of the next few years," Mounier wrote, "and once again independently of the continuing conflict [the war itself], will be an authoritarian Europe because too long it was a libertarian Europe." In a sense, France might have expected what it has gotten, Mounier's argument continues, a reaction against the sort of rapaciousness liberalism had weakly criticized yet allowed to flourish, a reaction "against the avarice and disorder of individualism"—even though, as both Mounier and Vidal realized, individual resistance is exactly the spirit that will encourage France finally to win. Yet, again, that "the Maginot Line ... turned out to be [a] weak illusion ... good only for fostering inertia in imagination" and that it was one of the "obstacles to the spirit" are not so much pro-German as distinctly French lines that would be "unsurprised" by or "prepared" for German force (Mounier, "Letter from France," *Commonweal* 33, 1 [October 25, 1940]: 11, 9). If I am correct in hearing echoes of Mounier, it would make Vidal's position complex indeed; Zeev Sternhell's reading of Mounier's personalism as evidence of the penetration of fascism into French society—which Sternhell, in *Neither Right nor Left: Fascist Ideology in France*, trans. David Maisel (Berkeley: University of California Press, 1986), argues was far deeper than historians have recognized—is presented in spite of the fact that Mounier was understood by Vichy as its enemy. For a rejoinder to Sternhell's reading of Mounier, see Saul Friedländer, "The Road to Vichy," *New Republic* 193, 25 (December 15, 1985): 26–33. Granting Friedländer's criticism of Sternhell's broad use of the term "fascism" to define Mounier's appreciation of German "Force"— "Germany against the West," he wrote, "is Sparta against Athens, the hard life against the pleasant life" ("Letter from France," p. 10)—it is surely reasonable, for the purposes of understanding Vidal's description of the situation for Stevens, to see in Vidal's own sense of "la Force" what would be called "defeatism" at the very least.

40. Vidal's long letter of March 2, 1940, described Ceria and his paintings for Stevens (Huntington, WAS2667); an invoice Vidal sent ahead of the painting is dated April 27 (Huntington, WAS2669). Ceria's *Harbor Scene* was sold from Stevens's collection in 1959.

41. The painting was purchased through Anatole Vidal's agency in 1938 (letter from Vidal to Stevens, March 26, 1939 [Huntington, WAS2656]). It is now in Holly Stevens's collection.

42. Letter from Stevens to Charles Henri Ford, April 9, 1939 (Texas, Ford Papers).

43. "[T]o be the master of disorder," he wrote Ford, "requires so very much more than to be the master of order" (ibid.).

44. This is the titular thesis of Richard Lingeman's *Don't You Know There's a War On?—The American Home Front, 1941–1945* (New York: G. P. Putnam's Sons, 1970).

45. Letter from Pach to Stevens, January 25, 1938 (Huntington, WAS1356).

46. Letter from Pach to Stevens, November 2, 1937 (Huntington, WAS1354).

47. For a full reading of Stevens's and Paule Vidal's buyer-agent relationship, see Alan Filreis, "Wallace Stevens and the Language of Agency: Still Life without Substance," *Poetics Today* 10, 2 (Summer 1989): 345–72.

48. Vidal, who noted "how I strive to follow your instructions minutely" (letter of April 6, 1938 [Huntington, WAS2657]), realized at the same time how difficult it was to paint visualities into words. After sensing that Stevens's Marchand seemed "not to have pleased you much," Vidal lamented: "Imagine the difficulty of my task, despite the knowledge I have of your tastes after seven years of relations" (letter of March 26, 1938 [Huntington, WAS2656]).

49. Letter from Pach to Stevens, August 11, 1930 (Huntington, WAS1353).

50. Pach sold a number of his paintings in 1949, and this was among them. *Exhibition & Sale at the Parke-Bernet Galleries*, January 6, 1949, item no. 4, p. 1 (Getty, accession no. 1949 Jan 6 NePaP).

51. Ibid., item no. 6, p. 2.

52. Pach later lent this painting to Hartford's Wadsworth Atheneum for a show, "French Romantic Painting: Delacroix and His Contemporaries" (October 15–November 30, 1952).

53. A study for the decoration in the French Chamber of Deputies; Pach reproduced this work in his edition of Delacroix's *Journal* (New York: Covici-Friede, 1937), p. 602; it too was put up for sale in 1949 (*Exhibition & Sale at the Parke-Bernet Galleries*, January 6, 1949, item no. 51, p. 28).

54. *Exhibition & Sale at the Parke-Bernet Galleries*, January 6, 1949, items no. 11, 57, 98 and pp. 4, 31, 62 respectively. One wonders if the Géricault Pach owned, *Horses in a Stable*, were not itself enough to assure Stevens that Pach was a model connoisseur of chaos, for the story Pach evidently liked to repeat about this painting suggested to Stevens the distinction between the artificiality of things "posed / For a vista in the Louvre" for the museum tourist and the ordinariness of "things chalked / On the sidewalk" for the sympathetic, local "pensive man" (*CP* 216): there were two *Horses in a Stable*, one in the Louvre and the other Pach's, and Pach took pride in asserting that his Géricault was the real thing, the closer of the two to the

depicted scene, as a curator of the Louvre had contended that "this picture [Pach's] was painted from nature and that the one in the Louvre was painted after this one" (Pach's foreword, catalogue for the first U.S. exhibition of Géricault [New York: Marie Sterner Galleries, November 16–December 5, 1936]; Pach lent to this show his *Horses in a Stable* [no. 18], and his anecdote is repeated in the foreword).

55. Walter Pach, *Ingres* (New York: Harper and Bros., 1939), p. 284.

56. Letter from Magda Pach to Stevens, November 22, 1939 (Huntington, WAS1360).

57. Evidence has been accumulated for a similar reading of "A Fish-Scale Sunrise" (1934) as a morning-after response to an evening of drink and dance that took Stevens, with Jim and Margaret Powers, from a restaurant-speakeasy to the Waldorf Roof. See Joan Richardson, *Wallace Stevens: The Later Years, 1923–1955* (New York: William Morrow, 1988), p. 116; and Brazeau's interview with Margaret Powers in *WSR* 90.

58. Both were published in Oscar Williams's *New Poems: 1940* (New York: Yardstick Press, 1941), pp. 157–63, 233–34. Williams "saw the green field of June shining" on a New Hampshire holiday, yet he could not help but recall hearing "the millennium of the Aryans foaming at spigots of beer" and "refugees praying to the hills of lead in the sky."

59. See James Baird, *The Dome and the Rock: Structure in the Poetry of Wallace Stevens* (Baltimore: Johns Hopkins University Press, 1968), p. 237 n. 5.

60. Holly Stevens, "Holidays in Reality," in *Wallace Stevens: A Celebration*, ed. Frank Doggett and Robert Buttel (Princeton: Princeton University Press, 1980), p. 109.

61. Baird's work was completed in 1968; the letter in question became available to scholars in 1975.

62. Letter from Elsie Stevens to Ida Smith Kachel Moll, July 1939 (Huntington, WAS4030).

63. It is indeed the starting point of Maurice Isserman's *Which Side Were You On? The American Communist Party during the Second World War* (Middletown, Conn.: Wesleyan University Press, 1982). See Florence Reece's labor song "Which Side Are You On?" (reprinted in *Years of Protest: A Collection of American Writings of the 1930's*, ed. Jack Salzman [New York: Pegasus, 1967], p. 100).

64. For a lucid description of the outmoded battlements, not only Polish but English and American, see Paul Fussell, *Wartime: Understanding and Behavior in the Second World War* (New York: Oxford University Press, 1989), pp. 4–7; on the dismemberment of the Polish cavalry, see p. 5.

65. In noting for Peter Brazeau that the poem "The News and the Weather" (1941) was derived from Stevens's attention to the radio and newspapers, Samuel French Morse recalled: "He listened [to] one program that intellectuals would be very snobbish about, one of these things like *All in the Family*—it wasn't that, of course, but something like it. He was capable of listening to these things and finding them amusing. He loved to listen to the radio" (from an unpublished, partly transcribed tape-recorded interview [Huntington]).

66. See *New York Times*, August 5, 1940, p. 15.

67. Terrence Des Pres, *Praises & Dispraises: Poetry and Politics, the 20th Century* (New York: Viking, 1988), p. 23.

68. Ibid., pp. 24, 25.

69. Adler, *The Isolationist Impulse*, see especially pp. 269, 270.

70. Bruce Bliven, "This Is Where I Came In," *New Republic* 93, 1025 (January 5, 1938): 246. To be sure, by the time Stevens delivered his lecture, Bliven and other liberals were leaving the isolationist camp, but his logic, according to Selig Adler, was characteristic of liberals within it for many months (see *The Isolationist Impulse*, pp. 298–300).

71. *New York Times*, September 27, 1940, p. 14.

72. Des Pres has in fact dated "Noble Rider" imprecisely, implying that it was given *after Pearl Harbor*: he notes that it was "a lecture delivered at Princeton and *first published in 1942*, at a time when grim messages of Europe were vexing the American dream of detachment" (*Praises & Dispraises*, p. 17; emphasis added). The more important fact here is that the lecture was written and delivered in April 1941. Des Pres's dating blurs the distinction between a popular and indeed official stance of American neutrality *before* Pearl Harbor on the one hand, and on the other, a feeling many if not most noncombatant Americans (and certainly Stevens) felt afterward, from 1942 through 1945—a psychological difficulty no less profound, surely, but very different in kind. In Des Pres's reading, then, Stevens's assertion, "I am thinking of life in a state of violence, *not physically violent, as yet, for us in America*," is unintentionally altered in meaning (*NA* 26; Des Pres, *Praises & Dispraises*, p. 30).

73. Des Pres, *Praises & Dispraises*, p. 29.

2. Formalists under Fire

The Soldier's War and the Home Front

1. Letter from Fernand Auberjonois to author, March 16, 1988.

2. "I met him often. I think I was there at a number of lunches that Barbara [Church] gave [in New York], but I also met him when he came to Princeton" (Fernand Auberjonois, interview with author, Los Angeles, December 22, 1987).

3. The Churches' willingness to help must have impressed Stevens, if only because in reporting the house full of guests Church was certain to add that he did not particularly like children. "Two babies and 2 girls from a former marriage and two women in the house," Church explained. "I always feel one should try a way of getting rid of them, perhaps drowning them as you do cats" (letter to Stevens, March 5, 1943 [Huntington, WAS3410]). Stevens could sympathize: like Stevens, Church "didn't like disorder in his life," Auberjonois noted (interview).

4. "I was probably the only contact between the war and them. And I could write through APO. From Paris others could only have sent things through people coming over to the States" (interview).

5. Letter to author, March 16, 1988.

6. Interview.

7. *France Speaks to America* ([New York]: National Broadcasting Company, [1941]), pp. 23, 11, [3]. Two contemporary studies of the power of wartime radio are Miles Henslow, *The Miracle of Radio: The Story of Radio's Decisive Contribution to Victory* (London: Evans, 1946); and Charles Rolo, *Radio Goes to War* (New York:

Putnam, 1942), especially the chapter "The Story of International Broadcasting," pp. 34–49; see also Lingeman, *Don't You Know There's a War On?* pp. 224–27.

8. Letter to author, August 18, 1988.

9. Letter to author, March 16, 1988.

10. In *Quarterly Review of Literature* 1, 3 (Spring 1944): 155–58.

11. Harvey Breit, "Sanity That Is Magic," *Poetry* 62, 1 (April 1943): 48.

12. Fackenheim, once a prisoner at Sachsenhausen, has argued that eyewitness accounts of wartime events may actually be less precise than *post facto* retellings (see "Sachsenhausen 1938: Groundwork for Auschwitz," *Midstream* 3 [April 1975]: 27–31).

13. This concept of testimony is informed by Barbara Foley's vigorous rejection of the thesis that in documentary fiction "history is ultimately unknowable, that stable general meanings do not inhere in particular instances." Especially helpful to my conception of the formal pressures brought to bear on Stevens's poem as it retains the young captain to close the gap between experience and imagination, war and home front, testimony and literature, is Foley's modification of Sidra Dekoven Ezrahi's idea that in testimony "assumptions about mimesis and historicity have accordingly been altered in order to compensate for this dislocation of the link between writer and reader." Ezrahi has argued, in *By Words Alone* (Chicago: University of Chicago Press, 1980), that there is "no analogous relationship between the world described in the text and the world inhabited by the reader" (Foley's paraphrase). Foley's response is: "But to acknowledge the difficulty of conveying a horrific experience . . . is not the same thing as to declare that reality itself has become 'fictual' " ("Fact, Fiction, Fascism: Testimony and Mimesis in Holocaust Narratives," *Comparative Literature* 34, 4 [Fall 1982]: 331, 332). Testimony emerging from survivors of World War II atrocities has been used shrewdly to define broader areas of wartime witnessing, including American novels and poetry written by combatants; in all such eyewitness accounts the necessity of describing the indescribable not only disrupts traditional generic expectations but often requires the sort of collaboration between witness and nonwitness that I argue is itself the subject of Stevens's poem. For a helpfully skeptical view of the problem of word-world interdependency in Stevens's political verse (or, rather, his poetic "views of the political"), see Melita Schaum, "Lyric Resistance: Views of the Political in the Poetics of Wallace Stevens and H.D.," *Wallace Stevens Journal* 13, 2 (Fall 1989): esp. 191–95.

14. "[E]n dehors des sursauts opérationnels, la vie d'une armée en campagne est monotone" (Fernand Auberjonois, "Ecrivains-soldats à Alger," *Journal de Genève*, February 27, 1987, p. 2).

15. The case for this influence has been clinched by Milton J. Bates, *Wallace Stevens: A Mythology of Self* (Berkeley: University of California Press, 1985), pp. 202–3, 247–65. David Bromwich has taken the Stevens-Nietzsche connection even further, in "Stevens and the Idea of the Hero," *Raritan* 7, 1 (Summer 1987): 1–27.

16. Bates, *A Mythology of Self*, p. 241.

17. Perloff, "The Supreme Fiction and the Impasse of Modernist Lyric," pp. 53–60.

18. Letter to author, March 16, 1988.

19. "Certes, on avait grand besoin d'écrire et de lire pendant ces années-là" (Auberjonois, "Ecrivains-soldats à Alger," p. 2).

20. "Mais à chaque retour à Alger on avait hâte de retrouver *Fontaine* et d'apprendre qui, en France ou en exil, avait écrit quoi, et sous quel pseudonyme" (ibid.).

21. "un tolérable purgatoire" (ibid.).

22. "*Fontaine* était le point de ralliement des Français, Anglais et Américains mobilisés ou en civil qui essayaient d'écrire durant les permissions" (ibid.).

23. "ce faisant, de se dégager de la gangue qu'est la vie militaire, même en temps de guerre" (ibid.).

24. Letter to author, August 18, 1988. The figure is repeated in "Ecrivains-soldats à Alger": "The balcony of the review *Fontaine*, 43 rue Lys du Pac, was a loge of a theatre. One stood there at about midnight during the black-out, glass of red wine in hand, to attend the bombardment of the port by the planes of the *Luft-waffe*." ("Le balcon de la revue *Fontaine*, 43, rue Lys du Pac, était une loge de théâtre. On s'y tenait vers minuit dans le *black-out*, verre de gros rouge en main, pour assister au bombardement du port par les appareils de la *Luftwaffe*.")

25. "Pendant les raids, au paroxysme des fusées" (Auberjonois, "Ecrivains-soldats à Alger," p. 2).

26. "[N]ous avions cherché en vain une élite culturelle" (ibid.).

27. "Je n'ai jamais rencontré personne qui l'ait vu tomber des cieux ou ramassé, mais un pilote de la RAF (Royal Air Force) avait risqué sa peau pour en lacher quelques dizaines de milliers. Ne dédaignons pas les gestes symboliques" (ibid.).

28. Letter from Church to Stevens, October 28, 1942 (Huntington, WAS3405).

29. In my interview with him, Auberjonois described this special issue of *Fontaine* in detail (the entries were generally "contributions about freedom").

30. In 1945, 12,133,455 Americans were uniformed personnel. As a percentage of the population, the figure of 16.93 percent is the highest in the nation's history (Morris Janowitz, *The Last Half-Century: Societal Change and Politics in America* [Chicago: University of Chicago Press, 1978], p. 187; for the percentage given, Janowitz uses a "Military Participation Ratio" and defines it in his table 6.2).

31. Alfred Knopf published *Parts of a World*. The long poems, "Notes" and "Esthétique du Mal," would not be collected in a trade edition until Knopf's *Transport to Summer* of 1947.

32. Letter from Katherine Frazier to Stevens, March 28, 1943 (Huntington, WAS664). In asking Stevens to write for Morse, Frazier conveyed to Stevens her strong feeling that those associated with the press who were *not* drafted would still be performing "intangible services" there; she was referring to Harry Duncan, her eventual successor, who had been temporarily deferred.

33. One reviewer of the book seems to imply this, citing the young poet explicitly as "Sergeant" Morse when quoting the maternal dedication (Sidney Cox, "Against Sickness of the Mortal Will," *Kenyon Review* 6, 2 [Spring 1944]: 293).

34. Samuel French Morse, interview with author, Milton, Massachusetts, January 7, 1983.

35. Quoted from a letter to Katherine Frazier in a letter from Harry Duncan to Stevens, March 14, 1943 (Huntington, WAS555).

36. Stevens's disposition did not merely serve to gather up his own optimism

about the war; he evidently sensed that Morse, who had been drafted on February 12, 1943—Stevens's letter was written on May 27—was "a reluctant member of the armed forces" (letter from Jane Morse to author, November 9, 1989).

37. "[W]e are looking at the situation with as much common sense as possible," Jane wrote her uncle at one point. "I want to be with him until the last possible moment, as once he goes, it will be a long time till we're together" (letter from Jane MacFarland to Stevens, May 23, 1943 [Huntington, WAS2715]).

38. Letter from John B. Stevens, Jr., to Wallace Stevens, January 19, 1943 (Huntington, WAS2295).

39. Letter from John B. Stevens, Jr., to Wallace Stevens, February 24, 1944 (Huntington, WAS2296). This letter had been opened by the military censor.

40. Letter from Anna May Stevens to Wallace Stevens, June 7, 1944 (Huntington, WAS2304).

41. On May 26, 1942, Anna May wrote this to Stevens from Oley, Pennsylvania (Huntington, WAS2302). John had left the country before a telegram announcing Laurie's birth could reach him.

42. Letter from Anna May Stevens to Wallace Stevens, March 3, 1943 (Huntington, WAS2303).

43. Letter from Anna May Stevens to Wallace Stevens, June 7, 1944 (Huntington, WAS2304).

44. Ibid.

45. Unpublished, partially untranscribed interview conducted by Peter Brazeau with Milli Sylvester (Huntington Library).

46. Typical of Stevens's own use of such euphemisms, this phrase was used in a letter to Nicholas Moore, an Englishman; Stevens had met Moore's mother, who was living in the United States in "prolonged exile" from Europe: he was glad "to know," he wrote, "that, at the bottom of *all the hubbub*, you are still alive and well" (letter from Stevens to Moore, September 15, 1943 [Huntington, WAS1225]). "Everyone is so deeply involved in *what is going on*," Stevens wrote to Kerker Quinn, without any other mention of the war, "that your answer to that question is something to be watched and studied"; the "question" was, How would a literary review respond to "what is going on"? (letter from Stevens to Kerker Quinn, October 2, 1940 [Illinois, Accent Papers]). Not surprisingly, the letters to Stevens after Pearl Harbor are full of similar usage: his niece, Jane, speaking of John Stevens's service in the Pacific, wrote Stevens of a time when "this *thing*" will be over (letter of October 24, 1943 [Huntington, WAS2724]).

47. For material on wartime propaganda here and elsewhere, I have relied on general information in A. H. Feller, "OWI on the Home Front," *Public Opinion Quarterly* 7 (Spring 1943): 55–65; and Sydney Weinberg, "What to Tell America: The Writers' Quarrel in the Office of War Information," *Journal of American History* 55, 1 (June 1968): 73–89.

48. At about the time Stevens saw Auberjonois on furlough, Church mentioned in a letter that he had telephoned Auberjonois at the OWI (letter to Stevens, March 10, 1944 [Huntington, WAS3435]).

49. Letter from Stevens to Philip May, January 22, 1943 (Houghton: May Papers, bMS Am 1543).

50. *Hartford Agent* 36, 1–2 (Midsummer 1943): 12–13, 15.

51. "We Pledge Ourselves . . . to Preserve Intact," *Hartford Agent* 34, nos. 1–2 (Midsummer 1942): 16.

52. Francis Walton, *Miracle of World War II: How American Industry Made Victory Possible* (New York: Macmillan, 1956), p. 373.

53. Susan B. Anthony II, *Out of the Kitchen and into the War: Women's Winning Role in the Nation's Drama* (New York: Stephen Daye, 1943).

54. Francis Walton has offered ample evidence that corporate managers were indeed unnerved (*Miracle of World War II*, pp. 372–77).

55. See, for instance, the *Hartford Agent* 35, 3 (September 1943): 31. That officers at The Hartford followed the trend noted by Francis Walton, and were disturbed by this influx of women, is purely speculation on my part. However, it is indisputably the case that a general alarm was sounded when the results of a study conducted by the Women's Bureau of the federal Department of Labor revealed that 75 percent of the women working had no intention of giving up their jobs; the response to this is described by Sherna Berger Gluck, *Rosie the Riveter Revisited: Women, the War, and Social Change* (Boston: Twayne Publishers, 1987), pp. 16–17.

56. One of Stevens's "From Pieces of Paper" jottings, quoted in George S. Lensing, *Wallace Stevens: A Poet's Growth* (Baton Rouge: Louisiana State University Press, 1986), p. 177.

57. For a general description of this invisible barrier, see Richard Polenberg, *War and Society: The United States, 1941–1945* (Philadelphia: J. B. Lippincott, 1972), pp. 146–50. To learn how the invisible barrier fell locally, I have worked with several detailed accounts of women's war-work in Hartford's insurance companies, transcripts of interviews conducted by the Center for Oral History, University of Connecticut: Esther Tracey, who began with the Aetna in 1942 (interview no. 126), and Teresa West, who found at the Travelers that women "had to fight sexist prejudices for higher job classifications" (no. 131).

58. A general description of changes in the character of wartime personnel at The Hartford is provided by Hawthorne Daniel, *The Hartford of Hartford: An Insurance Company's Part in a Century and a Half of American History* (New York: Random House, 1960), pp. 252, 255–56.

59. Unpublished portion of Peter Brazeau's tape-recorded interview with Wilson Taylor (Huntington).

60. "Of course," he noted of the liverwurst, "I only eat things of this sort on Sundays" (letter to Wilson Taylor, October 16, 1950 [Huntington, WAS3933]).

61. Letter from Stevens to Ronald Lane Latimer, May 10, 1937 (Chicago, Latimer Papers). This letter also refers to the "spasm of planting"; that was the "work" indeed that led to spending "most of the next day [a Sunday] dozing."

62. I am grateful to Linda Gutierrez for providing a transcription of this interview, and to Jill Janows and the Center for Visual History for permission to quote from it.

63. See Arthur A. Stein, *The Nation at War* (Baltimore: Johns Hopkins University Press, 1978), p. 57. Stein explains the comparison to the New Deal (p. 58). He also notes that neither the Korean War nor the Vietnam War saw any such sharp increase in government purchases for private goods and services: the figure of 47.3

percent offers dramatic contrast to the figure of 20 percent for 1952 and 19 percent for 1969.

64. Glenn Weaver, *Hartford: An Illustrated History of Connecticut's Capital* (Woodland Hills, Calif.: Connecticut Historical Society, 1982), p. 126. For a discussion of the general demographic shift, see Stein, *The Nation at War*, pp. 63–64.

65. *Hartford Agent* 35, 1–2 (Midsummer 1943): 5.

66. An exceedingly readable account of the function and impact of the War Damage Corporation is offered by Jesse H. Jones (with Edward Angly) in *Fifty Billion Dollars: My Thirteen Years with the R[econstruction] F[inance] C[orporation]* (New York: Macmillan, 1951), pp. 451–55. War-damage insurance, bolstering the services of 83 casualty insurance companies (as well as 546 insurers against fire), was suggested by Jones after Pearl Harbor because, "[t]o our knowledge, insurance companies were not prepared to write this character of coverage" (p. 451).

67. Stevens, "Surety and Fidelity Claims," *OP* 238.

68. A clear description of The Hartford's surety and fidelity business is offered by Daniel, *The Hartford of Hartford*, pp. 267–68. Brazeau provides a background to Stevens's work with surety and fidelity bonds in *WSR* 4–6, 12, 18. The Blanket Bond, also known inside the business as "dishonesty insurance," is described by George E. Foster, *Hartford Agent* 25, 5 (November 1933): 67. Prior to World War II this provision, which was designed exclusively to protect the employer, was defined as a "moral" argument against even petty forms of worker pilfering (take care of "the *Moral* side of the risk" was the particular slogan recommended in an article on the subject). During World War II nationalism supplanted moralism in the insurers' pitch for selling this form of protection. For the "*Moral* side" slogan, see J. Schmidt, Jr., on "Loss Prevention Service," *Hartford Agent* 25, 6 (December 1933): 84. Stevens's little essay "Surety and Fidelity Claims," in the *Eastern Underwriter*, briefly discusses variations on the investigation of insured dishonesty (*OP* 237–39). On the subject of employers' delight over crisis rhetoric: this suggestion is a controversial one, and certainly not provable at The Hartford; British insurers were apparently much more explicit about wartime coverage boons, going so far as to suggest that an advantage might be won from employers' dread of social unrest stirred by nationalism: "After the outbreak of war," two British insurance experts wrote between the world wars, "events which are subjects of common knowledge caused the insured public to modify its attitude. . . . The popular demonstrations which followed the sinking of the *Lusitania* and general indications of labour unrest caused apprehension to owners of property *and suggested protection by insurance against damage to property arising from such disturbances*" (Sydney Preston and Alexander Ernest Sich, *War & Insurance* [London: Humphrey Milford; New Haven: Yale University Press, 1927], p. 59; emphasis added).

69. Typical is a November 1937 *Agent* piece written at the height of anti–New Deal sentiment within the company. Celebrating the successful management of a surety bond worth many millions, one supervisor wrote: "It's refreshing, [in] these paternalistic days, to find people doing things for themselves" (Walter R. Whitford, "A '$220,000,000 Surety Bond,' " *Hartford Agent* 29, 6 [November 1937]: 103).

70. Daniel, *The Hartford of Hartford*, p. 236. The propaganda war waged against wartime individualism, because it went against the grain of cultural messages that

had always before encouraged the association of patriotism and financial success with self-reliance, was a particularly forceful common feature of corporate life. The "When You Ride Alone You Ride with Hitler" posters, for instance, urged a well-dressed white-collar worker to join a "car-sharing club" (Weimer Pursell, 1942, reproduced in Anthony Rhodes, *Propaganda, the Art of Persuasion: World War II* [New York: Chelsea House, 1976], p. 175).

71. For Stevens's support of social security, see his essay "Insurance and Social Change," *OP* 233–37. Evidence of other businessmen's opposition is plentiful: see B. M. Selekman, "The Social Security Act," *Harvard Business Review* 15, 2 (Winter 1937): 174–88, see 184 especially; and "Industry Out to Wage War on New Deal / Business Leaders Ratify Creed Built about Assertion American System Has Not Failed," *Hartford Courant*, December 6, 1935, p. 4.

72. *Hartford Agent* 35, 1–2 (Midsummer 1943): 23.

73. Alex B. Young, "Wartime Sales Methods in an Agency Which Has an Eye to the Future," *Hartford Agent* 35, 1–2 (Midsummer 1943): 10.

74. "Paper Situation," *Hartford Agent* 35, 8 (February 1944): 153.

75. Letter dated December 4, 1944. The original is at Princeton, in the Tate Papers; the carbon, retained in Stevens's office files, is at the Huntington.

76. Vivienne Koch, "Poetry in World War II," *Briarcliff Quarterly* 2, 6 (July 1945): 65.

77. Letter from Stevens to Philip May, January 22, 1943 (Houghton, May Papers, bMS Am 1543).

78. For the deputy's statement and the comparison of needs for heating oil and travel, see "90-Day Driving Ban Proposed in East," *New York Times*, December 6, 1942, p. 31.

79. *New York Times*, December 22, 1942, p. 1.

80. Letter from Stevens to Philip May, January 22, 1943 (Houghton, May Papers, bMS Am 1543).

81. Good measures of the intensity of this aspect of home-front propaganda are films released at this time suggesting the implications of travel-as-usual: one, *Is Your Trip Necessary?* (1943), asked citizens to restrict travel to make transportation (and oil) easily available to the military. For more on the "shock" felt by "many naive Americans who formerly thought of essential imports in terms of Havana cigars," see Adler, *The Isolationist Impulse*, pp. 322–24.

82. Two are: Richardson, *The Later Years*, pp. 109–12; and Bloom, *The Poems of Our Climate*, pp. 110–11.

83. Letter from Stevens to Philip May, January 31, 1940 (Houghton, May Papers, bMS Am 1543). "How happy you all seem to be down there [in Jacksonville]; how you go on living in a land of milk and honey, or, to be more exact, possum, sop and taters." See *WSR* 109.

The New Nationalism

1. Quoted by Edwin Alden Jewell in "The Problem of Seeing," New York *Times*, August 10, 1941, sec. 9, p. 7.

2. Serge Guilbaut, citing 1941 issues of the *MOMA Bulletin*, notes the dramatic increase in MOMA memberships; at the Metropolitan, attendance was up 15 percent in 1942 alone (*How New York Stole the Idea of Modern Art: Abstract Expressionism,*

Freedom, and the Cold War, trans. Arthur Goldhammer [Chicago: University of Chicago Press, 1983], p. 56). Much of the discussion of the new nationalism in painting in this section is indebted to Guilbaut's second chapter, pp. 50–99.

3. Typical of Stevens's letters that do list his intention of seeing exhibits, a letter to Church dated December 3, 1943, describes a planned visit to New York—"I have to buy suspenders, gloves and this, that and the other"—and notes his desire to see "the Blumenthal show, which opens on December 8th, and the pictures at Kno[e]dler's, etc., etc." (Huntington, WAS3529). "The Blumenthal show" was an exhibit at the Metropolitan Museum of Art of twenty-four Renaissance paintings and other items bequeathed to the museum by George Blumenthal; among them was Joos van Gent's *Adoration of the Magi,* a subgenre of continuing interest to Stevens ("Art Gifts to Be Shown," *New York Times,* December 5, 1943, p. 53; Edward Alden Jewell, "Blumenthal Art to Go on Display," New York *Times,* December 7, 1943, p. 24; on Adorations, see, e.g., *L* 608). The show Stevens planned to see at Knoedler's gallery on East 57th Street was explicitly connected to the war effort: Flemish, Dutch, and English masters were displayed to benefit the Citizens Committee for the Army and Navy (*New Yorker,* December 4, 1943, p. 4). A letter to Allen Tate confirms a 1942 visit to the National Gallery in Washington (July 6, 1943 [Princeton, Tate Papers]).

4. Letter from Stevens to Wilson Taylor, February 6, 1942 (Huntington, WAS3874).

5. This wariness dates back at least to the twenties, when he began to tire of visiting the annual exhibits mounted by the Society for Independent Artists, which Walter Pach helped organize. We know that the popularity of the 1922 show, held on the roof of the Waldorf Astoria, and described by the *New York Times* as "besieged" by the critics and the public, irritated Stevens. "This year's Independent Show," he wrote, "is a poor thing but it has grown almost fashionable and attracts large crowds" (letter from Stevens to Alice Corbin Henderson, March 27, 1922; reprinted in Alan Filreis, "Voicing the Desert of Silence: Stevens's Letters to Alice Corbin Henderson," *Wallace Stevens Journal* 12, 1 [Spring 1988]: 17, 18 n. 12); see "Independents' Art Draws Huge Crowd," *New York Times,* March 12, 1922, sec. 2, p. 1.

6. Quoted by Guilbaut, *How New York Stole the Idea of Modern Art,* p. 57.

7. Edward Alden Jewell, "The Realm of Art: Current Activities," *New York Times,* June 27, 1943, sec. 2, p. 6.

8. Eugene R. Gaddis, " 'The New Athens': Moments from an Era," in *Avery Memorial, Wadsworth Atheneum: The First Modern Museum,* ed. Eugene R. Gaddis (Hartford: Wadsworth Atheneum, 1984), p. 46.

9. A[lfred] M. F[rankfurter], "Vernissage," *Art News* 42, 1 (February 15–28, 1943): 7.

10. Letter from Stevens to Wilson Taylor, February 1, 1943 (Huntington, WAS3887).

11. Unpublished portion of an interview with Wilson Taylor (Huntington).

12. Letter from Stevens to Taylor, February 1, 1943 (Huntington, WAS3887).

13. *The Art and Life of Vincent Van Gogh: Loan Exhibition in Aid of American and Dutch War Relief,* compiled by Georges de Batz, with introduction by Alfred M. Frankfurter (New York: Wildenstein, 1943), p. 15.

14. Proceeds from the opening of this show went to the Fighting French Relief Committee and to France Forever ("France Will Benefit by Art Exhibition," *New York Times*, November 15, 1942, sec. 2, p. 1).

15. Stevens had seen the exhibit mentioned in the *New York Times*, and asked Taylor to send him the catalogue. It seems quite likely that Stevens attended the exhibit himself, though no confirmation of this survives (letter from Stevens to Taylor, February 6, 1942 [Huntington, WAS3874]).

16. Letter from Stevens to Wilson Taylor, November 18, 1942 (Huntington, WAS3882). Stevens had noticed, somewhat cynically, that "ART NEWS has its finger in this pie."

17. Letter from Stevens to Taylor, March 31, 1938 (Huntington, WAS3853); see also *L* 451.

18. Edwin Alden Jewell, "Cézanne Serves Resurgent France," *New York Times*, November 22, 1942, sec. 8, p. 9.

19. *Loan Exhibition of Paintings by Cezanne. . . for the Benefit of Fighting France* (New York: Paul Rosenberg and Co., 1942), pp. 13, 14.

20. Quoted by Gaddis, " 'The New Athens,' " p. 35.

21. Soby (d. 1979) himself recalled Stevens's interest in the Wadsworth Atheneum for Peter Brazeau in 1977: "Stevens went to the museum all the time. At noon hour, he'd wander around alone. He was almost furious if anyone interrupted him. He'd come every holiday. Very often on weekends. He wouldn't talk about the exhibitions. I kept trying to find out what artists he liked. There wasn't any way to tell except to follow him around the gallery and see where he stayed longest. . . . Stevens was a genuine lover of art" (*WSR* 118).

22. Goldschmidt's involvement was mentioned in "Cezanne Paintings Go on View Today," *New York Times*, November 18, 1942, p. 23.

23. Following Nazi decrees stripping Jews of further control of their own property, Reich tax authorities had issued an order for Goldschmidt's arrest for failure to pay the so-called Jewish flight taxes ("New Curbs Placed on Jews' Property," *New York Times*, December 6, 1938, p. 13). Stevens reported the Goldschmidt story to Wilson Taylor in a letter dated November 18, 1942 (Huntington, WAS3882).

24. Letter from Stevens to Henry Church, October 26, 1943 (Huntington, WAS3525).

25. *The Serene World of Corot: An Exhibition in Aid of the Salvation Army War Fund* (New York: Wildenstein, 1942), p. [2].

26. Letter from Stevens to Henry Church, November 18, 1942 (Huntington, WAS3504).

27. Soby was a devotee of Stevens's verse, following in particular Stevens's interest in the relations between painting and poetry. "I talked myself blue in the face about him. . . . He knew I admired him" (*WSR* 118).

28. This is not to suggest, however, that the Wadsworth Atheneum did not offer its own wartime exhibits. The well-received "Men in Arms" exhibit of 1943 was one.

29. "Museum to Offer Art Aid to Camps / Modern Art Institution Names J. T. Soby to Head work with Army and Navy," *New York Times*, January 28, 1942, p. 21.

30. "The Museum of Modern Art, at the present time, is being directed, I believe, by James Thrall Soby of Hartford. Soby is a very agreeable person. . . . [H]e

left Hartford, a year or so ago, to associate himself with the Museum during the war. He lives in Farmington [Connecticut], in a house specially arranged, I believe, to show his pictures." And, he added, "I am intensely interested in such of his pictures as I have seen" (letter from Stevens to Henry Church, December 3, 1943 [Huntington, WAS3529]).

31. Letter from Stevens to James Soby, September 16, 1940 (Texas, Charles Henri Ford Papers). This is a carbon copy that Stevens enclosed with a letter to Ford.

32. Letter from Stevens to Henry Church, December 3, 1943 (Huntington, WAS3529).

33. Soby recalled for Brazeau that at MOMA "I'd pass him in the gallery, and we'd talk a little while. . . . He'd ask me what I liked and what stood out. And he'd tell me what he liked most. Then he moved on. . . . I used to follow him through the gallery" (*WSR* 119).

34. Russell Lynes, *Good Old Modern: An Intimate Portrait of the Museum of Modern Art* (New York: Atheneum, 1973), p. 237. This was of course largely due to Nelson Rockefeller's association with both MOMA and the Office of Inter-American Affairs. "During the war the Museum," Lynes has written, "worked as much for Nelson Rockefeller as for anyone else" and became involved in "the export of American art" (p. 384).

35. MOMA under Soby also sponsored a National War Posters competition, followed by a group show. It is quite possible that Stevens saw this exhibit, which was held in November and December 1942, when he traveled to New York to see the Cézanne exhibit at Rosenberg's (*New York Times*, November 22, 1942, sec. 8, p. 9).

36. Quoted by Guilbaut from the *Road to Victory* exhibit catalogue (*How New York Stole the Idea of Modern Art*, pp. 88–89).

37. Indeed, Soby's own *After Picasso* (1935) was the principal reason why in the United States they were known as such. Alfred Barr noted of this book that "Mr. Soby is especially interested in the Neo-Romantics," and defined both Soby's thesis and the paintings he promoted as based on the "common rejection of Cubist esthetics[,] frequent dependence upon so-called 'literary' qualities of sentiment, anecdote, mood [and] . . . insistence in short upon the validity and interest of subject matter" ("Surrealists and Neo-Romantics," *Saturday Review of Literature* 12, 20 [September 14, 1935]: 6).

38. "[T]he fact is," he wrote Soby, "that XVIII of the MAN WITH THE BLUE GUITAR is the result of seeing one of your Bermans" (letter of September 16, 1940 [Texas, Charles Henri Ford Papers]). I have identified this painting as Berman's *Memories of Ischia* (now in the collection at MOMA); for a reading of the interartistic relation between Berman's painting and Stevens's poem, see Filreis, "Still Life without Substance," pp. 368–70.

39. Dorothy Dudley, reviewing the fourth issue of *VVV*, in *Chimera* 2, 4 (Summer 1944): 47.

40. Barr's dismissal is described by Lynes, in *Good Old Modern*, pp. 240–63.

41. For more on Sweeney's work at MOMA, see Lynes, *Good Old Modern*, pp. 75–76, 271–75. On Sweeney's relations with Stevens, see *WSR* 226–28.

42. *WSR* 119; Soby told Brazeau the story of Stevens's refusal to attend a party to which MacLeish was to be invited.

43. Fussell, *Wartime*, p. 173.

44. Milton Brown, "American Art a Year after Pearl Harbor," *Art News* 41, 14 (December 1-14, 1942): 9, 30.

45. Nicolas Calas, "America," in *Artists in Exile* (New York: Pierre Matisse Gallery, 1942), n.p.

46. James Soby, "Europe," in *Artists in Exile* (New York: Pierre Matisse Gallery, 1942), n.p.

47. Americans, Soby warned, may "want American art to have equal voice with that of Europe in the new world, but [we must] check th[at] ambition at this point, knowing that beyond lies the dread bait of imperialism which all men of heart must suspect" ("Europe," n.p.). In its bluntest form, the cultural imperialism that flourished after the war—in the second part of this study I will examine Stevens's response to it—was everything that Soby had feared in 1942. One art critic would gloat that "Europe has been prostrated" and that "[t]his country gives promise of being first to recover from the World War" (Howard Devree, "Straws in the Wind: Some Opinions on Art in the Post War World of Europe and America," *New York Times*, July 14, 1946, sec. 2, p. 4). Least damaged by war, this cold-war argument ran, the United States should take greatest advantage of the most severely damaged cultures, should invent and put forward a new national version of modernism while claiming its universality, its having no ideological axe to grind, and thus assimilate benevolently those "prostrated" cultures. In "Does Our Art Impress Europe?" Soby himself presented only a more polite version of the same idea: "Today . . . Paris has lost to a great extent its role as international arbiter of fame and quality in the fine arts. This is not a statement to be made gleefully" (*Saturday Review of Literature* 32, 32 [August 6, 1949]: 144). In 1948 readers of Soby's *Saturday Review* column were presented with this summary of the situation: "French art . . . is imprisoned in its parental house. . . . [T]he new school of Paris's great weakness is that it has become *too Parisian*" ("Report on Paris," *Saturday Review of Literature* 31, 33 [August 14, 1948]: 25-26). Soby's statements, like many others, revealed only a slight awareness of the new contingencies of value. The standards had shifted. The question to ask oneself of a new painting was no longer, How Parisian is its style? But, in the new terms, How *international* is the style? This meant, nevertheless, How uniquely *American* is its claim to having transcended the very idea of national style? It was not that the *world* now led France in the creation of the new manner that would be highly valued; obviously, the United States led France. How much more compelling, then, when placed in such a context, is Stevens's statement to Henry Church that "*France* leads *us* far more than we realize" (*L* 542). Stevens's keen desire to sentimentalize a Europe demolished, the very devastation that gave Americans the power to so valorize it, is the basis of Stevens's sentimental imperialism, and the essence of what the war would teach the postwar Stevens.

48. Samuel M. Kootz, *New Frontiers in American Painting* (New York: Hastings House, 1943), esp. pp. 57-64. Guilbaut interprets the frontier metaphor (*How New York Stole the Idea of Modern Art*, pp. 71-72).

49. James Thrall Soby and Dorothy Miller, *Romantic Painting in America* (New York: Museum of Modern Art, 1943), p. 16. Soby and Miller noted that during Cole's European travels he praised the work of Claude and Poussin. On Cole's dependence on European tradition: "Cole's art was based upon the 17th century

European tradition to a degree from which no love of New World scenery could completely free him," while at the same time Soby is sure to quote Cole's "patrioti[sm]": Cole decided that he had seen " 'no natural scenery [in Europe] yet which has affected me so powerfully as that which I have seen in the wilderness places of America' " (p. 16).

50. On Stevens's interest in Claude, see *CP* 134–35 and Bonnie Costello, "Effects of an Analogy: Wallace Stevens and Painting," in *Wallace Stevens: The Poetics of Modernism*, ed. Gelpi, pp. 77–78. On Poussin, see *CP* 219, *OP* 115, *NA* 152, *L* 229, and Costello, pp. 74–75; Stevens owned a copy of André Félibien's *Entretien sur Nicholas Poussin* (1929).

51. The Wadsworth Atheneum owned a number of Cole's paintings, including *View of Monte Video, the Seat of Daniel* (1828), *John the Baptist in the Wilderness* (1827), and *View of the White Mountains* (1827).

52. Oscar Williams, ed., *New Poems 1943* (New York: Howell, Soskin Publishers, 1943), p. vii.

53. Cole recounts the Chocorua legend in his *Sketch of My Tour to the White Mountains with Mr. Pratt*. A passage from this work is quoted in an annotation to Cole's *Chocorua's Curse*, an engraving of 1830, in a catalogue, *Thomas Cole, One Hundred Years Later*, prepared for the November 12, 1948, to January 2, 1949, exhibit at the Wadsworth Atheneum (pp. 47–48). See also Frederick Webb Hodge, *Handbook of American Indians North of Mexico* (New York: Pageant Books, 1960), 1: 287–88; and Samuel Gardner Drake, *The Aboriginal Races of North America, Comprising Biographical Sketches of Eminent Individuals* . . . (New York: Hurst and Company, [1880]), pp. 285–86.

54. For more on the image of Chocorua and a somewhat different reading of its influence on the poem, see Roy Harvey Pearce, *Gesta Humanorum* (Columbia: University of Missouri Press, 1987), pp. 135–44.

55. Stevens saved his copy of this the Spring 1944 issue (it is now part of the Huntington collection, RB440687); Stevens's own poem "The Creations of Sound" appeared in it (p. 33). Ralston Crawford's "Art Notes" (p. 83) offered this embittered view of the painter-soldier. The issue also included a line drawing by Crawford called "Lt. Loman Missing in Action, 19 August 1943" (p. 54). Crawford served as chief of the Visual Presentation Unit in the Army Air Force and was assigned to the India and Burma theatres; his *Bomber* and *Air War* (both of 1944) demonstrate Crawford's conviction that soldier-artists knew best how history in the making—destruction on a new scale—could be integrated into modern abstraction: "I don't mean the efforts of the quick sketch artist, but intelligent pictures *connected* with these events." See William C. Agee, *Ralston Crawford* ([Pasadena, Calif.]: Twelve Trees Press, 1983), plates 23, 24.

56. George Biddle has written an account of this outfit, *Artist at War* (New York: Viking, 1944). The assignment was "to obtain a pictorial record of the war in all its phases" (p. 2).

57. Van Wyck Brooks, "What Is Primary Literature?" and "Coterie-Literature," in *The Opinions of Oliver Allston* (New York: E. P. Dutton, 1941), pp. 211–46. "Chamber-of-Commerce spirit": Dwight MacDonald in "Kulturbolshewismus Is Here," *Partisan Review* 8 (November-December 1941): 442–51; reprinted as "Kul-

turbolshewismus & Mr. Van Wyck Brooks" in *The Memoirs of a Revolutionist* (New York: Farrar, Straus and Cudahy, 1957), p. 209n.

58. In an address delivered at the inaugural dinner of Freedom House on March 19, 1942, reprinted as "Divided We Fall," in *A Time to Act: Selected Addresses* (Boston: Houghton Mifflin, 1943), pp. 119–27.

59. In an address delivered at Faneuil Hall in Boston, November 20, 1940, reprinted as "The American Cause," in *A Time to Act*, pp. 105–16. "The integrity of words": p. 109.

60. Archibald MacLeish, *Prophets of Doom* (Philadelphia: University of Pennsylvania Press, 1941), a commencement address delivered at the University of Pennsylvania on June 11, 1941.

61. MacLeish, "The Country of the Mind," in *A Time to Act*, pp. 165–66.

62. Typical short notices reiterated MacLeish's indictment: a well-written "call to assumption of responsibility in an irresponsible world," offered by a man of letters as "erudite" and "finished" as MacLeish, was for many reviewers not something to be questioned but simply to be recommended—for most "a book not to be missed" (*Living Age* 359, 4488 [September 1940]: 92). But because MacLeish had so recently supported American intervention in Spain, the left paid special attention. The editors of the *Nation*, calling "The Irresponsibles" "a challenging, if bitter, document," asked scholars and poets to respond (*Nation*, May 18, 1940, p. 611). Max Lerner did so, and felt that "[m]ost of the scholars and writers of America deserve richly the drubbing" MacLeish gave them, though Lerner wanted to widen MacLeish's net to bring in the irresponsibility of the culture at large (*Nation*, June 1, 1940, p. 678–79).

63. *Nation*, June 8, 1940, p. 718.

64. Archibald MacLeish, *The Irresponsibles: A Declaration* (New York: Duell, Sloan and Pearce, 1940), pp. 5, 6.

65. Important to my own analysis of the new nationalism is the perception—the view most likely to have been Stevens's—of broad intellectual alliances that, notwithstanding their unholiness, divided American intellectuals in distinct halves as no other debate did in this period. Yet what was commonly termed the "MacLeish-Brooks" group, it must nevertheless be clear, was not in any sense an agreeable throng. No account follows the twists in the argument better than Raymond Nelson's, largely from Brooks's view, in *Van Wyck Brooks: A Writer's Life* (New York: E. P. Dutton, 1981), pp. 234–47.

66. See, for instance, the responses to Brooks gathered in the February 1942 issue of *Partisan Review*; among the respondents were William Carlos Williams, Lionel Trilling, John Crowe Ransom, and Allen Tate.

67. MacLeish, *The Irresponsibles*, pp. 19, 22.

68. Ibid., p. 3.

69. Professor Thorp provided me information about his (and Allen Tate's) relationship with Henry Church, in an interview on May 7, 1986, in Princeton, New Jersey.

70. *Nation*, June 1, 1940, p. 682.

71. Professor Thorp, in our interview, could not remember if the subject of "The Irresponsibles" was raised during Stevens's 1941 visit to Princeton. Margaret

Powers recalled for Peter Brazeau that she heard Stevens speak of MacLeish "frequently" (unpublished portion of interview [Huntington]).

72. See, e.g., MacLeish, *The Irresponsibles*, pp. 6–7.

73. Brooks, "Coterie-Literature," pp. 240, 245, 244.

74. Allen Tate, "On the 'Brooks-MacLeish Thesis,' " *Partisan Review* 9, 1 (January-February 1942): 38–47.

75. Quoted by MacDonald, *Memoirs of a Revolutionist*, p. 212.

76. Weldon Kees, "Parts: But a World," *New Republic* 107, 13 (September 28, 1942): 387.

77. Quoted by Kees (ibid., p. 388). While no specific evidence survives to date "Girl in a Nightgown" precisely before the war—it was not published before *Parts of a World* was issued, and no dating can be established from Stevens's published or unpublished letters—we do know that the contents were arranged more or less chronologically. The poem seems to have been written in 1938.

Allen Tate's Western Front

1. Tate recounted this in a letter to Donald Stanford, June 26, 1975 (Stanford, Donald E. Stanford Papers, 86–077/3).

2. Letter from Tate to Stevens, December 7, 1949 (Huntington, WAS2384).

3. Letter from Tate to Stevens, March 18, 1947 (Huntington, WAS2374). The poems Stevens published in *Arizona Quarterly* and *Pacific* were "Wild Ducks, People and Distances" (*CP* 328–29) and "Two Tales of Liadoff" (*CP* 346–47) respectively; he published five poems in José Rodríguez Feo's *Orígenes* in 1946.

4. Stevens's response to the emergence of Robert Lowell is a case in point; see *SM* 46.

5. The poetic relationship between Williams and Stevens is also an important one, certainly, as Glen MacLeod (*Wallace Stevens and Company*, pp. 77–91), Albert Gelpi ("Stevens and Williams: The Epistemology of Modernism," in *Wallace Stevens: The Poetics of Modernism*, pp. 3–23), Paul Mariani ("Williams and Stevens: Storming the Edifice," in *A Usable Past: Essays on Modern and Contemporary Poetry* [Amherst: University of Massachusetts Press, 1984], pp. 95–104), and many others have pointed out.

6. Twice Stevens wrote Tate with messages for Blackmur: *L* 393 and letter of July 6, 1943 (Princeton, Tate Papers).

7. Gordon and Tate "used to come fairly often, and everybody used the [Churches'] swimming pool, . . . a great attraction" (interview with Fernand Auberjonois). Auberjonois also recalls: "I was closer to Tate than to anyone else."

8. Letter from Tate to Bishop, March 12, 1943 (*The Republic of Letters in America: The Correspondence of John Peale Bishop & Allen Tate*, ed. Thomas Daniel Young and John J. Hindle [Lexington: University of Kentucky Press, 1981], p. 205). Auberjonois recalls not merely that the Churches "were very nice to Allen Tate," but that "I think the *Mesures* lectures were meant in fact to help Allen also" (interview).

9. Letter from Tate to Marianne Moore, October 20, 1945 (Rosenbach, Moore Papers, V:57:31).

10. Accounts of the New York "group" and Stevens's general attitude toward aesthetic affiliation are offered in Glen MacLeod's *Wallace Stevens and Company* (see pp. 19–41, 45–53) and Joan Richardson's *Wallace Stevens: The Early Years* (New York: William Morrow, 1986), e.g., pp. 400–401, 463–71.

11. Letter from Blackmur to Tate, February 16, 1932 (Princeton, Tate Papers). In this letter Blackmur discussed his essay "Examples of Wallace Stevens" (*Hound and Horn* 5 [January-March 1932]: 223–55) and suggested that Tate, because he had adopted a coherent theory, could have handled Stevens more systematically. He asked Tate to explain how critical "conviction," which Tate had and he lacked, could "make my handful of essays a single weapon."

12. Letter from Ransom to Tate, April 19, 1940 (*Selected Letters of John Crowe Ransom*, ed. Thomas Daniel Young and George Core [Baton Rouge: Louisiana State University Press, 1985], p. 268).

13. Penn Warren saw dangers in this academic trend, though he was certain to add that "these dangers seem trivial in comparison with the potential gains" ("Poets and Scholars," *Nation* 155, 7 [August 15, 1942], 137).

14. Mary Colum, "The New Books of Poetry," *New York Times Book Review*, March 22, 1942, p. 9. When she got to Stevens's contribution, she could only say that he was "like the others"—wordy and abstract.

15. Letter from Cleanth Brooks to Tate, dated "July 1942" (Princeton, Tate Papers). Brooks added that Colum, Van Wyck Brooks, and Joseph Wood Krutch had just then "discovered some of the books of modern criticism."

16. Colum, "The New Books of Poetry," p. 9.

17. Donald Stauffer, "Writers and the South," *New York Times Book Review*, September 14, 1947, sec. 7, p. 5.

18. "Socially he could be abysmally rude," Tate wrote in 1977. "Once at a party in Princeton he insulted Caroline" (letter to Ashley Brown, July 19, 1977 [Ashley Brown]).

19. Letter from Tate to Donald E. Stanford, July 7, 1971 (Stanford, Donald E. Stanford Papers, 86–077/3).

20. Letter from Tate to Stevens, January 9, 1948 (Huntington, WAS2377).

21. Letter from Tate to Stevens, December 7, 1949 (Huntington, WAS2384).

22. Ibid.

23. Allen Tate, *The Winter Sea* (Cummington, Mass.: Cummington Press, 1944), p. [4].

24. Letter from Donald E. Stanford to Tate, May 7, 1975 (Stanford, Donald E. Stanford Papers, 86–077/3). The point had been made by Radcliffe Squires, "Will and Vision: Allen Tate's *Terza Rima* Poems," *Sewanee Review* 78, 4 (October-December 1970): 549.

25. Tate, *The Winter Sea*, pp. [5], [7].

26. Letter from Tate to Donald E. Stanford, May 12, 1975 (Stanford, Donald E. Stanford Papers, 86–077/3).

27. Letter from Tate to Stevens, December 7, 1949 (Huntington, WAS2384); this is one of the letters Tate retained in a carbon copy (Princeton, Tate Papers).

28. Letter from Stevens to Tate, December 9, 1949 (Princeton, Tate Papers).

29. Letter from Tate to Stevens, January 9, 1948 (Huntington, WAS2377).

30. Letter from Tate to Ashley Brown, July 19, 1977 (Ashley Brown).

31. Letter from Cleanth Brooks to author, December 8, 1989.

32. *WSR* 174. Brooks had written Stevens to assure him that "there is nothing at all to apologize for"; Brooks insisted that he could not "possibly have taken offence at anything that you said on that occasion" and that Stevens should "wipe out this quite imaginary offence" (letter from Cleanth Brooks to Stevens, January 18, 1951 [Huntington, WAS440]), only later deducing that Stevens had insulted Tate in the first place and evidently at some other event (it is Brooks's recollection that Tate had not attended the New Haven affair).

33. *Sewanee Review* 61 (Summer 1948): 367–69; *OP* 256–59.

34. Letter from Tate to Stevens, March 4, 1947 (Huntington, WAS2373).

35. In the lecture "The Effects of Analogy," *NA* 112–13. Even this slight Tate remembered for years, though he said incorrectly that when quoting Ransom and himself Stevens "does not favor the reader with our names" (letter to Ashley Brown).

36. MacLeish himself tended not to name names in his wartime remarks, though there had never been a question about his disagreement with Tate. Something of their antagonism can be gleaned from Tate's "Aeneas at New York: To Archibald MacLeish" (1932), the little-known companion to "Aeneas at Washington," as from Tate's "Not Fear of God" (1932), in which Tate decided that *Conquistador* was "morally obsolete" (in MacLeish's words). See *Letters of Archibald MacLeish, 1907–1982*, ed. R. H. Winnick (Boston: Houghton Mifflin, 1983), p. 249; and Robert S. Dupree, *Allen Tate and the Augustinian Imagination: A Study of the Poetry* (Baton Rouge: Louisiana State University Press, 1983), pp. 146–47.

37. Letters from Tate to John Peale Bishop, May 24 and 30, 1940 (in *The Republic of Letters* ed. Young and Hindle, pp. 166–67).

38. In 1943 he wrote Bishop about Pound: "I can imagine myself holding, as I have held and do hold, views of my country that go deeply against the current grain; but I cannot imagine myself, in time of war, emotionally identifying myself with my country's enemies, whatever the causes of the war may be." It should be emphasized that here he "base[d] this feeling" not on ideological agreement with the Allied effort but on the practical notion "that it can never be a good thing for a nation to lose a major war" (letter from Tate to Bishop, September 6, 1943 [ibid., pp. 213–14]). In any event, Tate did attempt to get a naval commission in 1942.

39. Letters from Tate to Bishop, May 30 and July 8, 1940 (ibid., pp. 166–67).

40. His comment on the "parallel between the Brooks-MacLeish school and Dr. Goebbels' Hitler-inspired attack on 'modern' art" led to his bold conclusion that "[i]t is wholly irrelevant whether a nationalist-patriotic censorship of the imagination is set up in the interest of democracy or of totalitarianism"; this was further than MacDonald or other detractors of "the 'Brooks-MacLeish Thesis' " would go ("On the 'Brooks-MacLeish Thesis,' " p. 38).

41. Tate's comment was quoted by Coleman Rosenberger in a review of Lowell that appeared in the Wallace Stevens issue of *Voices* near the end of the war. Rosenberger put "little trust" in Tate's agrarianism or in "Lowell's Catholicism," though

he did show how one could admire Lowell's formal achievement and leave aside both the ideological implications of his Catholicism and his endorsement by Tate ("Lowell, [Selwyn] Schwartz, Gustafson," *Voices* 121 [Spring 1945]: 50–51). Stevens's poems appeared on pp. 25–29. Tate's review has been reprinted in *The Poetry Reviews of Allen Tate, 1924–1944*, ed. Ashley Brown and Frances Neel Cheney (Baton Rouge: Louisiana State University Press, 1983), pp. 210–11.

42. For Tate's definition of "relativism in history," see "Liberalism and Tradition," in *Reason in Madness* (New York: G. P. Putnam's Sons, 1941), pp. 206–7, 215; on relativism as a form of solipsism (or "any other *ism* that denotes the failure of the human personality to function objectively in nature and society"), see "Narcissus as Narcissus," p. 136; on "collectivism" and positivism, see p. 215 esp.; on social realism, see, e.g., "Tension in Poetry," p. 65. Kenneth Burke prepared a similar list of Tate's hatreds in his review of *Reason in Madness* and Ransom's *The New Criticism* ("Key Words for Critics," *Kenyon Review* 4, 1 [Winter 1942]: 132).

43. Allen Tate, "The State of Letters," *Sewanee Review* 52, 4 (October-December 1944): 612.

44. *Sixty American Poets, 1896–1944*, ed. Allen Tate and Frances Cheney (Washington, D.C.: [Library of Congress], 1945), p. 156. "There can be little doubt that Stevens and Eliot are the most impressive poets in the modern movement in English."

45. "M. M.," *Catholic World* 156 (January 1943): 501.

46. Louis Kronenberger, "American Letters: A Restricted View," *Nation* 155, 22 (November 28, 1942): 592.

47. For Cowley's pertinent response to the charge that the Office of War Information was "the principal refuge of what [one conservative critic] regards as the radical and subversive elements within the government," see Malcolm Cowley, "The Sorrows of Elmer Davis," *New Republic* 108, 18 (May 3, 1943): 591.

48. Kronenberger, "A Restricted View," p. 592.

49. This was to be Oscar Williams's "The Poets' Choice." Williams's prospectus called for an election of and among poets that would be "impartial and democratic." Elected poets would then be graded A, B, or C and given space accordingly, A's receiving twenty to thirty pages, B's ten to fifteen, C's four to seven (unpublished typescript, "Plan for a New Anthology by Oscar Williams," enclosed with letter from Williams to Horace Gregory [January 1942?] [Syracuse, Gregory Papers]). At this point, Williams noted, he was about to approach Stevens.

50. Kronenberger, "A Restricted View," p. 592. There can be little doubt that *American Harvest* made itself clear as an example of the way in which the "aesthetic" or "New" critic would go about putting together an anthology. Carlos Baker's favorable notice observed that Tate and Bishop "have chosen to dispense with the usual explanatory apparatus of the historico-critical anthology"—a real turn, we see in retrospect, in the very business of designing anthologies; that such a turn would be made in a *wartime* anthology was all to Tate's point. Moreover, Baker's positive statements about such a principle were made alongside a somewhat negative response to Hemingway's *Men at War* anthology of war stories, in which some of the selections were, Baker noticed, more history than literature—literary writing that served as " 'news that stays news' because [in Hemingway's view] it is true both

to itself and to its constituents." The juxtaposition of Tate's and Hemingway's wartime anthologies made for an analysis that bespoke the entire nationalist-formalist controversy in sum ("Anthologies of Mars and Midas," *Sewanee Review* 51 [January-March 1943]: 160–63).

51. Joseph Warren Beach, *New England Quarterly* 16, 1 (March 1943): 139.

52. Malcolm Cowley, "The Banquet," *New Republic* 107, 16 (October 19, 1942): 506.

53. Quoted by Daniel Aaron, *Writers on the Left* (New York: Avon, 1961), p. 353.

54. Howard Mumford Jones, "An Outpouring of Americana," *Saturday Review of Literature* 25, 43 (October 24, 1942): 17, 16.

55. Letter from Tate to Bishop, November 2, 1942 (*The Republic of Letters*, ed. Young and Hindle, p. 195).

56. Alfred Kazin, "Criticism at the Poles," *New Republic* 107, 16 (October 19, 1942): 492–95.

57. Ibid., pp. 493, 494, 495.

58. For example: "Allen Tate's South was remarkably like Michael Gold's Russia" (ibid., p. 493).

59. The term was established as commonplace in the *Partisan Review* of January-February 1942.

60. In a letter of May 2, 1941, Schwartz wrote Tate to criticize the way in which, in the *Reason in Madness* essays, Tate misrepresents his opponents' positions in order to attack them (*Letters of Delmore Schwartz*, ed. Robert Phillips [Princeton: Ontario Review Press, 1984], p. 112).

61. Letter from Schwartz to Ransom, February 11, 1943 (ibid., p. 153).

62. Ransom himself described the difference accurately: "I'd like to repel any idea of a political 'strategy' behind [*The New Criticism*]. I wanted it to have *no politics at all* [Ransom's emphasis]. I don't think the Positivists will regard me as a convert, unless they are grateful for small favors, which I think they are not" (letter to Tate, May 23, 1941 [*Selected Letters of Ransom*, ed. Young and Core, p. 282]). On Kazin's claims to centrist politics: the portion of *On Native Grounds* published in the *New Republic* amply showed this: "Whether written on the extreme left or extreme right," Kazin wrote, ". . . criticism became a totalitarianism in an age of totalitarianisms, rather characteristic of the times [the thirties] in its rigidity and pride, and not the easiest to live with" ("Criticism at the Poles," p. 492); that this indicated Kazin's position, in effect, as an ally of the nationalists was clearest when he stated that both extremist criticisms "vented so much passion upon literature *while betraying their essential remoteness from it*" (p. 493; emphasis added). In other words, a new, ostensibly postideological criticism, steering between extremist totalitarianisms, established new contact with the world.

63. Cleanth Brooks, "Allen Tate," *Poetry* 66, 6 (September 1945): 325, 326, 329. By the phrase "the failure of nerve" Brooks was referring particularly to an article of that name by Sidney Hook in the January-February 1943 *Partisan Review* and generally to the series of related "Failure" essays written by those stung, as one of Tate's allies put it, "by the anti-positivist bee." Stevens evidently read the series; he

told Church (*L* 441) of his response to Hook's "The New Failure of Nerve" and John Dewey's "Anti-Naturalism in Extremis."

64. Burke, "Key Words for Critics," p. 130. Burke called this a "novel twist": "Were I to suggest a slogan for [Ransom's] version of the poetic state, it would be not *e pluribus unum* but *ex uno plura*" (p. 131). Ransom's political analogy can be found in the chapter on I. A. Richards in *The New Criticism* (Norfolk, Conn.: New Directions, 1941): Ransom warned that he is taking "advantage of the condition of the reader's mind at this time"—major ideological conflict—in offering "a 'topical' metaphor." The result, in this political context, is an attack on the nationalists even more pointed than Burke's review suggests; finding that the poem, though like the democratic state, "restrains itself faithfully from a really *imperious* degree of organization," and that scientific discourse (what Burke simplified as "prose") does not regard its member parts as citizens, Ransom concluded with a swipe at nationalist poets and positivist critics who called for responsibility: "So much for the responsible poets. The responsible critics would be the thinkers who should consider that the most blinding of all illusions is the habit of regarding scientific discourse as comprehensive of the whole range of cognition" (pp. 43–44).

65. Tate, "Tension in Poetry," in *Reason in Madness*, pp. 77, 64. He unites Symbolists and Metaphysicals to this effect, e.g.: "'Tis madness to resist or blame / The force of angry heavens flame" (p. 78). For another use of "unity," see "Narcissus as Narcissus," p. 136.

66. Burke, "Key Words for Critics," p. 130.

67. Cleanth Brooks, who gave a paper at the symposium, reported to Tate that "the historians didn't care to fight," even though one of them, Yale's Frederick Pottle, had been designated—evidently by nationalist Norman Holmes Pearson—to "be the big gun" for the historicist side (letter from Brooks to Tate, dated "Monday" [September 1941] [Princeton, Box 13, Tate Papers]). Pearson would not merely generally represent the confluence of the antiformalist and nationalist arguments; he would doubtless represent it for Stevens, who was familiar with Pearson's work from 1938 and later came to know him well (a connection of some literary-political consequence in the fifties).

68. See *Selected Letters of Ransom*, ed. Young and Core, p. 284.

69. Donald Stauffer, "Cooperative Criticism: A Letter from the Critical Front," *Kenyon Review* 3 (Winter 1941): 142.

70. Letter from Brooks to Tate, [September 1941] (Princeton, Tate Papers).

71. Stauffer, "Cooperative Criticism," p. 143.

72. *New Poems 1943*, ed. Williams, pp. 240, 240–41, 241–42.

73. Malcolm Cowley, "War and the Poets," *New Republic* 113, 9 (August 27, 1945): 258.

74. *New Poems 1943*, ed. Williams, p. vii.

75. Ibid.

76. Harry Roskolenko, "In the Pity," *Quarterly Review of Literature* 2, 1 (1945): 358.

77. Stevens quoted by Williams in *New Poems 1943*, p. v. Stevens's statement was first published in *Parts of a World* (New York: Alfred A. Knopf, 1942), on the

last page (facing p. 182). It has been reprinted in *The Palm at the End of the Mind: Selected Poems and a Play*, ed. Holly Stevens (New York: Alfred A. Knopf, 1971), p. 206; and *OP* 241–42.

Poetry and the Actual World

1. Letter from Church to Tate, February 11, 1942 (Princeton, Tate Papers).

2. For more on the connections between the Church chair memorandum and Stevens's concept of the supreme fiction, see Bates, *A Mythology of Self*, pp. 212–13.

3. Letter from Ransom to Tate, January 28, 1942 (*Selected Letters of Ransom*, ed. Young and Core, pp. 289–90). In fact Ransom had thought of Tate's friend Church as a possible donor as early as January 16, 1941 (p. 276), when Ransom asked Tate if Church would "do a discriminating thing for us" and hoped Tate would "give me some good dope." But Ransom's approaches had not succeeded by the time he thought of Church again in early 1942. For more on the wartime troubles of the *Southern Review*, see George Core, "Remaking the *Sewanee Review*," *Chattahoochee Review* 8, 4 (Summer 1988): 72.

4. Cleanth Brooks described for Tate at one point how the *Southern Review* was operating on a "hand-to-mouth basis" (letter from Brooks to Tate, December 31, 1941 [Princeton, Tate Papers]).

5. Letter from Ransom to Tate, February 6, [1942] (*Selected Letters of Ransom*, ed. Young and Core, p. 291). Ransom had already discussed with Church "the possibility of his assuming some editorial place and being responsible for some foreign-literature part of the K.R." (letter from Ransom to Tate, November 15, 1941 [*Selected Letters of Ransom*, p. 286]).

6. Letter from Ransom to Tate, February 6, 1942 (ibid., p. 291).

7. Letter from Ransom to "Cleanth and Red," March 30, 1942 (Beinecke, Southern Review Papers).

8. Interview.

9. Letter from Church to Tate, April 1942 (Princeton, Tate Papers).

10. Letter from Ransom to Tate, July 12, 1942 (*Selected Letters of Ransom*, ed. Young and Core, p. 298).

11. Letter from Church to Stevens, May 31, 1943 (Huntington, WAS3418). See also *Selected Letters of Ransom*, ed. Young and Core, p. 292.

12. Letter from Ransom to Tate, February 6, [1942] (*Selected Letters of Ransom*, ed. Young and Core, p. 291).

13. Letter from Church to Stevens, May 31, 1943 (Huntington, WAS3418).

14. Letter from Church to Stevens, December 31, 1942 (Huntington, WAS3408).

15. Letter from Ransom to Tate, May 16, [1942] (Princeton, Tate Papers).

16. Letter from Church to Stevens, December 31, 1942 (Huntington, WAS3408).

17. *Selected Letters of Ransom*, ed. Young and Core, p. 297.

18. Even though Church attended some meetings with Princeton deans, he was always dependent on the availability of Thorp and Tate. Tate served as Church's guide through Princeton's administrative hierarchy, advising him as to the form and tone of their meetings with Deans Gauss and Stewart (letter from Church to

Tate, September 24, 1943 [Princeton, Tate Papers]). While Cleanth Brooks received an informal letter from Church and a formal invitation from Gauss, he knew who was really behind it: "My special thanks to you," he wrote Tate, ". . . you must have had a great deal to do with it" (letter from Brooks to Tate, January 30, 1941 [Princeton, Tate Papers]).

19. Tate, in his introduction to *The Language of Poetry* (Princeton: Princeton University Press, 1942), identified *Mesures* and briefly explained its suspension (p. viii).

20. Letter from Church to Stevens, January 25, 1942 (Huntington, WAS3396).

21. Stevens saw *High Tor* on Saturday, March 20, 1937. While deeming it a "farce," he saw that Anderson's effort had been to balance imagination with reality (letter to Morton D. Zabel, March 27, 1937 [Chicago, Zabel Papers]). The reviews had already emphasized the political realities represented in the verse play: Stark Young noted that Anderson showed how "the full exercise of creative imagination can bring it into a reality" ("High Tor and Highty Tighty," *New Republic* 89 [February 3, 1937]: 411), and *Newsweek* felt compelled to mention that the character played by Burgess Meredith, a leftist, was "driven by his hatred of capitalism" (*Newsweek* 9, 3 [January 16, 1937]: 32).

22. The file was released to Herbert Mitgang under the Freedom of Information Act (*Dangerous Dossiers: Exposing the Secret War against America's Greatest Authors* [New York: Donald I. Fine, 1988], p. 149).

23. Joseph Wood Krutch, "The Theater and the War," *Nation* 153, 19 (November 8, 1941): 464. A negative but informative review—with details about the play's concentration camp—was Wolcott Gibbs's "Nor Good Red Herring," *New Yorker*, November 1, 1941, pp. 45–46.

24. This "reprieve" was so much of an apparent change that even Church felt vaguely that Anderson "does not seem to fit into the picture" (letter to Stevens, January 25, 1942 [Huntington, WAS3396]).

25. Kenneth Burke, "The Tactics of Motivation," *Chimera* 1, 4 (Spring 1943), 37–53. Imagining possible American responses to "the situation after the war," Burke criticized in advance the sort of "dissipation" that leads to "tak[ing] whatever satisfactions are nearest at hand and let[ting] things go at that: a kind of lapse into 'isolationism,' not merely as regards international politics, but as regards collective planning of any sort. . . . Ironically, liberal education is being questioned most drastically precisely at a time when the world will have the greatest need for it. That is, the liberal education is needed insofar as it is 'global' and 'mediatory' " (pp. 37–38, 39).

26. The lecture was published as "The Study of Symbolic Action" in the first issue of *Chimera* (1, 1 [Spring 1942]: 7–16), a journal published at Princeton and edited by a number of graduate students and recent graduates of the English department and the Creative Writing Program.

27. Tate evidently had made the introductions to the speakers in the first series (see *L* 383). He did not leave Princeton until after the 1942 academic year; Burke's lecture was given in the spring of that year.

28. Burke made his call for reconciliation in his review of Kazin's *On Native Grounds*, in *Chimera* 2, 2 (Autumn 1943), citing Kazin's attack on Ransom in the

book, paraphrasing the formalist counterattack, and finally urging the two positions to "bring . . . [their] many aspects into closer relationship with one another" (p. 48).

29. Letter from Ransom to Tate, April 22, [1942] (Princeton, Tate Papers).

30. *Selected Letters of Ransom*, ed. Young and Core, p. 285.

31. Letter from Ransom to Tate, March 20, 1941 (Princeton, Tate Papers).

32. William Troy, *Partisan Review* 9, 2 (March-April 1942): 170.

33. Ibid.

34. Colum, "The New Books of Poetry," p. 9.

35. Stauffer, "Writers and the South," sec. 7, p. 5.

36. The clipping was found laid into Stevens's copy of the volume (Huntington, RB440456).

37. Elizabeth Drew, "Use of Words," *New York Herald Tribune Books*, April 5, 1942, p. 21.

38. Quoted in the Princeton University Press advertising pamphlet for the book; Stevens saved his own copy (Huntington, RB440456).

39. Tate, *The Language of Poetry*, p. vii.

40. The relation between Richards and the American New Critics was complex, of course, and had its own line of development from the early thirties, when Cleanth Brooks, who admired Richards's *Principles of Literary Criticism* so much as to have read it a dozen times between 1927 and 1931, told Tate that "you might have used I. A. Richards to support your position instead of considering him on the other side" (letter from Brooks to Tate, April 19, [1931] [Princeton, Tate Papers]). By the war years, Brooks was urging Tate, who had always been suspicious of Richards's positivist methodology, to rethink the relation as a matter of shrewd consensus-building. By the time of the 1941 *Mesures* series, Tate was being sincere when he wrote that it was something of a requirement for such gatherings to include Richards as a principal, if somewhat rival, master. For more on the similarities between Tate and Richards, judged by someone who heard both speak in the *Mesures* series, see R. P. Blackmur, "San Giovanni in Venere: Allen Tate as Man of Letters," *Sewanee Review* 67 (Winter 1959): 618–22 esp.; while Tate in 1940 described Richards's method as supplying a "hocus-pocus of impulses, stimuli and responses," Blackmur decided that generally "Richards and Tate eat one bread" (pp. 621, 622).

41. Brooks told Tate he was pleased that Tate had spent some time reviewing Richards's career in early 1941. Brooks evidently felt that such willingness on Tate's part, and the fact that both the special Princeton audience and "the general topic, 'The Language of Poetry' " would be congenial for agreement among formalists, and, not least, that Richards had "come a long way in our direction," were sure signs that the *Mesures* lectures would be the occasion for rapprochement (letters from Brooks to Tate, January 30, 1941, and February 13, [1941] [Princeton, Tate Papers]).

42. Tate, *The Language of Poetry*, p. 74.

43. Tate apparently worked closely with the press on the project. He, evidently with Church, made "minor revisions" in the text of Stevens's "Noble Rider," which the editors at the press were sure to note were the work of Tate and Church (letter

from Virginia M. Heide of the Princeton University Press to Stevens, September 22, 1941 [Huntington, WAS1403]).

44. Princeton University Press pamphlet.

45. A full, persuasive reading of the relations between "Notes toward a Supreme Fiction" and Richards's *Coleridge on Imagination* is offered by B. J. Leggett, *Wallace Stevens and Poetic Theory: Conceiving the Supreme Fiction* (Chapel Hill: University of North Carolina Press, 1987), pp. 17–41.

46. I. A. Richards, "The Interactions of Words," in *The Language of Poetry*, ed. Tate, p. 66.

47. I. A. Richards, *Coleridge on Imagination* (Bloomington: Indiana University Press, 1960; first ed. 1934), pp. 149, 86.

48. Letter from Tate to Stevens, October 4, 1941 (Huntington, WAS2344).

49. See Melita Schaum, *Wallace Stevens and the Critical Schools* (Tuscaloosa: University of Alabama Press, 1988), pp. 80–82.

50. John Crowe Ransom, *The World's Body* (Baton Rouge: Louisiana State University Press, 1938), p. 59.

51. Alfred Kazin was one who thought of the two observations as a pair (*On Native Grounds: An Interpretation of Modern American Prose Literature* [New York: Reynal and Hitchcock, 1942], p. 434).

52. *Harvard Advocate* 127, 3 (December 1940): 31.

53. Letter (carbon) from Tate to Zabel, April 19, 1944 (Princeton, Tate Papers).

54. Winters's "Wallace Stevens, or the Hedonist's Progress," arguing that Stevens's manner had degenerated after *Harmonium*, was just then being published in *The Anatomy of Nonsense* (1943).

55. Elizabeth Drew and John L. Sweeney, *Directions in Modern Poetry* (New York: W. W. Norton, 1942), pp. 72–77. Drew and Sweeney did include a section entitled "The Nineteen Thirties," but no reference to Stevens's more recent work is to be found there.

56. G[eoffrey] E. G[rigson], "The Stuffed Goldfinch," *New Verse* 19 (February–March 1936): 18–19.

57. Delmore Schwartz, "Instructed of Much Mortality," *Sewanee Review* 54 (Summer 1946): 440–41.

58. William Van O'Connor, "The Politics of a Poet," *Perspective* 1 (Summer 1948): 204–7.

59. This is not to suggest, however, that O'Connor did not also feel a commitment to the idea of poetry as war effort of which Tate would disapprove. Indeed, O'Connor, who knew Karl Shapiro in New Guinea and spoke of *V-Letter* before it appeared in 1944, wrote Tate enthusiastically of war poetry. Because he saw Tate's observations of Shapiro quoted in an article on war poetry, O'Connor seems to have assumed that Tate agreed with statements made there favoring the subgenre (letter from O'Connor to Tate, August 8, 1944 [Princeton, Tate Papers]).

60. William Van O'Connor, "Tension and Structure of Poetry," *Sewanee Review* (Autumn 1943): 556, 561, 558–59.

61. There are many descriptions of the differences between agrarianism and the New Criticism; I am interested in the shifts in the rhetoric that Ransom in particular used to rationalize the change in relation to literary-political debates, and for

this point a basic summary is Paul Conkin, *The Southern Agrarians* (Knoxville: University of Tennessee Press, 1988), pp. 127–38.

62. Kazin, "Criticism at the Poles," p. 495; the passage was reproduced in *On Native Grounds*, p. 434.

63. Kenneth Burke, *Chimera* 2, 2 (Autumn 1943): 47–48. On the editorial board of *Chimera* were William Arrowsmith and Frederick Morgan; both had been Tate's students in the Creative Writing Program and both knew Church at least to the extent of having been guests at Cleveland Lane.

64. He was an associate professor of English at Harvard. During the war he published poetry in the leading journals; *Shakespeare and the Nature of Man* appeared in 1942.

65. Theodore Spencer, "The Alumni," delivered before the Harvard Chapter of the Phi Beta Kappa in May 1943 and reprinted in *American Scholar* 13, 1 (January 1944): 26–34. Stevens's Phi Beta Kappa poem was "Description without Place."

66. Their fistfight seven years earlier is surely an example of contrasting personalities; see *WSR* 97–99, 143, and Richardson, *The Later Years*, pp. 124–25.

67. That he liked to think of Hemingway as a poet may indicate, among other things, that Stevens had had nothing to do with the novels; no Hemingway novel remained in his library, nor is one mentioned in published or unpublished letters. Certainly the later work would not come recommended by his sort of reader; José Rodríguez Feo later referred to *Across the River and into the Trees* as "detestable" (*SM* 183).

68. Letter from Stevens to Church, January 9, 1941 (Huntington, WAS3486). Marjorie Perloff aptly suggests that by January 1941 it was untenable to continue referring to a person primarily as "a Jew"—let alone as "an Austrian Jew" after the Anschluss or as "a Jew and a Communist" after Hitler's destruction of several European communist parties—and still claim that "I have not paid any attention to their political beliefs" (see "The Supreme Fiction and the Impasse of Modernist Lyric," pp. 42–45). That by 1943 Stevens was prepared to nominate Rahv without such qualifications is surely a sign of the shift from his pre–Pearl Harbor position.

69. "One of Allen Tate's predecessors at Princeton," Stevens explained, "was Archibald MacLeish, who is a close personal friend of Hemingway's. . . . If some one at Princeton could interest MacLeish (and he must have many friends at Princeton, including Dr. Gauss), it is quite possible that MacLeish could interest Hemingway" (*L* 412).

70. The list of speakers was reported to Stevens in a letter from Henry Church to Stevens, March 14, 1943 (Huntington, WAS3411).

71. The lecture was published in the July–September issue: Allen Tate, "Dostoevsky's Hovering Fly: A Causerie on the Imagination and the Actual World," *Sewanee Review* 51, 3: 353–69; these sentences appear on p. 356.

72. Ibid., p. 357.

73. Ibid., p. 359.

74. Ibid., p. 367.

75. Ibid., pp. 354–55. "Armies used to besiege towns by 'regular approaches'; or they took them by direct assault; or they manoeuvred the enemy out of position,

perhaps into ambuscade. These strategies are used today, for in war as in criticism the new is usually merely a new name for something very old. . . . When you have total war must you also have total criticism? In our time critics are supposed to know everything, and we get criticism on all fronts. Does this not outmode the direct assault? When there are so many 'problems' (a term equally critical and military) you have got to do a little here and a little there, and you may not be of the command that enters the suburbs of Berlin. At any rate, the world outside poetry, which continues to disregard the extent that it is also *in* poetry, resists and eludes our best understanding."

76. Ibid., p. 353.

77. Ibid., p. 362.

78. Ibid., p. 367. That Tate knew something of Burke's grammars can be deduced from Burke's letter to Tate, March 17, 1942 (Princeton, Tate Papers).

79. Tate, "Dostoevsky's Hovering Fly," pp. 368–69.

80. Ibid., p. 359.

81. Interview with author and Harvey Teres, New York, May 18, 1989; portions published as "An Interview with Stanley Burnshaw," *Wallace Stevens Journal* 13, 2 (Fall 1989): 109–21.

82. Letter from Burke to Tate, November 13, 1944 (Princeton, Tate Papers). Burke was obviously also thinking of the statements he would make about Stevens's Mount Holyoke lecture, "The Figure of Youth as Virile Poet," in *The Grammar of Motives* (New York: Prentice-Hall, 1945), pp. 224–26.

83. See *L* 445–46 and the letter from Church to Stevens, April 19, 1943 (Huntington, WAS3415).

Conversations with Refugees

1. Most prominent among critics who have criticized Stevens's essays in this way was A. Alvarez, who wrote in the *London Observer*: "Stevens could hardly come closer to impenetrability [and] . . . carried difficulty and allusiveness to their sticking place. . . . [T]he prose had no rhythm to sustain it in its twistings, . . . ingrown subtleties . . . [and] knotty allusiveness. . . . [H]e went on so much about reality because he was never altogether sure that, according to his own fastidious lights, it existed at all" ("Aesthetic Preacher," February 14, 1960, p. 21). Even when other notices were generally receptive to Stevens's lecture-essays, they assumed Alvarez's basic point that Stevens "lacked . . . a language for public communication." Babette Deutsch found some "dubious pages" along with admirable "plummy aphorisms" ("Pastures of the Imagination," *New York Herald Tribune Book Review* 28, 17 [December 9, 1951]: 4). Malcolm Bradbury sniffed "a rarefied air" in the essays: "they savour perhaps a bit too much of the closet" ("Towards a Supreme Fiction," *Manchester Guardian*, March 18, 1960, p. 8), while the *New Yorker* notice found "richness of allusion" but also the imagination as "monotonously a central subject" (February 23, 1952, p. 111).

2. Richard Eberhart, "The Stevens Prose," *Accent* 12, 2 (Spring 1952): 123, 124.

3. Ibid., p. 123.

4. That Wilson was present was the recollection of Alan McGee in 1977 (unpublished, untranscribed interview with Peter Brazeau [Huntington]).

5. Letter from Robert L. Ramsey to Stevens, July 12, 1943 (Huntington, WAS3362).

6. The handwritten manuscript of "The Figure of Youth as Virile Poet" (Huntington, Box 66, WAS4143). Compare with *NA* 64.

7. See *WSR* 183n.

8. And to some extent among American pragmatists and neorealists, as his *Pluralist Philosophies of England and America* had appeared in an English translation in 1925 (trans. Fred Rothwell [London: Open Court Company]); this study of William James and John Dewey included sections on Whitman, Royce, Lowes Dickinson, and Henry James, Sr.

9. A letter from Church to Paulhan, October 3, 1940 (Société Paulhan), puts a Swiss account at Paulhan's disposal; see below, p. 104.

10. It is also possible that Wahl was to be among the thousand "most seriously ill" prisoners freed from Drancy by the *Judenreferat* after the terrible outbreak of dysentery in the fall of 1941 (Michael R. Marrus and Robert O. Paxton, *Vichy France and the Jews* [New York: Basic Books, 1981], p. 253). When Stevens met Wahl at Mount Holyoke, stories were already circulating about his escape from the camp aboard a delivery truck (unpublished interview with Paul and Constance Saintonge [Huntington]). For a sense of the enormous difficulties facing French Jews who wished to emigrate, see Marrus and Paxton, pp. 161–63.

11. Interview.

12. Letter from Church to Tate, September 24, 1942 (Princeton, Tate Papers).

13. Quoted by Marrus and Paxton, *Vichy France and the Jews*, p. 253.

14. Letter from Church to Stevens, January 25, 1942 (Huntington, WAS3396); we know that by late February Stevens was receiving the journal (*L* 404).

15. "L'Actualité Littéraire," *Lettres Françaises*, July 1941, p. 46: Paulhan is reported to have been fired from *NRF*, having "aroused German suspicion" by his recent writings; Otto Abetz replaces Paulhan with Drieu La Rochelle. "L'Actualité Littéraire," October 1941, p. 37: Paulhan has been arrested and imprisoned; Wahl, "one of the masters of contemporary philosophy," is arrested and then sent to a concentration camp. "L'Actualité Littéraire," July 1942, p. 53: Paulhan is negotiating with Drieu La Rochelle a return to editorship of *NRF*, the (impossible) conditions being that Drieu would bring Gide, Claudel, and Valéry to the editorial board and that the review remain nonpolitical, "strictly literary."

16. Ibid., November 1942, p. 47.

17. Ibid., February 1943, p. 82.

18. Ibid.

19. Now with the Huntington's Stevens Papers, Box 66, WAS2677.

20. This is not to say that information about the French camps was unavailable: see Marrus and Paxton, *Vichy France and the Jews*, p. 347; and Walter Laqueur, "Jewish Denial and the Holocaust," *Commentary* (December 1979): 44–55.

21. Michael R. Marrus, *The Holocaust in History* (Hanover, N.H: University Press of New England, 1987), p. 154.

22. Systematic deportations began in the summer of 1942 (Marrus and Paxton, *Vichy France and the Jews*, p. 252). See also John F. Sweets, *Choices in Vichy France: The French under Nazi Occupation* (New York: Oxford University Press, 1986), p. 124.

23. Quoted in Frank Jones, "Writers and Defeat," *Partisan Review* 9, 2 (March–April 1942): 117.

24. Henri Focillon, *The Life of Forms in Art*, trans. Charles Beecher Hogan and George Kubler (New Haven: Yale University Press, 1942).

25. In *Wallace Stevens and Poetic Theory*, B. J. Leggett has argued convincingly that "Focillon is the presiding spirit of 'The Figure of the Youth as Virile Poet' " (p. 148).

26. "L'Actualité Littéraire," *Lettres Françaises*, July 1942, p. 54.

27. The *Partisan Review* ran Harold Rosenberg's "On the Fall of Paris," 7, 6 (December 1940): 440–48; William Peterson's "What Has Become of Them?—A Check-List of European Artists, Writers and Musicians," 8, 1 (January-February 1941): 59–62; and Victor Serge's "French Writers, Summer 1941," trans. Jean Connolly, 8, 5 (September-October 1941): 387–88. Also see Eugene Jolas, "Letters and Arts in Wartime Europe," *Living Age* 360, 4495 (April 1941): 113–21; and the anonymous "Letter from Paris," *Nation* 154, 2 (January 10, 1942): 39–40.

28. Letter from Church to Stevens, July 13, 1942 (Huntington, WAS3401).

29. Jones asked Stevens if he had read "Writers in Defeat" in the *Partisan Review*; Stevens replied, "I must have read it; I always read [*Partisan*]," calling it "[t]he only exception to the dreary scene" (*WSR* 130).

30. Unpublished, partly transcribed interview with Frank Jones conducted by Peter Brazeau (Huntington).

31. Frank Jones, "The Sorcerer as Elegist," *Nation* 155 (November 7, 1942): 448.

32. Letter from Church to Stevens, August 17, 1940 (Huntington, WAS3383).

33. Evident in a letter from Church to Stevens, October 9, 1940 (Huntington, WAS3386).

34. "Il me semble, s'agissant d'une revue où une large place a été faite dès l'origine aux Lettres allemandes (*Mesures* donnait à la fois le texte et la traduction des textes choisis) que les Autorités allemandes ne peuvent voir ce projet que d'un oeil favorable. Je suis tout prêt au demeurant à soumettre à qui de droit, sitôt rentré, la collection de *Mesures* (où il n'a jamais été traité, fût-ce par allusion, de sujets d'actualité, où la guerre même n'a jamais été mentionnée)" (letter from Jean Paulhan to Jean Lebrau, August 27, 1940 [Société Paulhan; courtesy Bernard Leuilliot]).

35. Ibid.

36. See the letter from Paulhan to Suarès of April 8, 1940, in *Correspondence Jean Paulhan André Suarès*, ed. Yves-Alain Favre (Paris: Gallimard, 1987), p. 296. Paulhan felt that if he could not successfully see Suarès's piece into print "the public could justly accuse me of treason."

37. Letter from Paulhan to Suarès, June 5, 1940 (ibid., p. 306).

38. Letter from Church to Stevens, October 8, 1940 (Huntington, WAS3385); it was at this point that Church was meeting with Dean Gauss to see about bringing Paulhan to Princeton.

39. Letter from Church to Stevens, November 14, 1940 (Huntington, WAS3388).

40. For providing me with this information and more on Paulhan's wartime experiences, I am grateful to Frederic Grover (letter to author, December 8, 1987) and Bernard Leuilliot (letter to author, November 16, 1987); see also Alexander Werth, *France: 1940–1955* (New York: Henry Holt, 1956), p. 143.

41. Letter from Church to Stevens, January 25, 1942 (Huntington, WAS3396). Church also seems to have misunderstood the precise reasons for Paulhan's arrest; it was for his work with *Résistance*. Auberjonois, who was reunited with Paulhan immediately after the liberation of Paris, remembers that it was quite a bit more involved than possessing "British tracts": "His role was that of a courier of getting people always to know what other people were doing" (interview).

42. Paulhan's account of his interrogation has been reprinted as "Une Semaine au Secret," in *Ouevres Completes* (Paris: Cercle du Livre Précieux, 1966), 1: 293–97; the quoted phrase appears on p. 294 ("Ils préparent surtout un groupement armé qui veut attaquer les Allemands").

43. As early as November 1939, Paulhan knew that Church in the United States "is pursuing *Mesures*" and "is calling for its naturalization" (*Correspondance Jean Paulhan André Suarès*, ed. Favre, p. 273).

44. Three letters from Church to Paulhan dated October 1940 did make it through, and are now holdings of Société Paulhan in Paris (courtesy Jacqueline Paulhan). The one describing Stevens's efforts on Paulhan's behalf is dated October 16.

45. Letters from Barbara Church to Paulhan, February 27, 1941, and [1942] (Société Paulhan).

46. *Correspondance Jean Paulhan André Suarès*, ed. Favre, p. 273; the phrase is "Ses lettres sont belles et chaleureuses."

47. Letter from Henry Church to Stevens, January 25, 1942 (Huntington, WAS3396).

48. Letter from Church to Stevens, January 18, 1944 (Huntington, WAS3433). That Gide did receive his copy of *Notes* has been confirmed by Fernand Auberjonois (interview).

49. "A Letter from Paris," p. 39. On Stevens's acquisition of Gide's *Journal*, see *L* 461, 602.

50. Letter from Church to Stevens, April 15, 1943 (Huntington, WAS3414). Church had sent Wahl a copy of the Cummington Press *Notes toward a Supreme Fiction* in the fall of 1942 (letter from Church to Stevens, October 28, 1942 [Huntington, WAS3405]).

51. It was just then, for example, that he wrote Samuel French Morse so positively that "[t]he lot of a soldier is one of the great experiences" (*L* 450).

52. Letter from Barbara Church to Stevens, January 27, 1943 (Huntington, WAS3564). Roosevelt and Churchill met with their Combined Chiefs of Staff at the Casablanca Conference, setting the strategy that would send Auberjonois, among many others, to Tunisia. Barbara Church's sense of the drama of the North African meeting was hardly overstated: Roosevelt's trip made him the first president to fly while in office, the first to leave the country in time of war, the first since Lincoln to visit an actual theatre of war.

53. "The Official Communique" was reproduced in full in the *New York Times*, January 27, 1943, p. 1.

54. A seemingly out-of-place quotation from Heraclitus in the anonymous prose of the *entretiens* brochure may have been identified as Wahl's at the conference: Wahl had a penchant for quoting Heraclitus that was obvious to anyone who

heard or read him. During his own *entretiens* lecture, titled "On Poetry" (and published later, in *Chimera* 2, 3 [Winter-Spring 1944]: 35–41), Wahl quoted Heraclitus (p. 39) so movingly that Stevens evidently wrote Wahl later to have the quotation repeated for him. Wahl obliged and Stevens in turn quoted the lines for Church, noting, "I feel the most intense desire to have a copy of Herakleites after that quotation" (letter of October 12, 1943 [Huntington, WAS3524]).

55. Brochure entitled "Les Entretiens de Pontigny," enclosed with a letter dated July 17, 1943 (Huntington, WAS632). The translated phrases are: "permanence des valeurs dans l'âme même de l'homme et dans la cité libre"; "des thèmes éternels et des circonstances actuelles"; "une métaphore chère à Shelley, les valeurs, comme les flammes, gardent leur identité sous des apparences sans cesse changeantes."

56. Klaus Mann, *André Gide and the Crisis of Modern Thought* (New York: Creative Age Press, 1943).

57. According to the recollection of Alan McGee (*WSR* 182).

58. Helen Patch, untitled note published in the all-Stevens issue of *Trinity Review* 8, 3 (May 1954): 35.

59. Mrs. Church fondly recalled Stevens "under the trees . . . on the lawn" (letter from Barbara Church to Marianne Moore, January 12, 1950 [Rosenbach, Moore Papers, V:10:23]). For Moore's recollection, see "On Wallace Stevens," *New York Review of Books* 2 (June 25, 1964): 5–6; *The Complete Prose of Marianne Moore*, ed. Patricia C. Willis (New York: Viking, 1986), p. 582.

60. Alan McGee (*WSR* 182) and Constance Saintonge (*WSR* 184). Saintonge had the impression that Stevens "flew in for a minute and went out," that he was "bor[ne] away . . . the minute it was over." In fact Stevens remained for the afternoon session on politics and political theory; see below.

61. Marianne Moore, "Feeling and Precision," *Sewanee Review* 52, 4 (Autumn 1944): 499.

62. Marianne Moore, "A Bold Virtuoso," in *Complete Prose of Marianne Moore*, p. 445. "Eulalia," she says, figures in Cohen's poem "Le Grande Clarté du Moyen Age": "A virtuous maiden was Eulalia, / Beautiful of body, more beautiful of soul." There is no other evidence of Stevens's previous familiarity with Cohen's work.

63. Letter from Church to Stevens, August 24, 1943 (Huntington, WAS3426). This may have been due as much to Church's feeling slighted that Cohen had "never heard about MESURES before" as to Cohen's politics.

64. "Cot Assumes Mission," *New York Times*, November 13, 1943, p. 6. Cot returned to Algiers in November.

65. Letter from Church to Stevens, August 24, 1943 (Huntington, WAS3426). On September 1, 1943, Stevens quoted Church's remark to Bishop, identifying Church as "a friend of mine": letter from Stevens to Bishop (Huntington, WAS206).

66. Letter from Stevens to Bishop, August 25, 1943 (Huntington, WAS205).

67. Letter from Church to Stevens, August 24, 1943 (Huntington, WAS3426).

68. Letter from Bishop to Stevens, August 31, 1943 (Huntington, WAS203).

69. Letter from Stevens to Alfred A. Knopf, May 2, 1944 (Huntington, WAS3150).

70. Letter from Tate to Marianne Moore, April 26, 1944 (Rosenbach, Moore Papers, V:57:31).

71. John Peale Bishop, "Entretiens de Pontigny, 1943: Introduction," *Sewanee Review* 52, 4 (Autumn 1944): 493, 495–96.

72. Ibid., p. 495.

73. Ibid., p. 498.

74. Ibid., p. 495.

75. Bishop read to his 1943 audience an old paper: "The Discipline of Poetry" was first published in the *Virginia Quarterly Review* 14, 1 (Winter 1938): 341–56.

76. Ibid., p. 350.

77. Ibid., p. 346.

78. Ibid., pp. 346, 348.

79. Ibid., p. 356.

80. Ibid., p. 353.

81. Ibid., pp. 348–49: "Baudelaire looked about him in the streets of Paris, in the poor streets, . . . even in the common ditch of the dead who have died poor. . . . [N]either T. S. Eliot nor Allen Tate would be today what they are had it not been for Baudelaire." Bishop, of course, had war-effort credentials. In 1941, as publications director of Nelson Rockefeller's Office of the Coordinator of Inter-American Affairs, Bishop was the official force driving his and Tate's *American Harvest*; see his assertion, not unlike Soby's, that "[t]he future of the arts is in America" ("The Arts," *Kenyon Review* 3 [Spring 1941]: 179–90). And "It is not too much to say," Tate later recalled, "that the war hastened [Bishop's] death. Not being a man of action he had few of the public outlets which some of his friends seized to get themselves through" (Tate, "John Peale Bishop: A Personal Memoir," *Western Review* 12, 2 [Winter 1948]: 71); Stevens read Tate's memoir and associated it with the Mount Holyoke conference (*L* 579). Still, even when Bishop was working with Rockefeller's group, it was felt that "Bishop is *too thick with Tate* to be of much use" to poets and critics starting up nationalist projects (so wrote Norman Holmes Pearson to John Gould Fletcher, January 22, 1943 [Arkansas, Fletcher Papers]; emphasis added).

82. Bishop had left word that he hoped Edmund Wilson and Tate would take charge of the unpublished manuscripts. Monroe Wheeler turned over to Tate the manuscripts of the Mount Holyoke lectures (letter from Tate to Marianne Moore, April 26, 1944 [Rosenbach, Moore Papers, V:57:31]). There seems to have been negotiation for possession of the Stevens typescript even before Bishop's death, with Tate informing Bishop at the end of 1943 that Henry Church had persuaded Stevens to send the Mount Holyoke talk to the *Sewanee Review* (letter of December 23, 1943 [*The Republic of Letters*, ed. Young and Hindle, p. 219]).

83. Letter from Tate to Stevens, May 11, 1944 (Huntington, WAS2355).

84. Letter from Tate to Moore, April 26, 1944 (Rosenbach, Moore Papers, V:57:31).

85. Rorty's many wartime articles would have made his radical views perfectly clear, e.g., "Advertising Rides the War" (*Common Sense* 12, 12 [December 1943]: 436–40). See also Wald, *The New York Intellectuals*, pp. 54–55.

86. Letter from Tate to Moore, May 1, 1944 (Rosenbach, Moore Papers,

V:57:31). This was not, of course, the explanation Tate gave when annotating Bishop's introductory essay; he told readers of the *Sewanee Review* that the editor "regrets" that Rorty's and Wahl's (and Bishop's) papers had been published elsewhere (*Sewanee Review* 52, 4 [Autumn 1944]: 493 n. 1).

87. Tate, "The State of Letters," p. 610.

88. Cleanth Brooks, an admirer of Tate's editorship, wrote Tate that he was "a little disappointed" with the *entretiens* in *Sewanee* (letter from Brooks to Tate, November 5, 19[44] [Princeton, Tate Papers]).

89. Wahl, "On Poetry," p. 36.

Ode to the Dutch Dead

1. Letter from Ransom to Tate, May 16, [1942] (Princeton, Tate Papers).

2. John Crowe Ransom, mimeographed "War Letter," May 20, 1942, p. 2 (Princeton, Tate Papers). Stevens, a *Kenyon* subscriber, received a copy of this solicitation.

3. Fernand Auberjonois knew this (interview).

4. Letter from Church to Stevens, April 15, 1943 (Huntington, WAS3414).

5. Jean Paulhan, "Escritores Presos en París Ocupado," *Sur* 12 (November 1944): 55–59.

6. Letter from Church to Stevens, January 16, 1945 (Huntington, WAS3449).

7. Letter from Church to Stevens, May 31, 1943 (Huntington, WAS3418); for Stevens's reply, see *L* 450.

8. Letter from Tate to Stevens, November 23, 1942 (Huntington, WAS2348).

9. Letter from Ransom to Tate, January 28, 1942 (*Selected Letters of Ransom*, ed. Young and Core, p. 289). Ransom told Tate that Kenyon College sought "extra budget money" for the aeronautics course as a means of stabilizing enrollment in a time when "the boys and the parents" want the curriculum to have "military features" (letter from Ransom to Tate, February 6, [1942] [*Selected Letters of Ransom*, p. 291]). Ransom did discuss the issue briefly in print, mentioning pressures put on a literary venture "because of the increased expense of a curriculum accelerated for war" (J[ohn] C[rowe] R[ansom], "War and Publication," *Kenyon Review* 4, 2 [Spring 1942]: 218).

10. Letter from Tate to Stevens, November 23, 1942 (Huntington, WAS2348).

11. Letter from Tate to Stevens, October 21, 1942 (Huntington, WAS2346).

12. Core, "Remaking the *Sewanee Review*," p. 73; Core's essay recounts the complex story of Lytle's interim editorship.

13. Letter from Tate to Bishop, October 20, 1942 (*The Republic of Letters*, ed. Young and Hindle, p. 193). Stevens briefly discussed the goings-on at *Sewanee* in a letter to Church on November 11 (*L* 428).

14. Letter from Ransom to Alexander Guerry (*Selected Letters of Ransom*, ed. Young and Core, p. 295).

15. Just as "Dutch Graves" came in, Lytle complained to Tate that Tate did "almost everything for the magazine" and that "this has worried me a little" (*The Lytle-Tate Letters: The Correspondence of Andrew Lytle and Allen Tate*, ed. Thomas Daniel Young and Elizabeth Sarcone [Oxford: University Press of Mississippi, 1987], p. 196). George Core has written that Tate decided "to become an unusually

active advisory editor, . . . with results little short of spectacular. But to what extent he was responsible for securing various contributions, and to what degree Lytle was, it is now impossible to determine" ("Remaking the *Sewanee Review*," p. 73).

16. On December 14, in a letter to Tate, Stevens refers to "your taking on THE SEWANEE REVIEW at the present time" (Huntington, WAS2391). A letter to Stevens dated October 26, 1942 (Huntington, WAS2347), suggests that by then Stevens might have sent a handwritten note to (or telephoned) Lytle to confirm his intention to send the poem to *Sewanee*.

17. Letter from Stevens to Tate, December 14, 1943 (Huntington, WAS2391).

18. Letter from Lytle to Tate, October 16, 1944 (*The Lytle-Tate Letters*, ed. Young and Sarcone, p. 204).

19. "Of Interest to Libraries," *Sewanee Review* 51 (Autumn 1943): 614.

20. Letter from Tate to Stevens, December 8, 1942 (Huntington, WAS2349).

21. Tate, "Narcissus as Narcissus," in *Reason in Madness*, p. 140.

22. That Stevens placed Tate's December 8 letter in his copy of *Reason in Madness* reinforces the suggestion that the new poem was written with Tate's critical reading of his "Ode" in mind.

23. The phrases are Eric Bentley's in "Kahler and Mumford," *Kenyon Review* 7, 1 (Winter 1945): 144, 145.

24. Allen Tate, "The Fallacy of Humanism," *Hound & Horn* 3, 2 (January-March 1930): 243. In "Liberalism and Tradition," Tate criticized historicist methods as follows: "The positivist procedure . . . becomes profoundly unhistorical when it argues, as it often does argue, that the medieval plowman was rationalizing his hard labor with worship of the Virgin at Chartres: the historian reads into the past his own moral disunity" (*Reason in Madness*, p. 214). This antihistoricist argument became familiar to Stevens; he soon found it in Eric Bentley's judgment, in a review we know Stevens read (*L* 481), of Erich Kahler's *Man the Measure* and Lewis Mumford's *The Condition of Man*. Bentley used Kahler to complain about the " 'popular trend in the modern writing of history that tends to equalize and level all epochs' " ("Kahler and Mumford," p. 148). Writing for Ransom's *Kenyon Review*, Bentley pointedly backed the New Critics' use of the "extraordinary tools of modern investigation" and called for a *"new critical historiography"* that would stand "parallel to the new criticism of poetry" (p. 148; emphasis added).

25. Allen Tate, "The Present Function of Criticism," in *Collected Essays* (Denver: Alan Swallow, 1959), p. 7; and "Miss Emily and the Bibliographer," p. 54.

26. Allen Tate, *Collected Poems, 1919–1976* (New York: Farrar, Straus and Giroux, 1977), p. 20.

27. Tate, "Narcissus as Narcissus," in *Reason in Madness*, p. 136.

28. Ibid., pp. 140, 136.

29. On Zweibrügge: letter from Stevens to John Z. Harner, July 17, 1945 (Huntington, Box 73, File 6). On Jean Henri/Johann Heinrich: letter from Stevens to Frank E. Lichtenthaeler, October 24, 1944 (Huntington, Box 73, File 20).

30. Letter from Elizabeth Stevens MacFarland to Stevens, December 11, 1941; originally filed and now preserved with Stevens's pencil notes (Huntington, WAS1076).

31. Letter from Stevens to Elizabeth MacFarland, December 19, 1941 (Huntington, WAS1094).

32. By late 1941 he knew from Davis's *History of Bucks County* and other sources that Dirk Hanse Hogeland, on his father's Barcalow side, commanded the vessel that brought him from Holland to New Amsterdam and that he settled in Flatbush in the mid-seventeenth century; his grandson Direk was the one who emigrated to Bucks County.

33. Letter from Floyd DuBois to Stevens, June 11, 1942 (Huntington, Box 72, Folder 22).

34. Its receipt is confirmed in a letter from Stevens to Lila James Roney, January 11, 1943 (Huntington, Box 74, File 5). See Milton Bates, "To Realize the Past: Wallace Stevens's Genealogical Study," *American Literature* 52, 4 (January 1981): 610; and Peter Brazeau, " 'Hepped on Family Ties': Wallace Stevens in the 1940s," in *The Motive for Metaphor: Essays on Modern Poetry*, ed. Francis C. Blessington and Guy Rotella (Boston: Northeastern University Press, 1983), pp. 37–47.

35. Letter from Stevens to Jane MacFarland, December 3, 1943 (Huntington, WAS2762).

36. So Stevens read in John A. Zellers, "A Brief History of the Zeller Family" (1945), p. 11; Stevens's copy of the pamphlet is filed in Box 74 at the Huntington. The events described took place in 1708 and 1709.

37. Göring's speech was reported and excerpted in the *New York Times*, October 5, 1943, pp. 1, 4; the threat was prominently covered in the *Times* as late as November 1 (sec. 7, p. 31).

38. George Core's phrase in "Remaking the *Sewanee Review*," p. 76.

39. Letter from Tate to Stevens, August 14, 1944 (Huntington, WAS2356).

40. Letter from Stevens to Tate, August 17, 1944 (Princeton, Tate Papers). Raymond Mortimer, "The Elizabethan Background," *New Statesman and Nation* 25, 637 (May 8, 1943), 310.

41. Letter from Tate to Stevens, November 30, 1944 (Huntington, WAS2358).

42. Allen Tate, "Emily Dickinson," in *Reactionary Essays on Poetry and Ideas* (New York: Charles Scribner's Sons, 1936), p. 19.

43. Ibid., p. 20.

44. Ibid., p. 19.

45. Ibid., p. 21.

46. "X" is usually assumed to be Eliot. Harold Bloom, for instance, states that in the poem "X or Eliot is massively (and prophetically) dismissed" (*The Poems of Our Climate*, p. 151).

47. In "Tension in Poetry," the essay in *Reason in Madness* Stevens evidently knew best (*L* 393), Tate made himself perfectly clear on the point: "For, in the long run, whatever the poet's 'philosophy,' however wide may be the extension of his meaning—like Milton's Ptolemaic universe in which he didn't believe—by his language shall you know him" (*Reason in Madness*, pp. 75–76). This is not to suggest that Tate would uniformly resist praising a poetry of ideas in such polemical, clear terms. Note, for instance, how a positive notion of a poetry of ideas excludes the sort of "point of view" that is commonly understood to define the concept: Emily Dickinson's poetry, Tate wrote, "*is* a poetry of ideas, and it demands of the reader a point of view—not an opinion of the New Deal or of the League of Nations, but an ingrained philosophy that is fundamental, a kind of settled attitude that is almost extinct in this eclectic age" ("Emily Dickinson," p. 3; emphasis added). While here,

in the opening paragraph of the essay, Tate can claim Dickinson's work to be "a poetry of ideas," by the end of the same essay he is arguing that "[l]ike Miss Dickinson, Shakespeare has no *opinions*" (p. 21). The difference between idea-as-"opinion" and idea-as-"idea" is equal to that between externalities irrelevant to literary greatness and inner truths that support it. Again, of Dickinson, Tate wrote: "Miss Dickinson's ideas were deeply imbedded in her character, not taken from the latest tract" (p. 16).

48. Letter from Tate to Stevens, January 15, 1944 (Huntington, WAS2353).

49. Allen Tate, *The Vigil of Venus* (Cummington, Mass.: Cummington Press, 1943), p. [2]. Tate had sent Stevens a signed copy of this book (Huntington, RB431837).

50. Letter from Tate to Ashley Brown, July 19, 1977 (Ashley Brown).

51. Letter from Tate to Donald Davidson, February 3, 1943 (*The Literary Correspondence of Donald Davidson and Allen Tate*, ed. John Tyree Fain and Thomas Daniel Young [Athens: University of Georgia Press, 1974], pp. 337–38).

52. An inscribed copy, now part of the Huntington collection (RB440404).

53. "[T]he principal poem . . . did not particularly attract me when I first read it," he wrote Duncan (*L* 488). And: "When I first read SEASONS OF THE SOUL, I did not particularly like it," he wrote Tate in acknowledging Tate's gift of the Cummington edition (*L* 487). Duncan later quoted Stevens's comments in a letter to Tate (letter of January 2, 1948 [Princeton, Tate Papers]).

54. F. W. Dupee, "Frost and Tate," *Nation* 160 (April 21, 1945), 466.

55. Alfred Kreymborg, "The Shadow of Mars," *Saturday Review of Literature* 28, 12 (March 24, 1945): 33.

56. Lowell quoted by Radcliffe Squires, "Will and Vision: Allen Tate's *Terza Rima* Poems," p. 554.

57. R. P. Blackmur, "Notes on Eleven Poets," *Kenyon Review* 7, 2 (Spring 1945): 343–44, 343.

58. Louise Bogan, "Verse," *New Yorker*, April 7, 1945, p. 81.

59. Horace Gregory, "On Vitality, Regionalism, and Satire in Recent American Poetry," *Sewanee Review* 52, 4 (October–December 1944): 584.

60. Blackmur, "Notes on Eleven Poets," p. 344.

61. Lines 31–33; the scene is the ghastly suicides' wood, in the second ring of the seventh circle.

62. Letter from Tate to Stevens, November 23, 1942 (Huntington, WAS2348).

63. Letter from Donald Davidson to Tate, March 21, 1943 (*The Correspondence of Davidson and Tate*, ed. Fain and Young, pp. 338–39).

64. Blackmur, "Notes on Eleven Poets," p. 345.

The War-Poem Business

1. See Terrence Des Pres, *The Survivor: An Anatomy of Life in the Death Camps* (New York: Oxford University Press, 1976), especially the extraordinary third chapter, "Excremental Assault," pp. 53–71.

2. The exceptions to this generalization are both numerous and important, to be sure; Paul Célan, his verse often breaking down into a stammer and finally suggesting silence, is one. But even Nelly Sachs's famous poem—"This can be put on

paper only / with one eye ripped out"—which Alvin Rosenfeld rightly calls "the most costly *ars poetica* I know" (*A Double Dying* [Bloomington: Indiana University Press, 1980], p. 32), is nevertheless *ars poetica*. The position Rosenfeld offers in *A Double Dying* and the one offered here agree, it should be noted, in rejecting such conclusions as Reinhard Baumgart's and Michael Wyschogrod's—namely, that literature from or about the camps "imposes artificial meaning on mass suffering . . . 'by removing some of the horror' " (Baumgart) and that "poor art . . . must result . . . [from] [a]ny attempt to transform the holocaust into art" (Wyschogrod). See *A Double Dying*, p. 14; and Wyschogrod's "Some Theological Reflections on the Holocaust," *Response* 25 (Spring 1975): 68.

3. The typescript is divided into three groups. The concentration camp poems make up the last nine pages. The first page is inscribed by Wahl to Stevens: "A Wallace Stevens / En profonde reconnaissance pour les moment qu'il nous a donné bien vive sympathie / Jean Wahl" (Huntington, Box 66, filed with WAS2677).

4. Letter from Stevens to Alfred A. Knopf, May 2, 1944 (Huntington, WAS3150).

5. Marrus and Paxton, *Vichy France and the Jews*, p. 253.

6. See Des Pres, *The Survivor*, chapter 2, "The Will to Bear Witness," a convincing accumulation of many survivors' statements about the overwhelming desire to ward off the silence that was itself a strategic weapon in the Final Solution.

7. "[TÉMOIN MALGRÉ MOI:] Et me voici jeté au milieu de ces luttes: / 'C'est juste,' 'c'est bien,' 'c'est droit.' / Je dis comme les autres, / Malgré moi je porte témoignage."

8. Wahl, "On Poetry," p. 36.

9. "[PAS D'ISSUE:] Jours affreux à vomir et sans aucune issue."

10. These were sonnets 1 and 5.

11. "Vérité, tu n'es belle que sous la menace."

12. Lawrence Langer, *The Holocaust and Literary Imagination* (New Haven: Yale University Press, 1975), esp. pp. 82–84; Rosenfeld, *A Double Dying*, esp. pp. 25–32.

13. Rosenfeld, *A Double Dying*, pp. 25–26.

14. Primo Levi, *Survival in Auschwitz*, trans. Stuart Woolf (London: Collier, 1959; first published, 1958), pp. 102–3.

15. Elaine Scarry, *The Body in Pain: The Making and Unmaking of the World* (New York: Oxford University Press, 1985), pp. 45–51.

16. Letter from Henry Church to Stevens, April 29, 1944 (Huntington, WAS3438).

17. Letter from Ransom to Stevens, June 15, 1944 (*Selected Letters of Ransom*, ed. Young and Core, p. 316).

18. Quoted by J[ohn] C[rowe] R[ansom] in "Artists, Soldiers, Positivists," *Kenyon Review* 6 (Spring 1944): 276.

19. Ibid., pp. 276–78.

20. New York: Devin-Adair, 1945, p. 158.

21. In his introduction, Williams proclaimed his judgment that Stevens was among the Americans who provided "perhaps the best documentation of the approach of war that any literary period has produced" and warned "us of the dangers

and necessities of the coming peace" (*The War Poets* [New York: John Day Company, 1945], pp. 9, 10).

22. Koch, "Poetry in World War II," p. 76.

23. *New Poems 1942: An Anthology of British and American Verse*, ed. Oscar Williams (Mount Vernon, N.Y.: Peter Pauper Press, 1943), p. 13.

24. "The true poets," Williams claimed, "began the Battle for Democracy, with full war warnings, more than a decade ago" (*New Poems 1942*, p. 11), with that decade reaching back well beyond Hitler's coming to power in 1933—to 1929, Williams declared, when, remarkably, the "best war poetry, *for this war*," was already being written (ibid., p. 12; emphasis added). This inexplicable remark was obviously intended to reply to those who criticized American poets for having acted irresponsibly as National Socialism was beginning to rear its head.

25. Ibid., p. 11.

26. Ibid., pp. 165–72.

27. *The Poetry Reviews of Allen Tate*, ed. Brown and Cheney, p. 206.

28. *New Poems 1942*, ed. Williams, pp. 14–15.

29. Ibid., pp. 117, 191.

30. *The Poetry Reviews of Allen Tate*, ed. Brown and Cheney, p. 207.

31. *New Poems 1943*, ed. Williams, pp. v, vii.

32. Ibid., p. vii.

33. John Peale Bishop, reviewing *New Poems 1943* for the *Nation* (October 16, 1943, pp. 446–47), and Milton Klonsky, in *New Republic* (September 20, 1943, p. 399), both praised Moore's poem without mentioning Stevens at all. Bishop believed Moore's poem "succeeds because . . . she finds the heart of her matter in her own responsibility for [others'] having to fight."

34. Susan Schweik, "Writing War Poetry Like a Woman," in *Politics and Poetic Value*, ed. Robert von Hallberg (Chicago: University of Chicago Press, 1987), pp. 159–83.

35. *The Complete Poems of Marianne Moore* (New York: MacMillan, 1967), p. 138.

36. Koch, "Poetry in World War II," p. 82.

37. *The War Poets*, ed. Williams, p. 6.

38. *New Poems 1944*, ed. Williams, p. v.

39. F. T. Prince, *Collected Poems* (New York: Sheep Meadow Press, 1979), p. 55.

40. *New Poems 1944*, ed. Williams, p. iv.

41. See Mona Van Duyn, "Wartime Attitudes and Platitudes," *Poetry* 64, 6 (September 1944): 339–43: she found many poems "written in wartime which ha[ve] *nothing but* a 'message' of soothing assurance to offer [their] readers," and she deemed them "dangerous" (p. 340). Another detractor was Vivienne Koch, whose review of Shapiro's *V-Letter and Other Poems* and A. M. Klein's *Hitleriad* praised Shapiro for his "determination *not* to become a 'war poet' " ("Poets Look Beyond the War," *New York Herald Tribune Weekly Book Review*, October 29, 1944, p. 14). Jarrell was not convinced: "You'd think Shapiro would have written something good about [the war], but I suppose his goofy ideas about the war as a subject for poetry have kept him from it" (letter to Oscar Williams, undated [late 1944?] [Houghton, Oscar Williams Papers]).

42. John Peale Bishop had declared his belief that Williams's use of the war-poem designation was not intended "to describe the book, but to sell it" (*Nation* 157, 16 [October 16, 1943]: 446).

43. Roskolenko, "In the Pity," p. 356.

44. The title of his review in the October 2, 1944, *New Republic*, p. 435.

45. Letter from Morse to Gordon Cairnie, August 24, 1944 (Houghton, Grolier Book Shop Papers, bMS Am 1897.1 [174]).

46. Matthiessen, "Not All New, Some Good," p. 435.

47. Ibid., p. 436.

48. Koch, "Poetry in World War II," p. 76.

49. He had been reading Serge's "The Revolution at Dead-End (1926–1928)," trans. Ethel Libson, *Politics* 1 (June 1944), where he found the sentence "I followed his argument with the blank uneasiness which one might feel in the presence of a logical lunatic." Konstantinov told Serge of treachery that had undone Lenin's Central Committee, its source being unnamed "powerful capitalists" in the United States. Knowing that repelling this plot would require "an inquisitorial genius," Konstantinov went to the committee with evidence of the plot; he was deported to Siberia in the early thirties. For Serge, as undoubtedly for Stevens, the counterconspiratorial thinking evinced by Konstantinov was proof of "a psychological phenomenon unique in history" (p. 150). Jan Pinkerton identified the source in "Stevens' Revolutionaries and John Addington Symonds," *Wallace Stevens Journal* 1, 3/4 (Fall-Winter 1977): 129 n. 1. Stevens first jotted down Serge's statement in his commonplace book; see *Sur Plusieurs Beaux Sujects: Wallace Stevens' Commonplace Book*, ed. Milton J. Bates (Stanford and San Marino: Stanford University Press and Huntington Library, 1989), p. 79.

50. This is precisely Helen Vendler's suggestion: the epilogue, she argues, "perhaps would not have been appended to *Notes* if the war had not made some external justification of poetry seem necessary" (*On Extended Wings: Wallace Stevens's Longer Poems* [Cambridge: Harvard University Press, 1969], p. 205).

51. Ruth Lechlitner, "Poetry in Time of War," *New York Herald Tribune Books*, September 27, 1942, p. 16.

52. Garden City, N.Y.: Doubleday, Doran and Co., 1942, p. 1.

53. Northrop Frye, "Poetry," *Canadian Forum* 22, 261 (October 1942): 220.

54. Letter from Stevens to Philip May, January 22, 1943 (Houghton, Philip May Papers, bMS Am 1543).

55. Letter from Tate to Stevens, November 30, 1944 (Huntington, WAS2358). He wrote again in December: "I feel exactly as you do about writing a prose statement on poetry and war. But Williams will be able to get out an anthology ... because many people can't resist blowing off on any subject whatever" (December 18, 1944 [Huntington, WAS2359]).

56. Letter from Stevens to Tate, December 4, 1944 (Princeton, Tate Papers); *L* 479n gives "politically" for "potentially."

57. "[T]here are a few poems on the subject of war," he wrote (letter from Stevens to Robert Tucker, February 15, 1954 [Huntington, WAS2428]).

58. James Clifford, *The Predicament of Culture: Twentieth-Century Ethnography, Literature and Art* (Cambridge: Harvard University Press, 1988), p. 13.

59. A jotting in his notebook, "From Pieces of Paper," quoted by Lensing, *A Poet's Growth*, p. 188.

60. Clifford, *The Predicament of Culture*, p. 14.

61. Letter from Tate to Oscar Williams, October 17, 1944 (Houghton, Oscar Williams Papers, bMS Am 1513).

62. A party was held at the Gotham Book Mart on the evening of June 19 to celebrate the publication of the book; many of the contributors were invited (undated invitation to Willard Maas [Brown, Maas Papers]).

3. Description without a Sense of Place

1. The speech was published in *Virginia Quarterly Review* 21, 4 (Autumn 1945): 483–96.

2. Ibid., p. 494.

3. Ibid., p. 493.

4. Ibid., p. 496.

5. Now at Harvard.

6. Letter from Theodore Morrison to Stevens, March 7, 1945 (Huntington, WAS910).

7. Letter from William C. Greene to Stevens, March 19, 1945 (Huntington, WAS913). Stevens learned at this early point that he would share the platform with Sumner Welles and that Stevens's Poem would precede Welles's Oration.

8. Or about thirty minutes, a figure I arrived at by calculating from Stevens's own estimation, later, that it took him more than three minutes to recite one canto of "Notes toward a Supreme Fiction" (letter from Stevens to Robert Tucker, February 24, 1954 [Huntington, WAS2431]).

9. Letter from Theodore Morrison to Stevens, March 13, 1945 (Huntington, WAS911).

10. Archbishop Francis J. Spellman, for instance, speaking at Fordham University on June 13, honored individually 166 students and alumni killed in action up to that date ("Fordham's Needs Put at $17,000,000," *New York Times*, June 14, 1945, p. 14).

11. I have cited Nicholas Murray Butler, speaking at Columbia ("Butler Talk at Columbia," *New York Times*, June 6, 1945, p. 14); Robert C. Clothier, at the New Jersey College for Women ("President of Rutgers Addresses New Brunswick Graduates," *New York Times*, June 11, 1945, p. 21); Ralph Sockman, at New York University ("N.Y.U. Graduates Hear Dr. Sockman," *New York Times*, June 11, 1945, p. 21); Armistead Dobie, at the University of Virginia ("Dobie Discusses Spirit of Youth," *Charlottesville Daily Progress*, June 25, 1945, p. 2); and Arthur Vanderbilt, the University of Pennsylvania speaker ("Dean Deplores Political Apathy," *Philadelphia Inquirer*, June 29, 1945, p. 13).

12. The PBK ceremonies traditionally have taken place two days before commencement and have been open to the public. It is very likely that Stevens heard a PBK Poem or two during his years as a Harvard student.

13. LaFarge's "The Great and Marching Words" was later published in the *Saturday Review of Literature* 26, 30 (July 24, 1943): 16; Spencer's "The Alumni,"

in *American Scholar* 13, 1 (Winter 1943–1944), 26–34; and Scott's "Contradictions in an Ultimate Spring," in *To Marry Strangers* (New York: Thomas Y. Crowell Company, 1945), pp. 2–8 (quoted lines: p. 2).

14. Vendler, *On Extended Wings*, pp. 218, 219; Bloom, *The Poems of Our Climate*, p. 239; Joseph N. Riddel, *The Clairvoyant Eye: The Poetry and Poetics of Wallace Stevens* (Baton Rouge: Louisiana State University Press, 1965), pp. 199, 198.

15. Michael T. Beehler, "Meteoric Poetry: Wallace Stevens's 'Description without Place,'" *Criticism* (Summer 1977): 241.

16. Ibid., p. 245.

17. Daniel Bell's is the eminent version of the idea; in *The End of Ideology: On the Exhaustion of Political Ideas in the Fifties*, rev. ed. (New York: Collier, 1962; first published, 1960), it is most clearly delineated on pp. 393–407.

18. Vendler, *On Extended Wings*, pp. 220, 218.

19. The rituals may have seemed even more rigid to Stevens than to others. The letters arranging the 1944 visit of Winfield Scott make no mention of the appropriate dress for the occasion, a concern that Acting Secretary Greene, in Stevens's apparently special case, had anticipated; nor does Morrison's letter of invitation to Scott bother mentioning the *lack* of custom as to topic (letter from Morrison to Scott, January 21, 1944 [Brown, Scott Papers, HA21894]). Morrison's correspondence files are housed at Harvard (HUG 4582.505); the PBK poems, and associated materials for the 1940s, are filed with the Phi Beta Kappa papers (Harvard).

20. Welles, "Vision of a World," p. 489.

21. Paul Rosenfeld, "History for Art's Sake," *Nation* 149, 2 (July 8, 1939): 50. There is no special evidence that Stevens read this piece; his general interest in Rosenfeld's work is confirmed by the essay (*OP* 246–47) he wrote for the commemorative volume *Paul Rosenfeld: Voyager in the Arts* (1948).

22. Letter from Stevens to Henry Church, June 17, 1944 (Huntington, WAS3537).

23. Letter from Church to Stevens, August 5, 1943 (Huntington, WAS3425).

24. Letter from Church to Stevens, April 24, 1945 (Huntington, WAS3452).

25. It has been summarized by Peter Novick in *That Noble Dream: The "Objectivity Question" and the American Historical Profession* (Cambridge: Cambridge University Press, 1988), pp. 300–311.

26. Letter from van Geyzel to Stevens, June 6, 1941 (Huntington, WAS2454).

27. Meyer Schapiro, "The Revolutionary Personality," *Partisan Review* 6 (1940): 474.

28. This is chapter 5 of part 3 of Wilson's book *To the Finland Station: A Study in the Writing and Acting of History* (Garden City, N.Y.: Doubleday and Company, 1940).

29. Schapiro, "The Revolutionary Personality," p. 467.

30. Ibid., pp. 475, 468, 469.

31. Welles, "Vision of a World," pp. 494–95.

32. Letter from Stevens to van Geyzel, May 26, 1938 (Huntington, WAS2472).

33. Frederic Prokosch, *Voices* (New York: Farrar, Straus and Giroux, 1983), p. 53.

34. Clifford, *The Predicament of Culture*, p. 10.

35. Randall Jarrell, "Reflections on Wallace Stevens," *Partisan Review* 18 (May-June 1951): 341.

36. Letter from Stevens to van Geyzel, May 27, 1948 (Huntington, WAS2484). The Ceylonese van Geyzels descend from Frans van Geyzel of Belgium, who married the daughter of Angelo Pegalotti, an Italian, and Dominga Perez, who was of Sinhalese or of mixed Sinhalese-Portuguese stock. The van Geyzel clan was not primarily English, although, like many Burghers, Leonard was educated at Cambridge. The genealogy of the Ceylonese van Geyzels, through the first decades of the twentieth century, was published in the *Journal of the Dutch Burgher Union* 10, 3 (1917): 70–79. I am grateful to Percy Colin-Thomé, president of the Dutch Burgher Union in Sri Lanka, for his help with the van Geyzel family tree.

37. By 1954, when Stevens used this last phrase, he was actually referring to the way in which the sense of "Ceylon as a fortress" was "considerably shaken" by the "Communists . . . growling not only at your back door but all around the house" (*L* 838).

38. Letter from van Geyzel to Stevens, October 14, 1941 (Huntington, WAS2455).

39. Edward Said, *Orientalism* (New York: Pantheon Books, 1978), p. 158.

40. The issue of South Asian poetic theory preoccupied Stevens. Was there one? Having been exposed, undoubtedly at Harvard, to a generation of orientalist scholars, such as F. Max Müller, who tended to view poetic embellishments as largely meaningless ornament, and studied texts to accumulate data for the historical reconstruction of ancient beliefs, Stevens was surprised to find that Eastern poetics was extensive. After he purchased Arthur B. Keith's *History of Sanskrit Literature* (Oxford: Clarendon Press, 1928) in 1940, he wrote: "I had no idea until I looked over Keith's book that poetics had occupied scholars in the East to the extent that appears to be the case. When I was young and reading left and right, Max Müller was the conspicuous Orientalist of the day, and, as you must know his things, I think you will agree that Oriental poetry was at a great disadvantage" (*L* 381). Van Geyzel made it quite clear where he stood on the issue, pointing out for Stevens that even if many of the Ceylonese lived in the "steamy mess" Stevens imagined (*L* 353)—that is, without the European influence—at least they were "familiar with the classics of their own poetry. You can't say that about Europe" (letter of March 27, 1940 [Huntington, WAS2453]).

41. Stevens's copy is now part of the Huntington collection (RB440407): Leonard Woolf, *The Village in the Jungle*, 5th ed. (London: Hogarth, 1931; first published, 1913).

42. Ibid., p. 283.

43. Ibid., p. 299. Stevens's apparent acceptance of the naturalism of Woolf's novel generally ignores van Geyzel's warning that "its scope is limited." It was van Geyzel who had sent the novel as a present (letter from van Geyzel to Stevens, May 16, 1938 [Huntington, WAS2450]).

44. In Stevens's poetry, "inhuman" does not mean inhumane or unkind, but nonhuman (or, occasionally, superhuman); it is less a term of value than of description. In "The Idea of Order at Key West" it modifies the ordering, parsing muse,

"Inhuman, of the veritable ocean" (*CP* 128). The "author" of "Credences of Summer," a poem written shortly after "Description without Place," is "inhuman" because he has reached the point where he can reflect on or be reflected in nature without emotionalizing it (*CP* 377).

45. This is precisely the view of van Geyzel's friend Professor E.F.C. Ludowyk, whose introduction to the Oxford University Press edition of *The Village in the Jungle* (1981) notes that Woolf's "views, at the time advanced, on such subjects as British colonial policy" were compromised by the "moral judgement" made in the story—that "the jungle is 'evil.' " "Unfortunately," writes Ludowyk, "this indictment runs counter to the real nature of the jungle as both the jungle-dweller and the white Hamadoru [a character in the novel], who is a hunter, know." Ludowyk criticizes as racially biased in itself Woolf's use of the word *slinking* "no fewer than six times in a few pages"; the effect of such repetition is merely to "suggest furtive and sinister movement" and to undermine other successful efforts at ethnographic precision (pp. viii, ix).

46. The cautious tone van Geyzel used to reject Stevens's characterization of Ceylon as a "steamy mess" indicates this strategy. "There is a good deal of foundation for your suspicion that these parts might be very largely a steamy mess," van Geyzel replied to Stevens. "They are; *but if people have got to work all out merely to keep alive* one can[']t expect them to bother much about how things look. That they continue to preserve certain graces, even a few, is, I think very creditable. . . . That England or Europe is capable of civilizing anything seems at this juncture to be very questionable" (letter of March 27, 1940 [Huntington, WAS2453]; emphasis added).

47. Letter from van Geyzel to Stevens, October 14, 1941 (Huntington, WAS2455); the pamphlet was enclosed with this letter.

48. Gananath Obeyesekere has labeled this general trend the "Protestantization" of Sri Lankan Buddhism ("Religious Symbolism and Political Change in Ceylon," in Bardwell L. Smith, ed., *The Two Wheels of Dhamma: Essays on the Theravada Tradition in India and Ceylon*, AAR Studies in Religion 3 [1972]: 58–78; see esp. pp. 61–62).

49. The Ven. Nyanatiloka Maha-Thera, *Essence of the Buddha's Teaching* ([Ceylon]: Bauddha Sāhitya Sabhā, [1941]), pp. 2, 10. See Lynn de Silva, *Buddhism: Beliefs and Practices in Sri Lanka*, rev. ed. (Colombo: Wesley Press, 1980; first published, 1974), p. 104.

50. The old Arabic name of the island, "Serendib," is the source of the English word "serendipity," playing on Ceylon's reputation as an accidentally discovered place of savory prizes.

51. Angus Holden, *Ceylon* (London: George Allen and Unwin, 1939), p. 22.

52. Ibid., pp. 27, 14. Holden surely knew he was quoting Mrs. Heber out of context: her "classic lines" remained a popular Christian hymn for many years and were meant to indicate God's "lavish kindness" and not hotel porters' relative ineptitude.

53. Ashley Gibson, *Cinnamon & Frangipanni* (London: Chapman and Dodd, 1923), p. 14.

54. As I have already noted, I use the term as Thomson, Stanley, and Perry do in a somewhat different context in *Sentimental Imperialism: The American Experience in East Asia* (1981).

55. Gibson, *Cinnamon & Frangipanni*, pp. 31–32. It must be noted that Gibson's style is not in the least unusual; much of the travel writing about Ceylon—and there is a strong tradition of it—reads quite similarly. An anthology produced by the U.S. Information Service and the American Embassy in Sri Lanka, *Images of Sri Lanka through American Eyes: Travellers in Ceylon in the Nineteenth and Twentieth Centuries* (ed. H.A.I. Goonetileke, foreword by U.S. Ambassador Christopher Van Hollen [Colombo: USIS, 1976]), offers a generous sampling. From Moncure Daniel Conway's *Thy Pilgrimage to the Wise Men of the East* (1906), for instance, this: "I shall always think of Ceylon as an Eden, and of the Sinhalese as happy children who have not yet eaten of that tree which Pessimism calls Consciousness" (p. 194). Not included in the USIS anthology, but possibly familiar to Stevens, is Albert C. Bushnell's account of his tour of the Far East, *The Obvious Orient* (New York: D. Appleton and Co., 1911). (The Hartford Bushnells, long one of the city's most prominent families, were of general curiosity to Stevens.) Bushnell's Ceylon "is probably the most happy and prosperous colony in Asia. The native Sinhalese appreciate the fact that [under the English] they have the greatest security and the least taxation in their history; and there is no [native] legislative body to queer the governor. . . . The situation of Ceylon fits it to be a pleasure city for other continents" (p. 298).

56. Renato Rosaldo, *Culture & Truth: The Remaking of Social Analysis* (Boston: Beacon Press, 1989), p. 69.

57. Gibson, *Cinnamon & Frangipanni*, pp. 22–23.

58. The term "imperial anti-colonialism" is William Appleman Williams's; see especially the second edition of *The Tragedy of American Diplomacy*, pp. 18–50. Thomson's, Stanley's, and Perry's concept of "sentimental imperialism" is derived largely from Williams (*Sentimental Imperialism*, pp. 132–33).

59. See Lentricchia, *Ariel and the Police*, pp. 204–6, 231–39 esp.; and Fredric Jameson, "Wallace Stevens," *New Orleans Review* 11, 1 (Spring 1984): 10–19. Jameson's ambition is to engage what he calls "the Third World material in Stevens" in "an analysis of the transformation of the 'sphere of culture' and its 'autonomy' . . . in the contemporary world," and to study "the relationship between modernist language and forms and the emergence of the imperialist world system in the 'monopoly stage' of capitalism," for his projected book on the 1960s (p. 10). Reading Stevens's early poem "Tea" (*CP* 112; 1915), with its "sea-shades and sky-shades / Like umbrellas in Java," Jameson writes:

> There is . . . a subterranean relationship between the "umbrella in Java"—the fantasy of the exotic holiday—and the "umbrella *from* Java," the luxury item whose own capacity to generate images, daydreams and semic associations lies in its origins in a distant place and culture, and in the momentary function of a Third World handicraft industry to produce just such objects of consumption for the First World. . . . [T]he Third World material in Stevens is . . . a fundamental piece in the overall system, the way by which the latter comes to know a global closure and thus a universality (both Hartford *and* Yucatan, both First and Third Worlds) on which its other procedures depend. . . . [B]y

means of this crucial meditation of Third World material, a bridge is made between image and word (by means of place-names), and a transformation of purely social and cultural objects ... back to Nature and virtual landscape, since they all come to be associated with exotic *places*. (p. 15)

In the second part of the two-part chapter on Stevens in *Ariel and the Police*, Lentricchia describes Stevens's "later poetry [a]s a form of gourmandizing, but deliberately teased out and emptied of satisfaction, a sustaining of overwhelming appetite: the thrill sought is the promise of thrill, not the thrill bought" (p. 204). Stevens's "late poetry of deferred desire," Lentricchia writes, "is not the escape from gourmandizing, it is its perfection" (pp. 205–6). Lentricchia refers to van Geyzel on pp. 237–38.

60. Lensing, *A Poet's Growth*, p. 235.

61. Vendler has noted Stevens's use of "the rhetoric of climax" in this canto (*On Extended Wings*, p. 186).

62. Ibid.

63. Gibson, *Cinnamon & Frangipanni*, pp. 67, 69.

64. Ibid., pp. 64–65.

65. Letter from Simons to Stevens, January 14, 1940 (Huntington, WAS86).

66. Letter from Simons to Arthur Powell, November 21, 1942 (Chicago, Simons Papers).

67. Letter from Simons to Stevens, August 15, 1940 (Huntington, WAS91). "Hi was a guileless man and what would now be called an 'open' person," Simons's daughter, Sylvia, has said. "He was a hero-worshipper and his hero was Stevens" (letter to author, February 11, 1983).

68. In his earliest surviving attempt to explicate his own poems for an inquiring correspondent, he paused to assert, "I hate like the devil to write like this" (Filreis, "Voicing the Desert of Silence," p. 16). He later came to realize the necessity of critical explications; still, his acceptance of the procedure, as a "principal form of piety" (*L* 793), was not unequivocal. Even when he offered Simons detailed explanations, the poet-explicator relationship was guided by Simons's "[k]nowing your [Stevens's] *disinclination* 'to explain things' " (letter from Simons, January 14, 1940 [Huntington, WAS86]; emphasis added).

69. A well-known version is provided by Terry Eagleton in *Criticism & Ideology* (London: Verso, 1978; first published, 1976), pp. 13–16, 21–25.

70. Stevens's collection of Ceyloniana included Francis de Croisset's *La Féerie Cinghalaise* (1926). See *L* 327.

71. Letter from van Geyzel to Stevens, June 6, 1941 (Huntington, WAS2454). Brogan, the Cambridge political scientist, published his small book, *U.S.A.—An Outline of the Country, Its People and Institutions*, with Oxford University Press. Brogan himself recognized "the absurdity of describing the United States ... in so small a place" (p. [6]).

72. Percy Colin-Thomé, a friend of van Geyzel, informs me that nothing came of the plan to involve Eliot (letter of April 12, 1989). On Edwin Arnold, see the letter from van Geyzel to Stevens, March 27, 1940 (Huntington, WAS2453); on Eliot, the letter of June 6, 1941 (Huntington, WAS2454).

73. Clifford, *The Predicament of Culture*, p. 231.

74. Letter from Percy Colin-Thomé to author, July 1, 1988.

75. Letter from van Geyzel to Stevens, June 6, 1941 (Huntington, WAS2454).

76. While it is true that during the war van Geyzel was cut off from his regular Western contacts—his correspondences and subscriptions to the *New Yorker* and *Partisan Review*—and while a plain fact that with German submarines active in the shipping lanes personal letters were always at risk of perishing at sea, Ceylonese in general actually had unprecedented interaction with Western culture during the war years. "For the first time," writes E.F.C. Ludowyk, "Ceylonese came in contact with the white man as an ordinary human being, stripped to the waist in tropical heat and working on the same laborious tasks they knew only too well" (Ludowyk, *The Story of Ceylon* [London: Faber and Faber, 1962], pp. 266–67). See also Zeylanicus (pseud.), *Ceylon: Between Orient and Occident* ([London]: Elek Books, 1970), p. 193.

77. Stevens's reference to the East in his Harvard poem thus coincides with Welles's concern over "the rising forces" in the same region. Stevens may have read about the Welles thesis, as the newspapers described the undersecretary's pre-June speeches in sufficient detail. The *New York Times* covered one April engagement as follows: "In his speech ["Roads Forward to World Peace"] Mr. Welles warned against making a peace settlement too hastily, and asserted that unless the proposed international organization found a solution for *the rising forces of nationalism in the Near and Far East* it was not likely that there would be any extended period of peace in those areas" (April 18, 1945, p. 25; emphasis added). See also Welles, *Time for Decision* (New York: Harper and Brothers, 1944), pp. 297–304.

78. H.A.I. Goonetileke, "The Long Afternoons of E.F.C. Ludowyk: Interludes of Memory," *Lanka Guardian* (Colombo), 11, 12 (October 15, 1988): 21–22; and 11, 13 (November 1, 1988): 17–18. I am grateful to Professor Goonetileke for allowing me to read this essay in typescript.

79. E.F.C. Ludowyk, *The Footprint of the Buddha* (London: George Allen and Unwin, 1958). The others are *The Story of Ceylon* (London: Faber and Faber, 1962), and *The Modern History of Ceylon* (London: Weidenfeld and Nicolson, 1966).

80. Goonetileke, "Interludes of Memory."

81. He consulted directly with Leavis when eventually putting into place at Colombo a modified version of the Cambridge Tripos; see E.F.C. Ludowyk, "The English Department, 1921–56," *Journal of the English Association of Sri Lanka, and the Association for Commonwealth Literature and Language Studies* (Sri Lanka), no. 3 (1980): 1–6.

82. See E.F.C. Ludowyk, "Mixed Thoughts on an Asian University," *Universities Quarterly* 12, 4 (August 1958): 393–95.

83. Ibid., p. 394. If Ludowyk was at all sensitive to the charge of methodological imperialism, it was the result of a defensive reaction against those who suspected the curricular changes. "To prevent misunderstanding," he wrote in *Marginal Comments* (Colombo: Ola Book Co., 1945), "it should be said that it was never intended that a 'new dispensation' should be offered here" (p. i). He was also capable of apologizing for having "referred throughout to the work of Dr. I. A.

Richards and Dr. F. R. Leavis in a way that might suggest to the reader unfamiliar with it that they were canonical authority" (p. ii).

84. Ludowyk, *Marginal Comments*, p. xxii.

85. E.F.C. Ludowyk, "The East-West Problem in Sinhalese Literature," *Yearbook of Comparative Literature* 6 (1957): 35.

86. Letter from H.A.I. Goonetileke to author, May 26, 1988. For more on the influence of Richards and Practical Criticism on Sri Lankan poetics, see Ranjini Obeyesekere, *Sinhala Writing and the New Critics* (Colombo: M. D. Gunasena and Co., 1974). See, for instance, the section on the critical theorist E. R. Sarathchandra (pp. 38–53), whose "position [sometimes] seems merely that of one who vaguely synthesized the positions of several modern western critics such as Richards, Leavis, Empson and others" (p. 52). Ludowyk, Obeyesekere notes, "introduced the New Criticism—then new even in England—to the students of his department," and under Ludowyk's guidance Leavis, Richards, Yeats, Eliot (replacing Shelley, in New Critical manner), and the Metaphysical poets (supplanting Milton) "became part of the standard reading for the course" in Colombo (p. 30).

87. Van Geyzel's contribution is acknowledged in *Marginal Comments* (p. iv).

88. Letter from van Geyzel to Stevens, with Ludowyk enclosure, March 18, 1945 (Huntington, WAS2457).

89. Letter from H.A.I. Goonetileke to author, May 26, 1988.

90. For more on Ludowyk's debt to Richards and Practical Criticism, see Godfrey Gunatilleke, "Ludowyk as Teacher—Some Reflections on Literature as Knowledge," in *Honouring E.F.C. Ludowyk: Felicitation Essays*, ed. Percy Colin-Thomé and Ashley Halpé (Dehiwala, Sri Lanka: Tisara Prakasakayo, 1984), esp. pp. 20–22.

91. Letter from Ludowyk to van Geyzel, enclosed with letter from van Geyzel to Stevens, March 18, 1945 (Huntington, WAS2457).

92. He carefully read and annotated his own copy of *Coleridge on Imagination* (1934), and undoubtedly read Richards's *Mesures* lecture, "The Interactions of Words."

93. It was not unusual for people of van Geyzel's elite racial and social status to be familiar with Marxist rhetoric. The Ceylonese left wing during the war years was indeed led by upper- and upper-middle-class men who had come to Marxism through their university days in England. See N. Sanmugathasan, *A Marxist Looks at the History of Ceylon* (Colombo: Sarasavi Printers, 1974), p. 46. These men, van Geyzel among them, viewed the Soviet role in the war quite favorably; van Geyzel told Stevens that "if the Russian Government had not concentrated its power at considerable costs to socialist ideals the outcome of this war would have been too horrible to contemplate" (letter of March 18, 1945 [Huntington, WAS2457]). Van Geyzel's interest in the left should have been clear to Stevens. He criticized the *Partisan Review* on the grounds that "the anti-Stalinites [at *Partisan*] do not really make out a sufficiently convincing case" (letter of June 6, 1941 [Huntington, WAS2454]). He was always suspicious that American capitalism contributed to the causes of war: "There seems to be little doubt that Big Business scheming is at the back of all the muddle" (letter of October 14, 1941 [Huntington, WAS2455]).

While welcoming American influence in the postwar world, he added that "it would depend on which America won. A victory for Wall Street + the City would in the long run be as disastrous as a victory for the Nazis" (letter of June 6, 1941). The bipartisanship, or evenhandedness, of van Geyzel's political ideas was increasingly typical of a Ceylon that by the mid-fifties had become ideologically heterodox; so notes François Houtart, in *Religion and Ideology in Sri Lanka* (Colombo: Hansa Publishers, [1974]), supported by the following statistic: during the cold war, the Ceylonese vote at the UN sided 34 percent of the time with the United States and 42 percent of the time with the Soviet Union (p. 245).

94. Letter from van Geyzel to Stevens, March 18, 1945 (Huntington, WAS2457). Neruda served in Colombo as Chilean consul in 1929 and 1930, when he befriended a clique of English and Burgher intellectuals and artists associated with Lionel Wendt. As Wendt was a close friend of Leonard van Geyzel, it is almost certain that van Geyzel had come to know Neruda during this period. For more on Neruda's relation to Ceylon, see Pablo Neruda, "Passional Pavilions and May Monsoons," in *Lanka, Their Lanka: Cameos of Ceylon through Other Eyes*, ed. H.A.I. Goonetileke (New Delhi: Navang, 1984), pp. 11–17; and Neruda, *Memoirs*, trans. Hardie St. Martin (New York: Farrar, Straus and Giroux, 1977), pp. 89–101.

95. Ludowyk, *Marginal Comments*, pp. 138, 29. The role of the New Critic in Ceylon, he felt, was that of a doctor called too late to his patient: "Deficiency of words is a stage of underdevelopment which might be expected to respond to treatment. The conversation of most boys in higher forms of schools makes one feel that even the 850 words of [I. A. Richards's program of] Basic English would be a strain on their language capacities" (p. 28).

96. Princeton, Tate Papers.

97. Horace Gregory, "An Examination of Wallace Stevens in a Time of War," *Accent* 3 (Autumn 1942): 57. Hi Simons, "The Genre of Wallace Stevens," *Sewanee Review* 53 (Autumn 1945): 566–79.

98. Quoted in Paul Mariani, *William Carlos Williams: A New World Naked* (New York: McGraw-Hill, 1981), p. 498.

99. Kenneth Burke, "The Vegetal Radicalism of Theodore Roethke," *Sewanee Review* 58 (1950): 68–108.

100. Ransom, "Poets without Laurels," in *The World's Body*, p. 59. Tate's decision to publish "Description without Place" did send mixed signals to the poetry world. Williams was astonished and angered by the poem, as we will see. John Gould Fletcher thought this meant "that Sewanee review (that bad paper) reversed its stand of a year ago—in favor of understandable poetry—and went off the deep end for Stevens!" (letter from Fletcher to Norman Holmes Pearson, April 4, 1946 [Arkansas, Fletcher Papers]).

101. Letter from Allen Tate to Donald E. Stanford, May 12, 1975 (Stanford, Donald E. Stanford Papers, 86–077/3).

102. Letter from Tate to Stevens, July 3, 1945 (Huntington, WAS2362).

103. Ransom's poem was reprinted as "Crocodile" in *Selected Poems* (New York: Alfred A. Knopf, 1969), pp. 65–67.

104. Probably a handwritten note that Tate did not save; only dictated and type-written materials, of course, survived in Stevens's office files as carbons (now at the Huntington).

105. Letter from Stevens to Tate, June 27, 1945 (Princeton, Tate Papers).

106. Letter from Tate to Stevens, July 12, 1945 (Huntington, WAS2363).

107. Letter from Williams to Vazakas, November 11, 1945 (Beinecke, Williams Papers, Za Vazakas).

108. Clifford, *The Predicament of Culture*, p. 4.

109. Letter from Williams to Walter Arensberg, April 4, 1944 (Huntington, HM39556).

110. Letter from Williams to Stevens, July 21, 1944, in *The Selected Letters of William Carlos Williams*, ed. John C. Thirwall (New York: McDowell, Obolensky, 1957), p. 229.

111. Mariani's phrase (*A New World Naked*, p. 499; see also p. 517).

112. Williams's position was familiar to Stevens from the forthright statements in *Contact* on the primacy of place: "If Americans are to be blessed with important work it will be through intelligent, informed contact with the locality which alone can infuse it with reality" (Williams, "Sample Critical Statement," *Contact* 4 [Fall 1921]: 18).

113. See Mariani, *A New World Naked*, p. 498.

114. Such an interpretation seems to be supported by Welles's reasons for favoring generous American aid to the devastated countries of Europe: such generosity will open up new American markets. "For the higher [the] living standards [of European nations] the greater is their demand for those products of our own factories and farms which we here are able to produce more efficiently and in better quality than anyone else" (Welles, *Time for Decision*, p. 409). Charles Maier, a counter-revisionist, argues that one can accept the revisionists' thesis that the United States forced its aid on Europe "without accepting the larger revisionist accusation of a pervasive neo-colonialism"; and he cites Sumner Welles's *Time for Decision* to support his reading ("Revisionism and the Interpretation of Cold War Origins," in *Perspectives in American History* 4 [Cambridge: Harvard University Press, 1970], p. 331).

115. Said, *Orientalism*, p. 32.

116. Ibid., p. 154.

117. Ludowyk, "The East-West Problem in Sinhalese Literature," p. 31.

118. Letter from van Geyzel to Stevens, August 30, 1945 (Huntington, WAS2458).

119. Ibid.

4. Cuba Should Be Full of Cuban Things

1. "Thinking of a Relation Between the Images of Metaphors" (as "Unidad de las imagenes"), "Chaos in Motion and Not in Motion" ("El caos movil e inmovil"), "The House Was Quiet and the World Was Calm" ("La casa y el mundo en calma"), and "Continual Conversation with a Quiet Man" ("Conversación con un

hombre silencioso") were first published in the Winter 1945 issue of *Orígenes* (2, 8: 3–6). Their first English publication came as "Four Poems" in *Voices* 127 (Autumn 1946): 4–6.

2. "aquellos momentos de creación en los que el germen se convierte en criatura y lo desconocido va siendo poseído en la medida en que esto es posible y en que no engendra una desdichada arrogancia" (*Orígenes* 1, 1 [Spring 1944]: 5).

3. The "intent to universalize" was most clearly articulated by José Lezama Lima, for instance in "Señales: Alrededores de una Antología" ("Signs: Outlines of an Anthology"), *Orígenes* 9, 31 (1952): 65.

4. "Por primera vez entre nosotros, lo contemporáneo no era una nostalgia provinciana" (ibid., p. 66).

5. "He ahí el detalle, la situación, los impensados agrupamientos, tocando, como arañazo y despertar creadores, la ajena imaginación poética; inequívoco signo de universalización, aparecer en las transmutaciones y misterios imaginativos de otros creadores muy alejados de nuestra latitud y paisaje" (ibid., p. 67).

6. In *Orígenes* 1, 3 (October 1945). The painting is now in the National Museum of Art, Havana.

7. "nada rendida al halago ... sí de exprimir lo que había en nosotros" (José Lezama Lima, "Notes: Lozano and Mariano," *Orígenes* 1, 4 [December 1944]: 44).

8. For a reading of one of these paintings, a watercolor of pineapples, in relation to Stevens's "Someone Puts a Pineapple Together," see Filreis, "Still Life without Substance," pp. 370–71.

9. I am grateful to Sienah Wold for this characterization. See note 24 below.

10. "Estamos, pues, y a esto quería llegar, los poetas de mi reciente Antología, muy lejos de constituir esa exquisita especie de evadidos que algunos imaginan. Tan lejos, por los menos, como lo estamos de ser los desarragaidos seguidores de las últimas escuelas europeas. Semejante asociación de equívocos no ha de parecer arbitraria si consideramos que una misma acusación de frialdad, de oscuridad y hermetismo recae, más o menos vagamente, sobre aquellas escuelas y sobre lo central de neustra actitud poetica" (Cintio Vitier, "Ten Cuban Poets," *Orígenes* 5, 18 [Summer 1948]: 41).

11. "una poesía del destierro y de la fidelidad" (ibid., p. 43).

12. Indeed, it was a place Stevens had come to—twice. He spent "the greater part of a week" in Havana on business in 1923, staying in a hotel room that "looks out over the Prado, a short boulevard running down to the Malecon or sea-wall." He took each of his meals at a different restaurant, certain to describe for his wife the luncheon he was served at El Telegrafo, in the following delicious detail: "a big glass of orangeade, a Cuban lobster, banana bread, cocoanut milk ice cream and a pot of Cuban coffee." He found "good cigars" as "cheap as dirt." The whole visit, a digression from business dealings in Miami, made him "feel rather sinful" (*L* 235). His second visit, a briefer and less sinful stop, came later in 1923, when, as he told Rodríguez Feo, "my wife and I stopped there for about a day on the way to California by way of the Canal" (*L* 483–84; see also *L* 241).

13. Bishop's essay about George Valdés appeared in *Orígenes* 2: 6 (July 1945): 27–32.

14. For a full reading of this poem as a response to the Stevens–Rodríguez Feo correspondence, see *SM* 18–21. The letter that found its way into the poem has been reprinted in *SM* 133–34.

15. This reading is supported by Stevens's immediate interest in the bootblacks of Havana. If "everything here," he wrote from Cuba in 1923, "is an object of interest," that interest could focus on a special kind of subservience—subservience that was somehow proud and lazy both: "the bookblacks *sit down* when they shine your shoes" (*L* 235).

16. The bootblack appeared in Stevens's introduction to Morse's book as follows: "[T]here develops a curiosity about the perceptions of others. . . . The fact is that the saying of new things in new ways is grateful to us. If a bootblack says that he was so tired that he lay down like a dog under a tree, he is saying a new thing about an old thing, in a new way. *His new way is not a literary novelty; it is an unaffected statement of his perception of the thing*" (*OP* 243; emphasis added).

17. Rodríguez Feo also called himself a "savage" (*SM* 69) and once paid Stevens the high compliment of addressing a letter to "My dear Primitive" (*SM* 193).

18. Speech of June 13, 1910, reproduced in *Parliamentary Debates*, 5th series, 17 (1910): 1140–46; quoted by Said in *Orientalism*, p. 33.

19. Joseph Conrad, *Heart of Darkness* (London: Penguin, 1973), p. 33.

20. Vitier, "Ten Cuban Poets," p. 41.

21. José Rodríguez Feo, interview with author and Beverly Coyle, New York City, October 17, 1983. Winters wrote of "The Mechanical Optimist" of 1936 that "the victim of the irony is very small game, and scarcely worthy of the artillery of the author of 'Sunday Morning' " (*In Defense of Reason* [Athens: Swallow Press/ Ohio University Press, 1987; first published, 1943], p. 446).

22. The charge that Stevens is "the Whistler of Amer. poetry" was Horace Gregory's, in "An Examination of Wallace Stevens in a Time of War," *Accent* 3 (Autumn 1942): 60.

23. These were published as "New Poems," in *Voices* 21 (Spring 1945): 25–29. With "Paisant Chronicle" were "The Pure Good of Theory," "A Word with José Rodríguez-Feo [*sic*]," and "Flyer's Fall."

24. In an interview on October 18, 1983, Rodríguez Feo speculated on the possibilities of Stevens's perceptiveness in this matter, and he discussed the subtle ways in which he tried to clarify the issue, in 1946 or later, without, so far as he could tell, any success. Rodríguez Feo's homosexuality was not merely a personal matter, of course, but an aesthetic one, as the homosexual thematics of the *origenistas* were central to their development and achievement as a group—as to their political identity. The private poetic language that developed among them, later conjoined with other such styles under the rubric "neo-Baroque," added to the strength of their manner and identity as well as to the accusations of hermeticism made against them. By coming out to Stevens, in short, Rodríguez Feo would have been contributing to a dialogue already well under way between them, about the problems engendered by the *origenista* aesthetic, problems Stevens knew well from his own struggles with claims made against his apparently secretive language and manner. For more on Lezama Lima's aesthetic, see Severo Sarduy, "The Baroque and Neobaroque," in *Latin America and Its Literature*, ed. César Fernández Moreno

(New York: Holmes and Meier Publishers, 1980), pp. 115–32. I am grateful to Marci Sternheim for her suggestions on this point.

25. See Stevens's letter of September 30, 1946, to Charles R. Barker (*L* 534), in which he partially describes his research into the Zeller family history during the previous month. See also *WSR* 112.

26. For a reading of Rodríguez Feo's prose poem "The Closed Door" in relation to San Miguel de los Baños, see *SM* 22–23.

27. Interview with Rodríguez Feo, October 18, 1983.

28. Oscar Rodríguez Felíu had translated Stevens for *Orígenes*; so had Eliseo Diego and Cintio Vitier (*SM* 47).

5. The Postcard Imagination

1. Adlai Stevenson's positions on foreign policy might have been something of a surprise to Stevens. In Hartford, giving a September 18, 1952, speech at the Bushnell Memorial Auditorium, a talk later dubbed "The Atomic Future," Stevenson sounded a great deal indeed like Eisenhower, despite strenuous efforts to distinguish his ideas from the general's on so many other counts: "We all know the character of the men in the Kremlin—their fanaticism, their ruthlessness, their limitless ambition"; "To my Republican listeners I would say: the atomic adventure *transcends partisan issues*" (*Major Campaign Speeches of Adlai E. Stevenson, 1952* [New York: Random House, 1953], p. 138; emphasis added). A week before the Hartford speech, Stevenson had said: "I do not believe there is any fundamental issue between the Republican candidate for President and myself . . . [in] the basic direction our foreign policy has been following . . . to prevent the expansion of Soviet dominion" (p. 43).

2. "The Green Plant," appearing in the December 6, 1952, issue of the *Nation* (175, 23: 519–20), was submitted along with six other poems on November 12 (*L* 764). "St. Armorer's Church from the Outside" appeared in the October 1952 issue of *Poetry*. To support my argument that the poem is based on Stevens's exchanges with Barbara Church *through September* the submission of the poem would have to be surprisingly close to publication time. Indeed, according to materials in the *Poetry* collection at Chicago, the October issue was delayed, at least in part because it was at that point the largest single issue in the magazine's history (celebrating the fortieth anniversary of its 1912 founding). The printers complained that "Oct. Poetry copy about 2 weeks late" (letter on Midway Printing Co. stationery [Chicago, Poetry Magazine Papers 1936–1953]).

3. A representative of George Marshall was visiting Ireland in September 1948, bearing "gifts like the Greeks," as McGreevy reported to Stevens. But since Ireland did not seem to McGreevy to require such economic aid (it was already "lousy with money," he said), he concluded that in an election year the Truman administration was "putting it out that we were all in such a dire danger from the spoiled priest of the Kremlin," Joseph Stalin, because "[t]hey [the Democrats] must be worried by [Progressive party challenger] Henry Wallace." Still, McGreevy assured Stevens that Ireland "need have no poor at all" and that "we could do it with Joe *and* George" (emphasis added; letter from McGreevy to Stevens, September 28, 1948 [Huntington, WAS148]).

4. Letter from Vidal to Stevens, September 28, 1948 (Huntington, WAS2831).

5. Letter from Vidal to Stevens, July 1, 1950 (Huntington, WAS2847).

6. It was now published as a small book (Paris: Éditions de Minuit, 1951). Stevens had read some of Paulhan's letters to the CNE in 1948, copies having been sent him by Barbara Church. See *Sur Plusieurs Beaux Sujects*, ed. Bates, p. 93; and *L* 574.

7. For more on the impact of Paulhan's *Lettre*, which Stevens read immediately after it was published in 1952, see Werth, *France: 1940–1955*, p. 287; and Herbert R. Lottman, *The Purge* (New York: William Morrow, 1986), pp. 234–42.

8. Letter from Barbara Church to Stevens, August 18, 1952 (Huntington, WAS3610).

9. See Nicholas Watkins, *Matisse* (New York: Oxford University Press, 1985), pp. 214–16.

10. January had been "a dismal month, very cold and though we have a well heated house (oil) I cannot forget the millions of Europeans freezing. If I were a sadist, I suppose it would be all right. . . . [I]t is remarkable how people bear up" (letter from Barbara Church to Stevens, February 14, 1947 [Huntington, WAS3567]). Dean Acheson's Delta Council speech may be the best example in modern American diplomatic history of naturalized rhetoric offering up what some who study political language have called the "legitimative symbol" (B. Thomas Trout in "Rhetoric Revisited: Political Legitimation and the Cold War," *International Studies Quarterly* 19, 3 [September 1975]: 251–84; esp. 263–64). Acheson described European devastation primarily as "acts of God," stressing what Mrs. Church saw, the harsh winters that had swept northern Europe and England, and interpreting them as both sign and reason for American aid. Acheson's speech, in short, was an address to farmers about "the weather," but it served to legitimize a natural metaphor for "the news"—for a new national policy in a trope already quite familiar to Stevens from his struggle with isolationism. Here and elsewhere, then, I am arguing that one of Stevens's rhetorical habits was the political recognition of "the weather" as a self-legitimizing symbol of "the news." Acheson's speech has been reproduced in full in Joseph Marion Jones, *The Fifteen Weeks: February 21–June 5, 1947* (New York: Harcourt, Brace and World, 1955), pp. 274–81.

11. Letter from Stevens to Allen Tate, October 14, 1946 (Princeton, Tate Papers).

12. Although he supposed the Churches, when they saw Ville d'Avray after there had been "a variety of soldiers in your house for five years," would be "wild" to come back to the United States, he was fully confident that "everything can be made bright and shining once again" (*L* 527).

13. A photograph of this farmhouse, taken *circa* 1948, was found, after Stevens's death, laid into his copy of Rilke's *Lettres à un jeune poete*. On the back of the photo Barbara Church has noted that this family farm was located in southern Bavaria, near Toelz. "It was my sister's during the war to keep it out of the Nazis' hands," she wrote there (Huntington, Box 66).

14. "I must go to Munich and see my sister and her children and the ruins," she wrote Stevens (letter of April 14, 1948 [Huntington, WAS3572]).

15. For her 1948 return to France, she booked passage on the USS *Washington*, "a tourist boat," she told Stevens, "one class only." From this experience she received a genuine thrill: "the tour is very democratique[,] . . . the crowd motley,

irish, tchecoslavaque mostly . . . [and] students. . . . Everybody talks with everybody" (letter of April 14, 1948 [Huntington, WAS3572]).

16. Though at first she doubted the efficacy of such ritual behavior, she generally shared her sister's deeply emotional response to the ruined churches, and she increasingly valued and retained "a tender feeling for the enthusiastic, very religious childhood I passed through. I used to go to early mass everyday in a beautiful 15th century little church in a Bavarian village. The last war has destroyed it, not a [direct] hit but it trembled and shook through the explosions and finally the tower crumbled" (letter to Stevens, June 19, 1950 [Huntington, WAS3592]).

17. She had observed that "[n]early all of St. Malo is destroyed" (letter to Stevens, September 18, 1948 [Huntington, WAS3575]).

18. Letter from Barbara Church to Stevens, September 30, 1948 (Huntington, WAS3576).

19. For these and other details of the French recovery, I have relied on C. F. Miller, "Europe Now," *American Federalist* (March 1949): 10–12, 28.

20. Charles Mee cites this observation in a letter from George Kennan to Marshall, dated June 6, 1947, now at the Marshall Library, Lexington, Virginia (*The Marshall Plan*, p. 90). See also Kennan, *Memoirs, 1925–50* (Boston: Little, Brown, 1967): aid to Europe was meant to have a "significant psychological effect" (p. 335).

21. If European reconstruction were to be defeated in Congress, or even merely delayed, Marshall's planners warned, Europeans would "suffer a *cultural and spiritual* loss incalculable in its long-term effects" (emphasis added). The memo, designated "PPS 4," dated July 23, 1947, has been reprinted in *Containment: Documents on American Policy and Strategy, 1945–50*, ed. Thomas H. Etzold and John Lewis Gaddis (New York: Columbia University Press, 1978), pp. 107–14; the quoted phrases can be found on p. 108. The Marshall Plan seems to have officially inaugurated cultural-psychological warfare in the nonmilitary contest between the United States and the Soviet Union.

22. The rhetoric of exhaustion is written into the very first planning memo, PPS 1, dated May, 23, 1947, reprinted in *Containment: Documents*, ed. Etzold and Gaddis, pp. 102–6. The actual plans for implementation are still immature here, yet the psychological thesis is already evident: aid will respond to "a profound exhaustion of physical plant and of spiritual vigor" (p. 102). The word "exhaustion" would be repeated by nearly every proponent of the plan.

23. The eight-thousand-word telegram, sent from Moscow to Secretary of State Byrnes on February 22, 1946, is reprinted in *Containment: Documents*, ed. Etzold and Gaddis, pp. 50–63. It proposed that Soviet power was "neither schematic nor adventuristic" and "can easily withdraw—and usually does—when strong resistance is encountered at any point," and suggested that such resistance come in part in the form of "courageous and incisive measure[s] . . . to improve self-confidence . . . *of our own people*" (pp. 61, 63; emphasis added).

24. Obviously, then, I am not arguing that the confusion or mixing of reconstructive motives in Stevens's work of this period is somehow the result of a lack of ideological acuity. Cold-war historiography provides a number of accounts of the rhetorical confusion that resulted from various members of the Truman administration explaining the ERP in public speeches, in congressional hearings, and to

journalists. Most members of Congress, Richard Freeland has written, "seemed surprised that the Administration would try to sell the program as profitable to the U.S., when so much of the public rhetoric depicted E.R.P. as an exercise in American self-sacrifice" (*The Truman Doctrine and the Origins of McCarthyism: Foreign Policy, Domestic Politics, and Internal Security, 1946–1948* [New York: Alfred A. Knopf, 1972], p. 260). My own survey of the daily and weekly journalistic accounts that Stevens is most likely to have seen (from Hartford and New York) confirms Joyce and Gabriel Kolko's generalization that for the American public the rhetoric of "unprecedented generosity" was put first (anticommunism second, economic integration last) (*The Limits of Power: The World and United States Foreign Policy, 1945– 54* [New York: Harper and Row, 1972], p. 359). As for the ERP's significance as anticommunism: if this was not indeed its primary appeal, it nevertheless was quite evident. By 1950 the Marshall Plan had come to be so closely identified with domestic anticommunism that it was used in loyalty-security cases, by ex-radicals under investigation, as a means by which to prove their hatred of communism (Eleanor Bontecou, *The Federal Loyalty-Security Program* [Ithaca: Cornell University Press, 1953], pp. 131–32, 226–34).

25. By "the Jews" Stevens is referring, of course, to Jewish settlers in Palestine. The 1945 loan to England amounted to $3.8 billion and was even more controversial than Stevens suggests, for the key to the agreement was not so much containment by itself as its association with the economic dismantling of the British empire, American negotiators having gotten "weary London officials" to promise to disengage much of the colonial trading bloc; see, e.g., Walter LaFeber, *America, Russia and the Cold War, 1945–1984*, 5th ed. (New York: Alfred A. Knopf, 1985), p. 11. Kennan's thesis was not available to the general public until it was published in the July 1947 issue of *Foreign Affairs* as "The Sources of Soviet Conduct"; see Kennan, *Memoirs, 1925–50*, pp. 354–55.

26. Theodore White's *Fire in the Ashes: Europe at Mid-century* (New York: Sloane, 1953) offers a detailed account of journalistic enthusiasm for the ERP.

27. He felt the extra tax burden in 1948, and warned Mrs. Church that the Democrats might realize they would remain in office only by promising to tax the rich to attract the lower-class vote—by, as he put it, "taking A's money and giving it to B." If this goes on "long enough," he added, "we shall all be reduced to such a dead level that politics won't matter" (*L* 604). Four years later a letter he wrote José Rodríguez Feo implied that U.S. revenues raised for European aid were being abused by the cultural diplomats: "I have been working at the office, nothing else: complaining a little about it but content, after all, that I have a solid rock under my feet, and enjoying the routine without minding too much that I have to pay a respectable part of my income to the government in order that someone else representing the government may sit at the Cafe X at Aix or go to lectures at the Sorbonne." Written several days before Eisenhower was inaugurated, this letter refers specifically to liberal spending: "The Democrats, if they are Democrats," Stevens continued, "have gone to incredible lengths in introducing their conception of things into American life and practice" (*L* 767).

28. For this and other characterizations of the conservative opposition to American-inspired European reconstruction, I have relied on Ronald Lora, "A View from the Right: Conservative Intellectuals, the Cold War, and McCarthy," in *The*

Specter: Original Essays on the Cold War and the Origins of McCarthyism, ed. Robert Griffith and Athan Theoharis (New York: New Viewpoints, 1974), pp. 61–62; Freeland, *The Truman Doctrine*, pp. 178–86; Robert A. Taft, "The Republican Party," *Fortune* 39 (April 1949): 118; and Adler, *The Isolationist Impulse*, pp. 384–86.

29. Mee, *The Marshall Plan*, p. 257. For more on industrial dismantling, see John Gimbel, *The American Occupation of Germany: Politics and the Military, 1945–1949* (Stanford: Stanford University Press, 1968), pp. 20, 22, 32, 78, 248.

30. Two years later he still thought Truman's election a "misfortune," writing then to Barbara Church: "Truman, with his politician's desire for money and power, alarms one" (*L* 684). In the 1952 election, when Stevens voted for Eisenhower ("Stevenson was not my man"), he could still not resist a comment on Truman (and Roosevelt): "Even in the case of Eisenhower, however, I should be cautious because we ought to have a little prose in the White House *after all the poor poetry, to say nothing of the music*" (*L* 765; emphasis added). The perception that Dewey opposed "a New Deal for the world," as the ERP was often called, was a strong one. John Foster Dulles, a Dewey supporter, spent a good deal of his time in Europe calming the fears of European allies that a Republican victory in November 1948 would be, in Dulles's phrase, "a return to 'isolationism' " (Dulles, *War or Peace* [New York: Macmillan, 1950], p. 132). For Dewey's actual position, see Richard Norton Smith, *Thomas E. Dewey and His Times* (New York: Simon and Schuster, 1982), pp. 469–70.

31. Walter LaFeber, in providing a definition of the origins of American "Open-Door Imperialism," speaks of an " 'economic vacuum' that, like all vacuums, invited invasion" (*America, Russia, and the Cold War*, p. 4).

32. Undoubtedly Stevens borrowed the political argument in this letter of August 14, 1950, from that morning's *New York Times*, where it was reported that the Republican leadership in Congress had found a way of endorsing their own version of containment through economic reconstruction while still denouncing Truman's (and the Democrats') approach to these otherwise unquestioned goals ("Text of G.O.P. Senators' Statement Charging Foreign Policy Bungling in Europe, Asia," p. 10).

33. Some historians have emphasized the economic interpretation of the origins of the cold war, especially since the publication of William Appleman Williams's *The Tragedy of American Diplomacy* in 1959. A summary of the economic theory indebted to Williams, and its shortcomings, is given by Bradford Perkins, "The Tragedy of American Diplomacy: Twenty-Five Years After," *Reviews of American History* 12, 1 (March 1984): 1–18. See also John Lewis Gaddis, "The Emerging Post-Revisionist Synthesis on the Origins of the Cold War," *Diplomatic History* 7, 3 (Summer 1983): 171–90; and Michael J. Hogan, "American Marshall Planners and the Search for a European Neocapitalism," *American Historical Review* 90 (February 1985): 44–72, esp. 44–45, 71–72. Hogan is among the first to show in detail "how American leaders . . . applied their corporative strategies to the management of foreign policy" (p. 44).

34. Quoted in D. F. Fleming, *The Cold War and Its Origins* (New York: Doubleday, 1961), 1: 478. The speech used what Joyce and Gabriel Kolko describe as "studiously vague terminology" (*The Limits of Power*, p. 367). For more on the

rhetorical climate authorizing Marshall's Harvard speech, see Trout, "Rhetoric Revisited: Political Legitimation and the Cold War," pp. 267–71.

35. Fifty-six percent of the Americans polled considered the ERP an act of charity; and only 8 percent thought it was really designed to "curb communism," a promoted rationale. The pollsters themselves did not report or seem aware of Americans who considered the ERP designed to meet American economic goals. For more about this and other public-opinion polls, see Freeland, *The Truman Doctrine*, p. 262; and Martin Kriesberg, "Dark Areas of Ignorance," in Lester Markel et al., *Public Opinion and Foreign Policy* (New York: Harper and Brothers, 1949), esp. pp. 52, 54–55.

36. The ERP, Spender observed, "has done a great deal to swing the political choice away from Russia" ("We Can Win the Battle for the Mind of Europe," *New York Times Magazine*, April 25, 1948, pp. 35, 15).

37. There were finally thirty-one cantos in the poem. Stevens read portions of it on November 4, 1949, before the Connecticut Academy of Arts and Sciences; these eleven cantos, including the twenty-eighth, were published in the *Transactions* of that academy in December (vol. 38, pp. 161–72). Stevens had written John Crowe Ransom on June 27 to report that he had finished composing the poem (Huntington, WAS1542), yet earlier comments suggest that his manner of adding new sections to it was "intermittent" and improvisational, for example: "I . . . intend to keep studying the subject and working on" (*L* 639).

38. *Souvenirs and Prophecies: The Young Wallace Stevens*, ed. Holly Stevens (New York: Alfred A. Knopf, 1977), pp. 70–71. See also Filreis, "Wallace Stevens and the Crisis of Authority," esp. pp. 575–76.

39. Letter from Barbara Church to Stevens, July 3, 1949 (Huntington, WAS3580).

40. Letter from Barbara Church to Stevens, August 13, 1949 (Huntington, WAS3581).

41. Adam Ulam, *The Rivals: America and Russia Since World War II* (New York: Viking, 1971), p. 124.

42. Geoffrey Hodgson, *America in Our Time* (New York: Random House, 1976), p. 76.

43. Enclosed with the letter of August 13, 1949 (Huntington, WAS3581).

44. Postcard from Barbara Church to Stevens, June 25, 1949 (Huntington, WAS3579).

45. Enclosed with Huntington, WAS3581. She was actually in or near Nussdorf, about a half-hour's drive from Salzburg.

46. Letter from Barbara Church to Stevens, July 3, 1949 (Huntington, WAS3580). As for the source of the phrase "Rome after dark," it is probably Barbara Church's friend McGreevy, who had visited there six months earlier and written Stevens extensively about it (e.g., in Huntington, WAS151: "Being there is like being part of a flag," he wrote).

47. Letter from Stevens to Barbara Church, September 16, 1949 (Huntington, WAS3717).

48. Henry Wallace, "Too Little, Too Late," *New Republic* 117, 14 (October 6, 1947): 12.

49. Toward the end of Mrs. Church's 1949 trip, for instance, Stevens told her he was grateful she had helped him suppress the postcard imagination: "The picture you sent me takes me away from the cliches of Germany—the castles on the Rhine; the arches in the cities, etc." (letter of August 23, 1949 [Huntington, WAS3716]).

50. Robert von Hallberg, *American Poetry and Culture, 1945-1980* (Cambridge: Harvard University Press, 1985), pp. 62–63. The chapter entitled "Tourists" has helped me put Stevens's tourism poem in literary and cultural perspectives (pp. 62–92).

51. "The State of American Writing 1948," *Partisan Review* 15, 8 (August 1948): 856. The other respondents were Ransom, Blackmur, John Berryman, Robert Gorham Davis, Leslie Fiedler, Clement Greenberg, Lionel Trilling, and H. L. Mencken (pp. 855–94). Stevens's response has been reprinted in *OP* 312–15. It should be noted that, according to Schwartz's letter of March 23, 1948, inviting Stevens to be part of the symposium, Stevens was free to disregard any of the questions that did not interest him. The answers, Schwartz added, should "be cast in the form of a discussion" (Huntington, WAS1720).

52. "The State of American Writing," *OP* 314–15. This must be likened to the response to the cold war more politically active writers were calling for, such as Spender, whose plan for winning "the Battle for the Mind of Europe" entailed first and foremost the intellectual's recognition that "it is not a struggle between his own country and another country or a struggle within his own country between parties. It is a struggle going on *in his own country* between two *outside* forces: Russia and America" ("We Can Win the Battle for the Mind of Europe," p. 15; emphasis added).

53. Davis's contribution argued that such a challenge was needed: through his own "organic, dynamic, historical sense of literature in society" (p. 866) he observed that the recent eclipse of the literary Marxists of the thirties, who "had little real influence on the teaching of literature in the colleges," by the "more fashionable teachers"—using Brooks and Warren textbooks or imitations of them—emphasizing textual explication," was itself "historically conditioned" ("The State of American Writing," pp. 868, 867, 869). In short, Davis stood by a form of materialism in order to pick his particular fight with the Soviets.

54. Letter from Barbara Church to Stevens, August 18, 1952 (Huntington, WAS3610).

55. The case of the Italian farmers has indeed been identified as the classic instance of the failure of ERP aid to trickle down; Mrs. Church's observation is acute, and gave Stevens an unusually good view of American reconstruction at its weakest. One of the ERP's goals in Italy was to raise the production standards of Italian farmers by urging them to use chemical fertilizers, but Italian farmers could not afford chemical fertilizers because they were made, as Theodore White put it, "by obsolete processes in obsolete plants." These "stubborn, persistent problems" in Italy the ERP could not solve, as the chemical cartel producing the unnecessarily expensive fertilizer resisted efforts to lift trade barriers, and the result by the end of the 1952 growing season, the time of Barbara Church's visit, was precisely what she saw and described for Stevens: untended small farms, the farmers having withdrawn to the cities. White, *Fire in the Ashes*, pp. 68, 67; Aylmer Vallance, "Report

on Italy: The Clock Runs Down," *New Statesman and Nation* (October 28, 1950): 385; Colston E. Warne, "Italy: Pauper or Convalescent," *Current History* (November 1948): 274–78.

56. Stevens knew that the *Nation*'s editorial positions carried over to its literary department at least insofar as they implied a sense of what poetry was and was not "appropriate" for the *Nation*; this was certainly the impression Randall Jarrell gave him when "A Pastoral Nun" was rejected outright as "not very appropriate for the Nation" (letter from Jarrell to Stevens, July 1946 [Huntington, WAS946]).

57. Huntington, WAS3612. For descriptions of San Gimignano predating both world wars, see Edmund G. Gardner, *The Story of Siena and San Gimignano* (London: J. M. Dent, 1905), pp. 344–65.

58. Letter from Stevens to John L. Sweeney, September 23, 1954 (Houghton, bMS AM1641).

59. "What he wrote about [Ireland] mystified me," Sweeney told Brazeau, "because I knew he hadn't been there. I did tease him about writing on a subject he was not immediately in touch with, teasing as I did about 'The Irish Cliffs of Moher' and the other poems [set in Ireland]. Why didn't he come to Ireland and join us there? . . . [H]is idea of Ireland . . . would be diminished if he had seen the real thing" (*WSR* 228).

60. In this respect the difference between the tenor of the Barbara Church–Stevens letters and that of the Church-Moore letters is astonishing. Mrs. Church felt comfortable enough with Moore to send her poetry, including a poem about the anxieties of being a tourist (quoted above as an epigraph) and an attempt at translating Emily Dickinson into French (letter to Moore, May 29, 1951 [Rosenbach, Moore Papers, V:10:23]). In return she received open expressions of sympathy from Moore: "As for your not being a poet, that is the one foolish thing I have ever known you to say. Really, Barbara! . . . Everything you say shows the poetry and imagination of your thinking" (letter from Moore to Church, March 13, 1952 [Rosenbach, Moore Papers, V:10:23]). She did not describe for Stevens the difficulties she had at directors' meetings of her late husband's firm Church and Dwight (the baking-soda company); to Moore she spoke plainly of what it was like to be a woman in such a setting. During one board meeting, she told Moore, she broke her usual silence to oppose the most senior director: "[O]ne has to say what one thinks even if one is *not* convinced of one's own rightness, the curious thing was that we two women Directors sided with the younger generation. Why? I think because wom[e]n stick less to tradition and do consider the practical side—" (letter from Church to Moore, December 19, 1951 [Rosenbach, Moore Papers, V:10:23]). Moore replied: "There is so much in life which coerces us to be corrupt, and you meet it strongly" (letter of December 30, 1951 [Rosenbach, Moore Papers, V:10:23]).

61. And it was a perspective to which Barbara Church was especially sensitive. When describing for Marianne Moore an evening in a beer hall in Bavaria, she closely observed how some French friends who had joined her family "were glad to be amongst us and not just onlookers, *outsiders*" (letter of September 15, 1951 [Rosenbach, Moore Papers, V:10:23]; emphasis added).

62. David Riesman and Nathan Glazer, "The Intellectuals and the Discontented Classes—1955," in *The Radical Right*, ed. Daniel Bell (Garden City, N.Y.:

Doubleday, 1963), p. 106. For a survey of the affiliations between the antipolitical political climate and a "New Rear Guard" in American poetry, see James E. B. Breslin, *From Modern to Contemporary: American Poetry, 1945–1965* (Chicago: University of Chicago Press, 1983), esp. pp. 46–51.

63. "The Marshall Plan," writes Norman Markowitz, "seemed to offer a version of the world New Deal that had been so important to popular-front liberalism" ("From the Popular Front to Cold War Liberalism," in *The Specter: Original Essays on the Cold War*, ed. Griffith and Theoharis, p. 106). The National Association of Manufacturers feared "a T.V.A. on the Danube" (quoted by Adler, *The Isolationist Impulse*, p. 385).

64. Stevens wrote: "I want to say how pleasant it is that so prodigious a traveler should eventually come back and how much that coming back means to all your friends, whose traveling you do for them" (letter to Barbara Church, October 18, 1951 [Huntington, WAS3760]).

65. Letter from Ebba Dalin to Stevens, October 17, 1954 (Huntington, WAS257). She quotes from *CP* 135, line 17.

66. Letter from Stevens to Dalin, October 26, 1954 (Huntington, WAS263).

67. Ibid.

68. Letter from Stevens to Dalin, January 30, 1947 (Huntington, WAS259). I wish to acknowledge Beth Dalin, of Halmstad, Sweden, for providing information used as the basis for this portion of the chapter.

69. Ibid.

70. See Geir Lundestad, *America, Scandinavia, and the Cold War, 1945–1949* (New York: Columbia University Press, 1980), pp. 296–302, 324–28.

71. "[T]he kind of winter one thinks of as appropriate to Sweden," he wrote Ebba Dalin, was "a huge night with all sorts of prismatic things" (letter of October 26, 1954 [Huntington, WAS263]).

72. Letter from Dalin to Stevens, October 14, 1952 (Huntington, WAS256). Lloyd Hustvedt, of St. Olaf College, provided me with a translation of the Swedish newspaper article, written by Ingrid Renman.

73. Letter from Stevens to Dalin, October 21, 1952 (Huntington, WAS262).

6. Last American Occasions

1. Roy Harvey Pearce, "Wallace Stevens: The Life of the Imagination," *PMLA* 66, 5 (September 1951): 561–82. The essay has been reprinted in *Wallace Stevens: A Collection of Critical Essays*, ed. Marie Borroff (Englewood Cliffs: Prentice-Hall, 1963), pp. 111–32; the quoted phrases can be found on p. 126.

2. The evidence for this is discussed by George H. Nash, *The Conservative Intellectual Movement in America since 1945* (New York: Basic Books, 1979), pp. 97, 372.

3. James Burnham, *The Struggle for the World* (New York: John Day, 1947), p. 182.

4. "1955 Harvard International Seminar, Guest Speakers" (Harvard, International Seminar Papers, Box 4, UAV 813.141.25).

5. Letter from Stevens to Henry A. Kissinger, June 27, 1955 (Huntington, WAS984).

6. Letter from Kissinger to Stevens, June 21, 1955 (Huntington, WAS983).

7. George F. Kennan, "International Exchange in the Arts," *Perspectives USA* 16 (Summer 1956): 8–16; the address was originally delivered at a symposium sponsored by the International Council of the Museum of Modern Art on May 12, 1955.

8. For more on Angleton, Pauker, *Furioso*, and the X-2 group at Yale, see Robin W. Winks, *Cloak & Gown: Scholars in the Secret War, 1939–1961* (New York: William Morrow, 1987), pp. 333–35. On Pearson, see pp. 247–321; Pearson's close connection to Angleton's *Furioso* is confirmed in a letter from Pearson to John Gould Fletcher, September 4, 1941 (Arkansas, Fletcher Papers).

9. John Pauker, "A Discussion of 'Sea Surface Full of Clouds,' " *Furioso* 5, 4 (Fall 1950): 36–46. I characterize Pauker's essay as I have despite his claim that it counters Blackmur's and especially Ransom's readings; when Angleton published the essay in *Furioso*, an editor's note was added asserting that Pauker's reading "demonstrate[s] that 'Sea Surface Full of Clouds' *does* contain what might be called a value-proposition . . . or, has political, social and ethical implications" (p. 36); yet the essay itself demonstrates nothing of the kind.

10. Hayden Carruth, "Stevens as Essayist," *Nation* 174 (June 14, 1952): 584.

11. Responding to an essay about him published in an undergraduate magazine, Stevens suggested that in "Angel Surrounded by Paysans" the angel is not the angel of the imagination but "the angel of reality." He went on: "For nine readers out of ten, the necessary angel will appear to be the angel of the imagination and for nine days out of ten that is true, although it is the tenth day that counts" (*L* 753).

12. A useful overview of cold-war liberalism is presented by Norman Markowitz, "From the Popular Front to Cold War Liberalism," in *The Specter: Original Essays on the Cold War*, ed. Griffith and Theoharis, pp. 90–115.

13. The 1948 prize—awarded in 1949—had been recommended by the Fellows in American Letters of the Library of Congress; after the controversy stirred by the selection of Pound, the administration of the prize was transferred from the Library of Congress to the Yale University Library. The 1950 award was given to Ransom. For information on Yale's firm goal, in President Charles Seymour's words, of "re-establishing this prize" after the Pound fiasco, which Seymour explicitly mentioned, I have consulted letters from James T. Babb, Yale librarian and member of the committee to administer the prize, to Conrad Aiken, who served on the Committee of Award that chose Stevens (February 13 and March 30, 1950 [Huntington, Aiken Papers, AIK1726–27]), and a Yale University News Bureau press release, dated February 14, 1950, #448 (Beinecke).

14. Untitled review of William Van O'Connor's *The Shaping Spirit*, *New England Quarterly* 24, 1 (March 1951): 125.

15. Robert Hillyer, "Treason's Strange Fruit," *Saturday Review of Literature* 32, 24 (June 11, 1949): 9–11, 28; and "Poetry's New Priesthood," *Saturday Review of Literature* 32, 25 (June 18, 1949): 7–9, 38.

16. Letter from Stevens to Tate, October 20, 1949 (Princeton, Tate Papers).

17. Letter from Tate to Stevens, October 21, 1949 (Huntington, WAS2383). By this time Stevens was surely familiar with Tate's position on the Pound award from Tate's statements published in successive 1949 issues of *Partisan Review*

("The Question of the Pound Award: Allen Tate," 16, 5 [May]: 520; and "Further Remarks on the Pound Award," 16, 6 [June]: 666–68).

18. Letter from Pearson to Burnshaw, April 27, 1973 (Texas, Burnshaw Papers).

19. Richard Eberhart, "Reflections on Wallace Stevens in 1976," *Southern Review* 13, 3 (Summer 1977): 417.

20. It was awarded jointly to Williams and MacLeish.

21. Hillyer, "Poetry's New Priesthood," p. 38.

22. Letter from Stevens to Norman Holmes Pearson, [December] 1952 (Beinecke, Pearson Papers).

23. 22 U.S.C. 1431.

24. Interview with Fernand Auberjonois, December 22, 1987.

25. Nancy Lenkeith's charges were reported in "State Department Voids Curb in McCarthy Study of 'Voice,' " *New York Times*, February 21, 1953, pp. 1, 7. Auberjonois's denial was quoted in "3 'Voice' Officials Deny Red Leanings," p. 7.

26. That he was "examined in executive session" on February 28, 1953, was reported in "2 'Voice' Officials Hit Program Rule as Boon to Soviet," *New York Times*, March 1, 1953, p. 28.

27. Letter from Stevens to Barbara Church, April 10, 1953 (Huntington, WAS3788). Mrs. Church was a tireless promoter of Auberjonois: "[H]is speeches on the Voice of America," she wrote Marianne Moore, "are often very good indeed" (letter of May 29, 1951 [Rosenbach, Moore Papers, V:10:23]).

28. Interview with Auberjonois.

29. "3 'Voice' Officials Deny Red Leanings," p. 7. I have quoted Harold Berman, chief of the central news desk, and Donald Taylor, a supervisor in the same department.

30. Ibid.

31. Victor Navasky, *Naming Names* (New York: Viking Press, 1980), pp. 314–29.

32. Interview with Auberjonois.

33. A request to the USIA under the Freedom of Information Act in 1988 confirmed that Theodore Streibert invited thirty-three American writers to participate in the program, including James Farrell, William Saroyan, John Marquand, and Dorothy Canfield Fisher. If other materials were saved from this program, they were later lost or destroyed; nevertheless I wish to thank Myron Baskin of the U.S. State Department for his energetic assistance in the search, and for providing me a general sense of Pauker's USIA work.

34. "This Is Connecticut," *Hartford Courant*, July 21, 1955, p. 10.

35. Ibid.

36. The typescript of "Connecticut Composed" is a holding of the Huntington (WAS2306); Bates rightly selects it as copy-text (*OP* 302–4).

37. For generalizations in this chapter about what John Higham called "The Cult of the 'American Consensus,' " I have relied on Higham, "Beyond Consensus: The Historian as Moral Critic," *American Historical Review* 67, 3 (April 1962): 609–25; and Mary Sperling McAuliffe, *Crisis on the Left: Cold War Politics and American Liberals, 1947–1954* (Amherst: University of Massachusetts Press, 1978), esp. pp. 70–74.

38. At Yale, Pauker was already preparing his line-by-line reading of "Sea Surface Full of Clouds"; he had written to Stevens for the glosses, which Stevens provided, though not without warnings about the problems of intentionality arising in close readings (*L* 389–90).

39. The Bicentennial Committee made a point of noting that it "has received no reply from any of . . . [the] countries behind the Iron Curtain [or from] China." See "Economic Parley at Columbia Set," *New York Times*, May 23, 1954, p. 50; and "Columbia University Bicentennial, 1754–1954" (Columbia, Bicentennial Papers, Box 1).

40. Letter from Stevens to Horace Taylor, November 3, 1953 (Huntington, WAS2115).

41. Letter from Taylor to Stevens, November 6, 1953 (Huntington, WAS2110).

42. "Proposal for a Poetry Reading Series," unpublished typescript in the University Archives, University of Massachusetts at Amherst, Robert Tucker File, p. [1].

43. I wish to thank Professor David R. Clark for providing me with transcribed copies of this and other documents pertaining to Stevens's "New England Anthology" recording.

44. Professors Leon Barron, Richard Haven, and Tucker had driven to Hartford to meet with Stevens at his office.

45. Letter from Stevens to Robert G. Tucker, February 15, 1954 (Huntington, WAS2428).

46. William Van O'Connor, *The Age of Criticism, 1900–1950* (Chicago: Henry Regnery, 1952), p. 131 (in a chapter that had been published separately in 1951); W. K. Wimsatt, "Exhuming the Recent Past," *Sewanee Review* 62 (1954): 352–53. For O'Connor's definition and defense of postwar liberalism, see "Lionel Trilling's Critical Realism," *Sewanee Review* 58 (1950): 482–92.

47. Quoted by Eva Cockcroft, "Abstract Expressionism: Weapon of the Cold War," *Artform* 12 (June 1974): 41.

48. "Proposal for a Poetry Reading Series," unpublished typescript, p. [1] (Massachusetts, Tucker File).

49. Letter from David Clark to author, July 10, 1989.

50. Letter from Richard Haven to author, July 10, 1989.

51. Letter from Clark to author.

52. Ibid.

53. Letter from Haven to author.

54. See Robert Tucker, "Freedom, Joy & Indignation: Letters from E. E. Cummings," *Massachusetts Review* 4, 3 (Spring 1963): 497–528.

55. "New England Poets Taping Programs Stressing American Concept of Free Man," *Daily Hampshire Gazette* [Northampton, Mass.], [May 1954]; a partly dated, unpaginated clipping in the University Archives, Massachusetts.

56. Quoted from a report on the Fund for Adult Education, *New York Times*, September 27, 1954, p. 61.

57. Alice Widener, "Who's Running the Ford Foundation?" *American Mercury* 76 (June 1953): 5, 4.

58. "NAEB Grants-in-Aid Agreement," unpublished typescript (Massachusetts, Tucker File). For more on this crisis, see Walter Goodman, *The Committee: The Extraordinary Career of the House Committee on Un-American Activities* (New York: Farrar, Straus and Giroux, 1968), pp. 379–81; and Stefan Kanfer, *A Journal of the Plague Years: A Devastating Chronicle of the Era of the Blacklist* (New York: Atheneum, 1973), pp. 260–66.

59. "Like Sandburg, [MacLeish] has declared, 'The People, Yes!'; and he has spoken forthrightly in his poetry (as well as his prose) for those rights and liberties guaranteed to free men under our Declaration of Independence and our Bill of Rights" ("Proposal for a Poetry Reading Series," p. 2 [Massachusetts, Tucker File]).

60. "New England Anthology" brochure, p. [2] (Massachusetts, Tucker File): "A peculiarly American rebel, Cummings attacks with sometimes brutal irony those aspects of American life which he feels are unworthy of America or of Man" (p. [2]).

61. "Proposal for a Poetry Reading Series," p. 2 (Massachusetts, Tucker File).

62. Ibid., p. 4.

63. Letter from Haven to author. "Joe McCarthy didn't understand th[e] concept [of freedom]," David Clark has written, "but that doesn't mean we didn't" (letter to author).

64. Letter from Tucker to Stevens, February 16, 1954 (Huntington, WAS2420).

65. Letter from Tucker to Stevens, February 19, 1954 (Huntington, WAS2422). The second paragraph of this letter quoted in full Varley's and Haven's message to Stevens; Tucker identified them as "[t]he two men here who are considering how best to order the total script for your program."

66. Letter from Stevens to Tucker, February 24, 1954 (Huntington, WAS2431).

67. Harold Bloom, " 'Notes toward a Supreme Fiction': A Commentary," in *Wallace Stevens: Critical Essays*, ed. Borroff, p. 86.

68. See, for instance, *WSR* 147.

69. Samuel French Morse, interview with author, Milton, Massachusetts, January 7, 1983.

70. Interview with Samuel French Morse.

71. *Trinity Review* 8, 3 (May 1954): 24.

72. Helen Vendler, "The Qualified Assertions of Wallace Stevens," in *The Act of the Mind: Essays on the Poetry of Wallace Stevens*, ed. Roy Harvey Pearce and J. Hillis Miller (Baltimore: Johns Hopkins University Press, 1965), p. 176. For a reading of "Not Ideas" as a "triumph" of "a reality outside the mind," see Leggett, *Wallace Stevens and Poetic Theory*, pp. 198–200.

73. Letter from Stevens to Tate, November 12, 1941 (Huntington, WAS2388).

74. William Van O'Connor, *The Shaping Spirit: A Study of Wallace Stevens* (Chicago: Henry Regnery, 1950), pp. 3–22. The phrase "Hartford fortress," quoted from Will Vance ("Wallace Stevens: Man off the Street," *Saturday Review of Literature* 29 [March 23, 1946]: 8), is repeated by O'Connor on p. 20.

75. Letter from William Van O'Connor to Cleanth Brooks, August 19, 1949 (Syracuse, O'Connor Papers).

76. Letter from Stevens to Eberhart, February 9, 1953 (Dartmouth, Eberhart Papers).

77. Eberhart, "The Stevens Prose," p. 123.

78. *Richard Eberhart: Selected Poems, 1930–1965* (New York: New Directions, 1965), pp. 48–49. A typescript of the poem is enclosed with a letter from Eberhart to Stevens, October 21, 1953 (Huntington, WAS344).

79. Letter from Stevens to Eberhart, October 27, 1953 (Huntington, WAS358).

80. Herbert Read, "Originality," *Sewanee Review* 61 (1953): 537.

81. Ibid., p. 541.

82. Ibid., p. 543.

83. Ibid., p. 539.

84. Ibid., p. 551–52.

85. Huntington, RB440483.

86. Letter from Stevens to Eberhart, January 25, 1954 (Dartmouth, Eberhart Papers).

87. Gerald Weales, "Furtive Marks on Paper," *Commonweal* 59, 16 (January 22, 1954): 409. Weales's comparison to Stevens was quoted by Eberhart in his January 31 letter to Stevens (Dartmouth, Eberhart Papers).

88. Letter from Eberhart to Stevens, January 31, 1954 (Dartmouth, Eberhart Papers). For more on Eberhart's distinction between will and inspiration, see Daniel Hoffman, "Hunting a Master Image: The Poetry of Richard Eberhart," *The Hollins Critic* 1, 4 (October 1964): 2–3.

89. Read, "Originality," p. 533.

90. Letter from Stevens to the *Times Literary Supplement*, August 17, 1954 (Huntington, WAS2411).

91. "Presence of an External Master of Knowledge," *Times Literary Supplement*, September 17, 1954, p. 20; *OP* 131–32.

92. Letter from Babette Deutsch to Stevens, June 1, 1954 (Huntington, WAS2119).

93. Letter from Stevens to Horace Taylor, June 9, 1954 (Huntington, WAS2117).

94. A typescript and two inconsistently corrected carbons are holdings of the Huntington Library; "knowing" replaced "grieving" in all three.

95. "Monitored Calls Stir New Debate in McCarthy Case," *New York Times*, May 22, 1954, p. 1.

96. "McCarthy Asserts He Will Testify," *New York Times*, May 23, 1954, p. 45.

97. Hundreds of events were planned by the various bicentennial committees; five major conferences included the one on economics Horace Taylor chaired. The CBS Radio network put on a program called "Man's Right to Knowledge" on four spring Sundays; and the Bicentennial Committee sponsored "Through the Iron Curtain" each Wednesday on ABC.

98. *New York Times*, January 6, 1954, p. 28.

99. Quoted in a flier entitled "Columbia University Bicentennial, 1754–1954" (Columbia, Bicentennial Papers, Box 1).

100. One such event was a late-March conference, called "The Rights of Free Americans," where the participants discussed "questions of wiretapping" and the "use or misuse of the First and Fifth Amendments, government loyalty programs, and subversive lists" ("Columbia Parley of Students Set," *New York Times*, March 21, 1954, p. 48).

101. "Publisher Maps a Way to Peace," *New York Times*, February 17, 1954, p. 14.

102. Undated *Bicentennial Clipsheet* (Columbia, Bicentennial Papers, Box 6).

103. Sulzberger quoted in "Publisher Maps a Way to Peace," p. 14.

104. Draft statement, "Man's Right to Knowledge and the Free Use Thereof: A Statement Concerning Its Theme Prepared by the Columbia Bicentennial Committee," undated (Columbia, Bicentennial Papers, Box 11).

105. From the text of Eisenhower's speech at the Columbia bicentennial dinner, at the Waldorf-Astoria, May 31, 1954, reprinted in the *New York Times*, June 1, 1954, p. 18.

106. Ibid.

107. Lucy Beckett, *Wallace Stevens* (Cambridge: Cambridge University Press, 1974), p. 205.

108. Michael Beehler has helpfully explored the problems and possibilities of a text that "takes place within a framing horizon of italics that itself encloses another frame formed by quotation marks," and finds, appropriately, that "Ulysses's *voice* is itself a recitation of a certain *writing*" (*T. S. Eliot, Wallace Stevens, and the Discourses of Difference* [Baton Rouge: Louisiana State University Press, 1987], pp. 164, 165; emphasis added).

109. Willard Thorp, *American Writing in the Twentieth Century* (Cambridge: Harvard University Press, 1960), p. 225.

110. Jarrell, "Reflections on Wallace Stevens," pp. 340, 343.

111. See, for example, the much-discussed symposium *Our Country and Our Culture* (1952), which featured some writers with radical pasts expressing the wish to be reintegrated into American society.

112. Randall Jarrell, "The Collected Poems of Wallace Stevens," in *The Third Book of Criticism* (New York: Farrar, Straus and Giroux, 1969), p. 65.

113. Jarrell, "Reflections on Wallace Stevens," pp. 343–44. Compare the rhetoric of exhaustion here to that in Bell's *The End of Ideology*, e.g., pp. 403–5.

114. Jarrell, "Reflections on Wallace Stevens," p. 344.

115. Breslin, *From Modern to Contemporary*, pp. 30–37.

116. *New England Quarterly*, March 1951, p. 126.

117. The point was a commonplace. The editorial statement introducing the book version of "Our Country and Our Culture," the *Partisan* symposium, put it this way: "[M]ost writers no longer accept alienation as the artist's fate in America; on the contrary, they want very much to be a part of American life" (*America and the Intellectuals* [New York: (Partisan Review) 1953], p. 3).

118. For more on this disavowal, see H. Stuart Hughes, "The End of Political Ideology," *Measure* 2, 2 (Spring 1951): 146–58; for Hughes, "humanity has been betrayed by ideology" itself, and the "basic conflict" in the fifties was "*between* ideology and democracy" (emphasis added).

119. Jarrell, "Reflections on Wallace Stevens," p. 338.

120. For a reading of this poem as a rejoinder to Alice Corbin Henderson's work with Native American poetics, see Filreis, "Voicing the Desert of Silence," pp. 9–10.

121. Jarrell, "Reflections on Wallace Stevens," p. 340.

122. Bell, *The End of Ideology*, p. 302. To the extent that there was a consistent view of Stevens at the *Partisan Review*, it was based on this shared sense of his trajectory through the decades: Wylie Sypher described it long before Jarrell, in a 1946 essay stressing Stevens as a misologist, averting ideas and conveying his minute details from period to period with undiminished remoteness and euphoria only somewhat dampened by the ferocity of the times: "[H]e is one of the more cogitative pagans of the 'twenties roving amid the sharper violences of the 'forties" ("Connoisseur in Chaos: Wallace Stevens," *Partisan Review* 13 [Winter 1946]: 85, 86).

123. Bell, *The End of Ideology*, p. 300. Joseph Riddel is right to suggest that, in the long view (Riddel wrote in 1965), "[i]t is unfair to Jarrell to identify him with those who cannot abide the later Stevens"; Riddel notes Jarrell's *Yale Review* essay of March 1955, "contrite and admiring," praising "The Rock" poems ("The Contours of Stevens Criticism," in *The Act of the Mind*, ed. Pearce and Miller, p. 261; see also *Randall Jarrell's Letters*, ed. Mary Jarrell [Boston: Houghton Mifflin, 1985], p. 405). Still, the passage from 1951 to 1955 was a long one; by the time of Stevens's death the critical habit of preferring early Stevens to late had been fully reinforced by other—though related—intellectual forces of the time.

124. Elizabeth Green, "The Urbanity of Stevens," *Saturday Review of Literature* 34 (August 11, 1956): 12.

125. William Van O'Connor, "Wallace Stevens on 'The Poems of Our Climate,'" *University of Kansas City Review* 15 (Winter 1948): 107.

126. See Novick, *That Noble Dream*, p. 323.

127. "Stevens is usually labelled a 'difficult' poet," O'Connor wrote in 1948. "The label need not be a pejorative. T. S. Eliot ... said that 'Our civilization comprehends great variety and complexity ...'" ("Wallace Stevens on 'The Poems of Our Climate,'" p. 105).

128. For this point, O'Connor was referring to Auden on Yeats (ibid.).

129. O'Connor, "The Politics of a Poet," p. 205.

130. Alexander Werth, "Marriage in Russia," *Nation* 166, 17 (April 24, 1948): 436–37. See O'Connor, *The Shaping Spirit*, p. 63.

131. O'Connor, "He Dared to Speak for the Imagination," p. 7.

132. O'Connor's papers at Syracuse include regular letters from Cleanth Brooks and Allen Tate, and a few from O'Connor to Brooks; the Tate Papers at Princeton contain O'Connor's letters to Tate. It was Cleanth Brooks whom O'Connor told that one of the reader's reports at Regnery judged O'Connor's Stevens harshly because of its obvious debts to the New Critics; the reader had said, as O'Connor informed Brooks, "something like this: 'The study is outrageously aesthetic and in the Empson–Cleanth Brooks line of literary analysis.'" Brooks's response was: "I'm familiar with this kind of objection of course. They load the term *aesthetic* and use it to damn you with" (marginal comment in a letter from O'Connor to Brooks, August 19, 1949 [Syracuse, O'Connor Papers]).

133. For more on O'Connor's understanding of the relation between "complexity" and the New Critics (who, he said, "recovered a sense of the density of language"), see his review of Arms's and Kuntz's *Poetry Explication*, "A Valuable Checklist," *Poetry* 77, 5 (February 1951): 289–91.

134. Peter Viereck, "Stevens Revisited," *Kenyon Review* 10 (Winter 1948): 155.

135. See Nash, *The Conservative Intellectual Movement*, pp. 65–68, 80–82, 114–17.

136. O'Connor made this position quite clear in the late forties and early fifties; see, e.g., "Social and Activist Criticism," *New Mexico Quarterly* 21, 1 (Spring 1951): 36–52, in which he attacked the thirties-style "economic interpretation" of culture (pp. 45–47) while praising Trilling's postwar integration of "the social aspects of literature" and "respect for literature as an art" (p. 52). Like many another cold-war liberal, he wanted to remain open to the cultural possibilities of the left (such as the theme of the artist's alienation from the middle class) while being sure to condemn Red Decade radicalism. "The chief effort [among poets] to break out of the circle of isolation," he wrote in 1947, "came with the political and economic upheavals of the thirties. Unfortunately, the pendulum swung too far the other way. . . . [P]olitics tended to . . . forc[e] out aesthetic, philosophical or even broadly human interests" ("The Isolation of the Poet," *Poetry* 70, 1 [April 1947]: 36).

137. O'Connor, "The Politics of a Poet," p. 207.

138. William Van O'Connor, "A Vessel on the Open Sea," *Poetry* 81, 2 (November 1952): 139, 140. In surveying the "contours" of Stevens criticism from the vantage of 1965, Joseph Riddel rightly viewed O'Connor's great claim for "Owl's Clover" with skepticism, pointing to O'Connor's "misplaced emphasis on the doctrinaire," and noting that O'Connor fails to distinguish "the relation of this poem to its period" ("The Contours of Stevens Criticism," p. 255). My point is that O'Connor *did* consider "Owl's Clover" in historical and political context, but that it was a context supplied wholly by his own period: a fifties' thirties induced O'Connor to claim greatness for a poem precisely because of its "doctrinaire" repudiation of radical doctrine.

139. Eberhart, "Reflections on Wallace Stevens in 1976," p. 418.

140. Letter from Eberhart to Stevens, October 19, 1954 (Huntington, WAS349).

141. Pearce, "The Life of the Imagination," in *Wallace Stevens: A Collection of Critical Essays*, ed. Borroff, p. 112.

142. Ibid., p. 120.

143. Quoted by Pearce (ibid., p. 132).

Entries under "Stevens, Wallace" primarily give information not found elsewhere in the index. Works otherwise unidentified are Stevens's.

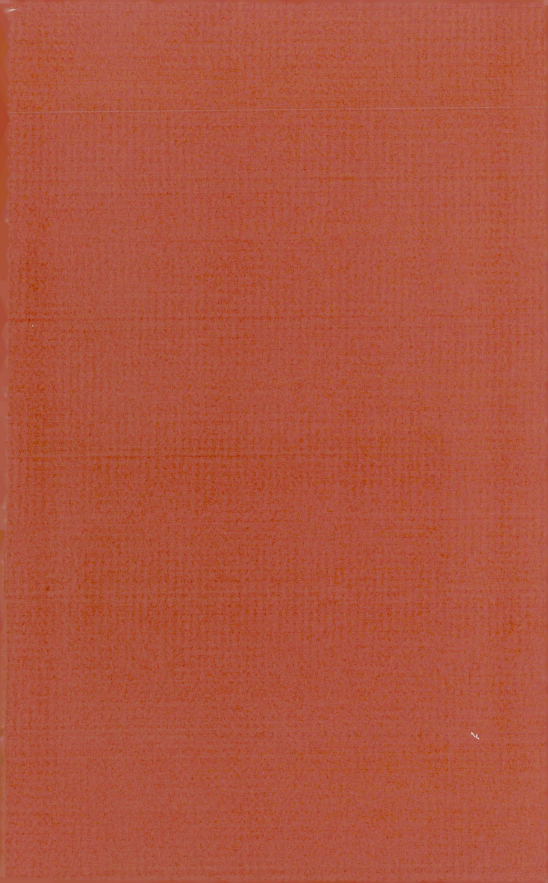